ം

This first printing

of

TOWARD GETTYSBURG

A Biography of General John F. Reynolds

is signed by the author

ം

TOWARD GETTYSBURG

A Biography of General John F. Reynolds

Toward Gettysburg

A Biography of General John F. Reynolds

Edward J. Nichols

The Pennsylvania State University Press, 1958

TO THE MEMORY OF

Colonel J. F. R. Scott

U.S. ARMY (RETIRED)

Acknowledgments

This biography of General John F. Reynolds was made possible at the outset only through the interest and cooperation shown by the late Colonel J. F. R. Scott, U. S. Army (Retired). A grandnephew of the general, Colonel Scott had kept together and added to the papers and correspondence first assembled by one of Reynolds' sisters. After his death in July 1954, Mrs. Scott put all the Reynolds material in the writer's hands for as long as needed. Anyone who has worked on a biographical subject can estimate the worth of this kindness. The papers have since been given to the Fackenthal Library of Franklin and Marshall College, Lancaster, Pennsylvania. Both Mrs. Scott and Mrs. J. J. Kline, of Fort Wayne, Indiana, a grandniece of General Reynolds, have furnished much essential information about the family.

Special thanks are also owed to the following members of the faculty and staff of The Pennsylvania State University: Dr. Philip S. Klein (History) for every manner and kind of assistance; Dr. Warren W. Hassler, Jr. (History) for a most knowledgeable reading of several chapters; Dr. Joseph G. Rayback (History) for his help and encouragement; Dr. John S. Bowman (English) both for his careful reading of manuscript and for making available the letters of his grandfather, Thomas W. Dick; Mr. C. S. Wyand (Executive Assistant to the President) for the use of his select personal library of Civil War literature; both Mrs. Margaret Spangler (Assistant Librarian) and Mrs. Harold F. Graves for generous help in providing hard-to-get source material.

Mr. George Palmer (Foreign Desk, *The New York Times*) earns the writer's deep gratitude, not only for his detailed reading of manuscript, but for many other useful services.

Thanks are also due Mr. William H. Price, Jr., for preparing the four maps.

Others who made important contributions are three historians of the National Park Service: Dr. Frederick Tilberg (Gettysburg), Mr. Francis Wilshin (Manassas), Mr. Ralph Happel (Fredericksburg); Mr. George H. S. King, of Fredericksburg, Virginia; Mr. Prentiss Price, of Rogersville, Tennessee; Mr. Charles F. Bowers, of Frederick, Maryland; Mr. James W. Moore, National Archives, War Department Records; Mr. M. Luther Heisey, Lancaster Historical Society, and Mr. Herbert Anstaett, Librarian, Fackenthal Library, Franklin and Marshall College, Lancaster, Pennsylvania; and Miss B. Elizabeth Ulrich, Reference Librarian, the State Library at Harrisburg, Pennsylvania.

Finally, to Mrs. E. J. Nichols, the most, *most* grateful thanks!

Contents

Illustrations

TOWARD GETTYSBURG

A Biography of General John F. Reynolds

CHAPTER I

Restless Subaltern

Young John Fulton Reynolds wrote home to Lancaster, Pennsylvania, from his new school in Lititz in the autumn of 1833. He was all of twelve miles away.

> Our school rooms are beautifully enlightened by patent lamps, and we can read and write in any part of the rooms. . . . Mr. Beck has been lecturing on Pneumatics which was very interesting to me, he explained to us that air had a coular [sic] and showed us how the Boilers on Steam-boats burst, and how the water was conveyed into the boiler, and a great many other things. There was an exhibition of wild Beasts last week to which we all went and were very much pleased. I think I have improved very much since I am here and I think every boy ought to improve here every oppertunity [sic] for to do so is given us. . . .[1]

Thirty years later, in marching half an army up toward Gettysburg, Major General Reynolds would write orders and dispatches much improved in composition. But the qualities of character underlying the words in this letter would carry over intact from the boy to the man. Deadly serious about his schooling, he would one day be deadly serious about soldiering. Satisfied now of his progress in Mr. Beck's classes, he would one day be as confident of his military capacities. And until the July morning when his decision would bring on the greatest battle of the Civil War, Reynolds' burning urge to "improve every opportunity" marked him above all else.

In 1833, John and his younger brother James had reason to be proud of their school. It once belonged to the Moravian Society, which

3

conducted it along with a seminary for young ladies. John Beck had taken over the boys' education in 1815, and his reputation soon reached beyond the state. In classes the Reynolds brothers sat next to boys from Ohio, Maryland, Virginia, and from as far away as the Carolinas and Louisiana. The Lancaster County historian Daniel Rupp found the quiet village ideal for boys because it offered no temptation for getting into mischief. He also approved of the instruction—". . . the great difference between Mr. Beck's method, and that of similar schools, attempted in imitation of his, has always been his sociable and parental intercourse with his pupils, by which means he gains their esteem and affection."[2]

John was lucky in other ways besides the family's choice for the boys' schooling. The Reynolds had early roots in Lancaster. His father's line went back to the widow Mary Ferree. She had fled with other Huguenots from the lower Palatinate to Holland and from there to England. In London she so impressed William Penn that he took her to see Queen Anne. As a result, Mary Ferree's flight from persecution ended happily, for by 1712 she held 4,000 acres in what shortly became Lancaster County.[3] This land was so fertile that farmers raised "quantities of wheat, barley, flax and hemp, without the help of any dung."[4]

The Protestant Irish began moving into the region early in the eighteenth century. Listed among the family names were Moore, Fulton, and Reynolds. John's grandfather Reynolds married a granddaughter of Mary Ferree. The Moores and the Fultons entered on his mother's side. His mother was a Moore, and the boys could boast about their grandfather Samuel, who fought at Brandywine and Germantown as a captain in the Continental line.[5]

The boys were also lucky in having a father of some prominence. After a successful printing venture in Philadelphia John Reynolds, Esq. had come to Lancaster, where he now owned and published the *Journal*. He had already served twice in the state legislature at Harrisburg. Among other duties at present he was attending to local business affairs for his friend James Buchanan.[6] The rising young senator in Washington had recently got an appointment as midshipman for one of John's older brothers. If all continued to stand well in this safe world of Andrew Jackson, opportunity might eventually come in the way of other Reynolds sons.

Finally, Lancaster was a pleasant place to live. In summer a boy could swim in Deep Hole or Ranck's mill dam southwest of town. He could catch all the sunfish, suckers, pike, and bass he wanted along the banks of the Conestoga[7] or in smaller creeks like Cocalico, Hammer, Chiques, and Copper Mine.[8] There was skating at Graeff's Landing in

winter, and the hills almost everywhere around made ideal runs for
coasting.[9] In 1833 boys of John's age would find plenty to do in this
lively town of 8,000 people. Lancaster had been making firearms and
the famous Conestoga wagons since before the Revolution and still did,
along with railroad cars, harness, nails, whiskey, and snuff. Shops and
stores took up the two blocks of King Street on either side of the court-
house square. Young hunters like the Reynolds boys could admire the
double-barreled shotguns in the windows of George Mayer's store.[10]

The Reynolds house at 42 West King Street was among the largest in
town. It had to be. Lydia Moore Reynolds' thirteenth child would be
born here in 1835. Four had died in infancy and one son, William, was
now a midshipman at sea. That left seven still at home, ranging in age
from Sam at nineteen down to baby Harriet.[11] The birth of the last
child, Eleanor, was two years away. These brothers and sisters could
make good use of the 250 feet of yard stretching from the rear of the
house to the alley. In winter there was the snug warmth of the second-
floor ballroom. The house, three stories high with five windows across
the front, had an interesting Colonial entrance with a fine fanlight above
the door.[12] In a town where fewer than a third of the homes rose more
than a single story the Reynolds place ranked among the best.

All in all, it was a comfortable life for John Reynolds, and with
Christmas near he was even more enthusiastic about his school. He was
glad to hear that his oldest sister Lydia liked her school too, also that
her handwriting showed improvement. Then he continued:

> James and myself are likewise much pleased with our situation; we
> are in the care of very kind people and we have a very fine school;
> the school is very large at present, and there are 74 boarding boys
> here; we have three teachers;[13] the boys are divided into three apart-
> ments. Last evening Mr. Beck closed the lecturs [sic] for this year;
> the subject was morals and good manners; he first told us what
> awkwardness in society was, and then he told us how to conduct
> ourselves; he told us all the virtues that adorn a good mans [sic]
> character; he said above all was Religion, then Humility, Mercy,
> Justice, Purity of Heart, Charity, Generosity, Truth, and Cheerful-
> ness; after he had illustrated these he told us to beware of Anger,
> Revenge, and Avarice, and told us to what such vices might lead
> us. . . . I think I have never passed the evenings happier and more to
> my advantage than I have done since the first of November. . . .[14]

Mr. Beck did not make the mistake of relying merely on morals and
good manners. ". . . Yesterday evening he lectured on Electricity, but
as the atmosphere was not favorable many Experiments failed; but we
all got several shocks and stood on the insulating stool, and electric fire

then discharged from every part of our body."[15] There were sports too, especially riding, which John loved. Only three years before, Mr. Beck had set aside an acre plot for playing ball and gardening. Then he made a riding course and bought two ponies. There was probably less fighting over the rakes and hoes than over who would ride; at any rate, the mounts were disposed of before John left the school.[16] Although the principal did not say why he discontinued the riding exercises, it is a likely guess that too many vegetable plots lay fallow or rank with weeds as long as the ponies were around.

The spring of 1834 found John still happy about school but disappointed that none of the family had been out for a visit. "I think you ought to come while the flowers are in blossom in the Grave yard," he wrote his mother on May 1; "you never saw anything so handsome." His father's friend Mr. Coleman was coming for his own two boys and then all the school would go on a fishing "frolic" unless it rained. Final examinations were near and John even thought they would be interesting. "The boys have made a number of Paintings and architectural Specimens—James and I will be examined in Grammar, Geometry Mensuration Geography and Astronomy and in the afternoon we must speak." At least the absence of commas would not matter when John talked.

So far, nothing particular in John Reynolds' makeup suggested the future soldier. Earnestness, dedication, and confidence were useful traits in any field. John did respect authority, of course. Mr. Beck obviously constituted THE WORD, and John's father deserved the most dutiful progress reports. But respect for one's elders was commonplace in those days, though it might ease the transfer to respect for military rank. Some better clue to the coming soldier was needed, especially in a boy who never saw anything so handsome as the flowers in the graveyard.

One near phobia did crop up in John at this stage, one that would bear importantly in army life. He suddenly became preoccupied with his health. A Lititz physician used to say that no doctor could hope to make money out of the schoolboys while Mr. Beck had charge of them. He was constantly preaching health.[17] With John the lesson stuck, and soon he began to notice that other boys got sick. Robert Coleman had a bad cold; his brother William had the mumps.[18] Then John's own brother came down with a sore throat.[19] John reported their illnesses faithfully, but he was never sick himself, and his pride in his physical resistance increased as he grew older. For the rest, John was not much different from the other boys around him. He was kind, well liked, full of high spirits; he worked hard and played hard.[20]

After their second year at Lititz, John and James faced the prospect of a new school. John was fifteen now and could take care of himself farther away from home. He could also keep an eye on James, who was two years younger. But in July of 1835 he set out for Baltimore alone because his brother was sick again. He wrote home as soon as he got there because, he said, he was anxious to begin his classical studies with Reverend Morrison and he hoped James would soon be able to come. The school was Long Green Academy, situated about sixteen miles from the city. He got in a full day's fishing while he waited for his brother. This might have consoled him except that he and the other boys had to fish from the wharf because all the boats leaked.[21]

John was less happy at Long Green than he had been at Lititz. Early in September he already had vacation on his mind, and on the 9th he wrote his Aunt Lydia that he thought it would be a good idea if he and James could come home. Besides, they could bring their summer clothes and pick up their winter ones. He was having trouble with his suits and thought it about time he be allowed to buy them in Baltimore. ". . . If you make them by the measure at home they will be apt to be too small as my new black has ~~Busted~~ Bursted in the back in three or four places." For a young man on his way to reaching six feet in height this was no time to freeze the measurements of his clothes. Aunt Lydia was his father's unmarried sister. She had come over from her own place to help John's mother, who was sick. The boy thought a lot of her, and she might be just the one to get something done about those shrinking suits.

By December he was having trouble with his brother. "James did complain a little of his being sick," he said, "but I did not know anything of his eating and drinking so much for he the other day said he did not get enough to eat, but that is not so, for he and all of us have plenty to eat and as to the advice you gave him in your letter he says he does not intend to mind, he has become very bad."[22] This letter was addressed to his oldest sister. In a household with the mother sick even a girl of seventeen could try to hold her younger brothers in line. John said they had not commenced their French yet but had almost finished the first book of Euclid.

The year at Long Green ended at last and in 1836 the boys were back in Lancaster for a term at the academy. Being home would have other advantages besides assuring enough to eat for James. For one thing the hunting was better. The Reynolds boys had rifles and shotguns put into their hands early, but the region around Baltimore had proved so poor for game that John refused to go out. Once after a whole day his brother had come back with a single rabbit, another time with a possum.[23] In Lancaster County you threw away a bag like that. In October he could walk to the end of north Lime Street and find both golden and black-bellied plover. Over in Big Swamp in Clay Township he could shoot woodcock and quail. Quail would always be a favorite with John. Wild turkey were still plentiful, and when the snipe came north in March there was good shooting with the dogs. Of course hunting with dogs suggested ducks—mallards, canvasbacks, pintails, shovelers, and blue-winged teal.[24] The best duck country was over on the Susquehanna and down south a way, but it was worth the trip.

A boy in his sixteenth year was ready for girls, too. Lydia was old enough to have callers, both girls and young men. The Coleman boys had Sarah and Isabel for sisters, and Annie Reigart and Mary Elizabeth Lane were other girls close to John's age. Later, when he grew nostalgic for the "soirées" of these years, he kept asking to be remembered to these friends and to others like Sam Humes, Hal Hopkins, and John Hindman.

In the meantime John and his brother continued with their French and added advanced mathematics. Also, at the beginning of 1836 John's father had partly changed the way of life for most of the family. He sold the *Journal* to take over the management of the Coleman iron furnace at Cornwall. This meant giving up the house on West King Street and moving the family eighteen miles into Lebanon County. It was lucky for the children that Aunt Lydia still had her home in Orange Street next to the Reformed parsonage. Her place as well as the homes of friends would always be open to them in Lancaster. Of course John and James would have to stay in Lancaster to finish their year at the academy.

In May of the same year John Reynolds had got the chance to make an exciting trip. It was a horseback ride of over seventy miles from Lancaster to Philadelphia, by way of West Chester. But most of the thrill he expected was lost when he pulled up at the Durkee stables on his rented mount. The horse had gone lame in the fore shoulders and the man who looked him over held John accountable. What would Mr. Durkee himself say when he saw the animal? It had left the owner's Lancaster stable in good condition. What kind of wild jockey was this young Reynolds to be trusted with a horse? Tired as John was, he set down his fears in a note to his father, but by 8 o'clock he gathered courage enough to add a postscript: "Mr. Durkee has not yet come and I do not think he will come but keep the horse and say no more about it. Excuse this as I am very tired and wish to go to bed."[25] Nothing at all about whether he might have pushed the horse a little . . .

Although now at Cornwall, John's father still found time to handle Lancaster business for Senator Buchanan. Among the letters arriving from Washington came one which had been addressed to the senator but which he passed on to Reynolds with a covering note. The letter itself read as follows:

War Department
January 25, 1836

Sir

I have had the honor to receive your letter of the 20th inst. recommending young Mr. Reynolds for appointment to the Military Academy. But as you state he will not be sixteen till September next, and as the period for entrance into the Military Academy is in June, you will perceive from the enclosed copy of regulations, that he is too young to be selected for that institution this year.

Very respectfully
Yr Mo Obt Servt
(Signed) Lewis Cass

Buchanan's note began beneath the signature of the secretary of war. "I feel mortified that I had forgotten the regulation in regard to age. I am convinced that it is better for John that it is so. I shall endeavor if it be possible, to get an appointment for him in advance during the session."[26]

If John did make the academy in another year, all but one of the boys would have started their careers. Sam had gone over to Castle Finn in York County to run a Coleman furnace, and Will would finish his sea duty as a midshipman and report to the naval training school at Norfolk in the fall.[27] (Founding of the academy at Annapolis was still about ten years away.) With John at West Point, James would be the only son left at home. He and sisters Lydia, Jane, Kate, Harriet, and Ellie would have to help keep their parents and Grandmother Moore from being lonely.

Did John Reynolds look forward to life in the army? There was that maternal grandfather of the Continental line of course, and he idolized his sailor brother Will. Then why not choose the navy? Well, John liked horses for one thing, and horses hardly fit into the picture of a ship's bridge or the quarterdeck. He also liked hunting. Moving around the various army posts in the country would give him a chance to shoot game of every kind. But in the end, his own desires probably influenced the choice of the Military Academy less than the situation at home. John's father was not a wealthy man. A great deal of what he did have was tied up in land and in iron ventures spread out over four counties.[28] Given his large family of children to educate, he could easily see the advantages of providing some of it at government expense. It was especially tempting when he had such ready access to a senatorial ear.

Ulysses S. Grant had been sent to West Point in spite of his own doubts about the pleasures of soldiering.[29] The same was true of General George Gordon Meade, though his mother did have the grace to feel bad about it. She wrote her son: "Although in my ignorance I was cruel enough to send you to West Point, an act for which I shall never forgive myself, and never cease to regret, I did not dream that you would enter the army, my dear George."[30] At least if John did happen to feel any reluctance against accepting military life, he would be in pretty good company.

But whatever he thought or whoever made the final decision, the process of shaping an army career for John Fulton Reynolds ground along. On March 1, 1837, his father wrote the secretary of war, giving his "full and free assent" to the conditional appointment of his son as a cadet. He endorsed John's signing of the articles that bound him for a minimum period of five years in the service of the United States.[31] Then within a week the young man himself had a letter to send off to the secretary of war:

Lancaster, March 6, 1837

Sir

Yesterday I had the honor to receive from you a notice of my conditional appointment by the President as a Cadet in the service of the United States, requiring immediate information as to my acceptance or non acceptance of the same. I therefore hasten to assure you, that with great pleasure, I thankfully accept the appointment and shall report myself to the Superintendent of the Military Academy at West Point within the time specified.

I have the honor to be
with great respect
your obt servt
(Signed) John F. Reynolds[32]

Mr. Buchanan had held to his promise, and this time the appointment went through, as of June 30, 1837. John Fulton Reynolds would now be a soldier for the rest of his life. Judging from the tone of his letter, he was a willing recruit.

John began his cadet years in training camp that summer. From there he wrote his brother Will in August, expressing a thought that kept recurring in his letters throughout his years in the army—restlessness, the desire for change, to move on: "Our life in the tented field is nearly at an end for this year; on the 28th we are to have a military ball, and on the next day we go into Barracks. The Ball our class has nothing to do with, we are merely invited. I do not intend going as I do not know any persons at the Point. I begin to tire of living in Camp and wish we were in Barracks. I am very much pleased with my life here and think I shall continue to like it."[33]

The Military Academy had come a long way since Sylvanus Thayer found it "a drowsy school of supine students" in 1817,[34] but not far enough to find all the friends and support it needed. The main charge against it was still being repeated at the time Reynolds entered. West Point was a retreat for the pampered sons of the rich. In 1820 a resolution had been offered in Congress for abolishing the school.[35] Grant mentioned a similar bill, introduced in 1839, which he said he then hoped would pass.[36] In that year he was still a reluctant plebe. Even five years after Reynolds graduated the army's chief engineer lamented that the Academy was often denounced as inefficient, effeminate, and luxurious; also that it did not equip cadets for active field duty.[37] In the same year, 1846, a Congressional committee noted that in some respects the Academy was aristocratic in character and tendencies and that too many appointments were based merely on wealth or political influence.[38]

At least Reynolds did not represent wealth, any more than Grant or Meade did. Influence, yes, but as the committee went on to point out, abuses would not occur if candidates were selected only by proper standards.

In 1837 none of this doubt about his new school was any business of John's. Wealthy aristocrat, politically preferred or not, he had work to do. Even then he proved to be no better than an average student. In natural philosophy he once fell as low as 36 in a class of 57. In his third year he did better, getting up to number 15 in drawing and as high as 12 in artillery—that was field artillery, which involved horses. John obviously gave this course some extra effort. Still, there was no likelihood that he would graduate near the top of his class. In this respect he was closer to Grant, "Uncle John" Sedgwick, "Stonewall" Jackson, Joe Hooker, Winfield Scott Hancock, and scores of other good soldiers than he was to such models as Robert E. Lee, George B. McClellan, or Henry W. Halleck.[39] John Reynolds played it safe, graduating 26th, as near to the middle of the fifty-two members of his class as he could.

But scholarship aside, one long-time professor at the Point liked him at once and proved a good friend throughout Reynolds' life. As a cadet John impressed Henry L. Kendrick by his clear and independent thinking, his even temperament, and by his courtesy.[40] Among the cadets Reynolds made friends in his quiet way. William T. (Cump) Sherman knew him and liked him at the Academy.[41] One of John's closest friends was Joseph Irons, of his own class. He would sorrowfully note this soldier's death during the final campaign in Mexico.[42] Another friend in the same class, Charles P. Kingsbury, would do John a handsome turn in the same war.[43]

Cadet Reynolds neared the end of his four years' training in a mood of reflection, unconscious candor, an excusable hint of First-Classman conceit, and in his most elegant composition. It all came out in one letter, addressed to his sister Jane. He said he was serving his country in the capacity of Officer of the Day, comfortably seated before the fire in the guard room of the cadet barracks, ". . . for though it is a Spring month the aspect of this day does not bely the character of 'Stormy March.'" This setting put John in a mood for what he called consolatory reflection. He had only four months to go till graduation, ". . . but why is it so consolatory: you will ask." Then he was off:

> . . . Will you not leave the halls of your "alma Mater," and the friends and classmates you have acquired here, without one single regret? Yes! But it is a case of necessity! "Ne cipitas non habit ligem"—it cannot be avoided. We have lived the portion of our time allotted to us here—it was a part of the contract and we might have foreseen that this must occur—and as we entered into it voluntarily we are bound to fulfil it and bear with the result as best we may— all this taken together with the others. That we go at last in a short time to meet friends as dear to us and more closely connected and that tho' we leave scenes endeared to us by a thousand pleasing reminiscences; and return to those of our childhood and to our homes, like which there is no place—all this, I say, *must* tend to alleviate, and sweeten the "bitter tear of separation and sad fare-well" (perhaps forever, for we do not know how many years). You will not wonder at this pathetic strain, but appreciate, I know, when I tell you that I feel it, and that it is natural. . . .

With his pathetic strain out of the way, John was ready to answer a few questions. Yes, he had been drawing, though not what she supposed. He was drawing fortifications. ". . . this together with the study of killing (theoretically I mean, not practically) men by the hundred, have been no small part of our course here since Jan^y." He would have to postpone the drawings of the Point Jane wanted because several other ladies were ahead of her in their requests. John would tell her all about drilling when he got home, though he hardly approved of applying it to ladies—". . . it takes away much of that easy grace, and carriage, which constitute the chief part of their beauty."

Jane had asked if potatoes still gave him a headache. That started her brother off again, this time on "hashes." These meals were made from stolen food and eaten in the cadets' rooms at night. John assured her that if she could join one of their hashes "made from potatoes 'hooked' from the mess hall and cooked a la wick, always by the most skillful 'chef de cuisine,'" she would know that at last he was happy to accept the vegetable.

Next, a Lancaster marriage put John into a spell of puns and doggerel. This in turn required four lines of apology for his wrestle with the muse, which he ended by noting that poets, like musicians, never thrived at the Academy.[44]

John's letter of more than a thousand words finally closed, though except for taps and the fifty interruptions caused by his duties as Officer of the Day he might have been good for another thousand. But as it was he said he was ready to resign himself with all his cares and responsibilities "to the arms of Somnus."[45] His postscript pleaded for news from Lancaster. How was Mrs. Clarke, Mrs. Myer and family? How about Sam Hines, Hal Hopkins, and the others?

Now where was the plebe who would not go to the military ball in 1837 because he did not know anybody at the Point? And what about the John F. Reynolds who later earned a reputation in the army as a man of few words? Yet with all his showing off for a favorite sister, other qualities came through as well. The scraps of Latin from Long Green Academy, the quotation marks, and the punning rhymes could not cover John's pride in his performance of duty, his love for the Academy and for his family and friends.

Along with Reynolds, the class of 1841 included at least a half-dozen graduates who would be heard from—Nathaniel Lyon, Don Carlos Buell, Horatio Wright, Richard Garnett, I. B. Richardson, and A. W. Whipple. Preceding him by a year were Sherman, George Thomas, and Dick Ewell. A year after Reynolds some of those going out would be James Longstreet, William Rosecrans, John Pope, Abner Doubleday, George Sykes, John Newton, Seth Williams, D. H. Hill, Lafayette McLaws, and Earl Van Dorn. This class of 1842 was loaded with military promise. In 1843 Grant and Rufus Ingalls were the biggest names. Two fellow Pennsylvanians, Winfield Scott Hancock, and the cavalry leader Alfred Pleasonton, had come in as plebes during Reynolds' last year.[46]

Prospects for a subaltern just out of West Point were none too good in 1841. The Florida war against the Seminoles had gone on all the while Reynolds was a cadet, but now it had died out. In another year the army would shrink from about 12,000 to fewer than 9,000 men.[47] Promotion was so slow and the hope of rising even from lieutenant to captain so unlikely that in a single year 117 officers resigned. Both Albert Sidney Johnston and Joseph E. Johnston had left already; Meade was out; and others who would quit were Jefferson Davis, Braxton Bragg, Grant, and Cump Sherman.[48]

But in the fall of 1841 Brevet Second Lieutenant John Fulton Reynolds still moved happily into his first assignment—Battery (Company) H., 3rd Artillery, at Fort McHenry, Baltimore. His first *military* assignment, that is. On his way there—or rather out of his way—he took four girls and Robert Coleman to New Haven, Connecticut, by way of New York City.[49] "After making a safe *deposit* of the Young Ladies at New Haven," he wrote his father on October 3, "where I expect to hear that I have left them in a *haven* of enjoyment I have at length made my way to the end of my journey and I am now comfortably situated in our Drawing Room at Fort McHenry." John took no chances on his puns being missed.

He was enthusiastic about the quarters. He said the parlor was elegantly furnished and he had a bedroom to himself, though he did need bedding. "The Fort is situated in a beautiful spot and must be exceedingly pleasant in Summer but a little too cold in Winter." In the letter he included an itemized account of the New Haven trip. He listed fares, hotel bills, hacks, portage, more hotels and fares, along with "theatre for Robert $1." Last was an item of $8.25, a dress for Lydia. "Anne bought her a dress for which I paid her but could not get the other things for want of time." Just twenty days from his full commission as lieutenant and he had to shop for a girl. Only a doting brother would have submitted, even by proxy. In closing, John wanted to know how his colt was doing. "I wish I had him here," he said. But a week later he was complaining to his mother about weariness from being too much in the saddle. His job was superintending road repairs from the town to the fort, which for him meant sitting a horse rather than riding. Otherwise he had been too busy getting settled to go into Baltimore much, so he said he had made few acquaintances in the female line as yet. He had met his commander, Captain Samuel Ringgold. To Reynolds he seemed to be clever and offhand, though hardly sociable.[50]

Peacetime years produce thin military chronicles. Although the United States Army contributed impressively to exploration, surveying, road-building, and to the protection and consolidation of new territory, these enterprises did little toward making heroes. Lewis and Clark, Fremont, Pike, and a few others are remembered, but mostly the army lived its days anonymously in fort and barracks routine. Soldiers put up buildings and kept them in repair, constructed roads and maintained them, took care of horses and livestock, policed their areas, and drilled. The officers superintended the work. Meanwhile, letters home could not make enough of these chores to be worth keeping. The writers themselves were making neither headlines nor reputations. It was of interest only to Reynolds' family that he had not met many girls in Baltimore yet or that he badly needed the box of his household goods from home. So the record for several years was slight.

The young lieutenant's next tour of duty took him to St. Augustine, Florida. It also took him down with fever. Being sick was a strange and disquieting experience for Reynolds. How could this happen to him, a six-footer toughened by his years out of doors and the rigors of West Point training? But he was sick—very sick, as a letter from a fellow officer to his father proved:

At the request of your son, Lieut. J. F. Reynolds, U. S. Army, I very cheerfully undertake the task, which it is thought he had better not perform at present, of informing you of the reason for his not having written. . . .

On the evening of the 12th of July he was taken with symptoms of fever and since the morning of the 13th has been confined to his bed by a pretty severe attack of *bilious fever,* and tho' he has at no time been considered dangerous, he has suffered a good deal and it will require some weeks to recover his lost strength. This communication had been delayed at my request, as it was believed it would be more gratifying to you after the crisis had passed, which his attending physician is now confident of; and I am confident from having been in constant attendance on him that he is *far* better this morning than he has been since the first attack. . . .

You may rest assured that every attention has been and will be rendered him by myself and friends of whom we both have many of the kindest, and though we may not supply the vacuum which must exist from an absent family every gratification which can arise from the kindest attention of friends will be afforded him.[51]

The author of this sympathetic and friendly letter was, of all people, Braxton Bragg. This officer was already on the way to being one of the most widely disliked men in the army. Every sentiment Bragg expressed to the senior Reynolds was the opposite of qualities he habitually showed to everyone around him. In fact most of those who knew Bragg might suspect that this letter was a forgery. Yet here it was, in his own hand. Not only that, but he followed it with a shorter note in which the tone was equally warm: "It affords me great pleasure to inform you of the continued improvement of my friend Lt. Reynolds, he has been able to sit up some every day this week and to-day has been so well that he insists on walking some; he is still weak and much reduced but if his present appetite continues it will not be long 'ere he recovers all that has been lost. I think I may safely promise you that your next news will be from his own hand."[52]

Bragg's softness was only a temporary lapse, as Reynolds and others would soon find out. The family of another southern officer who saw Reynolds through this siege during midsummer of 1842 was that of Lieutenant William J. Hardee. Both he and his family did so much for the patient that eight years later Reynolds was happy that he could make some repayment for their kindness.[53] This certainly was a gratitude he could no longer have felt for Bragg.

The beginning of 1843 saw John Reynolds his old rugged self again. But now it was his turn to be concerned about his mother's failing health. Writing to his sister Jane on February 10, he said he was glad to know their mother had improved a little after visiting Lancaster. "As for the rest of the family I take it they all remain the same, that is, as far as one blessed source of happiness, health, is concerned." John could say this more fervently than ever now. He said he was finding St. Augustine very dull. ". . . Occasionally we have a Spanish dance upon which we manage to live for a while, that is, I mean it is excitement and pleasure to us here, much enhanced by being almost the only one we have." John admitted missing the old soirées of his Lancaster days. He thought about them often, he told Jane, but added that in all probability he would never get to enjoy them again.

The young lieutenant seemed depressed. "I cannot think *when* I shall be able to bid Augustine farewell again and only expect to do so in the event of some change in our military affairs." John ended his letter with a request. He was sending Sarah Coleman the music for some of the Spanish dances, which Sarah had promised to learn. For some reason or other it was important that Jane should learn them, too.

This new mood differed from John's high morale at McHenry. If it took only the second round of the endless shifts from station to station to affect his spirits, he was going to make a restless soldier. But luckily his goodby to Augustine came long before he thought. The "change in our military affairs" had begun. Both Mexico and the new Republic of Texas were already sending small forces across each other's borders in 1842. Nor did the talk of annexing Texas to the United States help relations between Washington and Mexico City.

Reynolds shipped up the coast to Charleston in April of 1843. Fort Moultrie on Sullivan's Island should have been all any young man could ask in the spring. There was good company in the garrison too, with Cump Sherman and George Thomas, the future "Rock of Chickamauga." John would find friends in both of them as well as in others. But two men were going to prove exceptions. General Erasmus Keyes later gave his opinion of the officers there when Reynolds came. Cump Sherman was too ambitious but attentive to duty and completely likable. Keyes called Thomas one of the greatest, both as a soldier and as a friend. And although he knew Reynolds only three months before leaving Moultrie, he claimed John as an intimate and "as amiable as he was brave."[54]

About one officer Keyes felt otherwise. Bragg struck him as being saturnine, morbid, and vitriolic. Admitting his intelligence and exactness in performance of duty, Keyes still disliked the southerner's dictatorial manner and lack of sociability.[55] These were all traits that Reynolds would unfortunately come to know. Bragg's surprising kindness at St. Augustine had to be compared with his more normal self.

Such a chance soon came at a banquet in Charleston. In giving one of the toasts, a local newspaperman named Stewart made the mistake of calling Bragg's North Carolina, among other things, merely a strip of land between two states. This was too much for Bragg's temper, as Cump Sherman reported the incident: "High words and a challenge passed—pistols for two, coffee for one the next morning—but John F. Reynolds and I, from remote and obscure regions like Pennsylvania and Ohio, were chosen peacemakers, and succeeded in getting Stewart to admit that North Carolina was a state in the Union, claiming to be Carolina, though not comparable to *South* Carolina. At all events we postponed the battle."[56]

Another officer Keyes expected to dislike he changed his mind about.[57] That was the other Sherman, Thomas W., who came to Moultrie with a reputation of being as difficult as Bragg. But although Keyes learned to like him, Sherman remained generally unpopular in the army.[58] What made all this important for Reynolds was that both Bragg and Thomas Sherman would in turn command his battery, and they would give him trouble.

In August of this summer of 1843 John's mother died. The visit to Lancaster had not helped enough. Lydia Moore Reynolds was only fifty years old. An obituary called her retiring and unobtrusive and said she disregarded all the allurements of a fashionable life to devote herself to her family. But bearing and raising thirteen children, of whom nine still lived, had left her little time for anything else. She did belong to the Ladies Benevolent Society of Lancaster, though it probably took John's Aunt Lydia to coax her in. Lydia was secretary in 1816.[59]

Mrs. Reynolds had passed her own reticence on to her lieutenant son. While there was little or no withholding in the letters John wrote home, he was less open and confiding with others. In the fishbowl existence of army life he always preferred quarters by himself. He never made friendships casually, though he was by no stretch anti-social. If nothing else, his early years of security and affection in the bulging Reynolds family saw to that. He could be companionable without losing the reserve that always marked him.

The young officers of the Moultrie garrison were always welcomed in the summer homes on Sullivan's Island. Such hospitality helped make Charleston one of the prized stops in the army's tour of the forts. And winter meant hunting on the mainland, which Reynolds looked forward to most. But one trip he made had bad results for his friend Cump Sherman. During a chase his horse got out of control and knocked him off under the limb of a tree. Riding up from behind, Reynolds found him on the ground in a tangle of bridle and saddle. Sherman had dislocated his shoulder. John managed to repair the gear and prop his friend back on the horse, then he led him slowly through the woods to a cabin. Their host had joined them by now and helped Reynolds fix up an old gig they found in the yard. In this contraption Sherman ended his deer hunt in a six-mile jounce he remembered painfully even after four long years of the Civil War.[60]

While the pleasant duty in Charleston continued, the situation south of the Texas border grew worse. Mexico had realized too late that the American colonists in her territory would one day lean toward union with their own people. When the annexation of Texas finally took place in 1845, Mexico City broke off relations with the United States. John had written that only a change in military affairs would get him out of St. Augustine. He escaped to Charleston without it, but now the change was ripening fast.

The Indian fighter and hero of 1812, old Zachary Taylor, got orders to assemble an army of occupation. He began the job in New Orleans and near the end of summer moved down the Gulf to Corpus Christi, on the south side of the Nueces River near its mouth. The army was in disputed territory and Lieutenant Grant, who was there, did not like it. "We were sent to provoke a fight, but it was essential that Mexico should commence it."[61] Reynolds, who had arrived with his artillery company, disagreed. Good Democrat that he was, he not only approved President Polk's tough policy but hoped he would follow through as energetically as Old Hickory would have done.[62]

When he wrote his sisters on November 14 Reynolds himself was full of energy. "I have been so much employed for the past two or three weeks in imparting my knowledge of horsemanship to 20 or 30 stupid Germans, Irishmen, &c, that I have had no time to answer your (that is: Jane's) kind letter before the present. In order that you may fully comprehend the above it may be necessary to tell you that our Company has at last been converted to a light Co. . . . So you can see that I am once more in my element, with horses." He was eager to get his men whipped into shape so he could go hunting. "Game of all kinds abound. Geese and ducks in the thousands. Deer in abundance. Tell Rob I have commenced slaughtering the 'Jack Snipe,' which, tho not very numerous (for they have not begun to migrate from the North yet) offered tolerable amusement." He was glad to hear that his two dogs at home were doing well, but added that they would be useless where he was now because of the brush and the lack of water.

Will and his wife Becky were in Italy, where John hoped they would have a pleasant winter in a more comfortable house than he had:

> Our tents are miserable. I have just been recorder to a board of Officers and we condemned the whole of them. . . . The rainy season has set in; it has been raining for a week and looks as if it might continue for the balance of the year at least. . . .
>
> I can imagine you all in the Old Ball Room with a large blazing fire—and snow enough on the ground to keep you there—while we are living in cloth houses (tell Ellie) without fires and everything green around us and at present we are actually making hay—that is we have to cut grass for our horses. Poor horses, how they must suffer from the rainy spell! Horses, fires, &c are all military enough and no doubt we would go into huts for the Winter if we had any timber to make them of. There is but little wood to be had, scarcely enough for cooking purposes and that has to be hauled 4, 5, or 6 miles and is so crooked it won't lie still when you put it down and therefore totally unfit for building purposes. . . .

John could never get through a 1,500-word letter without a pun. He wanted someone to send him the Lancaster papers and had been after James to mail them, ". . . but," he said, "his 'brief' is so extensive I suppose as to occupy all his time. If this is so I am glad of it but I fear his is literally a brief in all senses of the word." At least this meant that his brother had graduated from Marshall College, had completed his reading of the law, and had begun his practice in Lancaster. Meanwhile Sam had left the Coleman forge in York County and had gone out to Clarion County in western Pennsylvania to manage his father's Lucinda furnace. "Poor Lucinda," John called it and said he expected to find Sam in Texas any day now, having quit in despair. This property seemed to be the white elephant of the family investments, and it was finally given up.[63]

It would have been easy for John to make more point of training his men and providing for the horses than he did. His light battery of four 6-pounders called for a captain (now Bragg), two lieutenants, four sergeants, eight corporals, and sixty privates. It took forty draft horses to haul the pieces and caissons, and fifteen saddle mounts for the officers and noncoms. Adding two 12-pound howitzers, as was later done, increased the number of men to a total of 122.[64]

Mounted light artillery was new in the army, and one correspondent watched the efforts of Ringgold's, Duncan's, and Bragg's batteries with a skeptical eye. He objected to the notion that green recruits would suddenly begin riding like Cossacks once the magic words "light artillery" were put on paper in the war office. "The military authorities say that very few soldiers are fit for the light artillery arms—that it requires picked men, bold and expert horsemen—and that these only become good light artillerists after long practice in riding, driving, managing, and attending their horses, and in using the sabre." The correspondent also complained that men and officers both spent so much time in keeping their horses fed that there was little chance for drill.[65] This newspaperman obviously did not know Bragg. Reynolds could have reassured him on the last count.

By January of 1846 Taylor's army had gone into winter quarters. As Reynolds put it, they did this by turning their tents around to face the south. The whole country from Corpus Christi down to the Rio Grande was covered with water and kept him from getting any snipe. Then the dreaded "Northers"[66] came. The men had to bank earth up around the tents and pile chaparral on top to keep off the stinging, knife-sharp winds. "Many officers have stoves or fireplaces made of old barrels, camp kettles and other like in their tents," John wrote, "but as I am one of those careless and improvident ones I have neither. I have actually been sleeping on the ground until this cold spell drove me to have a bunk made and this is the extent of my comforts."[67] Since John was neither careless nor improvident, a better guess is that he liked it the hard way. It was a means of celebrating good health.

The aggressive tone of Polk's annual message to Congress pleased Reynolds and he thought it would also please his father. In Oregon it was going to be Fifty-four Forty or Fight, and Taylor just might have to turn the army about and march north to discourage Great Britain's ambition for territory. Or so the young lieutenant informed his sisters. He thought matters with Mexico would be settled peacefully now that John Slidell had been sent to negotiate with the Herrera government. With that forecast out of the way, John went on to describe Corpus Christi—and finally, himself:

> The eating houses are grog shops of the vilest kind and the Theatre is a low-flung company of strolling actors who are striving to keep from actual starvation, and everything else is in like proportion. Upon the whole, the *Ranche*—as it has grown up since we

Sketch of Lieutenant Reynolds by a friend at Corpus Christi, 1846.

have been here—is one of the Rowdyest [sic], most cut-throat places I have ever been in. . . . There is no law of any kind, save for the Bowie knife and pistol, which is rather uncomfortable for a civilized person.

Lydia in her letter appears to have a perfect horror of my appearance. This is not at all justified as I am looking better than I ever did and don't know that I was ever hideous. In proof of the contrary now, I enclose a sketch of myself by a friend here. Tho' I do not think he has succeeded in getting a likeness at all, it will serve to put you at ease about my being in any way the frightful looking being you imagine. I am glad Hal [Harriet] goes to school to Mr C. and hope Ellie will be a good scholar by herself.[68]

A postscript included John's regret at missing a wedding in Lancaster, at which he said he would have liked to dance. His alleged appearance might scare a sister, but John himself had no doubts about his social acceptability. Yet as a political prophet he was on shakier ground. Taylor's army did not have to move north in spite of the President and Manifest Destiny. On the other hand, neither of the groups then fighting for power in Mexico would listen to Slidell. So the military situation continued hottest right where Reynolds was encamped.

And on the eve of his first campaign Lieutenant Reynolds sounded like a young man who was ready. He was tough enough to sleep without heat; he was happy working with horses; and he was much handsomer than sister Lydia thought. His morale was high. It was a good way to begin a war.

CHAPTER II

Rio Grande and Points South

The winter of 1845-46 was harder on some of the army at Corpus Christi than it was on Lieutenant Reynolds. At one time twenty per cent of the men reported sick, and half the rest deserved to be. There was also a great deal of gambling, drinking, brawling, and much desertion.[1] Yet by the time Taylor began to move south at the government's urging Grant thought the stay in camp had been well spent. He said: "A more efficient army for its number and armament I do not believe ever fought a battle than the one commanded by General Taylor in his first two engagements on Mexican—or Texan soil."[2] Grant wrote this about forty years later, after having seen much more war, but another officer was just as enthusiastic at the time the army broke camp. There never was so fine an army, John Sedgwick wrote. "It is better organized, has a greater proportion of artillery, and is better equipped than any army we have ever sent into the field."[3]

Taylor started for the Rio Grande with about 2,300 men out of a total close to 4,000. He left behind the sick and enough troops to guard the stores and other public property. Seven companies of dragoons moved out first, along with the artillery, then the three infantry brigades, each a day apart. The march began in an enchantment of distant blue mountains, tree-fringed lakes, rich farmlands, and a profusion of flowers. Within a week this idyllic countryside changed to desert, with sand like burning ashes and a searing, vertical sun.[4] Taylor had picked Point Isabel, about 150 miles south of Corpus Christi, as his supply base. From there, another 25 miles took him to the Rio Grande.

On March 28 the army began to see the church towers of Matamoros. As the troops moved nearer, across the river they could see the house-tops crowded with people waving flags and could hear bugles sounding.[5] This was a gala greeting for an army about to sink its tent stakes into the extreme southern tip of the disputed territory. Actually Taylor resented the aggressive gesture he was supposed to maintain, and he tried to reassure the authorities in the town. He arranged a conference between the second in command of the two sides, but nothing came of it. "Well," Captain George McCall said, "General Taylor's orders were positive not to commence hostilities; so here we stood looking at each other" across 150 yards of water.[6]

General Ampudia now demanded that Taylor take his army back up to Nueces again, and on its *north bank*. The Mexicans refused to accept the Texas version of its southern border. When Old Zach refused to move, the tension mounted. Then General Arista took command of the troops in Matamoros and at once began sending cavalry across the river. They soon captured two companies of dragoons, killing several officers. That did it. Both sides recognized a state of war.[7]

Reynolds had been busy from the time the first tents went up on the river bank. Construction work again. Captain Mansfield's engineers had designed a large field work to be laid inside the U of a river bend overlooking Matamoros. Reynolds, Thomas, and the other officers spent a month working with the men to dig ditches, embankments, to set up gun embrasures, and build bomb proofs.[8] The job might take long hot hours and sweat, but John would never have reason to regret a minute of his toil.

Arista's next move was to cut off Taylor's line of supply from Point Isabel to the north. To prevent this and renew his supplies Taylor started back to his base on May 1, with 2,000 men. Reynolds stayed behind in the new fort with Bragg's battery. Four 18-pounders were also held back, along with the 7th Infantry. Altogether about 500 men were available in the defenses.[9] Major Jacob Brown was given command of the fort, and his orders called for him to hold out as long as possible. This was not particularly reassuring to the garrison. The Mexicans had thrown up four sandbag works to put a converging fire on the Americans, in addition to a larger work already opposing them. Suppose Taylor failed to get back? After all, Arista's force outnumbered the isolated garrison three to one, as the men knew well enough. McCall, who had gone along with Taylor, thought the fort could hold out,[10] but Lieutenant George Meade, also on the march, had his doubts.[11]

The Mexicans began bombarding the fort on May 3. For the first time in his life John Reynolds was under enemy fire. The booming sounds rolled up along the edge of the gulf to where Grant lay safe with Taylor. In a single paragraph of his *Memoirs* Grant later set down four words: "The war had begun." Then in the next passage he added: "For myself, a young second-lieutenant who had never heard a hostile gun before, I felt sorry I had enlisted."[12] This first blast of war impressed Meade too. He described part of the bombardment in a letter to his wife, enclosing a detailed sketch of the fort, river, town, and the enemy's works.[13] He had to make his report at second-hand, from information brought in by an officer sent back to the fort by Taylor. The old general was showing some anxiety of his own.

But the garrison left on the Rio Grande had its own reporter. At the end of the bombardment he filed his dispatch: "Camp Opposite Matamoros, May 13, 1846." It appeared in Niles' *National Register* of Baltimore on the sixth of June:

> . . . On the morning of the 3rd at daylight the Mexicans opened their batteries on our fort, or rather our grand entrenchments; from that moment it was right hot work until after 12 o'clock, when both parties had to cease until their guns would cool. Were you ever shot at, in front with a 12-pounder, on a flank with a 6-pounder, and a shell directed to burst over your head? If not, try it, just to properly enjoy a brandy toddy after the gun cooling begins. Well, after the refreshments the ball continued. . . . It was only 23 minutes after we commenced our fire before one of our 18-pound shot struck their 12-pound cannon directly in the muzzle, and knocked it, head, back, and stomach into the air 20 feet, and it was accompanied by legs, hands, and arms. Seven Mexican officers were wounded, and 8 privates who were around their piece killed. We have not heard from their 12-pounder since. . . .

Omitting the toddy and the flying anatomy, Major Brown's official report generally agreed with the correspondent's. He added that Bragg's 6-pounders found the range too great to be of use and so had been posted to repel any assault. One sergeant was killed.[14] Brown made his report on the 4th and two days later he was hit. On the 8th, with mortar shells dropping in from three sides of the enclosure, Major Brown died.[15] The fort took his name and today is the site of Brownsville, Texas.

The bombardment ended next day, but now it was the garrison's turn to hear Taylor's guns at Resaca de Palma. The general was fighting his way back from his base against 6,000 Mexican troops. At Palo Alto the day before, Grant and Meade had caught up with the war themselves. The enemy had given up the field in this first fight and were routed in the second. The men in the fort began seeing the Mexicans returning in flight on the evening of May 9. As they straggled back to Matamoros there was no ringing of bells in the town. The men of Fort Brown got their first good sleep in days. Aside from the loss of Major Brown and the sergeant, casualties were light—only thirteen wounded. Reynolds' battery lost four horses, and John lost some of his hair. He found the shelling too hot for so much head-covering, so he had it cut short. ". . . Of one thing I am certain," he wrote Jane, "I can never again, I don't think, be placed in a more uncomfortable situation than the one we have just got out of. I had rather be on ten battle fields than take another week's bombardment, such as we had in 'Fort Brown.' "[16] Another officer upped the number of battles he would rather have been through to twenty.[17]

General Taylor occupied Matamoros on May 18, then sat down to wait for the new volunteers that were to help him sweep southward. Watching them arrive in great number, Reynolds said, ". . . and the cry is 'still they come.' They must amount to about 6,000."[18] He would be saying more about the volunteers later, and so would the other West Pointers. But right now he was weary of the inactivity. He looked forward to the opening of the campaign, which he thought would be brief and glorious if carried out energetically. He wanted to get at the work and have it done with.

In the meantime John had visited the hospital at Matamoros. He was shocked to see the Mexican wounded, who had been left with little medical care and less food. He said they begged for money in tones of pity that would move a harder heart than a soldier's. Along with other officers he had given dollars away among them. "Who I say could look upon all this and not thank his God most devoutly and exclaim 'I am not a Mexican.' . . . How different would have been our fate if fortune had picked on the Mexican banner in these battles. The few who served to fall into their hands would have been the most unfortunate."[19]

Now John turned to matters at home. He was glad everyone was well and hoped they would continue to be blessed with that greatest of blessings, health! His grandmother had apparently been worried about his rugged habits. "Grandma I hope will not make herself uneasy about me," he wrote. "If I have to sleep in a mudhole in the rain all night, *occasionally*, I am used to it by this time and that you know is everything. I can take care of myself and if it should be our lot to be unfortunate why there's an end of it." That should reassure Grandma, but what about this idea of Jim's wanting to enlist? "He and Sam ought to stay at home—Will and I are enough in the service, I think." And how about Will? Had he been ordered to a ship yet? Becky was not to take it too hard if he should be. The Mexicans would not be apt to hurt the navy much, John thought.

He ended his letter on a festive note: "To-night we give a dinner in the City, to the Committee of the Legislature of Louisiana—sent out to thank Genl T and the Army—and at this moment our bands are playing the 'Star Spangled Banner,' 'Hail Columbia,' &c, in the Plaza. Good bye, my love to all and may God bless you is the prayer of your affectionate brother."[20]

For the first time in his brief spell in uniform Reynolds admitted to some doubt about an army career. President Polk had nominated thirty civilians as officers for a rifle brigade. John called it the grossest kind of insult to put them over the heads of men trained at the academy. ". . . If, after this business is over and our Country once more at peace with the world I can find anything to do in any other profession I had better avail myself of it and leave the service when all hope of advancement and distinction is denied one, no matter what hardships endured or what service rendered."[21]

John Reynolds would never leave the army. He might continue to grouse, like any good soldier, but he would stay in. Too much of the life appealed to him—the outdoors, the horses, and the physical activity in general. Even his restlessness had its military advantages. After a spell in camp he was always itching to be on the move. Enough marching and he was ready for camp again. Tent life would finally pall, and he looked forward to going into barracks. Stationed in the east, he would begin eyeing a western assignment. For most of his leaves he planned more and farther travel. This urge for change was always there, and it gave the army a surer hold on him than he probably realized.

Being single also helped Reynolds. Meade complained to no less a person than his wife about the disadvantages of marriage for an engineer officer. He said their duty kept them away from home so much.[22] This was just about equally true for the rest of the army. Thus far Reynolds had escaped the problem, although he was not indifferent to women when their society was available. Too many of his letters ended with requests to be remembered to Miss so-and-so, also to the Misses this one and that one. But Reynolds could lose himself wholly for long stretches in the male world of camp, barracks, marching, and fighting. It made him an ideal type for the army at the same time his independence was making army life easier for him.

In Taylor's camps the volunteers kept arriving. Before the end of

June the general was objecting that he would have to send most of them home unless he got means to supply them.[23] By fall he complained of having almost 20,000 volunteers but not one sack of flour.[24] Reports of their conduct were discouraging. "They are perfectly ignorant of discipline and most restive under restraint," Meade wrote his wife. "They are in consequence a most disorderly mass, who will give us, I fear, more trouble than the enemy. Already our guard-houses are filled with drunken officers and men."[25] A volunteer officer himself admitted that it took a stump speech to get even the slightest order obeyed.[26] According to a correspondent with the army, these new soldiers seemed to confuse the state of war with a state of license.[27]

This was the situation Reynolds might have had in mind when he advised his brothers Sam and Jim not to enlist. Without questioning their moral stamina, he could hardly see them as ready for sudden command—or for obedience either. Like other volunteers they would be trying to give orders or take orders from men on their own level. It resulted from a system that let men elect officers from their own ranks. Neighbor suddenly found himself commanding neighbor, often with their civilian status reversed. No wonder these citizen soldiers shocked the West Pointers. They were used to the kind of private one of Taylor's officers later described: "A large majority of them write their own names, so that there can be claimed for them, *for their class*, a high degree of intelligence. It is said many of them are foreigners; this is true, and in that they represent very perfectly the population of the country. . . . Soldiers cannot be associates for refined persons; but they ought now to be as much respected as it is the custom to despise them. When called upon for duty they do not count the cost."[28]

These peacetime enlisted men reacted properly to the kind of treatment they got—the guard house, flogging, and even execution.[29] The army knew how to make its foreigners, down-and-outers, and adventurers work and fight. Volunteers called for an entirely different approach. But in this war and in every American war to follow, the professionals from the Military Academy would learn to use them effectively or lose.

Along with the other officers Reynolds continued to worry the problem. He was reconciled to using volunteers only to repel invasion. To march them onto foreign soil was something else. "All the volunteers that have been here yet acknowledge their worthlessness and would be glad to get out of the scrape. They will not be caught in it again I warrant. It is not the fighting they object to, it is the hot weather and marching that has disgusted them, and this lying idle in camp subjected to the strictest discipline that has disheartened so many of them. I have no doubt they will fight well enough when it comes to that but that is not half of what we have to undergo in the field."[30] Unlike Meade, Reynolds was showing some understanding of the spot these volunteers now found themselves in. He even gave them credit for courage, a judgment he would have plenty of chance to test.

The next move for Taylor's army was toward Monterey. He made his first stop about a hundred miles inland from Matamoros, at a new supply base he had set up at Camargo. But the new location brought no relief either from shortage of supplies or from the presence of the volunteers. By the end of August tents for some 15,000 men sprawled out for three miles along a small stream which flowed into the Rio Grande. The air was stifling among the barren limestone hills. Temperatures went up to 112 degrees. Dust, insects, and the yelping prairie wolves tormented the citizen soldiers in camp. They fared so poorly under all these hazards that Taylor left 600 of them in the hospital and sent large numbers home before beginning the next leg of his march.[31] But at last he had an army more in scale with his transport and supply. The 6,000 men remaining were about evenly divided between regulars and volunteers. The missing included several thousand three-months' recruits who, Meade complained, had eaten up 240,000 rations.[32]

Reynolds had looked forward to this march since June, and he was not disappointed. "We are entering into a very beautiful country up here. It is quite broken and in some places quite picturesque. . . . The rugged mountains of the Sierra Madre appear with their bold fronts to the south and many woods and pure springs of clear cool water are to be found every few miles. This is so different from any of the country we have yet seen that we are all anxious to move forward."[33]

The region did seem to impress everybody, especially when the road began to climb beyond Cerralvo, halfway to Monterey.[34] The army wound through fields silk-ripe in corn and past orchards heavy with fruit. The soldiers saw trees most of them had never known— ebony, Brazil wood, pecan, and wild olive. When they reached their encampment at Walnut Springs, two miles north of Monterey, an Ohio volunteer made the ultimate concession: "A more suitable spot for a picnic could not be found in the vicinity of our own Dayton."[35] Even Old Zach took time out to admire the city itself.[36]

But not Grant. His eye was solely on a war. All he saw was what an army would have to attack. There was the city "backed by a range of hills of moderate elevation." There was the "Black Fort" out on a plain in front, its guns commanding "the approaches to the city to the full extent of their range."[37] Even the terminology was military. Grant also took note of the fortified heights to the west, the redoubts at the eastern end of Monterey, and the Plaza with its cathedral-turned-arsenal. The sandbagged roofs of the stout masonry houses, and the overlapping entrenchments fronting the whole, completed the scenery for Grant.

Bragg had his battery out the next morning. The officer from Dayton passed by while they were at work. "We paused in our walk to witness the morning drill of Captain Bragg's excellent company of artillery. The horses, as well as the men, seemed to understand their business perfectly; and being of 'fine bone and blood,' they whirled the guns and caissons over the plain with wonderful rapidity and ease."[38] John Reynolds' "stupid Germans and Irishmen" had apparently learned something after all.

Before reaching Monterey John had written that he expected to spend his twenty-third birthday there. "Who would ever have thought of this?" he asked. "I hope the next one will be spent in the U. S. some-where—I am not particular, almost anywhere will do. You must not think, however, from this that I am not in good spirits—that I always am so long as I am in good health. I have never been in better health than I am now, but I think I have been most long enough in this country."[39]

Early on September 21, 1846, Reynolds took his health and good spirits into the city to spend his birthday. He would celebrate the event by firing his 6-pounders from early forenoon until dusk. Taylor had started the battle the afternoon before, moving General William Worth out to the west with 2,000 men and two batteries of artillery. Meade with a party of engineers led his reconnaissance. Worth's orders were to turn the city's left flank, which would cut the city and Am-pudia's 10,000 troops from their supply route to Saltillo. What brought Reynolds into the fighting was Taylor's demonstration against the east end of town. By striking there while Worth was approaching the op-posite end, he hoped to divert attention from the main attack. But Taylor's first column of infantry ran into trouble. It went too far to the right of the main enemy defense, which was Fort Teneria. The advance quickly got tangled up in a maze of suburban gardens, narrow lanes, and high stone walls.[40]

The scrambled situation called for help, and both Bragg and Ran-dolph Ridgely were ordered in with their batteries. Captain John Kenly of the Baltimore volunteers saw Reynolds' section of two guns move in: ". . . it had come in by the way we had come, and met with a rough reception; it looked as if it had, and where it was now not much would have been left of it in a few minutes if not ordered out, which was done. To turn the leading piece was difficult in the narrow street; this was effected by lifting the gun carriage jam up to the wall of the house, in front of which it had been halted, by officers and men of the Baltimore battalion. This gun disengaged, the other followed it out onto the plain."[41]

Reynolds' pride would have resented help from volunteers, but it was the kind of frustration the artillery faced all day long. Meanwhile Taylor had sent another column into the east end. This force kept farther to the left and got into the rear of Teneria. Jefferson Davis with the Mississippi Rifles and another volunteer regiment from Tennessee stormed the fort. They got help from some of the first column that went in and soon captured it. While this fighting was in progress, Reynolds' gun section wheeled out to the north edge of town. About two hundred Mexican lancers had charged in over the plain from the Black Fort. The artillery was given the job of meeting this threat to the rear of Taylor's assaulting troops. So for a change Reynolds had a target out in the open, and a few shells sent the horsemen scattering back toward the fort.

But now Taylor ordered the 6-pounders into the streets again. If anything, their luck was worse than before, and Lieutenant Sam French reported the outcome:

> From this situation we were ordered out. In passing an opening in the works a shot killed the two wheel horses to one of the caissons, and Lieut. Reynolds and I with the men, threw, or pushed, the horses and harness into ditches on either side, and after we had done this and gone some distance, another shot passed through two horses of one of the guns. These horses were loosed, and with their entrails dragging, in agony of pain, I suppose, commenced eating the grass.
>
> Having gotten out, Bragg ordered me back alone to the ditch at the edge of the town to save the harness that was on the horses. I met General Taylor, who enquired where I was going. When told, he said, "That is nonsense," and ordered me back to camp. . . . I never forgave Bragg for that picayune order.[42]

And Bragg probably never forgave French for returning without the harness.

About this time there happened along the same officer who had admired the battery's snappy drill before the battle. What he saw now was different. The once proud outfit looked to be in a bad way—in fact a perfect wreck. "A few of his [Bragg's] artillerymen, and more than a dozen of his horses, were down in the same spot, making the ground about the guns slippery with their gasped foam and blood. The intrepid Captain and his men, though exposed the while to a galling fire, were deliberately engaged in re-fitting the teams and in stripping the harness from the dead and disabled animals, determined that not a buckle or strap should be lost upon the field."[43] Sam French no doubt agreed. But say for Bragg that he never lost sight of the tight supply problem. For want of a strap no battle would be lost if he could do anything about saving the strap.

Before the end of the day Reynolds got one more chance at a cavalry target. He and Bragg each took a gun to drive off another troop of lancers south of the small stream that ran through the town. By nightfall Taylor's foothold in the east end of Monterey was secure, thanks largely to the fall of Teneria. Except for the regular infantry and Ridgely's battery the general pulled the rest of his troops back into camp at Walnut Springs. On September 22 the only fighting that counted took place toward the west. Worth's division had got across the Saltillo road during the first evening, and at daybreak of the 22nd began storming the fortified heights in its sector. By nightfall Worth had taken this key to the defenders' position, forcing Ampudia to concentrate his troops in the center of town.

While Taylor was leaving the battle to Worth, Reynolds spent most of the day with his battery in reserve under a slight elevation in front of the town.[44] But not the whole day. The Black Fort out on the plain to the north discovered Bragg's location before long and shelled it for several hours with 18-pounders. It was not so bad at first, only spraying gravel and dirt from the rise in ground above. Then with the ground wearing gradually away, the position got too hot to expose the guns further, so the battery was ordered out along with its infantry support. Captain Kenly saw the dread in the faces of the artillerymen as they made ready for their dash under fire.[45] But Kenly was an infantry officer, whose soldiers had only to grab their rifles and run. It was quite another matter to struggle out over the exposed plain with the 6-pounders, caissons, and teams.

Shortly after daybreak on the 23rd, Taylor's regulars, Grant among them, began a touchy house-to-house advance from the east toward the fortified plaza in Monterey's center. General Worth was already cutting his way in from the opposite end of town. Cut was the right word, for his men smashed through the walls from one house to the next in order to avoid the raking fire in the streets.[46] If the pincers worked it would crowd Ampudia's force around the cathedral and end the fighting in a few hours. Meanwhile Reynolds was back again with the rest of the battery. This time they managed to work in close enough to shell two of the smaller fortifications and even had the cathedral in range before the day ended.

As on the first day, Reynolds thought that except for the howitzer

the guns got badly used up without much to show for the effort. The
6-pounders simply lacked the weight for the job. The adobe houses
merely flung back clouds of dust and lime, which blinded the men
and obstructed their view of targets. The tougher masonry houses
gave back nothing at all. Worse yet, the flat roofs sheltered Mexican
sharpshooters who kept trying to pick off the gunners and horses.
Reynolds put the battery's loss at 14 men and 22 horses for the two
days. In view of the hazards he thought they were lucky to get off with
as little punishment.[47]

Taylor pulled the battery out before dusk. By now his infantry on
both sides had got in far enough to mop up all except the resistance
in the cathedral itself. Worth's push from the west end was particularly
fruitful. His part of the offensive had gone well from the start although
it took hard fighting. He captured Monterey's two most important
defenses on the first day out—Federation and Independence hills—
and Meade thought he handled his men better than Taylor did when
he got into the town.[48] For a while, with the battle about over, it
looked as if the cathedral might last out the night. But before daylight
of September 24 Ampudia decided he had had enough and asked for
terms.

Taylor's generous armistice let the Mexicans march out of Monterey
with their flags, sidearms, personal property, and six guns. This kindness shocked the administration in Washington, and as criticism
mounted Taylor defended himself. He admitted that his instructions
hardly justified the terms he had offered. "The gallant defense of the
town, and the fact of a recent change in government in Mexico, believed to be favorable to the interest of peace, induced me to concur
with the commission in these terms."[49] Several weeks later he added
that he had wanted to avoid further bloodshed or harm to the citizens,
and that anyhow the enemy force was too large.[50] Taylor had in fact
taken the place with fewer men than Ampudia led, reversing the usual
ratio of attackers to defenders. American casualties were 128 killed
and 368 wounded.[51] The general got a good press at home for his
victory, as he had after Palo Alto and Resaca de Palma. The Whigs
were already talking up Old Rough and Ready for the presidency.

In refighting the battle around camp plenty of talk went on in
the battery over using light artillery in cramped city streets. For one,
Reynolds had his say: "In the first place our battery was ordered into
town on the 21st, with four guns, four caissons, and six horses to a
carriage. It was discovered that only one gun could be brought into
action, the remainder was therefore exposed to the fire from the enemy's
works without being of the least use. It was therefore ordered back

where it started from, and which it never should have left. . . ."[52] Certainly nothing in General Winfield Scott's *Instructions for Field Artillery, Horse and Foot* had prepared Reynolds or his battery mates for maneuvers like these. "By the left wheel" made some sense on the flat terrain of the drill ground, but the manual was silent on the handling of guns jammed up against house walls in mere alleyways.

Others besides the artillerymen themselves saw what they had to contend with in Monterey. One reporter thought bows and arrows would have done as much harm to the fortifications as shells from 6-pounders.[53] A historian felt that it was at least extraordinary to send batteries into narrow streets against heavy stone works and roofs filled with protected marksmen.[54] Yet, while Reynolds agreed with this criticism and knew it was Taylor who had put the guns in the town, he still could see no wrong in Old Zach's leadership. The general's military skill was and has been questioned,[55] but never by the young lieutenant.

In spite of its lack of effectiveness at Monterey, the artillery was rewarded for its hard try. Taylor's report had strong praise for both Bragg's and Ridgely's batteries, though without mentioning other names.[56] General David Twiggs, who led a division which attacked on the east end of town, was more specific: "Captains R. Ridgely and B. Bragg, and their subalterns, W. H. Shover, G. H. Thomas, John F. Reynolds, C. L. Kilburn, and Samuel G. French, deserve the highest praise for their skill and conduct."[57] To be cited favorably in official battle reports is lifeblood for professional soldiers. Reynolds would not be disappointed at sharing mention with a half dozen others. In his first active engagement (Fort Brown hardly counted) he was down in black and white forever. The war department took most careful note of individual performance as described in the records, so he knew he had made a good start.

There was other military action beside Taylor's in the summer of 1846. Colonel Stephen Kearny struck through New Mexico with 1,700 men, ran up the United States flag to claim Santa Fe, then pushed on into California. Breaking off from Kearny, Colonel A. W. Doniphan marched 800 troops south to whip the Mexicans at Barzito, Sacramento, and Chihuahua. General John E. Wool had more trouble in moving out of San Antonio with 1,400 poorly trained volunteers, but at least he was able to join Worth at Saltillo, which the Mexicans gave up after losing Monterey.

During a lull in Taylor's operations, which lasted through autumn, Reynolds was active in a favorite pastime—hunting. His usual companion was Sam French, and together they also located a good bathing spot in a hot spring not too far from camp.[58] Then in December, with the battery temporarily under George Thomas, they marched in a force of 2,000 men southeast toward Tampico, on the Gulf. A freshly recruited volunteer army under General Robert Patterson had been moving down from the Rio Grande to explore the mountain passes and the country in that direction. Taylor intended to join part of his troops with Patterson's, but other events kept him from getting beyond Victoria.

It was a wasted trek despite an elaborate review Taylor staged in the city square of Victoria. When Reynolds got back to Monterey, he wrote his brother Jim: "We had been sent ahead with the volunteers alone on the march down and had anything but a pleasant time of it—and now since we have returned we find all the regulars here have gone down the river with General Worth, so that we are likely to see enough of the volunteers yet. Will's idea of them is perfectly correct and I have no doubt those you speak of from Phila will turn out worse than the Baltimore boys."[59]

It was only later that Reynolds really learned what happened to those regulars. They had gone from Taylor for good. General Scott was gathering his "Army of Invasion" for the main drive into Mexico and he wanted troops—good troops. He had been nice enough to come down to Camargo, hoping to find Taylor himself before robbing him. But since the old general had already left on his march south, Scott's problem was simplified. He merely wrote out an order detaching the regulars, chiefly infantry, and marched them off. Reynolds insisted that Taylor had no knowledge of the plans for Scott's campaign and that if Washington had only informed him in time it would have saved the futile march toward Tampico. What upset Reynolds even more was that dispatches describing the new operations were intercepted by the Mexicans. "If they are not very careful at W.," he wrote, "they will get the Army *whipped* yet. Some of their ideas are so absurd that they are really laughable."[60]

In these remarks Reynolds was writing for the first time what he would say over and over again from 1861 to 1863. He never could accept the logic of a war directed by authorities remote from the field of operations. And at this point Washington was a long, long way from Mexico. But what about John's politics? Was good Democrat Reynolds getting Tayloritis along with the Whigs up north? He might quarrel with the administration on military grounds, but his family's political allegiance belonged to the "in's." John's benefactor, James Buchanan, would never question his government's strategy in regard to the war.

Santa Anna had returned from exile, and that could mean more trouble for what was left of Taylor's army. President Polk had let the former Mexican leader come back to his country—had helped him, in fact, on his promise to work for peace. It was Santa Anna's men who captured the dispatches and killed the small party bringing them to Taylor from Washington. So Taylor, having returned to the Monterey-Saltillo area, faced real trouble. The main offensive was about to shift south under Scott, which would leave his own troops a mere holding force. In the meantime his strength had been reduced to 4,700 men, mostly raw volunteers. Finally, Santa Anna was "working for peace" by building an army of 20,000, and meant to strike Taylor quickly in order to swing south against Scott's invasion from the Gulf.

Santa Anna impressed Reynolds. ". . . He knows what he is about I think and will give us more trouble than all the [other] Mexican generals together." Reynolds already had news of enemy activity. Mexican lancers had just captured two companies of Kentucky cavalry sent out on a scouting expedition by General Wool. The Americans were trapped about 25 miles south of Saltillo, at Agua Nueva. Reynolds showed his disgust: "The story goes that they were surprised and surrounded . . . at night. They had no precautions against surprise, had no pickets or sentinels and were taken asleep without firing a gun. . . . I think upon the whole we have the most careless, indifferent disposition to danger and less caution and watchfulness than any other people —the Mexicans can beat us altogether in this respect."[61]

Reynolds hardly needed the lesson of the Kentuckians' slack behavior, but it probably stuck in his memory. At least in later years no general ever surpassed him in his zeal for protecting soldiers in camp.[62]

Like most of the West Pointers, Lieutenant Reynolds was welcome at Taylor's headquarters. The general knew fighting at first-hand far better than they did, but he respected the professional training of these academy graduates. As for Reynolds himself, Taylor's adjutant general William Bliss had already written one of John's professors that "your young friend has the general's high regard and is the idol of his men."[63] Taylor confided freely with his officers, so when Reynolds wrote his brother Jim again on February 5, 1847, he had a full report on how his chief felt about things:

> General T. is perfectly disgusted with the part assigned to him here, of sitting down quietly in front of Saltillo for the Winter. He is also highly indignant at the attempt made by the administration to cover their late act of injustice to him by circulating through the papers that it was at Genl T's request Genl Scott was sent out to supersede him. True, Genl T. after the battles on the Rio Grande did inform the Dept. that he did not wish to be in the way of Genl S. or

interfere in any way with his being sent to take command of the army then, but with the distinct understanding that *he* would be permitted to serve under him in the active movements then contemplated. He certainly never expected the treatment he has now rec^d at their hands, withdrawing all the regular troops and the greater part of the volunteers to go upon a distant and dangerous expedition and leave him behind with a small force scarcely sufficient to hold the country he has conquered. This however is not the first instance of ingratitude they have been guilty of.

The estimate made by Reynolds of Taylor's strength at this time was 4,500 men. The force included sixteen pieces of artillery, all under the regular officers. But there was a change in the command of Reynolds' battery. George Thomas had to give way to Captain T. W. Sherman on February 14.[64] It was bad news for the subalterns. Reynolds, Thomas, and French had got out from under Bragg only to draw Sherman. And not the *good* Sherman either. William T. (Cump) Sherman had been put in the quartermaster department and kept in New Orleans before operations along the Rio Grande started. Bragg now led the battery Ridgely had until he was killed in a fall from his horse after the battle of Monterey. Ridgely was a great favorite among the artillerymen, and along with others, Reynolds and French sadly regretted his passing.[65]

John was finding it cold in Saltillo, especially with the scarcity of wood. He wondered why any people would put a large town on a hillside where there was no convenience of any kind except brackish water. He said the town was built of mud and was unprepossessing. The plaza with its inevitable cathedral and a few large buildings nearby were all he could find that made any pretension to elegance and comfort.[66] Reynolds wanted a warmer place that had plenty of wood, and good water. Yet when he moved on down to Agua Nueva some ten days later, neither the climate nor the countryside seemed to improve:

> We are now . . . situated in a large plain as barren and bleak as one can well imagine. We are now, the Mexicans say, in the middle of Winter, which usually lasts until April. I don't know when I have suffered more from the cold in many years than I have since we left Monterey to march for Victoria. It was exceptionally cold during the whole march and since we have been here we have had ice regularly every night and last night it tried its hand at snowing but did not succeed very well, further than to clothe some of the high peaks around us with a frosty mantle. Occasionally the sun will break through the clouds and remind us that we are yet in the vicinity of

the tropics—but only for a day—the next day comes a cold and chill-
ing Norther which reminds us of our homes in the north *very
forcibly. . . .*

I sleep on the ground with four blankets in a tent by myself. Three
of us mess together on what the Commissary furnishes—occasionally
varied by chickens and eggs which we get from the Mexicans—drink
nothing but pure *water* (the liquor in this country is a most villain-
ous compound)[67]—see very little or nothing at all of the Signoritas—
I have seen only one pretty face since I have been in the country, the
Spanish Counsel's [sic] daughter at Monterey—and wear no uniform
at all save a jacket and forage cap and then but rarely. . . . I talk very
little and very *bad* Spanish and do not dance at all. I have *seen* a
Fandango which is quite enough for me. . . .[68]

In that paragraph John hoped he was answering all the questions
the family had been asking. Of course it was Jim who had wanted to
know about the liquor and the women. He would probably be disappointed. In the letter John enclosed a copy of one of the maps found in
General Arista's baggage, which was recovered at Resaca. He said it
was the only one that gave any real idea of the country and he thought
Father might like to see it. He had left some vacant spaces which he
said were taken up on the original by coats of arms, etc., "inscribed
to the glory of Mr. Arista with 'El honor Mexicann se halla en Tejas,'
and like nonsense and bombast which I had neither time nor inclination
to copy."[69]

A young combat veteran who scorned wearing his uniform had no
time for the military frills of Mexican generals. John Reynolds had
seen duty in a foreign country for almost a year now. He had endured
a week's siege, fought in a three-day battle, and made the rugged
200-mile march down to Victoria. In his twenty-sixth year he had come
of age as a soldier. He had already earned praise from his superiors, he
was liked by his commanding general, and he was popular with his
men. It was certainly a good start. But so far the light artillery had not
been fairly tested. If the chance only came to fight the 6-pounders
under the right conditions, he was sure they would prove themselves.
Just let that opportunity come. It could mean a lot in John Reynolds'
future.

CHAPTER III

Six-Pounders at Buena Vista

Less than two weeks after John Reynolds went down to Agua Nueva he got into the biggest battle he would fight until fifteen years had passed. Santa Anna was on his way north. His army outnumbered Taylor's force by four to one, and it came on well equipped. For its leader it was all or nothing. By driving Taylor he could swing through to reclaim the whole Rio Grande valley. His booty would include stores of American munitions, provisions, camps, and all manner of public property. On the other hand, to lose would be to find himself a discredited adventurer. With a beaten army he could never hope to retreat over the desert he had just crossed. He had to win.[1]

Taylor knew Santa Anna was on the way. A reconnaissance on February 20 had touched his advance, but the Mexicans moved up so fast Taylor had to burn his supplies at Agua Nueva and pull out the troops stationed there. He withdrew them to the position already picked for making a stand. As a battlefield it proved to be about the most peculiar terrain two armies ever fought over,[2] yet Taylor trusted its rugged features to handicap his foe.

About a dozen miles north of Agua Nueva and half that distance from Saltillo lay Buena Vista, along the road which cut the valley of Encantado. The stark beauty of the area equaled its place names. Buena Vista itself consisted of a scattering of ranch buildings and a hacienda. Taylor prepared to defend a point some two miles south of Buena Vista. Here ravines to the left and deep gullies on the right pinched the road into a place called the Narrows. His center topped a plateau about eighty feet above the road on the left as he faced south.

The impassable gullies extending down from the mountains sealed him from attack on the west (his right). Taylor's center and left also fronted broken ground, but on this side of the road the slope up to the opposite heights was more gradual. The ravines were shallower and the ridges between them would allow some maneuvering. The main ridge, or plateau, leveled out for several hundred yards almost to the road. It was here that Old Zach set up headquarters.

Santa Anna chose Washington's birthday to start the battle. He drove in Taylor's outposts, then informed him that he was surrounded and demanded his surrender.[3] When Taylor refused to shame the memory of the first President by submitting, the Mexican general formed his infantry lines south of the main plateau and covered their flanks with artillery and cavalry. His first advance was toward the eastern mountains on Taylor's left. He put Ampudia with four battalions into this move, supported by a howitzer. It began an attempt he never gave up—to get past Taylor along the base of the mountain into Buena Vista. It would put him in the American rear and cut off supplies.

By the middle of the afternoon Santa Anna had succeeded well enough to open fire against the mounted Arkansas and Kentucky volunteers in an effort to outflank them. Heavy skirmishing followed and kept moving higher along the mountain until almost dark. At this point Taylor arrived from Saltillo, where he had been arranging for its defense, if affairs should come to that. He inspected General Wool's positions and, apparently satisfied, turned around and rode back to town.

Lieutenant Reynolds slept on the ground that night, with nothing but his overcoat and an extra cloak:

> . . . It was a bitter cold night and I had a slight inclination to a chill and was fearful I should be sick the next day. The morning sun shone on us so brilliantly as to remind one of Napoleon's sun at Austerlitz, and after being allowed to take a piece of ham and hard bread—for we had no fires and no wood to burn—we took our posts in line. . . . I never went into action in better spirits in my life, the excitement entirely dissipated any sign of a return of my chills—and tho' I know that our Arty was not as efficient as it should be, for we had only a few weeks ago received 30 recruits, so all our gunners, or cannoneers, were raw and scarcely drilled men who had never been in a fight, our drivers were the old soldiers we had at Monterey. I thought if only our volunteers would stand by our guns we need have nothing to fear.

About 8 o'clock the Mexican line formed beyond the brow of a slight ridge, which protected the ground they encamped upon, advanced in beautiful order making a sort of feint to advance upon the road, and then suddenly changing direction to their right, came up over the ridges across the plateau I spoke of before, on which our line was formed. I never in my life beheld a more beautiful sight; their gay uniforms, numberless pennants, standards and colors streaming in the sun shone out in all their 'pride and pomp.' . . .[4]

Along with the beauty, Reynolds also noted that the Mexican line appeared to be about three times as long as their own and four times as deep, not counting a second line in reserve. He was glad to find further that when the shock came the American volunteers stood up to it; "now giving way and again advancing, [they] maintained their ground against fearful odds for an hour or two."[5] Their behavior bore out Reynolds' prediction of the previous autumn, that so far as the fighting itself was concerned he had no doubt they would do all right.[6]

But for all the courage of the volunteers this first attack came close to disaster. The Mexicans partially succeeded in enfilading Taylor's left from the heights Ampudia had reached the afternoon before. Thus the weight thrown against both front and flank crowded the Arkansas and Kentucky troops back on Bowles's 2nd Indiana near the center. Finally they broke under the raking fire, which peeled away the support from three of Captain John Washington's guns under Lieutenant J. P. J. O'Brien. This young officer had the pieces up on the main plateau, where he hung on until he lost one. By day's end he became the hottest artillerist in a battle that made heroes of them all.[7]

It was this crisis that had rushed Bragg's and Sherman's batteries in from reserve, along with infantry, and it accounted for Reynolds' presence on the plateau. But much as he was needed there he soon had to be pulled out with two guns and hurried north toward Buena Vista. His task was to support May's dragoons in protecting a wagon train on the road. It meant close to a two-mile gallop, and by the time he got his guns into battery the Mexican cavalry were already being driven off. He still managed to catch them within range of spherical case shot. To make the best of the few moments left, Reynolds prepared the fuses himself at the caissons while Sam French directed the fire.[8]

Now he limbered up his two pieces and headed east of the ranch buildings, where more lancers had broken through to the American rear. Again he had to catch them on the rebound. "Although distant," a cavalry officer wrote, "they were not out of reach of Lieutenant Reynolds' guns. He brought his section into battery just below the hacienda and . . . he continued to play upon them with astonishing accuracy and great execution."[9] It was good work, but if Santa Anna ever got this far in rear with his infantry, the dragoons and 6-pounders would not be enough to keep them off.

Meanwhile the pressure kept mounting to the south, both on the plateau and on the ridges immediately behind it. Jeff Davis had formed his Mississippi Rifles below the brow of one of these ridges, where he was waiting for a column moving down to attack. Captain James Carleton, the same officer who had just liked Reynolds' handling of his guns, was impressed by the approach of this Mexican formation: "Every lancer sat erect, and kept his charger well in hand; and the whole brigade, preserving exactly its intervals and the direction of its march, moved forward with the ease and regularity of the best-drilled troops on a field-day. . . . It had a sort of air about it—an easy, nonchalant manner of going into the work,—which could not but recall to one's mind his ideal pictures of the cavalry of the olden days."[10]

But for all their poise and brilliance of color the lancers came on too slowly. Carleton thought they wanted to draw the American fire while still out of range. Instead, Davis held off until the column came closer and halted. Then he gave the order. Gradually the infantry fire, aided by guns which reversed position on the plateau, began to eat into the lancers' sweep. About this time Reynolds and May's dragoons roared panting back from Buena Vista and whipped into action. Bragg had already got in ahead with three pieces and Reynolds kept working to closer positions in support. He might not like his former captain, but he respected courage in any soldier. Besides, Bragg was well up in front and needed help. With the 3rd Indiana now throwing in its strength, the firepower was up to the job.

Between five and six thousand Mexicans were driven back to the base of the mountain. For a time the American artillery kept forcing them in the opposite direction from their main body. Then, apparently in an attempt to avoid being isolated, they broke out a white flag, hoping to buy time enough to backtrack toward their own lines.[11] Taylor's men slacked off their fire until they saw that the courtesy was not being returned, but this interruption assured the success of the Mexicans' ruse. Anyhow, Taylor's left was finally safe. The general himself had come up from Saltillo with the dragoons and Davis just in time to meet the threat. Now at last he was on location for the final push.

Santa Anna still had one more move—and he made it. He sent 12,000 troops against the center on the plateau. It was a final desperate try, but he had the reserves to throw in. To meet this new assault Taylor had to realign his force to the south again, the way he had begun the fight. The recent attacks had bent his lines back so far on the left that they faced almost due east toward the mountain. Fortunately his right had never been in trouble. In addition to the natural obstacles on that side he was solidly anchored by Washington's four guns in the road just below the plateau. This stout artilleryman had hurled back every-thing thrown against him since morning.[12] He even lent O'Brien another gun to replace the one his lieutenant had lost to the Mexicans.

For defense of the plateau Taylor had Hardin's 1st Illinois, Bissell's 2nd Illinois, McKee's 2nd Kentucky, Conner's Texans, and O'Brien and Thomas with their guns. But this force would be too small unless help arrived from the north—and soon. The infantry and the 6-pounders which had just done so well on the ridges behind the plateau were going to be needed. Out to the left the Mexicans were so close they could almost lay their hands on the muzzles of the 6-pounders. Once more O'Brien held on till the last minute, this time losing two more pieces.[13] The Illinois and Kentucky troops now tried to counter Santa Anna by a forward push of their own. Before they could make much headway they got pinned in a ravine near the road. Here they made a hard fight of it. Colonel Hardin went down and Colonel McKee was mortally wounded, as was also the son of Henry Clay.

"But by this time Bragg and Sherman, lashing and spurring their tired horses, came up from the North field. . . . Without support Bragg whirled his guns into battery only a few rods from the enemy, and Sherman followed his example. . . ."[14] The Mississippi Rifles and Lane's Hoosiers also double-quicked from the rear of the plateau. From then on it was a storybook finish for the Americans, and artillery made the difference. Seventeen guns swept the Mexicans with grape shot and canister. Although French lay wounded back at the hacienda, Reynolds, Thomas, and the others stood to the work with their captains until 5 o'clock. Santa Anna was through. Except for a fitful skirmish or two he had little army left when darkness and chill settled down into the valley of Encantado.

It was all right with Reynolds that Santa Anna had quit, and his letter to Jane covered what happened from there:

> . . . From the noise that night we rather imagined that the enemy was withdrawing from the field and were not a little glad to find it so the next morning. Our battery was in the advance on the plateau, and after being up the greater part of the night getting forage for the horses, and more ammunition, I lay down on the hard rocks with nothing but my cloak around me and snatched a few hours sleep, when the intense coldness woke me in the morning long before day-break. I had time to think of you all at home and how comfortable you were there, little thinking of the critical condition we were in. . . .
>
> This has been the greatest battle yet. I thought that at Monterey I had been in a pretty tight place but it was nothing to this. For eight hours incessantly we were in the hottest places and only one

officer touched. Lt. French got a pretty severe wound in the right
thigh but I think by no means a dangerous one. The rest of us
escaped unhurt, how I cannot imagine. The loss in our Company is
1 sergt, 2 corpls, 1 musician and 6 privates wounded, some mortally,
12 or 14 horses killed or wounded. We are pretty well used up, both
men and horses. . . .[15]

Reynolds' estimate of the day's losses among all troops was about
the same as Taylor reported on the sixth of March: 267 killed, 456
wounded, and 23 missing. Both put the Mexican cost at from 1,500 to
2,000 casualties.[16] In continuing his letter, Reynolds described the
enemy prisoners as miserable beings, who were half starved. They had
not eaten for two days, he learned, but were promised great feasting on
American provisions if they whipped Taylor. These poor soldiers
affected Reynolds in the same way as those he saw earlier in the hospitals of Matamoros. His only response was pity. He might have to shoot
Mexicans again, but it would be only to win, never to exult in the killing
itself. He could be determined and aggressive without hating. Sheer
lust for fighting was not in his heart. Instead of feeding on the peculiar
chemistry of battle fever Reynolds would always have to motivate his
actions from his head.

It seemed to Reynolds that the victory at Buena Vista should just
about end the war. He said many of the officers expected Vera Cruz,
down on the Gulf, to be abandoned. "I hope so," he added, "for both
Scott and Worth have tried to ruin Genl T and I hope the war will end
just in time to give them no further chance." At this point Reynolds was
higher than ever on his chief. "Let them do now what they will, Genl T
will be the next Presdt in spite of everything. The Administration have
also treated him in a shameful manner—however he only becomes the
greater the more difficulties thicken around him. I never saw him so
perfectly cool and determined in my life before. He was in a good
humor the whole fight, and appeared perfectly certain of gaining the
day."[17]

Captain Joseph K. F. Mansfield of the engineers agreed with Reynolds on the old general's behavior in the battle. He thought Taylor
fought Buena Vista without a mistake, though he "was made *ragged* by
the balls passing through his clothes."[18] In his own report, Taylor gave
full credit to the army. He was well aware of what the guns in particular had accomplished, and he named Reynolds among the officers
commended. General Wool was more to the point: "Without our
artillery," he said, "we could not have maintained our position a single
hour," and also: ". . . a section of artillery, admirably served by
Lieutenant Reynolds, 3rd Arty, played an important part in checking

and dispersing the enemy in the rear of our left. They retired before him whenever he approached them." Colonel May added praise for Reynolds' promptness, as well as for his steady and destructive fire. May held for the end of his report his "warmest thanks for the gallant and bold manoeuver in which he [Reynolds] rendered the most important and effective service." Captain Sherman, Reynolds' commander, said: "Lieutenants Thomas and Reynolds behaved nobly throughout the action, and their coolness and firmness contributed not a little to the success of the day."[19]

All these glowing words should have convinced Reynolds that he did well in the first battle that really gave him a chance. Fort Brown was a siege, with his battery (then Bragg's) practically immobilized. Monterey was a futile gamble in the streets. But Buena Vista was a field day in that he could fight his guns over open ground. At last he had caught up with the drill manual.

Reynolds' maneuvering on the 23rd was phenomenal. He began the day in reserve more than a mile north of the plateau. He was brought up from there to help fight off the first push against Taylor's center. Soon after that he was hustled to the rear again to protect the wagon train which was threatened near the hacienda. From there he kept moving gradually eastward as he spotted positions for holding the Mexicans in range. Now back south again, pounding toward the plateau. Along with Bragg he worked in almost to the mountain in support of Jefferson Davis. At the end he was back on the plateau itself to meet the final assault. A busy day, taken all together.

But Lieutenant Reynolds had a long time to wait before he would be as active again. From here on the war was General Scott's. He had occupied Vera Cruz at the end of March in 1847, and with 12,000 troops he began fighting his way west to the Mexican capital. Meanwhile Taylor's army lay idle, and Reynolds with it. At least he had more time to write. A comment from Jim got a quick response: "The account you refer to signed 'Buena Vista' was evidently written by *a man of Education,* but not as you suppose, by any lawyer in the Ky. Regt., tho' no doubt all lawyers must *be men of education.* It was written by Lieut. Kingsbury of the Ordnance Dept, a particular and intimate friend of mine."[20] But it would suit him just as well, Reynolds added, if the authorship were kept secret. While it was pleasant to see his own efforts so glowingly played up in Niles' *National Register,*[21] it might be embarrassing if it got about that the writer was an old friend of John's West Point years.

He was glad to see that celebrations were in vogue in the states, John told his brother, though he was not eager to be the cause of any more of them. It was all right with him if the war ended now. About Taylor's nomination for president he said: "Genl T's principles are of the Whig party; tho' a perfect Democrat in appearance and habit he differs from that party principally on the Bank question. He has never been much of a politician and I do not think cares much about politics. He has one good recommendation however, he is I believe perfectly honest and honorable in all his public dealings, which is more than can be said of many of the other political candidates."[22] After all, a nonpracticing Democrat like John Reynolds could accept the mild Whiggism of a great general like Taylor.

It was all right with Reynolds to have the fighting over for a while, but in an army merely marking time his old restlessness began to set in. He wanted to move. One chance might be an instructorship at West Point—if he could get one. This idea had first occurred to him the year before, and he had asked his father to look into the possibility. Now it semed more important than ever, with the weeks of inactivity dragging along. Spring, and still no word from home; nothing until the end of April:

Cornwall Apr 27th, 1847

My dear Son:

I wrote you in December last by Lieut. Edward Hayes of your Regiment, whom I met in New York, informing you what I had done and was doing in an endeavor to get you a situation at West Point, as you seemed to believe that with the taking of Monterey the war had or would most probably terminate. About the time I wrote you it was becoming evident that the war was not going to end as rapidly as you had expected and that further operations on the part of our forces would ere long take place. I therefore said nothing further about the West Point business thinking it would be better for you to take your chance in the further progress of the war. It is true that with yourself I felt some mortification that you were not to have a chance of gaining some distinction in the operations on the coast of Vera Cruz &c. But it has, I doubt not, turned out better as it is, you have had an earlier and better chance at Buena Vista than you would have had at Vera Cruz and you have been fortunate enough to have gained some distinction by your part in the desperate and bloody fight. . . .[23]

John's father had seen the account by "Buena Vista," as well as the reports of General Taylor and his subordinates. "I need not, I am confident, assure you how gratifying this has been to me and all the family." John's grandmother had been quite ill, his father said, and was most concerned for the boy's success and still more for his safety. An editorial notice had appeared in the Philadelphia *Pennsylvanian* stating that "Lt. Reynolds who rendered such opportune aid with his battery on the bloody field of Buena Vista and whose services are so handsomely noticed by Gen. Taylor in his official despatch, is a native and citizen of Lancaster in this state." The family were very proud of that too. Near the end of the letter John's father said: "I wrote to Mr. Buchanan mentioning your participation in the defense of Fort Brown, the taking of Monterey and the repulse of Santa Anna at Buena Vista— asking him if, on looking at your course, he felt freedom to do so, to say a favorable word for you at the War Department. . . ."[24]

By a "favorable word" Mr. Reynolds probably meant a brevet. Brevets were granted for gallantry in action or for meritorious service. But except under the most special circumstances they remained purely honorary. They offered neither more pay nor exercise of advanced rank. A brevet did serve to single a man out, however, especially when it rewarded gallant fighting. Reynolds had certainly fought well in two battles, but was it going to require the added help of a Mr. Buchanan to win a brevet? Of course, it was only because of Mr. B. that he was in the army at all. That was one way to look at it. Maybe political influence went hand in hand with a military career—all the way. Granting this, it was at least reassuring for John to have his father watching out for his best interests. But under these conditions could a brevet have any real meaning?

Reynolds reacted to the prospect of one in writing his brother Jim. "You have my thanks for your opinion relative to my being breveted. I am perfectly indifferent to it and care not whether I am included amongst those so distinguished or not. The system is a complete humbug and until it changes I believe it is to be rather more of distinction to be passed over than to be breveted . . . that is, amongst us who know the facts. With the people it may be different."[25] This sounded a little like rationalization on Reynolds' part. Congress would grant him brevets for services both at Monterey and at Buena Vista, but they were still a year away. An officer who felt he had been overlooked might easily take a defensive attitude. Meade also was skeptical about the value of brevets until he got one, though he seemed less cynical than Reynolds.[26]

The need for political assists in getting appointments to the Military Academy and in winning honors afterwards was fairly obvious. The important fact was the kind of men who got them. By now, in the two years of fighting below the Rio Grande, the evidence was beginning to show. Did Grant, Lee, Cump Sherman, Jackson, Longstreet, Thomas, Meade, Hooker, Reynolds, etc., accurately represent the material coming out of West Point? If so, not only did brevets make sense, but so did the Academy itself. Military writers have been fond of making long lists of these young officers to prove how well the Mexican War trained them to fight the big one that followed.[27] But the men from the Point did more immediate service by knocking out the old prejudice against the Academy.

". . . The nation is much indebted for a series of splendid victories; any one of which would more than compensate it for all the expenditures at West Point. That will be an unfortunate day for the Republic, when Congress, influenced either by motives of economy or the vile appeals of the demogogue, shall consent to abandon an Institution which has already done much to establish the reputation and extend the borders of the country."[28] A volunteer officer wrote this in 1853. Normally volunteers would hardly be expected to defend the men from the Point, but even another one came to their aid. The same Captain John Kenly who admired Bragg's artillery noted that that arm of the service in itself "reflected undying lustre on the Military Academy at West Point and proudly displayed the standard of its training. . . ."[29]

Although support like this helped, much more was needed. By 1860, with General Scott's famous "fixed opinion" in defense of the Point, the argument should have ended, but attacks on the Academy continued well beyond the Civil War.[30]

In the meantime one West Pointer got entangled with volunteers again. Reynolds became a sort of judge advocate, as he put it, in all the volunteer courts martial. The work meant a great deal of writing, which he quickly tired of, though he was kept at it all through the hot summer and into autumn. For once he was willing to admit some virtue in the study of law: "I have the benefit of the talents and experience of many distinguished brother chips of yours," he wrote Jim, "and altogether it is probably beneficial to me—this is some consolation."[31] But John was still not giving his brother too much by his admission.

There was plenty of writing to do in addition to court briefs. John was always about to get a letter off to Sam, or had just written Kate, or would soon acknowledge Harriet's last. As for the girls, he more often simplified the problem by addressing them all at once as "my dear Sisters." During this period if he wrote to only one of them, it was usually Jane. Lydia, like Sam, was too much his senior for the closer ties he felt with the others. Then too, Lydia now was a busy housewife and in fact had just made John an uncle. Of course for his younger brother he had real affection. He and Jim had been together most in growing up.

Still you had to enforce your two-year edge over a brother or he might get out of hand. John could be hard when he thought he had reason: ". . . from your not acknowledging the receipt of previous letters I feared that they had gone astray and for a man of business like your-self I think it strange that you should not have done so, especially the one enclosing the money, which you now do not make any particu-lar mention of, so that I am left to *infer* that *it* has been rec^d with the others. I had intended to employ you in another matter of business, but from *this* evidence of your attention, I am rather disposed to give up the idea."[32] A few years later he was going to find Jim's casual way with family business affairs even more exasperating.

The brother that John would have written to far oftener than he did was Will, but he was never sure of where to reach him. Lieutenant William Reynolds, U.S.N., was his hero and he included Will's wife Becky in his affection.[33] John's letters to the others always asked for news of Will and "Be" or had a message for them. So when a letter reached him from the "Steam Barque" *Allegheny* in the fall, it was opened eagerly. The postmark showed New Orleans, the farthest south his brother had got in trying to reach Vera Cruz in time for the occu-pation. After leaving Pittsburgh, his ship had been laid up too long in Memphis for refitting. He was greatly disappointed, as he explained to John:

. . . I did not expect to gain any honor or distinction, but merely wanted to be there, as a matter of business—to learn a lesson in my profession—one that seldom offers. I wanted, naturally, to be in the war, while it was going on. . . . There is no use to cry about it now, but I shall feel bad for a long time to come.

It has been a very high satisfaction to me, my dear John, to read the honorable mention made of you, in the various reports of Gen. Taylor, Gen. Wool, Colonel May, and in the letter signed "Buena Vista." It does much to console me, for my bad luck, that you have done your part so well, as to merit such particular praise, and the important share you had in that memorable and desperate battle, on the result of which greater stakes were hanging, than at either Vera Cruz or Cerro Gordo has deeply gratified your brother, your poor grandmother, who lived only long enough to hear of it, and whose last thoughts were of General Taylor and his army—and all your friends at home. Mr. Buchanan says "you deserve a brevet, and you shall have one, at the next session." So I presume you are secure of that cheap distinction and I am glad you will obtain it, as it seems to be the only honor in store for officers in the army. For the Navy, there are none.[34]

John would no longer have to assure Grandmother Moore that he was in good health even if he did sleep on the ground. But he was going to miss her. Will relayed other news from home too. Lydia and the baby were doing well at Lucinda, where her husband Nathan Evans had just sold 32 dollars worth of iron. The furnace was not doing so well as the family. Will wished he could get down to see John, the army, and especially a light artillery drill, but it would be impossible. "We cannot ship a crew. Sailors and all manner of men are in demand. The Quartermaster offers $25 a month and 1½ rations per day." His next orders, Will said, were for a cruise in the Mediterranean. "A piece of good fortune for me—a Lieut. of only 6 years standing. . . . These things go by favour however, very often, and I may as well profit, when a chance offers, as another."[35]

Well, John could reason, if his favorite brother was glad to take advantage of any special favor that came his way, what could be so wrong about accepting brevets? First they had to be honestly earned. Only after that could help from a Mr. B. in all conscience be accepted.

Will wanted a long letter in return for his own. He wanted to know how his brother lived, what he did, how many horses he had, whether he wore his Rio Grande spurs in the battles, and every other particular about him. In a postscript he announced the happy results of mating his Italian greyhound and the bitch. "The parents are the prettiest dogs in the world, and I have no doubt the pups will equal them."[36] Both Will and Sam still liked to get out into the fields with a gun. John's letters to them shared this interest, but it was a link that no longer held him and his younger brother. Jim seemed to have moved indoors for good.

In September of 1847 John Reynolds suddenly discovered he was a year older. "Who would believe it! It is now a year since the battle of Monterey! Who would believe that I am now twenty—I am almost ashamed to write it, however it is not my fault, so here goes—seven years old! Who would think that I have now been in this country more than two years! Two years in the best part of a man's life. I can hardly realize all this, yet, they are melancholy facts." What worried him most was seeing no end of the occupation. He had nothing but praise for Scott's victories, only now he wanted to hear about a peace. He thought there would be small promise in an armistice with a nation whose generals were all "unqualified liars." Anything short of real peace was meaningless.[37]

There had been more news from home, and what was best about it, *home* was moving from Cornwall back to Lancaster where it belonged. His father had bought a house on North Duke Street and hoped to have the family settled by the next summer. With Robert and William Coleman home from Europe there would be different arrangements at the furnace in Cornwall. John was glad to hear of Rob's return and said he ought to come down to see the war. He would be glad to share his tent with the visitor — also some of the game. "The most abundant is the 'plumed' Partridge, a bird I never saw before. It is very much like the northern bird in size, and has much the same flavour, but its plumage has a shade more of gray and has a plume or top-knot of gray and white on its head."[38] All this in a letter to Jane, whose interest in the color of game birds was slight at best. She would have to pass the letter on to her brother's friend. She could also be glad her brother had found some hunting. It might keep him from exploding.

In November John wrote to Jim, enclosing a check for $400. Apparently he had forgiven his brother's previous lapse. Two hundred and forty dollars were to repay a loan from Robert. The balance John wanted his father to have for any use he might find. "I am now out of debt and have more than I know what to do with. If we stay here much longer I shall send you some to invest for me, and as soon as I return I intend to make the 'grand tour of the continent.'"[39] The move from Cornwall had told him without any announcement that his father was through at the furnace. Buying a new home and beginning all over again in Lancaster could be expensive. As for the tour, if Robert Coleman could go to Europe so could John Reynolds.

Business matters were all right to trouble Jim about, but other subjects were suitable only for a sister. John sat down in his tent at the beginning of 1848 and started a letter to Jane:

> I cannot do less than to write an hour of this New Year evening to you all at home wishing you all a Happy New Year, hoping that you have had a Merry Christmas, and praying that this may be the last Christmas I may have to spend in Mexico, at least for some time! It makes the third since I saw you, and I begin to think, I must soon come to the conclusion — though I struggle against it most heroically, that I am looking old. Yes! Really getting old! This is leap year! is it not? Yes and I think I had better take advantage of it, seriously now, don't laugh, and authorize you, with full powers to make the contract, to receive proposals for me from any of the respectable white portion of the female population in your vicinity. I have only three conditions which it is necessary to consider: the applicant must be good looking, amiable, and have a small portion of what is usually termed common sense. I won't object to money, if she have any, neither do I make it a condition, tho' all things being equal you will decide for the monied one in preference to one without it. The contract to be fulfilled immediately on my return to the U. S., the whole object being to economize time, fearing that I may not reach there before the end of the year and I cannot possibly

wait for another leap year. Please make this known among your female acquaintances; understanding the term vicinity, which I have used before, to have its most extended signification. . . .

Interpreting *vicinity* too locally would rule out York or Lebanon counties, and Sarah Coleman might be in either. Some of the other girls he used to know around home must be scattered about more too. But with his sisters back in Lancaster there ought to be lots of visiting, and a brother's letters had a way of getting passed around—especially letters from a soldier brother at the front. The pencil sketch of Lieutenant Reynolds had gone the rounds two years before. He knew that because Sarah had wondered how many coats he was wearing in the picture. And he played it safe anyhow. He closed his leap-year contract by adding, "enough of nonsense."[40]

For the first months after the battle of Buena Vista Reynolds kept expecting the army to move south. Hope of active campaigning was all that kept up his morale. In May of 1847 he was sure Taylor would abandon Saltillo and his depots to strike down for a junction with Scott. By August, with the army still lying idle, he could see no other choice.[41] But when autumn ended the best weather for marching, and word of Scott's successes came in, he was ready to agree with Will that the administration had had enough of Taylor's triumphs.[42] His impatience grew and all his letters showed it. By the middle of February '48 he was desperate. "I am almost sick of the people of this country and everything in it," he wrote Kate on the 13th. "I can see no reasonable time when I may hope for the pleasure of seeing you at home. Under the existing state of things I should be very glad if I could be ordered to West Point in any capacity, tho' I would much prefer going there as an assist. instructor of Arty, than infy. This is the only possible way in which I could hope to leave here, and if a word can be said for me in this respect I would not object to it now. . . ."

If it took his father's help to get him out of Mexico, he would be glad to accept it. One more summer in the country would kill him, he said. It was giving him gray hair already and "the eccentricities of Capt. Sherman are becoming unsupportable."[43] He no longer cared where he went or what he did so long as it was somewhere else. He thought, for instance, that a light artillery officer ought to be sent north on recruiting service. Yes, he was perfectly willing to be that officer. He was sure one could be spared from the company just now, given the dead slack in activity throughout the area.[44]

In other words, to use a term familiar in his beloved Lancaster, Lieutenant Reynolds "wanted out"!

CHAPTER IV

Mountains, Mormons, and Dust

When John Reynolds reached Lancaster for the Christmas holidays of 1848, he was a brevet major. Senator Buchanan had written John's father in May the year before: "I shall take good care of John when the proper time arrives. He richly deserves a brevet; but the President without the Senate cannot give it to him."[1] Not just one, but two brevets came through before Reynolds left Mexico. One as captain dated back to the battle of Monterey, and one as major dated from Buena Vista.[2] So now, although he was not yet a captain in actual rank and pay, he could write "Brevt Maj" below his signature on all official papers.

Lancaster chose to show its pride in its new major by arranging a dinner to honor his services in the late fighting. A committee of forty-nine wrote him on December 27: "The undersigned, your fellow-citizens, having learned with much pleasure of your arrival in this your native city after an absence of a number of years in the service of your country, beg to offer you,—as a small token of their regard and admiration, for your brave and meritorious conduct in the several battles, including that of the memorable Buena Vista, in which you were engaged,—a social dinner, to be given at the White Swan Hotel on Saturday next, or any other day you may please to name more convenient to yourself."[3]

Familiar and prominent local names like Slaymaker, Muhlenberg, Reigart, Franklin, Humes, Fordney, Lightner, Lane, Myers, Ellmaker, Lewis, etc., should have tempted Reynolds to accept. Instead, with "characteristic modesty"[4] he declined in the following note: "Your letter of to-day, offering me a 'social dinner' was recd with deep emotions, and I regret that my short stay among my fellow-citizens of Lancaster compels me to decline the honor. Allow me to assure you that no feelings are more gratifying to the soldier than those excited by the approval of his fellow-countrymen; and that this testimony of your approval of my conduct in the service of my country will ever be most gratefully cherished by me."[5]

No doubt John's fellow citizens saw far less of him than did his family. A lot had changed in his four years away. He had left Hal and Ellie as children, and now they were young ladies. He missed his "venerable and beloved Grandmother"[6] Moore. Nobody would have been prouder of young Major Reynolds. Will's absence was of course disappointing, but he could greet his baby nephew and namesake if only Lydia and Nat Evans could get over for Christmas. Still, with Sam and Jim around to share the brandy and cigars after dinner, there would be plenty of help to fight the late battles all over again.

On January 15 Reynolds was back on duty at his new station, Fort Preble, in Portland Harbor, Maine. He could hardly have got farther from Mexico if he had been allowed to pick the spot himself. By the end of the month the garrison was snowed in, but John's only complaint was on the quality of the local cigars. "We can get nothing but trash here, which to a person who smokes as much as I do is not only disagreeable but injurious."[7] To guard his all-important health he wanted the mildest smokes Sam Witmer could send him from Lancaster. He was sorry to hear that all the neighbors at home had colds. "Why don't Jim recommend the Water cure to *them?* tho' in Miss Bryan's case I object to *cold water's* being thrown on so fair a subject."[8] Maybe John's Christmas attentions had gone beyond the family after all.

The first year at Preble went along well enough. He liked his commander, Major Robert Anderson,[9] and if the duties were routine they were at least familiar. He was being kept busy, he said, with work piled as high as his head.[10] Army paper detail never let up, from requisitions for heavy ordnance all the way down to one pair of flannel drawers, listed at eleven cents in Item No. 4 of the "Report of the proceeds of the sale of the effects of Prvt John Camp, late of Co. G, 3rd Arty . . . and hereby approved by John F. Reynolds, Brevt Maj. Comdg."[11] Like most officers Reynolds found desk work galling. All garrison duty was boring enough, but at least the hours he could spend in the saddle gave him exercise and kept him out of doors. For him, out of doors was where army life belonged.

In addition to his paper load John now had two more sisters to write to. Hal had just made him a scarf, which he told her was the envy of the whole garrison. But doting brother though he was, he cheated a little on space in his acknowledgment: "Imagine the rest of this sheet filled up with—thanks! Hal! thanks for the scarf!"[12] Later a letter from youngest sister Ellie put him in a vein of reminiscence:

I am glad to hear you have got over your home-sickness. You ought not to be unhappy—so near home and with so many of your friends with you, particularly in such a beautiful spot as Litiz, the name of which always brings to my mind some of the most pleasing recollections of my schoolboy days. I remember my boarding house just opposite your school—and the kind, good Mrs. Krumer [?], with a pleasure almost boyish, and think of the days free from trouble and anxiety, that I spent under her motherly care, as the most happy of my life. So will you, one day, think of those that are now passing with you. Do not lament them![13]

All the mellowness of twenty-nine years advising a girl of fourteen. But John Reynolds had taken part in battles, which added to his age. Combat soldiers tend to mature faster than their birthdays warrant. Fort Brown, Monterey, and Buena Vista gave an ancient cast to the faraway days under Mr. Beck. Ellie's brother was acting the fully arrived adult that he now was.

These two youngest sisters, Hal and Ellie, were moving in at just the right time to be spoiled by their brother. Jane was about to marry George Gildersleeve of Baltimore, while Kate had been visiting for longer and longer periods in Philadelphia. She liked somebody there more than casually.[14] Inevitably the older girls would be too busy with families of their own to suit a soldier who relied so much on letters. Home ties counted everything for him, and he needed Hal and Ellie to fill the threatened vacuum.

The customary peacetime squeeze for the army was on. In November of 1849 the quartermaster general in Washington cautioned Reynolds to keep the purchase of stores to a minimum. "The exhausted state of the appropriations for the Department and the difficulty of obtaining appropriations from Congress makes it necessary to observe the utmost economy in all our expenditures."[15] The government had already dismounted his own and all but two other light batteries of artillery, so Reynolds felt the pinch where it hurt. By the middle of the next year, while he was still in temporary command of the fort, he faced a good many unsettled public accounts. He was forced to admit that he was without a cent of government money to pay them.[16] This penury did nothing to glamorize a career in the army, and if Reynolds stayed in he would have to fight it at every turn.

But if he had trouble meeting the army's debts, he could still get out to hunt game. As long as he could line up a bird in his rifle sights Reynolds was all right. He had brought his pointer "Milo" from home, but Milo got after the wrong prey. Hal had made John a knitted jacket when she saw how much he liked the scarf. "The jacket was perfection itself," her brother wrote, "and was the admiration of everyone, particularly Milo. In a sudden fit of admiration one day he seized it in his mouth and paws, and no doubt would have reduced it to its original worsted in a short time, had I not rescued it. . . . But I have darned it up so that it scarcely shows at all, and with a lecture that I gave him at the time, and keeping it out of his reach, I think it quite safe from any further attempts on his part."[17]

For once the war department shifted Reynolds before he complained of restlessness. In fact, they moved him about pretty fast. He was sent from Preble down to Fort Adams, at Newport, Rhode Island, in 1852. By September of the following year he was in New Orleans, as aide to General Twiggs, the same officer who had conducted the wasted march to Victoria in 1846-47. John's stay here was notable for a special reason. He took sick for his second time. Almost everybody else did too. Yellow fever laid the city low and all who could got out. But Reynolds volunteered to remain as replacement for his friend Cump Sherman, who was waiting for his leave to come through. Sherman had tired of the dull routine and low pay of army life. Married, and with two small daughters, he was eager to get into business on the Pacific coast where gold was proving a bonanza.[18]

Several reasons could have prompted Reynolds to offer his services. Most important, he wanted Sherman's assignment as commissary of subsistence for the department. He also had the courage and high sense of duty to volunteer under adverse conditions. Abner Doubleday recalled afterwards that Reynolds' willingness to stay in the city through the epidemic was praised by other officers at the time.[19] Finally, it takes nothing away from Reynolds to guess that it never entered his head that the fever would get *him* down. His Florida spell should have told him otherwise, but his faith in his physical invulnerability never deserted him. Anyhow he did come down with fever, though he weathered it and was able to write home September 27, 1853:

> Since I became convalescent I have been over the lake, at Passcagoula and Pass Christian—where I spent a week most delightfully enjoying the sea breeze for the first time this year. . . . Since I wrote to you one of my clerks died of Black Vomit over the lake. He was only sick three days—he was a very worthy young man—from Ohio. He was afraid to remain in town and I let him go over the lake early in August, but this year the fever has been everywhere in the

vicinity—even on the plantations which have always been exempt in former epidemics.

Of the commissary opening Reynolds added: "If I don't get the appointment of C. S.—of which it seems I have a good chance—I will spend the next summer at home. That will be some consolation at any rate." Sherman also thought Reynolds would succeed him.[20] But when War Secretary Jefferson Davis made his choice he picked Captain Charles Kilburn instead. In time Reynolds' leave turned out to be less consoling than he expected, and his resentment over his rejection mounted.

John's father had died during the spring, while returning from a visit to Jane and her husband, George Gildersleeve, in Baltimore.[21] Reynolds had left for home the next day to be with the family. Now, five months later, he renewed his sense of loss in reading Will and Becky's letter, which Ellie had sent on to him. By way of answer he wrote her: "I read with feelings of brotherly love warming towards them, their deep expression of sympathy with us in the loss of our dear Father. I return you the letter; it is well worthy of their warm hearts and I trust we may all be influenced by the same filial love which we know has been a striking trait in the character of both Will and Be, and I look forward to the pleasure of meeting them and you all once more under the family roof as the greatest time has in store for us."[22]

Reynolds' last work before leaving New Orleans was with a board of officers appointed to inspect channel improvements at the mouth of the Mississippi. By Christmas of 1853 he was home and in January moved over to New York. At Fort Lafayette in New York Harbor he took command of two companies of the 3rd Artillery. At the end of March he was in charge of the post, but his men were being readied for California. Some of them had started out before, by sea, and were survivors of a shipwreck off Cape Hatteras. Among the two hundred or more who drowned was the skilful Captain Washington, defender of Taylor's right at Buena Vista. This time the companies would move by land across the continent. Of course Reynolds hoped to go with his command. After all, he had been no farther away than New Orleans for nearly four months.

So when his orders came, he was ready. He got vaccinated, bought two nice cages for Kate's birds, promised to sit for another daguerreotype, promised to write his sister Lydia, said he would see Mr. B's niece Harriet Lane at the Astor, and still found time to remind Ellie that she had failed to inform him of their aunt's health: ". . . you should always mention her; recollect that she is the only one left to us of the passing generation! Give my love to her, Miss Hal, Kate, Jane, when you write, and all friends in L."[23] With that Reynolds was off to Kansas City by rail.

At Fort Leavenworth, about twenty miles northwest of the city, Colonel Steptoe had assembled 300 men, including his teamsters, herders, and a detachment of cavalry recruits. The immediate responsibility for reaching the coast with this force, and with over four hundred mules, several hundred horses, and some eighty baggage wagons, fell to the quartermaster, Captain Rufus Ingalls. He was fortunate in the help he got from the other officers, including Reynolds, and he said so in his report to the secretary of war.[24]

The command left on June 1, 1854, over the already familiar Oregon Trail. According to Ingalls, trouble began almost at once. Before they had pushed a hundred miles the horses got distemper. Many of the recruits took sick from eating and drinking too much for men on the march. For a short time even cholera broke out. The weather was changeable, roads were muddy, and the horses, roped in strings of thirty behind the wagons, often tried to stampede. The mules were painfully slow on foot. But the small force inched on to Fort Kearny, which was reached on the 23rd. After resting two days the men moved out along the Platte River to the South Fork, where they saw their first Indians. They reached Laramie in the middle of July.

At Laramie a delegation of Sioux came into the fort to establish friendly relations. The Pawnees and the other tribes kept out of sight, Ingalls reported. He had problems enough without them. The worst of the journey lay ahead. Arid desert country stretched almost to the climb for South Pass in the Rockies. Ingalls saw his cavalcade come nearest breaking down in the Wahsatch Mountains, though with only a slight loss among the animals he finally got it down the 3,000-foot descent and into Salt Lake City on August 3. They had been on the road close to a hundred days and had covered more than twelve hundred miles.[25]

Of all this Reynolds had no time to write. He had just made his greatest march; he had seen his first Indians of the western plains; he had crossed his first great desert and bridged the Rockies. What he had seen and done deserved a detailed account, and he promised one to Hal. But Reynolds no sooner settled himself in Salt Lake City for the winter when another new experience crowded out everything else. With the other officers he attended several parties, one of them given by Governor Brigham Young, of the Utah Territory. "We of course met the 'Mormon Belles,' " he wrote, " and made the acquaintance of several families, yet this did not give us entree to their houses. . . . They are jealous of all Gentiles and of course discouraged any intimacy among their young people with us. This did not amount to much however, as there are very few people among them of any pretensions to respectability at all, and therefore it was not much of a deprivation."[26]

This was only the beginning. Reynolds would have several years in which to build up a hatred for the Mormons. But in this he only shared the view of other army officers, both in this spring of 1855 and three years later in the so-called Mormon War.[27] The government of Brigham Young did not welcome a visit by soldiers of a "foreign power." Young insisted as strongly on the independence of his people from Washington as the capital insisted on its jurisdiction over the territory. In fact, although his term was about to expire and under the law he could not succeed himself, he had defied the United States. "I am and will be governor,"[28] he protested.

Reynolds soon had a specific grudge against the Mormons. Colonel Steptoe's orders for the march out to Utah had included a search for the Indians who wiped out a party of army engineers under Captain Gunnison the previous summer. Steptoe had rounded up some of them during the winter and now chose Reynolds to bring them to Salt Lake City. This venture John did report to his sisters:

> At the end of February I had a rather exciting trip to Fillmore City to receive and bring up the Indians who murdered Captain Gunnison. I went down with twenty-two men then brought up five of them [Indians] in eight days, making 300 miles in that time. They have since been tried by the Mormons and found guilty of manslaughter only and sentenced to the penitentiary, tho' proof was positive and clear. But their jury were counseled by Brigham Young as to their verdict and thus they perjured themselves. May God have mercy upon them, they would hang two Indians for killing two Mormon boys last summer when there was scarcely any proof at all, but when a Gentile is murdered it is only manslaughter!! I cannot write the truth about these people here—but will sometime or other.[29]

No doubt the unfriendly and uncooperative Mormons helped bring Reynolds to an admission he had never made before in his thirty-five years: "I have been away from home a great deal in my lifetime, spent years in a foreign country, but never did I feel anything approaching to homesickness before—never did months drag their slow length along before as they have done here this Winter. Thank God it is over at last and we are preparing to go into camp once more and I hope by this day a week to be on the road to Rush Valley with the Command where we will await the coming of grass to start across the country."[30] Reynolds had a cure for homesickness. Go somewhere else.

When the command did get off early in May, Colonel Steptoe had a new captain. Brevet Major Reynolds' regular rank had gone up from that of first lieutenant on March 3.[31] Fourteen years to advance three grades. He never even mentioned it in his letters home. Then while on the march to the Pacific he learned that his old captain, Braxton Bragg, had been commissioned a major of cavalry. Of course he would have to give up his light battery of the 3rd Artillery to take it, but if he did, Reynolds wanted it. His own company was still dismounted. Bragg's, on the other hand, had kept its full equipment, including horses. The chance of getting it was worth an all-out try, and Reynolds pressed hard. ". . . A Light Battery, the very thing of all others that I wish for—by my services in that arm and I trust, my reputation in the Army, I have every claim to this particular Company."[32]

In short, John wanted his brother Jim to get some of his political friends to go to Jeff Davis and plead his case. ". . . Remind him how last year he did me a great injustice when in the face of every military recommendation he overlooked my application and services when he appointed my junior, Capt. Kilburn, to the Commissary Dept. I shall be very much tempted to resign if I am treated unjustly this time."[33] So two years had not eased Reynolds' bitterness at missing out on the commissary. It was no help either that Sherman had got out of the army as soon as his leave was up. These were lean years to stay in, and any officer who felt unrewarded could be trigger-ready to quit.

If Jim Reynolds could put his brother's record in front of the right people, it might be a way to ensure justice. And Jim had reached a position to be useful. In Pennsylvania Democratic councils his word carried enough weight that he could offer advice to the next President of the United States.[34] He had also turned down a judgeship on the state supreme bench.[35] Attorney James Reynolds was already a busy and influential man, and he was going to be busier now that his brother wanted Bragg's battery.

When John Reynolds reached Fort Yuma, California, at the end of August, he heard that Bragg had turned the cavalry assignment down. Half of the last two hundred miles had been a steaming desert march, with the thermometer hitting a 120 degrees, but the new captain was even hotter on getting the light battery. Now rumor had it that Bragg was resigning. Reynolds was desperate. "Jim I hope received my letter, and acted upon it, and if he hears of Bragg's resignation I hope he will try and do something so as to get me the Company. I am satisfied of one thing now. In the Army, merit is no recommendation and political influence is everything. I have given it a fair trial and give it up. The less you do, the more worthless you are, the more favors you can obtain and the more apt you are to be advanced. . . . I may say that I have never been so fully disgusted with the Army as within the last twelve months."[36]

This was bitter talk for a true career man like Reynolds. His present location, it might be added, did nothing to improve his temper. Yuma lay at the juncture of the Colorado and Gila Rivers, where any summer breeze boiled over desert sands from all directions. Besides, even the rugged Reynolds was tired. He had marched more than twelve hundred miles since leaving Salt Lake. Worse yet, it was impossible to relax by hunting, he said. "Tell Sam and Robt that quail abound here in the greatest numbers, but with the thermometer 110° in the shade they are unmolested by dog or gun."[37] This represented the ultimate frustration for Reynolds. Fortunately the autumn brought him activity, and for a change without marching. In October he went up to San Francisco, where he shipped on the steamer *California*, bound for his new post at Fort Orford, Oregon. He hit rough weather on the way north, and when the ship arrived at the mouth of the Columbia River it bore out a prediction of Mr. Beck's. Twenty-two years before, at Lititz, he had explained "how the Boilers on Steam-Boats burst." Now Reynolds experienced the practical application of this theory. The ship caught fire from the explosion of the boilers and for some time became unmanageable, drifting helplessly close to the bar. ". . . But by almost a miracle we did not strike," Reynolds reported, "and in a few minutes sufficient steam was got up in the other boiler and the fire subdued, so that we crossed the bar and got inside the heads, when a strong tide and current obliged us to anchor."[38] This was not the end. After landing Captain Keyes and his company in Puget Sound, the vessel burst a steam pipe, then was struck by a gale. With a patched-up engine it took sixty hours for the *California* to limp back to San Francisco.

Keyes, who no doubt had missed Reynolds' early instruction in the bursting of ships' boilers, was more impressed by the accident. He noted how the pilot quit the bridge at the most critical moment, leaving the ship to flounder. If she had struck the bar all lives would have been lost, he said. The fire itself terrified many of the soldiers. Only the help of the army officers and others who refused to panic made it possible for Captain Dall and the crew to save the ship. Keyes added that eight or ten shipmasters among the passengers assured him they had never survived a greater danger.[39]

San Francisco merely put Reynolds back where he had started from. It took a second try early in 1856 for him to make Fort Orford. The post lay about sixty miles up the coast from the southern boundary of the present state of Oregon. Although it rained a great deal he found the location healthy and a happy change from Yuma's searing skies. No sooner was he settled than John got after his brother again. "Tell Jim I expect to hear from him whether he has done anything in the way of securing the promise of Mr. Davis to give me the Light Co. of the Rgt. in case Bragg resigns, which I understand he will do on February next. I hope he has not neglected it. Tell him to write at once."[40]

Meanwhile a campaign lay ahead. Trouble had been breaking out off and on between white settlers and the Indians of the Rogue River region south of Orford. Philip Kearny had fought them in 1851, and his biographer called them the most wicked, warlike, and most difficult to subdue of all the tribes on the Pacific Coast.[41] But when Reynolds went with his men to join the troops under Colonel Robert Buchanan, they spent more grueling days flushing the Indians out of the virgin mountain areas than they did in fighting them. The official report told its own story. Reynolds' Company H, along with a company of infantry, killed twenty Indians. Another dismounted artillery company killed five more.[42] This was hardly warfare, though the terrain made the operation a rough one.

By the middle of June, Colonel Buchanan was on his way up to Fort Orford with most of the troops and a number of captives. Reynolds and Captain Ord remained "to collect the old, the lame, the blind and halt," as Reynolds put it. "There is still one of the worst bands out yet in the upper country who say they will not come in and they will I suppose have to be hunted down, which in this country will prove an interminable undertaking."[43]

If Jefferson Davis was slow in recognizing Reynolds' services, the citizens of Orford were not. Before he had been back a month he received the following letter: "Representing a portion of our fellow citizens who, desirous of manifesting the high esteem in which you are held by them, as an officer, and for the interest shown by you for us, during our defenceless condition while you were in command of the Military Post, at this place,—we ask your acceptance of the accompanying gold watch, as a small token of our high consideration and regard."[44] The testimonial was signed by a committee of thirteen, none of whom apparently noticed the frightening ambiguity of the adverbial clause.

The award to Reynolds was well intended nevertheless. People in the vicinity of this westernmost fort on the continent had good reason to value their military garrison. The growth of new territories hinged on the stability brought in with the troops. Captain and Brevet Major Reynolds rated only company command in the war department's eyes, but here at Orford he and his few men could spell the difference between prosperity and ruin, or even death. Twenty Indians killed was a poor measure of the worth of Company H. The lives and property, both white and Indian, that were saved by its presence counted most.

The Indian fighting done, Reynolds could go back to his worry over getting Bragg's battery. He was sure that the 3rd Artillery's colonel, George Bauman, had recommended him for it, but what about Davis? The strain was beginning to show in Reynolds' prose: "I have the strongest claim to it of any Capt. in the Regt; and should Mr. Davis give it to anyone else I do not see that there is any chance of ever getting justice in the army—and shall think it almost time to think of leaving it, that is, should, as I am almost positive he has, the Col. of the Regt. recommended me."[45]

Bragg had in fact resigned. He had resisted, he said, until he was disgusted and worn down. Like Reynolds he had been bitter for a long time.[46] For one thing he had expected to be upgraded earlier, and his resentment at being sent out to chase Indians in impossible places with 6-pounders was equally as great. Now the war department was replacing light artillery with long-range guns. "The finest battery I ever saw was destroyed in two years at the cost of $100,000."[47] Knowing perfectionist Bragg, it is easy to accept his own high opinion of his unit. So Bragg was through and in the end his Battery C, or what was left of it, went to Reynolds. After all the straining and waiting it was an empty triumph, but at least it brought him east again. In his new post at Fort Monroe, Virginia, it hardly mattered that he would continue to be without mounts and that the guns were fixed.

Before Christmas of 1856 Reynolds was comfortably situated in a cottage by himself and ready to plan for the holidays at home. There would be a lot to tell the family. He had seen the new territories of the west, lived among the polygamous Mormons, visited booming San Francisco, and had even fought Indians, small affairs though they were. He could never begin to put into letters all he had seen and done. The telling required a family circle. But where would his family be? Lancaster was no longer home. The house on North Duke Street remained closed most of the time, pending settlement of the estate. Hal and Ellie spent their time with one or another of the married sisters. Jim preferred his own bachelor's quarters at the corner of Prince and Marion. The failing Aunt Lydia had her own place of course, so where could they all come together?

Nearly ten years before, John had written: "I can imagine you all so comfortable in the old Ball Room with a blazing fire—and snow enough to keep you there." That was how he remembered Christmas then, and the way he longed to have it now. John was a Lancaster boy and always had been. At thirty-six a man could begin to feel alone. After more than two years away he wanted to come home, but where was home? Although he tried to re-create one, at least for the days he could be there, nothing worked out. On December 15 he had to write Hal: "I am sorry Sam cannot get up a gathering at Christmas and if no one is to be at L. I do not think it worth my while to come." Thus, in one sentence he closed out a part of his life. From now on he would spend his leaves at Kate's in Philadelphia or with Jane and George at Baltimore.

In April Aunt Lydia died. With her passing, the older generation of the family was gone. When John found he could not reach Lancaster for the funeral, he wrote: ". . . I regret it the more because I have not been present at the death of any of the members of the family. . . . And Aunt being the last connection between us and the past, I did hope to be able to join your sorrowing circle and follow her remains to the grave."[48] Now he could be sure his Lancaster days were over.

Reynolds' stay at Monroe was pleasant enough. He found plenty of quail in season, and he enjoyed the parties at the hotel whenever navy ships nudged into Old Point. He liked the change from the rough and lonely outposts of the frontier. Baltimore and Philadelphia lay within easy reach, with Washington closer yet. Now that James Buchanan was President, his niece Harriet Lane had come down from Lancaster. As hostess in the White House she of course welcomed visits by the younger Reynolds girls. So when John went up to the capital during the summer to show Hal and Ellie about, he was invited to call with them.[49]

But although trips to the cities helped, and he liked his life at the base, it would hardly be Reynolds not to plan for a move. He was thinking about six months' leave. If Sam could get off they might take a trip somewhere, maybe spend part of the winter in Florida. Events failed to work out that way, however, and when Christmas of 1857 arrived Reynolds spent it with Kate and Harry Landis. Hal and Ellie had come for the holidays too. They all hoped Jim would appear, especially because he had been dawdling in the settlement of their father's estate. John definitely wanted an accounting, at least for the two unmarried girls. The fact that he soon might be on his way across the continent again made it all the more important that affairs be concluded.

The day after Christmas Reynolds wrote his brother: "We are all very much disappointed that you did not make your appearance at Christmas; hope you had as pleasant a day as we have had. Sam has told me that you have promised to have a settlement with the girls on

Monday week. I wish to say that in view of my prospects for Utah in the Spring I will be very glad if you will include me in the same. I would not like to go so far away again and not know something about the Estate and the means the girls may have to depend upon." John had already turned over to Hal and Ellie the interest from his investments in state and city bonds. In almost a refrain he kept telling them to use the money as their own.[50] Home or no home, John Reynolds was still a good brother.

Sure enough it was to be Utah again in the spring of 1858. In his eagerness to strike out on the road once more, Reynolds probably forgot some of his distaste for Mormons. He spent the interval before leaving in recruiting new men, seeing to their proper training, and providing the company with mounts. Ellie, who was visiting with Jane in Baltimore, got a five-line note from Fort Monroe on the 13th of April. Her brother wanted eight or ten good ready-made shirts, colored, and a dozen pair of good socks. He would be through Sunday to pick them up on his way to take the cars for Leavenworth.

Whether Reynolds remembered the Mormons or not, they would give him little reason to change his opinion of them. Since his last trip friction had increased between the Church government and the officials in Washington. General Albert Sidney Johnston had already been out in June of 1857 to see that the laws of the United States were obeyed. The Mormons countered by burning off Johnston's grazing lands wherever they could. They refused to sell him supplies, and in October destroyed seventy-five of his wagons, driving off the horses. Johnston went into winter quarters at Old Fort Bridger with about 2,000 men. But the Mormons had already burned the buildings and suffering was acute. The general lost hundreds of mules, oxen, and horses through exposure and starvation.[51]

The worst would be over before Reynolds got as far as Salt Lake City. It was May when he reached Leavenworth. He had eighty-six men and seventy-seven horses to start with from there—but no artillery. Bragg's celebrated Battery C without guns! Oddly Reynolds made no complaint at the time. In writing Ellie he was more interested in describing the post. "This is quite a busy place you may imagine. Horses, mules, oxen and teams going all day long. Every one here seems to be looking for Uncle Sam's money. . . . And the most inflated prices are asked for lots in town, which is situated just beyond the Gov. Reserve and near where in '54 I encamped when not a sign of a house was visible or anything like cultivation. . . . It is now at the height of its prosperity, and I think is ordained to have a smash of some kind. Things cannot be kept up in this unnatural state a great while."[52] Reynolds was describing the army boom town that has been familiar to every generation of soldiers. He added that he was glad his books had come safely and wished he knew whom to thank for sending them. He was happier yet to hear that the Lucinda mine had sold so well. "If Sam or anyone has money for me," he concluded, "I wish it put in some safe and good stocks and given to yourself [Ellie] and Hal, for your joint use of the interest."

The command moved over the same route Reynolds had traveled before. The same muddy roads, the same delays to wait for teams to catch up, the hunt for grazing land—even the same stops: Kearny, the Fork of the Platte, Laramie, then desert and the climb to South Pass. This time Reynolds was bored, although he reported to Ellie at every break in the march: June 3, 1858—heartily tired of Leavenworth and relieved to be on the prairies once more; June 28—ox teams too slow; hoped Mr. B. would put no faith in the Mormons; hoped Lydia and family would settle near Lancaster now that Lucinda was sold; glad to hear Sam had settled Aunt's estate so satisfactorily; now maybe Jim would also settle; July 21—did not trust the "quiet aspect" of Mormon affairs; August 13—expected forty more days of marching to put them in Salt Lake City; grazing scarce; hard on horses.

By the last of September Reynolds was in Camp Floyd, about fifty miles from Salt Lake City. On the 25th he wrote his sisters, this time in care of Hal: "I am now encamped with my Battery in the Camp of General Johnston, and begin to feel at home already, glad that our trip, a tedious one and not well managed, is over. Reno's Battery that you saw mentioned is the battery that is now mine. He is an ordnance officer in the Staff and therefore not entitled to command troops. He had no right in law to the Battery while I was by law made Lt. of Artillery (Illegally deprived of my right by Mr. Davis) and therefore I claimed this Battery, which I now have the pleasure of being encamped behind."

Offhand, and especially to the nonmilitary, Reynolds' insistence on his right to the battery might seem callous. But it was not merely that always unpretty act of "bumping" a junior in rank. A good soldier like Reno must have seen the justice at once. Whether he did or not, army headquarters' Special Orders No. 52 were quite clear on the matter: "Captain and Brevet Major Reynolds' Battery C of the 3rd Artillery is directed to proceed to Leavenworth for horses and thence to Utah to receive guns, caissons, and other material from a detachment of ordnance, in whose charge they have been placed by the commanding general in Utah." The orders went further, and however outraged Reynolds may have felt he could hardly have improved on the argument made in his own defense by the head of ordnance himself:

The efficient performance of his ordnance duties will occupy Brevet Captain Reno's time and that of his ordnance detachment. It was not supposed that he would be diverted from these legitimate and proper duties to be assigned to those which pertain properly and exclusively to the artillery. Every consideration of justice and propriety demands that all batteries of artillery, and especially those in active service, should be manned and served by artillery troops, under the direction of officers of that arm; and the assignment of such duties to ordnance officers and soldiers, or to any other, is wrong. It is also adverse to the interest of public service, inasmuch as it tends to lessen the artillery *esprit de corps*, and assigns very important military service to troops who cannot be supposed to take much interest in it, or to be as efficient for its performance as those to whom it legitimately pertains.[53]

At Camp Floyd Reynolds' "family" consisted of two servants, a horse, and a mule. He thought his budget was high, with eggs and butter at fifty cents a pound, potatoes two dollars a bushel, oats two dollars, and hay twenty dollars a ton. The animals, he complained, especially threatened to eat him out of pocket. Still, every pay brought him more money than he could spend, and he had more funds to invest. As for the camp itself, it was "Dust! Dust! Dust! nothing but Dust!"[54]

It seems strange that in coming to Utah Reynolds could have marched out of Leavenworth muttering merely about Mormons. What about "Bleeding Kansas," where the Civil War was rising to a boil right under his feet? He had crossed part of this territory twice in four years, yet never a word in his letters about what was exploding there. Names like Lawrence, Lecompton, and Topeka were already old headlines in the eastern press. Colonel Cooke of the 2nd Dragoons had almost captured Osawatomie Brown in 1856.[55] Guerilla fighting still went on along the Kansas-Nebraska border, in spite of efforts by the army to stop it. Of course Reynolds' Mr. B. was in the White House and the Kansas-Nebraska Bill with its popular sovereignty had been a Democratic bill.[56] The platform stood for noninterference in the territories. Did that help to explain why vigilantes in neighboring Kansas posed less a threat in Reynolds' eyes than the disciples of Brigham Young?

Around camp there was bound to be talk pro and con about slavery. The question sharply affected officers, both north and south. Camp Floyd itself was named for the new secretary of war, who was suspected of rigging the service to favor the slave states whenever and wherever he could.[57] As a Pennsylvanian Reynolds' position ought to have been obvious, but he faced a division of loyalty. With the new Republican party accusing Buchanan of softness toward slavery, the old friend and patron of the Reynolds family was deeply in trouble. It was a situation likely to keep the cautious Reynolds silent, at least for the moment.

Besides, by February he had a more immediate complaint. He had turned his horses over to the quartermaster department for winter feeding and was dissatisfied with their condition when he got them back. ". . . Such a plight as they are in is enough to make one sick almost—if not sick at heart, sick of the service, such service at least as we have out here. The men are well enough off, and the horses might have been too, if they had been properly cared for. If I am lucky I expect to get them all through the winter until grass comes, when they will recruit very rapidly on the green 'bunch grass' of these valleys. I am very glad to have the care of them again as it gives me something to occupy myself about."[58]

As for news from home, Will had been in poor health for several years, but now an operation on his leg had seemed to help. He was still on duty in the Pacific Islands. "Will and I remain the only wanderers," John wrote, "tho' I am afraid from the account of his leg his wanderings are somewhat stayed. Our Winter is fast wearing away and we are looking anxiously for Spring, tho' what we expect to gain by it one could not tell if asked the question. It is dreadfully monotonous here, and the season makes but little difference in our daily occupations."[59] This marked the first time Reynolds ever showed doubt about the therapy of change—either in season or location.

To create some excitement Reynolds celebrated February 22, 1859, by firing off a full battery salute and the next week took part in a review of the full command at Camp Floyd. "It was quite pleasant in morning at reveille, but commenced snowing slightly just as we were getting under arms. The storm steadily increased and before the Review was over there were three or four inches of snow on the ground, and on us too. There were a few cold hands and feet among us, I can assure you." But the winter was almost spent and he had found the barracks most livable. "You city people cannot appreciate the comfort of a warm house, never having lived out of one. I am only waiting until the weather gets settled a little to commence drilling."[60]

By May Reynolds reported both horses and battery in fine shape. He also admitted that he had gone into gardening on a small scale. When this soldier was reduced to gardening it was certainly time for

him to move. And move he did. He left Camp Floyd on June 27 and
covered 838 miles in seventy-one days. This brought him to Fort Dalles
on the Columbia River, about 200 miles in from the coast. From there
the battery shipped 90 miles farther west to Reynolds' new station at
Fort Vancouver.

Now Reynolds was farther away than ever from the ferment over
slavery in Kansas and in the east and southeast. To the north of him
a brief excitement had stirred up between England and the United
States over ownership of a small island between British Columbia's
Vancouver Island and the American mainland.[61] But by the time Reynolds reached his post the trouble had quieted down. His first job was
overseeing the construction of quarters and stables, and he found
himself with a "thousand and one things to do which no one else can
do as well as oneself."[62] Then in December the work slacked off and
the fort was icebound for a month. When mail could get through
Reynolds had leisure to answer. He also had time to plan. Unless he
went back east in the summer he would certainly make every effort to
ship out to Honolulu. There he could see for himself how brother Will
was doing.

In Lancaster there was still the matter of the estate. Jim managed
only to distribute the money in dribbles. John threatened that if he
could just get there he would take care of the settlement himself.
To Hal and Ellie he wrote: "As for any that belongs to me, I have
already told you to use it as if it were your own. Jim I feel must have
some account of his stewardship which he should produce in justice
to himself." His next paragraph changed the subject. "Our little excitement on this side of the continent has quietly settled down, while
on your side I see things rather interesting. I think if they could hang,
along with old Brown, Gerrit Smith, Wendell Phillips, and a few more
of the abolition stripe, it would effectually stop this agitation for a
time, at least."[63] So Reynolds had finally caught up with the coming
Civil War, if so far only barely.

CHAPTER V

To Serve in Any Capacity

In 1859 Vancouver was about as safe as anywhere outside the South for damning abolitionists. But farther east the familiar events leading to the Civil War rapidly increased their tempo. At Charleston in April the southern delegates withdrew from the National Democratic party. Its North and South wings then went their separate ways, each holding a convention in May. The following month northern Democrats nominated Stephen Douglas of Illinois for President and accepted his doctrine of popular sovereignty. Let the new territories decide the slavery issue for themselves. How could the South object to that? But in choosing John C. Breckinridge the party's southern wing even denied territories the choice of keeping slavery out. Two other parties had meanwhile declared themselves. The Union party picked John Bell and evaded the slavery question entirely. Lincoln, the Republican choice at Chicago, stood for prohibiting slavery in the territories.

Such was the political cast of the country when Reynolds came east in August. He found Lancaster split down the middle. The city was proud to have given the United States its fifteenth President, but it faced the doubtful record of his cabinet, as well as Buchanan's own timidity in forcing the issue with the hotheads of the South.[1] Old friends were now cutting each other cold on Duke and King and Queen Streets. Callers at Mr. B's "Wheatland" manse gambled their social status. Violence threatened any who talked secession. Midsummer of 1860 saw a Lancaster far from the snug, safe little world that Reynolds used to know.[2]

For Reynolds the problem was made especially acute. To the long record of friendship between his family and the Buchanans he could add the help rendered by Mr. B. in connection with his career in the army. On the other hand, Reynolds was a soldier pledged to defend his country—the Union of *all* the states. Now President Buchanan was under heavy fire for putting that union in jeopardy. Within three months the general of the army, Winfield Scott, would be pleading with Buchanan to defend the military posts in the South. Republicans would charge that this patriotic counsel was being ignored.[3] So if Reynolds preferred visiting in Philadelphia to choosing sides in his old home town, his reasons were understandable.

When his leave ended in September, the army could have sent Reynolds any number of places that would escape the torn loyalties near home. At Vancouver the year before only the loudest shouts of the abolitionists had reached his ears. On the frontier an officer lost himself in the chores at hand—feeding and quartering men and horses, caring for equipment, drilling. After dinner and a nip of brandy he could light up a cigar and lean into the paper work. Detail was escape in itself: canteen straps 82, bugles with extra mouthpieces 7, forage caps 42, hospital tent poles (sets of) 1,[4] expenses for administering oath to Sergeant J. M. Brooks, 33¢,[5] "and a thousand and one things which no one else could do as well as oneself."

But instead of landing at a station on the far outer rim of army posts, Major Reynolds drew West Point. He was assigned as Commandant of Cadets. Who appointed him? "I had only heard," he wrote, "that amongst the numerous applications for the place as Commandant here, my name was mentioned and decided upon after the failure to settle on any of the applicants. I am of course very much gratified that Mr. B. remembered me at all."[6] This further favor from an old patron came at an embarrassing time. It also set him down where the ferment of choosing sides would be going on everywhere around him, though fortunately the tension had barely begun to show as yet.[7]

Learning the job would be distraction enough at first. Reynolds wrote Ellie on September 20, describing his early impressions:

> I have been on duty here for a week trying to persuade myself that I shall like it but notwithstanding the kind reception I have met with on all sides from my friends here I have not made up my mind fully on the subject. . . . I shall try for a week or so longer the duties, which I find very disagreeable to me, so different from anything I have ever had before, and so confining, annoying, and various, that I have hardly yet had time to test them fully—then I can make up my mind as to whether I will remain or not. Of one thing I am certain, that the position to be filled is no *sinecure* for any one.

It is a most exacting one to the patience, industry and temper of any person, and of course very different from commanding men.

Colonel William J. Hardee, who had turned over the commandant-ship to Reynolds, had just outlined the duties of that position to a board of visitors. The Commandant of Cadets taught artillery, cavalry, and infantry tactics, equitation—or the veterinary science—and art, outpost duty, strategy, grand tactics, and army organization and administration.[8] This was quite an order, though not so rough as it sounded, for the C.C. did have assistant instructors under him. However, in addition he commanded all corps formations, parades, ceremonies, and reviews.[9] He was also the chief disciplinary officer at the Point.

At any previous time in his career Reynolds would have grabbed at this appointment. A dozen years before he was yearning to get back to West Point in any capacity.[10] When his friend Captain Bradford R. Alden became commandant in 1845, Reynolds called it "the highest and most honorable command for a Capt. in our service."[11] Among other qualifications, the Commandant of Cadets was to be chosen for distinguished service in the field with troops.[12] So now Reynolds was here, in the second highest position the Academy could offer, and still he had his doubts.

Nothing was likely to annoy him more than the system of demerits, which covered almost every move a cadet made. As commandant he was final arbiter on all charges, excuses, pleas, or whatnot that came up. During Reynolds' incumbency a board of visitors headed by Senator James D. Blaine protested that too many demerits were imposed for petty offenses. Failure of a cadet to fold back his bed properly or to draw the curtains back in his room each cost a demerit. Detection of tobacco smoke in his room meant four, and so on. One hundred demerits in six months brought dismissal. Senator Blaine felt that such a system would rob the service of many potentially fine officers.[13] Given several more years he could have cited Cump Sherman as one brilliant leader who as a cadet had barely squeaked by in his battle with demerits.[14] And a first classman now under Reynolds was having his troubles too. George Custer was tailing the class of '61 in both conduct and scholarship.[15] Yet like Sherman, Custer would be heard from soon.

For his assistants in military instruction Reynolds had good men. Alexander McD. Cook taught infantry tactics; Fitzhugh Lee, Charles W. Field, and Robert Williams, cavalry; and Charles Griffin, artillery. The board of visitors made no complaints about "tac." But in watching battalion drill they were shocked to see cadets casually dropping out of ranks whenever they found the evolutions too complicated. Responsibility for this slack performance normally lay with the commandant. In this instance, however, the board quickly tagged the cause. Cadets were no longer being cashiered for such behavior. With threat of dismissal removed, the effect on morale was obvious. In its final report the board devoted most of its stress toward stopping this lenient practice.[16]

When Reynolds first reached the Point in September, he lived for a while with his old friend and teacher, Dad Kendrick. The professor kept bachelor's quarters on the post, where over the years he took in numbers of former students who came back to visit or to work. He also liked a good drink.[17] Explaining his stay with Kendrick, Reynolds wrote: "Col. Hardee, whom I relieved here, had his family here and as it is rather early for them to go to their home in Florida I have not disturbed him in his house, where they will remain until the end of the month. I was under great obligation to some of the members of it when I was sick in St. Augustine and of course was very glad to have it in my power to make any return to them for kindness for which I have been so long a debtor."[18]

Hardee and Reynolds would be fighting on opposite sides within a year. But relationships like this, built up over years in the small peacetime army, were hard to break. They help explain the wrench in friendships brought on by the outbreak of the war. They also make it clear why leave-takings at the Point, even after the affair of Fort Sumter in the spring of 1861, took on a mood of sorrow rather than of bitterness.[19]

In spite of the mounting crisis Reynolds did not lose touch with family affairs. News from Will continued bad. If he should grow worse, John wondered what would happen to Becky. Honolulu was so far away. At home the estate was nearing settlement at last, although it required Sam's help. Jim had either given the job up, or had been given up. In thanking Sam, Reynolds wrote: "I have the account and shall preserve it as a matter of course, as well as Hal's and Ellie's. The latter shows I have received from the estate, if I can make it out rightly, about $3,666; this, with your account makes about $4,364.67. It is certainly not more than this and may not be so much."[20] The total settlement when it came could hardly exceed $50,000, which shared among eight brothers and sisters would be none too much. What mattered to Reynolds, of course, was getting along with the business. Since he had seemed to make Hal and Ellie his particular responsibility, he wanted to know how things stood with them.

Jim Reynolds was too busy with politics to fret over the details of the estate. In Lancaster he served Buchanan both as his lawyer and as a political aide. This second duty was being made especially delicate by Mr. B's current difficulties in Washington. As for the family itself, Jim had always been more distant than the others. His college, in fact, remembered him later as diffident and retiring. One of the two top students in his class, he was looked upon then and afterwards as an intellectual, stimulating to the few he chose as his friends.[21] Still a bachelor with his own place, he was a great reader rather than a mixer—strange behavior for a politician.

Sam likewise remained somewhat aloof from the family, even in his recent marriage, one which did not please the others.[22] But Sam was less complicated than Jim, and more approachable. Besides, he was the one brother John could rely on to grab up a gun at the first suggestion of duck or quail. The two youngest girls, however, found little in common with either Sam or Jim. Once the estate was settled and the house sold, Hal and Ellie would live with Kate and her husband in Philadelphia. Henry D. Landis, "Harry" to his brother-in-law, was partner in the going hardware firm of Vance and Landis. He had both the means and the warm nature to welcome his wife's two younger sisters to make 1829 Spruce Street their home.[23] From this time on it would also be as close to a home as John himself would ever know.

The election of Lincoln in November 1860 carried Pennsylvania into the Republican column. This put a strain on Reynolds' self-imposed neutrality, but throughout the winter he still hoped for a moderate course that might avoid war. He admitted that the tension was now affecting the Academy.[24] Then in Charleston Harbor Sumter was bombarded on April 13, 1861. On the 25th John wrote Ellie: "What history will say of us, our Government, and Mr. B's Administration makes one wish to disown him." For Reynolds that sentence hurt. Old loyalties were not easily broken off.

He looked for his stay at the Point to be cut short and thought the southern cadets would be gone in a month. Meanwhile he hoped Harry would stay in Philadelphia and take care of the family instead of joining his old local militia company of artillery. Two of the family in service was enough to begin with. At that rate they would at least last longer, he felt. Then he continued: "I have said but little, except among ourselves here, on the present difficulties that surround the Government but a more disgraceful plot, on the part of our friend B's cabinet and the leading politicians of the South, to break up our Government, without cause, has never blackened the pages of history in any nation's record."[25] With this indictment Reynolds finally wrote off the old family friend. The letter contained just one relaxing note: "Tell Rob I have been on the eve of writing him to know when he was coming up to pay his visit here and to say that I have reserved some of that good Monongahela in case he should drop in suddenly, and at all events will have something to steady his nerves at billiards, the only amusement we indulge in here."

Reynolds had saved his bitterest words for an officer he fought with at Monterey and Buena Vista:

> . . . Who would have believed when I came here last September and found Mr. Jeff Davis laboring with a Committee of Congress and civilians to *re-organize* the Academy; our national School! whose sons, never until the seeds sown by his parricidal hand had filled it with the poisonous weed of secession, had known any other allegiance than that one to the whole country, or worshipped any other flag, than that which has moved our own youthful hopes and aspirations and under which we marched so proudly in our boyish days—who! I say, would have believed, that he was brooding over his systematic plans for *dis-organizing* the whole country. The depth of his treachery has not been plumbed yet, but it will be.[26]

In this high but earnest rhetoric Reynolds arrived full circle from his earlier wish to see the abolitionists hanged.

The first scattered fighting of the Civil War began in May of 1861 and gathered momentum in June with small engagements at Philippi, West Virginia, and Big Bethel, Virginia. The seceded states had formed a government, with a constitution and a president—Jefferson Davis. The Union blockade of southern ports had been in effect, on paper at least, since April. Reynolds was serving his last month at the Point. Along with his normal duties, which were heavy enough, he was in the midst of student examinations and the annual inspection by the board of visitors, "to say nothing of the feminine visitors."[27] It would be a relief if he found the ladies less critical than the members of the board.

Orders to a wartime assignment were due any day, and Reynolds had reason to hope for them. When Pennsylvania went for Lincoln, Jim Reynolds went with his state. He had moved more quickly than his brother. He seemed already close enough to the new administration to apply a little pressure in John's favor on Simon Cameron. The new secretary of war was a Pennsylvanian himself. At least Jim had put a word in somewhere to earn his brother's thanks: ". . . You have been fortunate," John wrote, "in anticipating my wishes and inclinations in reference to my own case, tho' I will serve in any position the Gov. may call me to with all the energy and power I possess." Then he showed his confidence in his brother's talent for leaping political fences. If Congress permitted replacements for the resigned southern cadets, would Jim make an effort to have the son of his friend Mrs. Schermerhorn appointed?[28]

Another chance had just come to Reynolds that he would have jumped at in peacetime. Winfield Scott, commander-in-chief of the army, wrote him a personal note on March 7: "Several years ago I said to you that I should offer you the first vacancy for an aide-de-camp that might occur in my staff. . . . I now have the pleasure of saying that I shall be glad if you will accept it. I have thought of no one else for the place."[29] Reynolds turned the assignment down, though he never said why. The old warrior was infirm and crotchety, but he had been for some years. Besides, he was the sole authentic American war hero now living. At this time he was still solid with the administration too.[30] What must have frightened Reynolds off, of course, was horror at being trapped at a desk in Washington. If this war heated up, Reynolds wanted to be where the fighting was.

Meanwhile affairs were coming to a head. On June 11 John assured Ellie that he knew nothing officially about a promotion beyond what Jim had already told him. But in July his commission as lieutenant colonel came through, dated May 14, 1861.[31] He was ordered to New London, Connecticut, to recruit a regiment. *His* regiment. "I would, of course, have preferred the Artillery arm of the service, but could not refuse the promotion offered me under any circumstances, much less at this time, when the Government has a right to my services in any capacity."[32] In his last letter from West Point he wrote: ". . . I have had every expression of regret from both officers and Professors here at my leaving them, and what is more flattering, great rejoicing among the cadets at their being relieved of me."[33] Reynolds' humor aside, there was probably some truth in his statement. The strong-headed young egos on the Hudson could easily have found that their commandant knew how to ride herd.

What happened to the new lieutenant colonel in September typified the confusion in army command at Washington. Reynolds barely had time to absorb his promotion in regular rank before he was made a brigadier general of volunteers.[34] Then General George B. McClellan wired him at Hartford on the 4th. Did he accept the commission and if so when would he report to the department of the Potomac?[35] Reynolds did accept and Special Order No. 145 made it official. The order stuck exactly three days. Special Order No. 147 switched him toward Fort Monroe, on his way to the command of Hatteras Inlet in North Carolina. General Wool, the department commander there, hardly had time to thank Scott for sending him "such an able and experienced officer"[36] before McClellan got Reynolds back again by complaining over Scott's head to the secretary of war.[37] On the 14th he was instructed to "repair to Washington via. Baltimore by the Steamer 'S. R. Spaulding'" and to deliver four companies of artillery to General John Dix before joining his new command.[38]

This last order held, thanks to McClellan's persistence. The young major general was getting his way in the capital these days, as well as in the way of his chief, General Scott.[39] McClellan was topping the rise of one of the most disputed careers in American military history. He would soon become the "problem child of the Civil War."[40] In July he had headed a small army in West Virginia that gave the North its first real taste of victory in an otherwise disheartening start. Then the defeat of McDowell's 35,000 troops at Bull Run on July 21 left the administration nowhere else to turn. So to McClellan went the job of reorganizing the beaten units, along with the thousands of recruits piling into Washington from the loyal states.

When Brigadier General Reynolds finally reported, McClellan assigned him to the 1st Brigade of the Pennsylvania Reserves. The Pennsylvania Reserve Corps (actually only a division in strength) was the creation of the state's new governor, Andrew Gregg Curtin. No other governor exceeded his zeal in serving the Union. Sometimes in his anxiety for the safety of the Commonwealth he strained even Lincoln's patience.[41] The most unlikely rumor would find Curtin shooting frantic wires off to Washington. But his patriotic support of the President made it possible to put up with this alarmist quirk. The tolerance was deserved. Like other northern governors Curtin was able to give more than he was asked for in 1861. In April the President had fixed Pennsylvania's quota of troops at fourteen regiments. Curtin could offer twenty-five, and more if needed. He had already furnished the first organized force to reach Washington from any state.[42]

Formation of the Reserves resulted from a special session of the Pennsylvania legislature. On May 15 an act was passed to provide the "Reserve Volunteer Corps of the Commonwealth." It was to consist of thirteen infantry regiments and one each of cavalry and artillery. These were to be three-year troops, organized to defend the state. But an all-important addition to the act granted their availability to the national government in an emergency. Pennsylvania responded at once to the call for both men and money. By the third week in June two of the infantry regiments even took part in skirmishing near Cumberland, Maryland.[43] One of these regiments later became famous as the "Bucktails," named for the deer tails the men wore on their caps.

They were also called "Kane's Rifles," after one of their several commanders. These men had been rigidly selected to provide expert shots and skilled woodsmen for maneuvering in rugged country ahead of other troops.[44]

While the Bucktails were the pick, all the Reserve regiments added up to the best soldier material then available in the state. As secretary of war, Simon Cameron had watched their organization with interest. So had the assistant secretary, who knew them even better. He was Thomas A. Scott, vice president of the Pennsylvania Railroad, who had left Curtin's military staff to come to Washington. Both Cameron and Scott knew where to turn when the Union army was driven back from Bull Run to the defenses of the capital. In fact, they may have taught Curtin how to heat up the wires between Harrisburg and Washington. The fourth telegram was the most urgent: "Tomorrow wont do for your regiments. We must have them to-night. Send them to-night. It is of the utmost importance."[45]

Four regiments of the Reserves started at once. As fast as they arrived at the Baltimore and Ohio terminal on the night of July 22 they were rushed to the north bank of the Potomac. Another four regiments moved in on August 2. Within two weeks eleven Reserve regiments had encamped at Tenallytown, about six miles northwest of the city. General George McCall, their commander, had to appeal strenuously to Cameron to let them come into the Army of the Potomac as a division intact.[46] By succeeding he made the Pennsylvania Reserves the only entire division to keep its geographical identity throughout its three years of fighting. The objection to such organizations is the effect heavy casualties have on concentrated local populations. Its virtue of course lies in the spirit and high morale that come from a soldier's pride in his community and state. Its identity with Pennsylvania helped make the Reserves the best-known and most respected single division in the Army of the Potomac.[47]

Reynolds was on hand September 16 when the Reserves were formed into three brigades. He drew the 1st Brigade, consisting of four infantry regiments and the cavalry. Brigadier General George Gordon Meade got the 2nd Brigade, and the 3rd was put under temporary command until Brigadier General E. O. C. Ord would become available. Present total strength of the division was reported as 10,465 men. Reynolds could hardly have found a better assignment. McCall and Meade were not only Pennsylvanians but also familiar names from the Mexican War.[48] Reynolds and Ord had only recently rounded up Indians together in Oregon. Even the "Lancaster Guards" from his home county had been absorbed into the Reserves.

On the 17th he wrote his sisters that he expected to be permanently settled in camp within several days.[49] But by this time new orders had a habit of catching up with Reynolds. The war department was staggered by the task of finding competent officers for an army already numbering nearly a half million. The West Pointers left to the North were being stretched painfully thin, and the need had to be met by volunteers. The system of selecting them through regimental elections was not working out. Somebody would have to screen the obvious misfits. One result was Special Order No. 71, of September 20: ". . . a Military Board to consist of the officers herein named will assemble at Washington, D. C. at 10 o'clock on Monday the 23rd inst. to examine into the capacity, qualifications, propriety of conduct, and efficiency of all commissioned officers of volunteers who may be ordered before it."[50] The order was given by command of Major General McClellan and Reynolds' name headed the list of five members.

Three times in one month Reynolds had caught the eye of his superiors. After snatching him away from General Wool, McClellan was now putting the chief responsibility on Reynolds for weeding out poor officer material. When the Army of the Potomac's 5th Corps historian wrote of Reynolds years later, he must have had evidence like this in mind. "No brigade in the service could boast a commander giving brighter promise of a glorious career."[51]

Before long, Reynolds got around to the volunteers that made up his own brigade. The men showed good stuff potentially, but they were amateurs at war. As to the officers, a chaplain of the Reserves said they had been picked less for their knowledge of Jomini's *Art of War* than for the number of recruits they could bring in.[52] One result of the examining board may have been the schools of instruction for company and regimental officers. The Reserves' volunteers got training tactics and army regulations twice a week at regimental headquarters. Noncoms also were included in this attempt to give the division some military coloration at least. Drill went on endlessly.[53] By October 9 the Reserves moved from Tenallytown over into Fairfax County, Virginia, with McCall reporting them well equipped and well drilled. His command now totaled 11,255 men.[54] They marched into enemy territory as the bands played "Dixie" and cheers broke out along the columns, then they filed into Camp Pierpont west of the old Chain bridge near Langley. In this position the division anchored the extreme right of the Army of the Potomac.

It was a good position too, according to Reynolds, with an open field facing toward the enemy. ". . . Should they advance upon us here," he wrote, "posted as we are in front of our line of works and we cannot stop them, we may as well give it up as a bad job." Hardly a confident statement, but Reynolds distrusted his command. "I begin to agree with somebody who, writing in one of the papers said: 'You cannot make soldiers of volunteers.' I thought in Mexico that I would never have anything to do with them under any circumstances, and nothing but this state of things in the country would have induced me to take command of any body of them. In coming over here they proceeded at once to plunder and destroy everything in the houses left by the people. . . . I almost despair, from what I have seen of them since I have been here of our ever making an attack upon any of the positions the enemy may take up."[55]

A 12th Regiment sergeant in the Reserves also saw the destruction that disgusted Reynolds: "The country we inhabit is remarkable for its beautiful and picturesque scenery. When we first came over here the farms were in a high state of cultivation. But as the troops advanced the rebel occupants fled precipitously, leaving the plow in the furrow and the furniture in the houses untouched. Uncle Sam's boys took charge of all. I think by the time the Army of the Potomac deserts its shores, the sacred soil of Virginia will represent to the eye, one continued scene of desolation."[56] This eighteen-year-old proved a good prophet.

Reynolds had company in his doubts about the volunteers. Meade was equally pessimistic: "They do not any of them, officers or men, seem to have the least idea of the solemn duty they have imposed on themselves in becoming soldiers. Soldiers they are not in any sense of the word."[57] Years of commanding professionals in a peacetime army had spoiled the West Pointers. Even veterans of the Mexican War had forgotten what volunteers were like. Reynolds and Meade were only repeating their familiar complaints of 1846-48.

On October 18 the division was ordered to make a reconnaissance toward the village of Dranesville, about twelve miles west of camp on the Leesburg pike. Reynolds' brigade led the march, but he returned disgusted three days later. "They plundered and marauded most outrageously and disgracefully," he wrote. ". . . Of course it was stopped but not until great damage had been done. I see by the papers that great praise had been given Genl. McCall's division for being exempt from this stain upon our Army, our Country, and our character. Do not believe one word of the accounts, which must be written from here by some of the very scoundrels who were the leading characters of it. . . . I have an officer and 3 men in arrest for their plundering at Dranesville and hope to have them hung if I can."[58] Reynolds meant it. He would either bring his brigade to heel or would ask for a transfer to the Connecticut regiment he had recruited before coming down here. At least they were regular army—strictly prewar. He could understand those men and they knew what to expect of him. Of the Reserves Reynolds excepted only the Bucktails from his indictment. They acted something like soldiers, he said, despite their being considered the most unmanageable at first.[59]

Along with McClellan and McDowell, Reynolds could be classed as a kid-glove general.[60] Only the last two years of the fighting to come sanctioned the idea of total war. At the beginning it was to be fought by gentlemen's rules—that is, if the professionals at the top could make them stick. The men in McClellan's army knew where he stood in regard to enemy property whether it deterred them or not.[61] But it was in Reynolds' character itself for him to be shocked at vandalism. A home and its contents—furniture, clothing, silverware, pictures, books, mementos—were sacredly private. They did not belong among the spoils of war. Reynolds had never owned a home and had spent his adult years largely outside of one, so more than ever he felt its worth. Of course he was luckier than some of his raiding volunteers. He stemmed from solid family roots, with a community history successful enough to give meaning and values to his idea of home.

About noon of October 21 Reynolds unknowingly led his brigade away from the only sizable engagement involving any of the army during its seven months of training. A brigade of General Charles P. Stone's division crossed the Potomac above Leesburg where a Confederate force caught it at a disadvantage and badly hacked it up. Its commander was Edward D. Baker, an inexperienced volunteer officer but a prominent senator from California. He was killed, along with forty-eight others. The wounded, captured, and missing totaled half his brigade.[62] Reynolds said that he had been within a dozen miles of where the battle started only two hours after he left. He thought somebody had blundered, for he was sure McClellan never intended a river crossing or he would not have withdrawn the Reserves from the area.[63]

The loss of Senator Baker hit Washington hard, including Lincoln.[64] Who had committed the brigade to this senseless battle? For his own part, McClellan disclaimed any responsibility and defended his pulling out of McCall's division.[65] Meanwhile the move had cost Reynolds his first crack at the enemy. Meade was disappointed too. He admitted that a great deal of talk went the rounds over McClellan's decision. "For myself," he concluded, "I ask no questions and don't speculate."[66] Neither did Reynolds, though both he and Meade tended to support their general. Of course loyalty to the chief was a strong habit with

Reynolds, and his tolerance could stretch a long way for any leader before it broke.

Following this disaster of Ball's Bluff quiet returned along the Potomac. One day the wives of Generals McCall and Meade visited camp, and Reynolds put the entire division through a review in their presence. It was executed according to his own ideas of the proper formations and the distribution of large units. "It was a splendid success!" he wrote his sisters. It succeeded so well, in fact, that his plan was recommended for a grand review to include three divisions. No West Pointer had ever before maneuvered as many as 30,000 men at one time. In his letter Reynolds began describing how he aimed to put them through their paces, then decided it would be too complicated for girls. "I doubt whether this will be very plain to you," he said, and gave it up.[67]

He went on to simpler matters. He had just been photographed in uniform and would send them a print. "They are the best I ever have had taken *I think*." He was apparently still touchy about that daguerreotype of his Mexican War days. But in these new pictures he would be sporting a beard, short and bristling. The high cheek bones were the same, the eyes as dark and expressive. They said most for his face—a hard glint for temper or fighting, softer tones for girls, including sisters who hid good cigars in his pockets,[68] and of course for his friends. Since John Reynolds seldom smiled or laughed, it was mostly his eyes that gave the key to his moods.

He had bought another horse, and like the pictures he thought it was the best he ever had. A major going home on sick leave had sold it to him for $225. Now he had three mounts, although the government allowed brigadiers forage for four. This put Reynolds on the conservative side for an old lover of horses, but left him better off than his friend Meade, who had only two. "I should like much to have a really fine horse," Meade confessed to his son John, "but it costs so much I must try to get along with my old hacks."[69] In fact, he got along in other ways with less spanking equipment than Reynolds enjoyed. Much of it would have been wasted on Meade anyhow, for he lacked the straight, square-shouldered military presence of Reynolds. The artists for *Harper's* and *Leslie's* weeklies would never model their field officers from the stooped, bespectacled Meade.

For all his three horses Reynolds could not manage to get into a battle. On December 20 McCall had sent his 3rd Brigade, now under Ord, toward Dranesville again. The object was to drive out enemy pickets and gather forage for the animals. It happened that Confederate

General Jeb Stuart had about 1,200 men in the vicinity. A sharp though small fight resulted, lasting about an hour and a half. McCall himself got up before it ended, but by the time he ordered the brigades of Reynolds and Meade up from reserve Stuart had retired. Union losses were 7 killed and 61 wounded. The enemy reported 43 killed and 143 wounded.[70]

Particularly after Ball's Bluff, this little victory looked good in the northern press. McCall got a congratulatory letter from the secretary of war, and Governor Curtin hurried down to deliver his praises in person. Dranesville would soon make Ord a major general, but all that Reynolds and Meade could hope for was commendation for giving moral support. Ord's report described Reynolds' activity as follows: "I must not forget the prompt manner in which General Reynolds came up from Difficult Creek, some four miles off. He arrived too late, it is true, to take part in the affair, but the certainty that he would come with his brigade insured a victory and stimulated our men to earn it."[71] All Reynolds would see in this generous passage was, "He arrived too late." The best he could do, he wrote Ellie on Christmas, was to fight the battle over again at a dinner McCall was holding for his brigadiers that afternoon.

But he was finally going to see Will and Becky, and that would help. Reynolds had been watching ship arrivals in California, scanning the passenger lists. Their paths had almost crossed out there in 1855, when Will and Becky shipped out to the Pacific Islands. John was on his way to Orford at the time and barely missed them in San Francisco. Now on January 11, 1862, he rode into Washington from camp to meet them. It was a happy reunion. But in reporting to Ellie the following day, he had to admit his concern for his brother's health. "Will has not been well since he arrived. His duties took him to the top of the Treasury Building, which he accomplished twice I believe, much to his discomfort and probable injury. He looks badly, I think—tho' his doctors *here* give him great encouragement."

Ellie and Kate wanted to come down at once to see Will and Becky, but John advised against it, especially for Kate, who planned to bring the children. He warned them about smallpox and typhoid fever, which he said were around in the city. The girls had asked about expenses, as if they needed to care. He was host, he said. Besides, he had just received $300 from Dad Kendrick from the sale of the furniture he had left at the Point. He would be glad to throw that into the kitty for their visit, though he still thought it a bad time to come.

Hal and Ellie came anyhow, and their brother spent what time he could spare showing them about. But he found it tough commuting on horseback between camp and the Willard Hotel. He had to send in a note of regret on the 17th: "I intended coming in this evening, but having been out most of the day, I returned so much covered with mud that I am loath to make another trial of it to-day, as it involves cleaning up only to be muddied over again. So I will come to-morrow morning in time to take breakfast with you, that is by half-past 8 or 9 o'clock unless something should prevent my leaving or the weather prove too bad to be *faced* with my delicate Phiz! and you can wait till that late hour for your morning meal." Being with the family was relaxing for Reynolds, though his puns were as bad as ever.

The Army of the Potomac had swollen to 177,556 men present for duty by February of 1862,[72] but it had barely moved into enemy territory and had not fought an engagement larger than the lamented Ball's Bluff. The impatient Meade was saying, "When are we going to do something? . . . This condition of quiescence . . . is ruining the country. . . . This army is gaining nothing by inaction. . . ."[73] Along with the whole North, Lincoln was impatient too. His order of January 31, calling for McClellan to go forward, had failed to prod him loose. It took two more orders to stir him from Washington. The last one stripped McClellan from his command of all the Union forces, leaving him only the Army of the Potomac. And still he delayed. He wanted to be sure his command was ready for offensive operations before taking the field. But military judgment aside, the pressure for action made it politically unwise for Lincoln to let him stall any longer.[74]

Meanwhile the reaction reduced Reynolds to cheering victories won elsewhere. "What glorious news! the last three days have brought for the cause of the Union, from the South and West." He wrote this on February 18. His old 3rd Artillery mate, General George Thomas, had just set the Confederates back at Mill Springs, Kentucky. With help from a gunboat flotilla Grant had done more by taking Forts Henry and Donelson in Tennessee. But what especially impressed Reynolds was the navy's success along the coast of the Carolinas. "One good effect the gallant work of our navy has accomplished will be to show England that the spirit and pluck that *lowered* her proud banner so often in 1812 has not diminished in the last 50 years and will dissipate any idea of interference with the blockade if they even seriously contemplated any." Reynolds thought his brother's branch of the service was doing all right.

At last McClellan moved south to meet the enemy. The Pennsylvania Reserves broke camp on March 14th and advanced to Alexandria for further orders. They had sloshed through two days of rain and mud to get there. A week later Reynolds was sure they would be shipped out by water, and he thought he knew where. One of the four corps had already sailed, so he expected McDowell's 1st Corps, which now included the Reserves, to follow. He was glad to hear that Will was improving, he said, but felt he might as well give up hopes of getting into the war because it would probably be settled one way or another by events now in progress.[75]

Reynolds was as mistaken about his destination as he was about the length of the war. The rest of the army landed on the lower Peninsula of Virginia, just about where he thought it would and where it began the campaign to take Richmond in 1862. Then at the last minute Lincoln detached McDowell's corps because he decided that McClellan had left the capital too thinly defended. The dedicated but irascible Edwin Stanton had by now replaced Cameron as war secretary, and it was chiefly to him that McClellan made the first of countless protests. He complained that he was robbed of essential support. From this point on the relations between Washington and the Army of Potomac command began to deteriorate.

Holding McDowell back from the army lost Reynolds another chance to fight. Instead, the Reserves drew the duty of guarding the Orange and Alexandria Railroad south out of the capital, and worse yet, repairing track destroyed by the Confederates. Reynolds wrote a discouraging letter to his sisters from Catlett's Station on April 24. He said the weather had been terrible. Some of his brigade had spent as much as twelve hours riding flatcars in a snowstorm. In desperation he finally stopped the trains and put his men in huts left by the enemy in their retreat after the long stalemate in front of Washington. But this act of kindness only brought Reynolds trouble. A surgeon in his brigade was caught desecrating a Union grave on Bull Run battlefield.

"When I called him up to ask him about it," Reynolds continued, "he did not deny it, acknowledged that he had brought away some of the bones, but excused himself by saying they were rebels! You better believe I gave him a piece of my mind on the subject." To Reynolds the lie was as bad as the act itself. He was thinking once more of resigning his volunteer's commission and going back to his Connecticut regulars as lieutenant colonel. "I do not know what these men [the volunteers] will do in action under their officers, who appear to have no control over them under the most ordinary circumstances. . . . I have done all I could to correct these evils but must say without being able to effect much change for the better." Again he excepted only the Bucktails. Volunteers would never meet Reynolds' high and rigid standards for military behavior. They continued to exasperate him in 1862 just as they had in 1846. But in time he would relent a little.

Eventually General McDowell was allowed to include the taking of Fredericksburg as part of his defensive operations below Washington. Then after Stonewall Jackson began threatening the capital by his victories in the Shenandoah Valley, McDowell was given the Department of the Rappahannock. McCall, Ord, Shields, and Rufus King commanded the divisions in his corps. Ord had got his major general's commission. Meade thought he deserved it but added a comment to which Reynolds could say amen: "War is a game of chance, and besides the chances of service, the accidents and luck of the field, in our army, an officer has to run the chances of having his political friends in power, or able to work for him."[76] Reynolds seemed to have a "right" friend in his brother Jim, but at this stage both he and Meade would appreciate some of that luck in the field.

The Confederate troops pulled out of Fredericksburg when McDowell's corps advanced, and in May the Reserves went into camp about a mile above the city at Falmouth on the opposite bank of the Rappahannock. Reynolds said they marched down over the worst roads he had ever known. Since this included the highways of Mexico and the several thousands of miles he had covered in the American west, it told a great deal about Virginia roads in 1862, especially in spring. As to the inhabitants, he thought only the total destruction of their army would ever bring them to their senses.[77] And Reynolds said *army*, not homes, factories, stores, crops, orchards. The only objective was enemy soldiers. The ones on his side whipped or got whipped by those on the other. To him a war was simply military, in its most restricted sense.

This definition of warfare made Reynolds an ideal military governor from the standpoint of the 5,000 people of Fredericksburg. He was assigned to the post on May 26. Not that the population had been mistreated by either Generals John Patrick or Rufus King, who preceded him.[78] In fact Reynolds clamped the lid tight as soon as he had marched his brigade through the city to its camp on the heights beyond. Nobody could cross the Rappahannock without a pass from his headquarters, set up in the Virginia State Bank. He slapped an 8 o'clock curfew on all stores, hotels, and public places.[79] By these measures he hoped to control both the flow and consumption of liquor and to stop the smuggling through the lines, particularly of medical supplies.[80]

His fairness was bound to please reasonable citizens. He applied the curfew as impartially to his own soldiers, to the sutlers, and other northern traders, as he did to the local population. Except for curfew, people were not to be molested in any way as they went about their business. Yet Reynolds was no appeaser. On June 4 a flash flood washed out the temporary bridges and cut off the 1st Brigade from the rest of the division across the river. This gave hope to the more rabid secessionists that their city would be recaptured. But as soon as they began trying to stir up hostile demonstrations, Reynolds merely pointed to McCall's guns posted on the opposite bank.[81] That ended the trouble.

Reynolds himself had little to say about his sixteen-day rule over an enemy city. He wrote to Ellie on June 10:

> The people in Fredericksburg are secesh of the first water—the first almost we have seen of the real F.F.V.'s and tho' they were distant, the ladies especially, they behaved with much more dignity and propriety, than it appears they did in New Orleans.[82] A family of Washington's, on whose place I made my Hd. Qrs. before we moved over to Fredericksburg, were very sensible and sociable, and as there were two young ladies (not bad looking either) your friend Mr. Lamborn[83] became quite intimate with them. They had a brother in the army with Genl Pettigrew's command and as he was a prisoner were very anxious about him after the late battles.

The young ladies who caught Lamborn's eye were Jane Charlotte and Eugenia. The brother, Ferdinand, must have been captured at Seven Pines. They were children of William Temple Washington, whose grandfather Samuel Washington was a full brother of the President. If this failed to establish Reynolds' recent "hosts'" as sufficiently First Family of Virginia, there was Samuel's wife, the former Dolly Payne Madison. So it should not have surprised a young Federal brigadier to find these people deep-rooted in loyalty to their historic state.[84]

But other duty looked more important to Reynolds than policing civilians. Would he ever get into a battle? It was the only way to get ahead in the army, and the army was his life. McDowell's other divisions had seen action against Stonewall Jackson. Front Royal, Cross Keys, and Port Republic were new battle names in the Valley. Shiloh and Island No. 10 had been won in the west. New Orleans was in Union hands. Even McClellan had inched up the Peninsula after the long siege of Yorktown, adding Williamsburg and Seven Pines to the list. All this time McCall's men merely idled about in the rear. Along the banks of the Rappahannock they had ornamented their camps with arbors pleasantly shaded by boughs of cedar and pine.[85] They were comfortably settled for the summer.

This might be one way to ride out a war, but Reynolds had no taste for it. The rising military leaders of the North had all fought battles— Grant, Sherman, Thomas, Rosecrans, Buell, Pope, Burnside. Battles were building new reputations in Reynolds' own Army of the Potomac. Yet only by fighting could a Hooker or a Hancock make his mark. Somewhere back in these last fretting days Reynolds had been promised a division, if McDowell could make one available.[86] Ord's promotion had left Reynolds the senior brigadier of the Reserves, and with McCall in steadily fading health there was the chance of replacing him. If he could only get into a fight in the meantime! It was not in Reynolds' nature to doubt for a second that he would improve the chance.

The break came at last. He wrote his youngest sister from the steamer *Cannonius*: "We have just dropped our anchor in the York River below West Point, having embarked in the Rappahannock yesterday morning. To-morrow we will be up at the White House, where we march to join the Army before Richmond."[87] At this point Reynolds should have been happier than he had been for months, but if he was it hardly showed in what followed: "Stanton's operations I do not like at all. They had no business to interfere with McClellan in the first instance when he left for the Peninsula. . . . It makes me sick to think of the absurd ideas people have of military operations—I cannot write about them."[88] He was against robbing McClellan in order to chase Jackson.[89] But most of all, Reynolds was against Washington for having left him on the Rappahannock completely out of the war.

CHAPTER VI

Two of Seven Days

On June 12, 1862, Jeb Stuart rode into military folklore by beginning the first of his three raids around the Army of the Potomac. He moved out north of Richmond shortly after daybreak and that night camped near the South Anna River. Next morning his 12,000 cavalrymen cut east to Hanover Court House, then bore southeast. They easily scattered the first Union cavalry they met, at Old Church about fourteen miles along the route. Nine more miles would bring them to Tunstall's Station on the York River Railroad. As this linked McClellan's supply line from White House Landing, Stuart could expect trouble there. Still it was tempting. He might catch a supply train, and he could tear up enough track to cripple the Union army for days. And of course there was the White House base itself, just four miles farther on. Destroy that and McClellan would have to retreat.[1]

Stuart's decision to strike Tunstall's brought John Reynolds into the big-time theater of the war. He played a minor role, and for the glory of the dramatic Rebel leader, too close to a supporting one. But at least it was fighting. The brigades of Reynolds and Meade had landed at White House two days before Stuart left Richmond. The 3rd Brigade, now under a recent Reserves artilleryman, Truman Seymour, was delayed until the 14th. So was Meade himself, whose command sailed without him when McCall and staff crowded him off their transport at the last minute.[2] So Reynolds had marched the two brigades down the railroad past Tunstall's and by the 13th was encamped at Dispatch Station. That night under a brilliant moon the Confederate cavalry swept into Tunstall's. The small guard left at the depot was not enough, and Reynolds took after Stuart from eight miles away. What he did in the next hours had to serve for his first official report of action in the war:

Dispatch Station
June 15, 1862

Sir: I have the honor to report that, in obedience to orders from headquarters, I proceeded with my brigade on the night of the 13th instant up the railroad to Tunstall's Station, which place I reached just about midnight. I approached as quietly as possible, sending one regiment out to occupy the hill, which commanded the whole place, another through the woods to the left, the remainder moving down after the advance. On reaching the depot I found a car loaded with corn on a side track on fire and partially consumed; the telegraph poles on the cross-road thrown down and the wires severed; the bridge beyond the depot on fire. Both fires were at once extinguished, the platform of the car and part of the corn alone being destroyed. One dead body on the track near the depot run over by the train. . . . Another body afterward found in the woods with a gun-shot wound in the head. . . .[3]

Too late for fighting, and the two casualties turned out to be civilian laborers. It was not much of a start for Reynolds. Later Reynolds was joined by cavalry units under Generals Emory and Cooke. Philip St. George Cooke was a Virginian who stayed with the North, but his failure to catch up with Stuart at any point of the raid put him under suspicion.[4] Whether or not Reynolds already doubted Cooke's zeal, he was most careful in concluding his report: ". . . Though I did not assume any command over Gen. Emory or Gen. Cooke . . . I coincided with measures taken by Gen. Emory and gave him such assistance as was in my power. . . ."[5]

Following their futile chase of Stuart the Reserves moved up the Chickahominy to join the rest of the army. McClellan now fronted Richmond with a force of over 150,000 men.[6] At the same time his secret service was feeding him estimates that put Lee's strength as high as 180,000,[7] although the Confederates numbered closer to 90,000.[8] In addition, McClellan believed a rumor that Beauregard was on the way east to join Lee. His demands on the war department for more men grew so frantic that Lincoln tried both to calm him and scold him at the same time: ". . . the probability of your being overwhelmed by 200,000, and talking of where the responsibility will belong, pain me very much."[9]

But now most of McDowell's corps had been returned to McClellan, and it was up to him to make his big push. Lee beat him to it, however. He had learned from Stuart's raid that the Union right was exposed.

General Fitz John Porter had 30,000 troops on the north bank of the Chickahominy, split off from the main part of the army. Anchoring his extreme right were 10,000 Pennsylvania Reserves, who had moved up on June 19 to take position about a mile east of the village of Mechanicsville.[10] This was the flank that invited Lee. If he could wreck Porter's command before it got help from south of the river, he could roll up the entire right and separate McClellan from his base at White House.

This threat made the Reserves' position crucial. General Porter himself looked over the ground before leaving the details of providing its defenses to McCall, who in turn delegated the job to Reynolds.[11] The Reserves occupied a rise above the east bank of Beaver Dam Creek. It gave good cover for both infantry and guns and controlled the only approaches. While most of his men began digging themselves in, Reynolds sent patrols north of the village where Stonewall Jackson was rumored to be closing in. He could bring 18,500 men fresh from their miracles in the Valley to join the strike against McClellan's vulnerable right. Reynolds also occupied Mechanicsville and set guards at the bridges along the Chickahominy. Richmond and Lee lay only four and a half miles to the south.

On the 26th Porter returned to inspect the position. "Quite early in the day I visited General Reynolds," he wrote later, "and had the best reasons not only to be contented, but thoroughly gratified, with the admirable arrangements of this accomplished officer, and to be encouraged by the cheerful confidence of himself and his able and gallant assistants. . . ."[12] At last Reynolds smelled a battle and he was taking no chances. Now let them come on.

The morning hours passed hot and still. About 11 o'clock Reynolds learned that his cavalry pickets were being driven in from the north.[13] That could be Jackson, so he rode into Mechanicsville with Seymour to arrange for the withdrawal of his skirmishers and patrols to the field works across the creek. They were to move back gradually as they felt pressure, joining the eight regiments that manned the defenses. Meade's brigade was held a half-mile to the rear of the line in reserve. Additional support would come from Griffin's and Martindale's brigades of Morell's division if needed.[14] Five batteries of 10- and 12-pounders swept the slight rise west of the creek toward the village. They had been put into position by old artilleryman Reynolds, who knew something about posting guns.

Now Lee's men began to come up from the south. At that point, just when Reynolds thought he had everything under tight control, somebody misread one of his orders. It cost him almost a whole company, which failed to drop back from Meadow Bridge, got cut off and captured. By 2:30 the rest of the advance Reserves was scrambling back to the cover of its field works. Lee had uncovered the bridges over the Chickahominy, and the divisions of A. P. Hill, D. H. Hill, and Longstreet were pouring into Mechanicsville. If Jackson made his expected appearance on their left, Lee could throw four divisions at one. This certainly followed the maxim of applying overwhelming strength against a key point. But his instructions to the first Hill were to wait until Jackson was ready.[15] A. P. Hill planted artillery to hit the Reserves' position across the creek, and for awhile held out his infantry as ordered. Still no Jackson.[16] Finally, in his impatience to attack, Hill moved his leading regiments southeast from Mechanicsville on the road which crossed the creek at Ellerson's Mill. This would bring them in front of Seymour's 3rd Brigade on the Union left. Longstreet and D. H. Hill filed out by the upper road in the direction of Reynolds' brigade on the right. The battle of Mechanicsville, or Beaver Dam Creek, was about to open the "Seven Days" that ended McClellan's invasion of the Peninsula.

The volunteers from Pennsylvania waited behind their entrenchments. They had never fought a battle before. The Dranesville affair was too small to count. These unruly soldiers who had sickened Reynolds by their pilfering now had the chance to make it up. He had said back in April that "all they care about, to hear them talk, is fight, which under favorable circumstances they do very well—but not under adverse ones."[17] What were the circumstances on this steaming afternoon? Between two and three times their own number edged toward them from the village. But if Porter and McCall had picked their ground wisely, and if Reynolds had posted the men and guns to the best advantage, the odds should at least even out. Reynolds himself reported how his men behaved:

> . . . The enemy appeared in force about 3 P.M. and opened with his batteries from the high ground around Mechanicsville, impetuously assailing with greatly superior force and at the same time the right and left of our position by the roads leading from that place. He was repulsed in every effort to storm our position, as well as in an attempt to turn our right by the ford and old dam where he was handsomely checked by the 2nd Regt., Lt. Col. McCandless [Reynolds then shifted his lines to meet new attempts]. . . . The action continued with undiminished vigor and the repeated efforts of the enemy to carry our position by assault was in every instance signally repulsed. Genl. Seymour was equally successful on the left in maintaining his position and night closed the action with the enemy defeated and discomfited.

The conduct of the troops, most of them for the first time under fire, was all that could be desired and was creditable to their State and Country. I would particularly mention the conduct of Capts. DeHart, Smead and Cooper for the coolness and judgment in which they directed the fire of their batteries. Lt. Piper of Smead's Battery was severely wounded.

Cols. Simmons, Roberts, Lt. Col. McCandless and Major Stone, commanding Regts., behaved with great coolness and executed my orders with a soldierly spirit and promptitude very gratifying to me.[18]

This account was part of a rough draft Reynolds never finished. What happened to him the next day kept his first report of a battle from getting into the official records. But he had put his reappraisal of his volunteers in writing. Tough discipline had helped the whole division before it even marched up to Mechanicsville. Two Peruvian army observers saw the Reserves arrive at White House Landing and thought they were regular troops. Their response to commands belied their recent civilian status.[19] For their first real combat experience Reynolds had provided the most favorable conditions he could, and the volunteers repaid his skill and care. Soldiers like to be used economically as well as effectively. From now on respect and appreciation would grow between Reynolds and his brigade.

In reporting the battle Reynolds made more of the attack against the Reserves' position than did Lee. But Lee's report appeared almost a year after Reynolds wrote his, and after they both had fought bigger battles. Mechanicsville had not followed Lee's plan of coordinating his own advance on McCall's left and center with that of Jackson on the right. Jackson never got into the fight. A. P. Hill failed to attack in strength, while Longstreet and D. H. Hill delayed so long repairing Mechanicsville bridge that it was almost dark before they engaged at all. That was how Lee saw the battle. He admitted only that Ripley's and Pender's brigades got within destructive short range of Union rifle and artillery fire. Like Reynolds, he pointed out that his troops had never fought before.[20]

Confederate losses still were high, about 1,400 to fewer than 200 for the Reserves.[21] The 44th Georgia was practically knocked out, and the 1st North Carolina lost half its effective force. The Reserves' defensive position was simply too strong. Two infantry brigades with artillery, and three brigades in reserve and little used, had stood off at least seventeen brigades of Lee. Reynolds probably learned that his old archenemy, Mr. Jefferson Davis, had ridden out from his capital to see the fight. This would make the victory doubly sweet. But Reynolds could feel satisfied on any account. So could Seymour, who generously threw most of the credit to the senior brigadier: ". . . I may say that much of the credit of this day belongs justly to him; his study of the ground and ample preparation even to the smallest detail, justify his high reputation as a soldier, and his conduct of the right wing is worthy of all praise."[22]

McClellan found room in his long report of the Seven Days' battles to remark on Reynolds' successful resistance at Mechanicsville.[23] McCall finally got around to thanking him too, though in his first account he made more of Meade for some strange reason.[24] Meade did not even fight in the battle. Of course McCall could not help being aware of Reynolds' ambition for higher command. But then Meade was ambitious too.[25] Could the difference be that the senior brigadier was next in line of succession? McCall knew his own time was short, both on account of his age and his health. During the battle just over he had had to leave most of the actual direction to Reynolds. It must have hurt the old soldier to see what was bound to come.

Truman Seymour needed this battle more than the others. He was not a popular replacement for Ord, who would have been hard for anyone to succeed. The 3rd Brigade loved Ord and parted with him in sorrow when he moved up to division command.[26] Sergeant Dick of the 12th Regiment wrote: "You would hardly believe how the boys were attached to him. . . . Our present brigadier general is T. Seymour, formerly captain of artillery. The boys do not like him very well but I think in a short while he will become quite popular."[27] Time proved Dick to be right. Seymour's direction of the left at Mechanicsville was soldierly, as recognized by the reports. He would already be respected for that.

That was the battle. Now the Reserves' job was to get out. McClellan's invading army had gone on the defensive. With Stonewall Jackson prodding his touchy right flank above the Chickahominy, the Union general was changing his base. This meant abandoning White House Landing on the York River and retreating south across the Peninsula's swamps to the James. Once the Pennsylvania Reserves pulled out from the security of their defenses on Beaver Dam Creek, Lee and Jackson could hit them in the open. Withdrawing weary troops at night after a battle was tough work at any time. Reynolds described the movement in his unfinished report:

> . . . I rec[d] . . . the order to fall back with my command to Cold Harbor, taking the upper road, Genls. Seymour and Meade to take the lower. Hastily arranging with Genl. Seymour the manner of withdrawing our troops, we put our commands in motion at once and by daylight the Batteries had already cleared the roads. I held the road on the right with the sharp shooters and the Rifle Regt.,

[Bucktails] now reduced to 5 Comps; and Cooper's 4 pieces. Genl. Seymour held the left road in a similar manner. The enemy's skirmishers advanced as soon as it was light enough to see and occupied the edge of the woods in our front and kept up a spirited fire upon the position while they endeavored to fill the woods in rear with their troops preparatory to an assault upon our position. Our fire kept them in check while our artillery shelled the woods until the Brigade had cleared the Bridge and the stream by Nunnally's Mill. I then ordered the withdrawal of the rear guard from its position; in effecting this unfortunately 2 Comps. of the Rifle Regt., Capt. Niles, failed to get the order and were left behind in the rifle pits and after making their way some two miles to the rear were overtaken and made prisoners.

The services of Maj. Stone and Capt. Cooper in covering the withdrawal of the troops in the morning cannot be too highly extoled. They maintained their advanced positions alone for more than an hour in the face of greatly superior numbers and with a firmness and boldness that would have done credit to experienced veteran troops.[28]

In the confusion of preparing his army's retreat, McClellan still found time to wire Stanton that the Reserves had beautifully executed their change of position under sharp fire and with little loss.[29] But the division needed rest. Porter appreciated its condition and promised to hold it in reserve for the day. It took position about 600 yards in rear of the corps' new defense line near Gaines' Mill. Without counting the Pennsylvanians, Porter had 20,500 men to hold off an attack north of the Chickahominy. The rest of McClellan's army, over 80,000 men, lay south of the river.[30] So what happened to Porter would depend on how much help McClellan was willing to send over the bridges. The Army of the Potomac thus awkwardly straddled the river. Lee liked it that way, especially as he and Jackson planned to strike on the side where Porter stood alone.

Porter had anchored his left close to the river, then bent his line gradually east for about a mile until his extreme right faced to the north. This gave him an arc fronting west, its bulge toward the enemy. He had a swampy stream bed below him and good elevation for controlling the two approach roads. His bridges lay to the rear, if he needed them. It was a stout position, but in order to take full advantage of the ground Porter felt he had stretched his line dangerously thin.[31] Morell's division held the left and Sykes's division of U. S. regular troops covered the right. Artillery emplacements broke the line at intervals.

Noon of the 27th passed quietly, again in searing heat. The first sound of firing came from Gaines' Mill. Around 2 o'clock A. P. Hill beat back a stubborn Massachusetts regiment, rolling them into Porter's front at the juncture of Morell and Sykes. Then he tried for two hours to crack through, but without any other help. As at Mechanicsville, Jackson was supposed to coordinate his attack on the extreme right with that of Lee on the left. Again he delayed, until Lee finally sent Longstreet in about 4 o'clock to lift the pressure from Hill.[32] This diversion gathered enough power to become an attack of its own against Morell's left. By that time Jackson did get up and with D. H. Hill began to crowd Sykes on the right.

Up out of reserve went Reynolds, Meade, and Seymour. Their day off was over. Along the base of the slope that rose from the swamp, Porter's forward line had come apart. In the muck and water, and in the fog of smoke, units lost their organization. Officers could no longer see their men, let alone make the orders heard in the din of guns and musketry. By 4 o'clock only Slocum's division had been sent from the south of the Chickahominy in support of Porter.[33] It was not enough.

Meanwhile Reynolds threw in his five regiments wherever he could plug a hole. The 1st Regiment relieved Duryea's Zouaves on the lower ground in front, fought there for two hours, then ran out of ammunition. The 2nd plunged into the swampy woods to their left. Reynolds rushed the 5th and the Bucktails to the opposite end of the line where Confederate artillery pinned them down from only 500 yards away. His 8th Regiment pushed out front to help Warren's brigade of Sykes in the center of the buckling defense. Meade and Seymour, as well as McCall, spurred their horses back and forth along the front, posting regiments to block off the enemy penetration. Sunset found all but the 12th Regiment of the Reserves in the hottest of the fighting.[34] This was the only division that had fought the day before; then it had marched most of the night under fire, so today it had expected to rest.

And still Lee could pile in troops to exploit his gains. Their momentum increased with success until they wore away most of the Union left and center. Two all-out attacks staggered Porter near dark and ended his chances of holding the ground. Two additional brigades that McClellan had finally put across the river got up too late. The direction was now toward the bridges and retreat. As long as it could, Porter's lone corps had stood off the bulk of Lee's army practically without help from the three corps that lay to the south. McClellan refused to send more help because he was afraid of the pressure on his own front. Actually he faced half the number of men he kept idle on his own side of the river. In fact, McClellan's tactics at Gaines' Mill have not gone down well with military writers.[35] As of 5 o'clock of June 27, about the best McClellan felt he could do for Porter was to wire him: "You must hold on till dark."[36] Three hours later he wired Stanton too: "We are holding our own very nearly. Had I 20,000 fresh and good troops we would be sure of a splendid victory."[37] No word about the three corps he never put in. But that was for war department consumption. For Flag Officer Goldsborough, whose gunboats would protect McClellan's retreat when it neared the James, he had a different message, which included this sentence: "We have met a severe repulse to-day."[38]

Reynolds was still on the field after sundown. He had promised Major Roy Stone to relieve the Bucktails and the 5th. His men were terribly exhausted, Stone said.[39] Reynolds knew they were and was trying desperately to find help. That had been his job all afternoon. Shore up one gap and the cry for men came from somewhere else. This defensive surgery had scattered McCall's brigades too far to control. Aides and orderlies continually got lost, and with them the orders they carried. Meade's 11th Regiment fought almost till dark alongside the 4th New Jersey, both unaware that Confederates had swung around their rear. Too late they tried to go back but could not find their commands. They made over a thousand prisoners for Lee. Reynolds was still out there too, reposting a battery on the far right.[40] It would be dark before he could make his way south across the rear of the sifted line.

McCall's Pennsylvanians had spent quite a day for troops in reserve— 1,600 in killed, wounded, captured, and missing out of about 10,000. The old general was very pleased with their efforts and gave thanks to his brigadiers in his official report.[41] Porter himself was more specific as to one of McCall's brigadiers: "Previous to the arrival of Slocum," he wrote, "Reynolds, having repulsed the enemy on his front, and hearing the tremendous contest on his left, had, acting under a true maxim and with the generous spirit of the soldier, moved to the sound of the cannon, and led his men, regiment after regiment, where our hard-pressed forces required most assistance."[42] Reynolds never needed praise more. He had spent an unhappy night on June 27. His letter describing it was dated Richmond, July 3, and was the first letter he had found time to write in over three weeks:

> You will have learned something ere this reaches you of the battles before Richmond and most probably of my fate also.
> After the second day's fight, I had withdrawn my brigade from the action around "Gaines' Mill." I went with my Adj. Gen. to the right of the line to post the artillery, or to get it changed to a different position, where I remained till nearly dark. When in endeavoring to

return to my brigade, I found the left of our line had given way and the Confederate pickets occupying the ground I had passed over, and taking what I thought a direct course through the woods to our rear, became entangled in the swamp. With my horse wounded [his favorite sorrel] and unable to extricate him, I remained there through the night, and when day broke made another effort to regain the position of our lines, but was unfortunately unsuccessful and taken prisoner. We have since been in Richmond where we have been most kindly treated and cared for. My brigade in the first two days behaved well and our loss was not great; more in missing than in killed and wounded. The Capt. [Charles Kingsbury, his adjutant] is with me and is well.[43]

Reynolds' aide, Charles Lamborn, added what information he had picked up when he wrote Hal and Ellie two days later. He said he had seen his general as late as 6 o'clock at Gaines' Mill. They were together on the right of the line where Reynolds had ordered him to post two regiments that had been pulled out of action. Then the general rode toward the front, and none of the officers had seen him afterwards. Lamborn also had heard that Reynolds was being courteously treated.[44]

The Confederates were glad to catch this brigadier who had fought them so hard in two battles. His capture was announced by Lee's adjutant, and claimed by the pickets of General Winder; then more specifically by the pickets of the 4th Virginia, and finally by D. H. Hill.[45] Hill described Reynolds' reception at Confederate headquarters on the morning of the 28th. They had been messmates for more than a year in the old army, and tentmates for part of the time. He said no unkind word had ever passed between them. Then of his capture: "General Reynolds seemed confused and mortified at his position. He sat down and covered his face with his hands, and at length said: 'Hill, we ought not to be enemies.' I told him that there was no bad feeling on my part, and that he ought not to fret at the fortunes of war, which were notoriously fickle."[46] Reynolds apparently told Hill he had fallen asleep during the night of the 27th, but his letter to his sisters contradicts Jackson's biographer, who said Reynolds was asleep when caught— ". . . one of the most gallant of the northern brigadiers," Colonel Henderson added.[47] Small wonder if Reynolds had dropped off from exhaustion. He was on top of the only fighting the army did on the 26th, spent that entire night directing the move back, then added his harried day at Gaines' Mill.

Lamborn assured Reynolds' sisters that their brother was sorely missed by his men. "His coolness and bravery and his admirable disposition of the forces at Mechanicsville . . . are yet the constant theme of conversation about the camp fires. It is the highest aspiration of these men to fight again under Genl. Reynolds." The other two brigades of the Reserves were also aware of his high performance. ". . . And if he could return to-day to the command of the division he would be received with an earnest enthusiasm that no other man in the world could awaken."[48] Allowing for bias on the part of an aide for his chief, it still looked as if Reynolds had proved himself to the Reserves on June 26 and 27.

Certainly division command was inevitable for the senior brigadier if only he could be exchanged in time. Now it would come to him by default, even if he had been no more than competent. After Gaines' Mill the Reserves had fallen back south of the Chickahominy and continued toward the James with the rest of the army. On the 30th they had fought at New Market Cross Roads (also called Glendale or Nelson's Farm), where McCall was captured. This would make Reynolds eligible to succeed him in command. But more happened in this rugged fight. Meade was wounded and Colonel Seneca Simmons, who had replaced Reynolds, was killed. At one time during the long night Colonel R. B. Roberts was the ranking officer on the field. General Seymour had somehow got separated from the troops and could not resume division command until almost the end of the battle.[49]

The absence of Reynolds at New Market hurt the Reserves badly. Add the loss of McCall and Meade, and it is not surprising that they took quite a beating. They had to abandon their artillery and they lost about 25 per cent of the fewer than 7,000 who fought. Worse yet, General Hooker's report of July 15 accused the entire division of having been routed on his left. He called the Reserves "these demoralized people." Later McCall came to their defense, and he and Hooker fought it out in the official records.[50] McCall leaned heavily for support on the testimony of a captured division surgeon who quoted Longstreet as crediting the Reserves with saving the Union army on the 30th.[51] Porter also defended the division.[52]

It was a punched-out division, whoever was right. It had done more fighting in the first five of the Seven Days than any other division in the Army of the Potomac.[53] These Pennsylvanians deserved the rest they finally got when they were held out of the final battle at Malvern Hill. For once McClellan could spare them. His position was perfect and Lee lost heavily in attacking it.

Lamborn had hopeful news for Reynolds' family when he wrote them again from Harrison's Landing on July 7. Several wounded officers who had been released by the Confederates told him that the general might soon be exchanged. Lamborn wrote: "Men of all grades in the Reserves still come to me every day to ask if I have heard from 'The General,' if he is to be exchanged, and if I am sure they will let him command [them]. I think every man in the First Brigade would follow him to the Gates of Tophet if he would come and ask them." Lamborn even had hopeful news for himself. He had opened a package which came for Reynolds to see if it might go through the lines safely. It contained a half-dozen pairs of cotton socks and two soft woolen undershirts. Should the enemy refuse to let them pass, he said he was tempted to assume the right of war and confiscate them.

But Reynolds was luckier, for the package got through. He penciled a note to Lamborn from Richmond on July 30, thanking him for it, as well as for other favors. General McCall and Captain Kingsbury were well, he said, but all of them found the confinement irksome and were only buoyed up by the hope of soon rejoining the division. The officers had been forced to spend the last weeks in the notorious Libby prison. Later Reynolds gave the Joint Committee a detailed account of his stay in Richmond.[54] At first he had been properly treated, beginning with his reception by General D. H. Hill. He lived the first week in his room at the Spotswood House, which was a good hotel. But when McCall and a number of other officers were brought in, all of them were moved to a tobacco warehouse, where a space had been partitioned off for general officers. Several younger officers then tried to escape. As a result the Confederate captors marched every officer through the streets to Libby. Reynolds had made and would make longer marches, but none in which every footstep galled his pride the way this one did.

At Libby the officers were quartered regardless of rank. But the conditions that later made Libby infamous in the North had not yet set in. Reynolds and McCall were allowed to buy their own food and have it sent in from a boarding house. He never saw the prison rations, Reynolds told the committee. The officers all washed, ate, and slept in the same room, which he described as filthy. For him the final indignity was to be kept constantly under guard. He had given his word of honor not to try to escape. What more did they want? Reynolds wanted to fight this war "old army" style, and General Hill's courtesy had subscribed to it. But the authorities of Libby preferred a less tidy and less gallant version. If it made Reynolds a grimmer opponent when he got back to his troops, the South was the loser.

So far as it concerned Reynolds, the city of Fredericksburg seemed to accept his kind of war. When they heard he had been captured, a citizens' committee was formed to appeal for his release. On July 4, Mayor Slaughter and John Marye, Jr., started for Richmond with a petition signed by twenty-seven of the most influential men in Fredericksburg. It was a unique document, not only in purpose but in the nervous anxiety of its tone. How many drafts did this committee make before striking the exact balance it sought between toughness and mercy? The final effort was addressed to the Confederate secretary of war and it deserves partial quotation:

> . . . We feel called upon to testify that Gen. Reynolds exhibited in a marked and efficient manner a desire and a determination to so conduct his military command here as to conserve and protect so far as practicable the personal rights and domestic comforts of the citizens and thus to mitigate, so far as his actions could avail, the evils and annoyances which are incident to such an occupation. Your own military experience will suggest to you how materially such conduct as this on the part of a commanding officer could avail in saving our citizens from the countless ills which an unbridled and licentious soldiery might inflict upon a helpless population; and while, sir, neither his kindness and consideration or any other act or line of conduct pursued by the military authority now occupying our houses can avail in the slightest degree in modifying our sentiments touching the heinousness of our invasion or our devotion to our beloved cause and Government, yet we do feel that inasmuch as when we were prisoners in the hands of General Reynolds we received from him a treatment distinguished by a marked and considerate respect for our opinions and feelings, it becomes us to use our feeble influence in invoking for him, now a prisoner of our Government, a treatment as kind and considerate as was extended by him to us. We would therefore hope that he might be placed upon parole. . . .[55]

Whether the delicate mission of these twenty-seven citizens persuaded the war department at Richmond or not, it was as solid a tribute to its subject as it was unprecedented. Few men tried harder than Reynolds to be fair to others—even to enemies. It was as much a part of him as his fury when he thought others were being unfair to him. If he ever learned of this letter to Secretary Randolph, he would have been pleased. His only concern might be that some persons would accuse him of softness.

Reynolds was released in a general exchange of prisoners on August 13.[56] McCall returned to the Reserves at the same time. But the division commander was not as well as Reynolds had reported him in early July. The frenzied last five days of June had caught up with him. It was asking too much for a man in his sixtieth year to follow that pace with an additional six weeks in prison. McCall had never been a rugged soldier. He had taken a leave of absence once and had resigned once, each time because of poor health. When he reached the army again at Harrison's Landing, the war department would not risk returning him to field command.[57]

Reynolds wired Harry Landis on August 13 from headquarters. He was back with his division. Both McCall and he were received with bands and cheering—also with calls for speeches. The old general did manage to say a few words, but there is no record that Reynolds responded.[58] There were officers, and some good ones, who never sent troops into battle without the ring of oratory in their ears. Reynolds never made such speeches. He was satisfied simply to know that his men were ready for fighting.

On the night Reynolds returned, the 1st Brigade sergeants met and resolved to raise a subscription for a sword to be presented to him. "The money was freely given," a young officer wrote, "and placed in the hands of the author to procure the gift. It coming to the knowledge of the general, he refused to receive it, but being assured that it came from the men only, that there was no axe to grind and that no officer would attempt to make capital out of it, he consented. . . ."[59]

The sword, of course, would be some time in the making, so Reynolds had no need to worry in the meantime. Not a man or officer in the 1st Brigade would expect their general to relent over the slightest lapse in discipline, sword or no sword. The Reserves already had one for McCall, but since he had started for Washington on the 16th, he received the sword later at his farm near West Chester.

Now the division had a vacancy for a new major general. Seymour had led it since June 30, as acting commander. Young Sergeant Dick of the 12th Regiment thought Seymour's coolness under fire during the Seven Days had made him popular with the men, but two other soldiers were telling a different story to a Lancaster paper. One of them said: ". . . Our gallant Reynolds was the leading spirit of the day; wherever the thickest of the fight was there he was. . . ." The other correspondent objected to Seymour's taking partial credit for Mechanicsville when he was far to the left and hardly in the fight at all. Yet Seymour now had the division. They complained that under him it was fast losing its state pride. Why could Governor Curtin not find them a Pennsylvanian?

These two writers said Reynolds was the unanimous choice of the whole Reserves, rank and file. ". . . This man Seymour we do not wish to command us. The commanders of several regiments have written most earnest letters to Gov. Curtin. . . ."[60] Truman Seymour could hardly help being a New Englander, as they called him, and neither of them had apparently seen Seymour's generous tribute to Reynolds'

work at Mechanicsville. It was true that Seymour had claimed credit
for the battle along with Reynolds, but he was right.[61] What hurt
Seymour with the Reserves was not being a Pennsylvanian and not
having the personality to win the devotion of his troops. Finally, Reynolds was the ranking brigadier in the division. And if McCall was
jealous of him, Porter liked him and so did McClellan. He would be
the new commander.

Reynolds knew the Reserves were his when he wrote his sisters on
August 15. He was happy to be under the old flag once more and
hoped he had seen the last of Rebel tyranny. ". . . We are on our way
back to the Potomac to try to advance to Richmond by way of Fredericksburg and Pope's line. . . ." He disapproved of the move but supposed political considerations took precedence over military judgment.
Three days later he felt the same. ". . . I am very fearful of the operations in the valley. Pope's Army has not seen or met anything like
the force we know left Richmond before we did." How right he was.

Meade, now recovered from his wounds, had trouble catching up
with the division. He expected to join the command at Harrison's
Landing but found that it had already left the James. When he finally
saw Reynolds he was warmly greeted, he wrote his wife, and was
promised the 1st Brigade. ". . . Reynolds looks very well," he added,
"but complains bitterly of the want of courtesy shown him at Richmond."[62] Four days later, on the 21st, Reynolds officially assumed
command of the division opposite Fredericksburg. It had lost a third
of its men in the Peninsula and needed reorganizing to give it anything like equal strength throughout. Reynolds assigned Meade the
1st Brigade as he had promised, including the Bucktails; Seymour
got the 2nd; and the 3rd went to Colonel C. F. Jackson, who had led
the 9th Regiment.[63] The division still belonged to Porter's 5th Corps.

Now that Reynolds had a division the Army of the Potomac went
into temporary eclipse. The same Washington that angered Reynolds
by its interference had given McClellan up. Lincoln and Stanton felt
they had supported him in every way short of exposing the capital
itself. He had threatened Richmond for a month with the largest army
ever put into an American general's hands, and he had ended by
retreating. More than that, McClellan had protested to the last against
the administration. After Gaines' Mill he wired that if he saved his
troops he would owe no thanks to Washington. ". . . You have done
your best to sacrifice this army."[64] What that message failed to ac-
complish in antagonizing his superiors he made sure of by the pre-
sumptions of his letter from Harrison's Landing on July 7.[65] They
never quite trusted him afterwards.

Since only from the armies in the west could the government find victorious generals, two of them had been brought east. General Henry W. Halleck arrived at Washington headquarters on July 3 to become general-in-chief of the armies. John Pope, fresh from his success in opening the Mississippi above Memphis, was put at the head of the new Army of Virginia. It included McDowell's, Fremont's and Banks's corps, but when Fremont refused to serve under a former subordinate, his corps went to Franz Sigel. By the end of July Pope was able to report his strength at 56,000 ready for field duty.[66]

This army was assigned three tasks: to cover Washington and the Shenandoah Valley; to disrupt communications northwest of Richmond; and to draw off troops from McClellan's front. It had already succeeded too well in the last. By now Jackson was north of the Rapidan with 25,000 troops. Then on August 9, at Cedar Mountain near Culpeper, two divisions of Banks's corps stood him off for several hours in a sharp battle. But with Lee now beginning to push up from Richmond in force, Pope decided to draw back from the Rappahannock line to keep contact with McClellan.[67]

All these movements were under way when orders came for Reynolds to transfer the Pennsylvania Reserves from Porter to Pope's command. He might get into the fighting after all. He started the division for Rappahannock Station on the 22nd and reached Warrenton the next day. The tough seventy-mile march wore the men out, and they practically staggered into camp near the town.[68] A general with Pope who saw them arriving thought Reynolds' veterans showed the effects of their campaign in the Peninsula. "Their faces were bronzed, their colors pierced and torn with bullets, and their ranks thinned. . . ." But he added that there was great cheering when this battle-tested division moved in.[69] Samuel Bates, the historian of the Pennsylvania volunteers, wrote: ". . . Had Generals Franklin and Porter [of McClellan], who had a much shorter distance to march, shown the same enterprise and earnestness in moving their commands as was exhibited by the gallant Reynolds, a grievous defeat might have been averted."[70] Bates was referring to the second battle of Bull Run toward which all these armies were moving. It began to look already as if Reynolds' worshipful aide Lamborn was right in boasting that the Reserves would follow his general to Hell.

On August 25 Reynolds got his first chance to write his sisters. It was a quickly penciled note. He said the enemy was advancing against their position in great force and he expected an attack momentarily. ". . . Our situation is very critical. I think the whole movement from the Peninsula wrong and if the army is to be managed from Washington, I am afraid there will be nothing but failures as there have been formerly. No one can conduct a campaign at a distance from the field or without being in the actual presence of the operating armies. However, I did not intend this for any other purpose than to let you know where I am."

Now, not only one but two armies would be maneuvered on Virginia soil from Washington. Reynolds believed only soldiers should lead armies, and the armies should be led in the field. In another year Grant would agree. He would move the "office" of general-in-chief out of the capital to a front where at least half the war was being fought. Within months Reynolds' fierce opposition to remote control of military affairs was going to govern the all-important decision of his life.

CHAPTER VII

Heroics on Henry House Hill

The campaign of second Bull Run destroyed three military reputations and almost ruined a fourth—all of them Union generals. On the Confederate side it established Lee as a great leader, helped Longstreet, and added to Jackson's fame. Pope's jerry-built Army of Virginia made most of the wrong moves and had all the bad luck. Reynolds and his Pennsylvania Reserves suffered more than their share of this frustration. For five wearing days the division either marched or fought, or did both. Its appalling expenditure of courage and stamina far exceeded its results.

On the day Reynolds wrote his sisters about the army's perilous situation, the enemy was helping to prove him right. Lee sent the willing Jackson up along the Rappahannock to the west of Pope. By one of his typical marches Jackson got in behind Bull Run mountains and on August 26 about 25,000 men poured through Thorofare Gap in the rear of Pope's army. First they hit Bristoe Station, on the Orange and Alexandria Railroad. But the big prize lay up the track to the northeast—Pope's supply depot at Manassas Junction. General Winder with several hundred men and a cavalry force under Stuart plunged on ahead, tired as they were. The raid quickly paid off in 300 prisoners, eight guns, some 300 horses and 200 tents, besides immense stores of provisions and forage.[1] The Confederates also tore up track and knocked out several bridges.

This disaster in his rear changed everything for Pope. It meant reversing his position entirely. Instead of pushing southwest and deeper into enemy country, he must now start his troops up the parallel roads to the northeast. But since Lee had gambled in splitting his own army, there was a good chance of cornering Jackson's force alone. Destroying his command would cancel out any number of raids. Pope got his columns under way on the 27th, and that afternoon Hooker's division collided with Ewell's division of Jackson beyond Bristoe. Ewell made a show of resisting, then retreated to join his chief at Manassas. It was a good start for Pope. In a few hours he ought to be in contact with all of Stonewall's corps.

Porter was ordered to close up behind Hooker along the railroad. Meanwhile two other corps, Sigel's and McDowell's, marched on the Warrenton turnpike. Reynolds' division followed McDowell, once again under his command. Three more divisions under Kearny and Reno kept the same direction, though farther to the right. So Pope had all his columns heading northeast and spread like a net to pin Jackson down at Manassas. And if Jackson moved out of there, where could he go? He was outnumbered more than two to one.[2]

Throughout the 27th and the morning of the 28th long columns filed up the pike under the heat haze of August. Delays were frequent, as always when large bodies of troops congest along a single road. One member of the Reserves said it took until noon to cover five miles, and they had started at dawn. But early afternoon brought a more significant halt than the ones before. ". . . The report of a cannon was heard a mile in our front, and a shell flew over our heads, striking in a field on our right. Half a dozen additional shell and shot now came crashing and smashing around us. General Reynolds—brave fellow— was among us; and, with soldierly coolness and courage, he proceeded to arrange a line of battle."[3]

Accounts of second Bull Run note this brief contact with Confederate fire only because of what it foretold, but to Private Alonzo Hill it was a battle. A shell exploded in the midst of Company G of his 8th Regiment, killing three men and wounding five more. "One of our batteries, hastily taking a position, replied to the rebel battery, and the latter soon ceased to play. Line of battle was formed. . . . We could see dark lines of rebel infantry upon a range of hills a mile to our front, and a little to our left. We had very little doubt that a fight was at hand. . . . What therefore was our surprise, our amazement, our astonishment, our chagrin, when, after standing in line for half an hour, we were suddenly marched by the right flank, across the road, through a wood, over a hill and far away."[4]

Hill's surprise, amazement, and so on, were well taken, but McDowell's orders had to be followed. The division was to march to Manassas Junction along with Sigel's corps.[5] The trifling enemy force in their front, probably a reconnaissance, would only keep them from the main objective—Jackson. So after Cooper's rifled guns had driven the Confederates from the ridge,[6] Reynolds broke up his battle formation, the 8th gathered up its dead and wounded, and the Reserves moved off to the right. Reynolds and McDowell rode together at the head of the column.[7]

But Jackson's movements seldom accommodated the reasoning of his opponents. With Pope about to crowd him at Manassas, he began pulling out before daylight of the 28th, hours before his evacuation was discovered. He seemed to be heading for Centreville; at least he sent A. P. Hill's division there. By the time Pope caught up with this move, Sigel and Reynolds had already covered several miles in the direction of Manassas. But as it now looked advisable to make the strike at Centreville, Pope switched Reynolds and Sigel to the northeast. Back to the pike they started around 5 o'clock.[8] Reynolds followed Sigel on the Sudley Springs road, which would bring them in just east of Groveton. King's division of McDowell was luckier. His men had not yet turned off the pike and the new orders saved them the trouble. They could keep right on to Centreville.

Near sunset Reynolds heard firing from the vicinity of Groveton. This time he knew it was more than a mere reconnaissance. He paced up the speed of his column and spurred his horse ahead into the broken country to his left. Now he must have wondered about those guns they had brushed aside so casually a short while before. Should he have got permission from McDowell, who had just left to find Pope, to feel out the strength behind them? What he heard now was heavy cannonading and from almost the same position. But then Reynolds was new to this army of Pope's, and on temporary assignment at that. Who was he to question McDowell's orders from the general commanding?[9]

Even before Reynolds caught up with the fighting, it had pretty well died down. About dark he found General Doubleday on the pike and asked what troops were engaged. Gibbon's brigade of King, Doubleday told him. Then why had the rest of the division not been brought up in support? Some of them had been. "... But why don't you push all these troops up?" Reynolds insisted.[10] Years later Civil War historian Ropes also wondered why.[11] King's other two brigades took no part in the battle of Groveton. Gibbon, with only three additional regiments, had stood off the weight of five Confederate brigades at close quarters. At the end he had scarcely more than 1,200 of his 2,000 men, and 133 dead would never know the pride of the new name their outfit was on the way to earning—the Iron Brigade.[12] The three regiments attached to Gibbon lost almost half their strength.

The enemy of course was Jackson. A. P. Hill's retreat through Centre-ville in the morning had decoyed Pope out of position. Jackson's other two divisions had moved west of Bull Run and retired behind Grove-ton. Hill's men joined them north of the pike later in the day. Now Reynolds knew the source of the artillery fire that had caught him as he turned off toward Manassas. Any order from here on that read Centreville was obsolete, including the one he carried in his pocket. The changed situation gave some initiative to the Union troops closest to Jackson, who had to be whipped before Lee could join him. For Pope it meant reversing direction once more. Instead of being on the right flank of his army, Reynolds suddenly found himself anchoring its left. King was in his front on the pike. Ricketts' division was even farther in advance, guarding Thorofare Gap against Lee.

At this point King became the key man. He was closest to Jackson, and if he only held till the other divisions countermarched to support him, they would have Stonewall in trouble. This seemed so obvious to Reynolds that he saw King and explained how vital it was for the divi-sion to stay put. And Reynolds did more. Without orders he promised to bring the Reserves up early next morning. "His offer fully demon-strated that this fine soldier duly appreciated the importance of the position."[13]

He started back to his own men about dark. But even before getting out of earshot, he reported later, he heard King's division moving off.[14] After talking things over with his brigadiers, Rufus King had decided he was too isolated.[15] Troops promised in the morning without orders might never show up. So it was a bitter ride for Reynolds, picking his way through the broken country in the moonless night. He had no authority over King; he could only advise. And their corps commander was nowhere around. McDowell had ridden on ahead of Reynolds to see Pope at Manassas.[16] Behind him his three division commanders, each separated from the other, were left to their own decisions. When King slipped out from under Jackson's guns, it was Ricketts' turn to feel lonely and so he pulled away from in front of Thorofare Gap.[17] Only Reynolds planned to move forward instead of back. McDowell's absence from his corps was costing Pope on this critical night.[18]

Ironically, King was at least following the latest orders he had. By backtracking to Gainesville he could leave the pike and cut southeast to Bristoe Station. From there he could go up the railroad to Centre-ville. His orders said Centreville, and good soldiers obeyed orders. Reynolds' orders said Centreville too, but by following them once on this day he had missed Jackson. With Sigel's corps and McDowell's at hand, they could have caught Jackson while Lee was still pinned west of Bull Run mountains. Now it would take desperate counter-marching to bring Pope's scattered troops back to the new front near Groveton. No wonder Reynolds was ready to throw his orders away.

By the time he got back to his command at daybreak, he was a tired horseman. He was facing a crucial day without sleep. Reynolds drew rein as Sigel was starting off for Groveton with his corps. Pope at last knew where Jackson was. Sigel was moving out against him on orders just received. But what about the Reserves, who were as close to the enemy as Sigel? In fact, Reynolds and the German had the only troops anywhere in Jackson's vicinity. The Reserves' historian afterwards supplied his description of what Reynolds did: "With the spirit of a true patriot, and a generous soldier," Sypher wrote, "he did not delay action from doubt of authority to move. . . . From daylight till dark, with no higher orders than the consciousness of a deed well done, the General and his troops, marching and countermarching, moving against the flank, or straight to the front, fought the enemy driving his right wing from hill top to hill top until darkness put an end to the contest."[19]

Unfortunately, this glowing version of Reynolds and his men over-stated the facts. In the first place Reynolds' report of the campaign stated that Sigel requested him to cooperate in the attack, although the cantankerous Sigel never admitted it.[20] Reynolds also said McDowell came up at daylight to direct the Reserves' march on Sigel's left. So the attractive fiction of the leader whose only instinct is to move toward the enemy, orders be damned, is out. Unlike Groveton the night before, headquarters now knew where Jackson was and orders would have to come from there. It was not a situation that gave Reynolds any latitude. He itched to go in, but he was a thoroughly obedient soldier.

The usually careful Sypher was also off in his account of the fighting. The Reserves spent an unhappy day. On the morning of the 29th they went into battle on Sigel's left, just south of the Warrenton pike. Then Meade's brigade and Cooper's battery crossed the pike to a position on the same ridge held by Jackson's right behind Groveton. That put them up close where they fought for some time while Reynolds was bringing the other two brigades to their support. Sigel soon ran into trouble farther to the right and began calling for help. A brigade from Schenck's division was pulled out of line next to Reynolds to support Sigel. This left a gap which the Confederates quickly exploited. They finally drove the Reserves off the ridge, forcing them back to Schenck's remaining brigades somewhat in rear.[21]

Jackson held a strong defensive position behind an unfinished railway cut. It made a natural defense running about two miles in a north-easterly direction from a point just below Groveton. Sigel and Reynolds had been trying to force this line on Jackson's right. During the forenoon other Union divisions began arriving to fill out the line opposite the enemy's left. Pope came up about noon to direct the fighting. Because Jackson had moved back to take advantage of the railway cut, Pope thought he was retreating. He had been of this mind since earlier in the morning when he sent a joint order to Porter and McDowell at Manassas.[22] This turned out to be a celebrated order, one that Pope made use of later.

In spite of his optimism, August 29 would go badly for Pope. Sigel and Reynolds had both made some progress at first, and their small gains were matched farther to the right up to midafternoon. But neither then nor later could Pope get all his force in at once. If Porter came up from Manassas in time to join Reynolds on the left, Pope meant to make an all-out attack. He was still waiting for Porter's two divisions and an additional brigade when the day ended.

Meanwhile Reynolds was having trouble cooperating with Schenck's division of Sigel. In the middle of the afternoon he got orders to advance again. Sigel's corps had already been moved ahead, and as Reynolds' skirmishers began catching up, Schenck asked for help to outflank a Confederate battery. Reynolds responded by trying to work Seymour's and C. F. Jackson's brigades in close enough to drive it out. But he had to report that ". . . notwithstanding all the steadiness and courage shown by the men they were compelled to fall back before the heavy fire of artillery and musketry which met them both on the front and left flank, and the division resumed its original position."[23]

It took only part of a sentence for Reynolds to describe this withdrawal, but Schenck's adjutant gave it more space in his report. He complained twice about the Reserves having fallen back,[24] and one of the charges found its way into a Philadelphia newspaper a month after the campaign. This was the only time Reynolds was ever accused of leaving the enemy's front while other troops stood fast. It must have hurt, for although he ignored the news dispatch, he took pains to answer the charge in a letter to McDowell. He pointed out that Schenck's sending a brigade to Sigel had exposed his own men and forced him to pull back. He ended: ". . . I make these corrections to you without any desire to enter into a controversy in the papers on official matters."[25] To Reynolds' mind, refighting battles in print should be confined to military sources. McDowell completely sustained his division commander's judgment on the 29th.[26]

This wrangle was typical of the lack of harmony and coordination

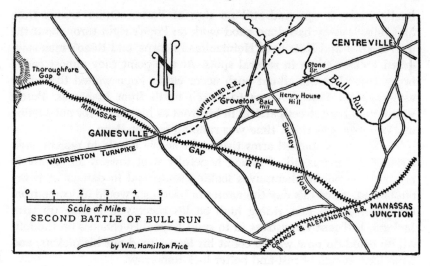

SECOND BATTLE OF BULL RUN

by Wm. Hamilton Price

existing in Pope's army. Ropes saw the trouble it caused him: "The advantage possessed by an army composed of troops who, for a year, have been organized as an army . . . in fighting an army that is a mere collection of three or four independent armies, or parts of armies, drawn together and organized as an army a few weeks before the first battle of the campaign . . . is enormous."[27]

For one thing, Sigel hated McDowell. It was even thought he suspected McDowell of treachery,[28] and a mad rumor ran through the army that Sigel had ordered him shot.[29] So Sigel's corps and Reynolds' division of McDowell each fought its own battle on Pope's harried left wing. The one attempt to cooperate had failed. In the beginning Sigel had isolated the Reserves by pulling a brigade out of line to shore up his right. Then Schenck called for help and Reynolds had sent men in until too much pressure drove them back. Later in the afternoon he began to wonder about this mounting opposition on his left. Schenck felt it too, but his adjutant said Reynolds refused to consult with them about how to meet it.[30] It semed that strangers instead of good neighbors had moved in next to each other.

The fighting of the 29th ended on the same disjointed note. King's division was brought up near sunset and thrown in on Reynolds' right. With support from Meade's brigade it made good headway at first, but in a little over an hour it was the same story again—too many Confederates now pouring south of the pike. Lee's Army of Northern Virginia had united. The fresh strength Reynolds and Schenck felt earlier was Longstreet. Toward night he punched holes in King's attack, then finally broke it up. And still no sign of Porter. Other troops from McClellan's army had done good work on Pope's right throughout the day. Hooker and Kearny of Heintzelman's corps, and Reno's men staggered Jackson's line in several spots. At one point they almost caved in his left.[31] But the all-out push never came. Pope waited the whole afternoon for Porter's corps to march north from Manassas. Porter would give Longstreet's arrival in his front as his reason for not getting up. Whoever was right, time was running out for Pope.

The Reserves stacked arms that night nearly a mile in rear of their starting point. Instead of facing hopefully west toward an enemy in retreat, they found themselves looking south and in danger of being outflanked. As of this day the names in headlines would all come from the Union right. Lee, riding high on his success in linking up with Jackson, had sent Longstreet in to spoil Reynolds' chances on the left. All he could do now was to count his losses, send out his pickets, and hope for a snatch of rest and better luck tomorrow.

Pope reported on how his army shaped up for the last day of second Bull Run: "On the morning of the 30th, as may be supposed, our troops, who had been so continually marching and fighting for so many days, were in a state of exhaustion. They had had little to eat for two days previous, and the artillery and cavalry horses had been in harness and saddled continually for ten days. . . . It may easily be imagined how little these troops, after such severe labor, and after undergoing such hardships and privation, were in condition for active and efficient service."[32] Of course when Pope wrote this, he was trying to explain why he lost. Much of the wasted marching and countermarching was his own fault, as was the destruction of his supply depot at Manassas Junction, which left his army short of food and forage. But his facts were right, and what they said for all his men included the Pennsylvania Reserves. "It must not be supposed," one of its soldiers said, "merely because I have not kept it before the reader, that we did not feel the pangs of hunger during all this time. We *were* hungry." Their last rations, enough for two days, had been issued almost a week before.[33]

On Saturday Jackson and Longstreet faced Pope's 65,000 with some 50,000 men in a line four miles long.[34] During the night Longstreet had drawn back from his advance against King and now looked east with most of his four divisions south of the pike. To his left, beyond a gap protected by artillery, Jackson's line remained about as it was on the 29th. Pope was still sure that Lee intended to retreat. He was deceived by Longstreet's moving back to rearrange his line.[35] Porter at last was up with the army and was to lead an attack down the pike, with Reynolds' division supporting his left in columns. Ricketts' division would cover Porter's other flank.

It was midafternoon by the time Porter advanced. South of the pike Reynolds began shelling the first ridge in his front, which lay opposite Groveton. He sent the Bucktails ahead to clear the way, then three more regiments. All of them got over the ridge but were stopped in a wood just beyond. Yesterday repeating itself already. Reynolds expected trouble because he had felt this wall of Confederates late on the day before. He rode up through his columns and left toward the far edge of the wood. He could see nothing there, so he spurred his horse out into the open field beyond. A spatter of fire showed him a line of enemy skirmishers. In rear of the skirmishers stood cavalry, waiting. Reynolds well knew what lay behind its screen—fresh infantry massed for an attack.

He had to take it all in at a glance, then get out. Union generals who made their own reconnaissance set up exciting targets. The riflemen raked the field over to reach him, but he made it to safety. Tearing along in Reynolds' wake, his orderly was not so lucky.[36] One soldier was so impressed by his general's daring that he laid Reynolds' escape only to the fact that his hour had not yet come.[37] Meanwhile Reynolds galloped right on back through the rear of his division to find McDowell. When he did he apparently wasted no words in damning Pope's notions about a Confederate retreat.[38] Some said he went directly to Pope, who refused to believe him.[39] But if Reynolds did go over McDowell's head to the commanding general, he omitted any mention of such a meeting, though possibly to avoid wrangling in print over a battle already fought. His description of his own role at second Bull Run was equally general in other respects, and modest enough to draw favorable notice.[40]

McDowell was quick to act on Reynolds' information, but his instructions for meeting the threat were no help to Pope. He took the Reserves from Porter's left near the pike and sent them back about three-quarters of a mile to Bald Hill. It was a fair position defensively, but the movement exposed Sykes's division and Hazlett's battery. Then, having detached Reynolds, McDowell also robbed Porter's other flank to build up the new defense south of the pike. Longstreet saw his chance and hurled his troops against this crippled front. Even though General Warren tried to plug the hole where Reynolds had been pulled out of line, it was too little and too late.[41] Porter's brigades would have to absorb the shock.

Stopping Longstreet now depended on two key points, both in rear on the left. Bald Hill was one of them.[42] On it were Reynolds and

McLean's brigade of Schenck. Just east over the Sudley Springs road was Henry House Hill. Here McDowell had placed two brigades of Ricketts' and several guns withdrawn from Porter's right. A stand-off defense on these two hills might save Pope's line if Jackson could be held on the north. So far Hooker, Kearny, and Reno, with help from Sigel, continued to pin him down by the same tough fighting they showed the day before.

Porter's front buckled around late afternoon. Hood's Texans struck Warren's thin line just south of the pike, bent it back, then swept through, headed for Bald Hill. Longstreet had the jump. Wilcox, Kemper, and Jones piled in on Hood's right. These were leg-weary troops from Lee's hard march to join his two wings, but they smelled victory and came on full of bounce. Old artillerist Reynolds had posted his guns to cover the maximum field of fire. By staggering Longstreet now, his Reserves and McLean's brigade could salvage much of what the last two days had cost. Or by merely hanging on long enough to blunt the attack or slow it up, they might at least keep Pope's army from being trapped. Its only line of retreat lay behind Bald and Henry House Hills.[43] Stone Bridge had to be held. One brigadier pushing in against Reynolds had been there before. "Shanks" Evans would like to add to his fame of first Bull Run. Reynolds of course would like to make some history of his own at this point. The Union left was overdue.

Soon the Confederate wave came rolling up toward Bald Hill in the wake of Porter's rout. When it smacked into Reynolds only a single brigade of the Reserves, along with McLean, was there to meet it. Orders again:

> . . . the commanding general, observing the attack of Porter to have been repulsed, ordered me with my division across the field to the rear of Porter, to form a line behind which the troops might be rallied. I immediately started my division in the direction indicated; but before the rear of the column had left the position the threatened attack by the enemy's right began to be felt, and the rear brigade, under Colonel Anderson, with three batteries of artillery, were obliged to form on the ground on which they found themselves to oppose it. Passing across the field to the right, with Meade's and Seymour's brigades and Ransom's battery, my course was diverted by the difficult nature of the ground, and the retreating masses of the broken columns, among the troops of Heintzelman's corps, already formed, by which time was lost and confusion created, which allowed the enemy to sweep up with his right, so far as almost to cut us off from the pike, leaving nothing but the rear brigade and three batteries of artillery of my division and scattered troops of other divisions to resist the advance of the enemy upon our left. . . .[44]

Reynolds had had a week to cool off before writing his account. What he must have thought of this maddening predicament at the time would be too hot for an official report. To be dragged off Bald Hill and sent on an impossible errand was pure waste of manpower at the time. In fact, Reynolds had actually planned to attack from his position before he was ordered out.[45] Instead, two-thirds of his division were brought away under fire only to disrupt Heintzelman's front and get tangled in the backwash of disorganized units shoving to the rear. They would have been too late to save Porter anyhow. So two brigades and a battery were literally thrown away when they could least be spared. To use Reynolds' understatement, they were ordered where they "were perfectly out of place."[46]

Somehow a staff officer from Pope managed to weave through the confusion of the retreat to locate Reynolds. Get the men and guns on Henry House Hill. It was the last possible defense on the left. A breakthrough there and Pope no longer had an army. "Reynolds' division was quickly extricated from the wreck of battle with which it had become entangled."[47] It moved in on the right of the hill. Two brigades from Ricketts under Tower were already there, along with a scattering of other troops and guns. Now that the day was nearly spent, maybe Reynolds had a spot where he could stand and fight. He could see division after division giving way and fading past in the gathering dark. Stone Bridge was secure to exactly the extent this final defense held on.

By the time Meade and Seymour, with Ransom's battery, got into position, the Confederate sweep had wrapped around Pope's shrunken left. The Reserves took the closing attack while facing south on the right slope of Henry House Hill. A private of the 8th Regiment saw his general and the two brigade commanders sitting their mounts beside the battery. He thought they were actually enjoying the prospect.[48] Whether enjoyment was the right word, at least for once in this campaign the Reserves were being properly used.

A slightly sunken lane partly protected the men, but when the shock came it took constant, rapid firing to check the heavy forces mounting the rise against them. Shortly both brigades began to stagger back. The 1st and 2nd Regiments were about to give way when Reynolds drove his horse into the line and grabbed the shattered flagstaff of the 2nd. Twice he rode up and down the entire front, waving the flag and calling for a charge.

This gallop along the lines suggested the engravings in the popular weeklies more than it did Reynolds.[49] The bristling mustachio, the blood-hungry eye, and the sword or tattered banner brandished toward the foe had no appeal for him. But the last frustrating days had conditioned him for any gesture that promised results. This final effort had to succeed. If Longstreet took Stone Bridge and the Bull Run fords he could choke off the way out, and the future for Reynolds could black out in the ruck of Pope's disaster.

"Reynolds, ever alert, driving his spurs into his horse's side, shouted his order: 'Forward, Reserves!' In a moment his troops, inoculated with his enthusiasm, swept forward and downward. . . . A mark for rebel sharpshooters, he seemed to bear a charmed life. . . ."[50] Many other Pennsylvanians, though with variations, recorded their agreement on how their commander pumped fight into the two brigades and sent them cheering and screaming down Henry House Hill.[51] "Old Army" Reynolds, self-conscious, scornful of show, had given his men the glory treatment when it counted. He had the physical and mental equipment for the job and he made it work. But it needed all the help it got from the other units on the hill. Buchanan's regulars from Sykes had come up; Tower's brigades of Ricketts were there; Reno had brought men in; and wherever a Union gun found a field of fire it had done its handsome best.[52] Longstreet's attack sputtered out in the darkness.

Still trapped back near Bald Hill, the Reserves' 3rd Brigade had done its part to wear down the Confederate advance. This brigade, as Reynolds reported, failed to get out with the other two. It simply went to work where it got caught, sticking it out till Kern's battery lost its four guns and Kern himself had to be left wounded on the field. "It was here," Reynolds wrote, "that the most severe loss of the division was sustained, both in men and material. . . . Colonel Hardin, commanding the Twelfth Regiment, was here severely wounded. The brigade under Colonel Anderson sustained itself most gallantly, and though severely pushed on both front and flank maintained its position until overwhelmed by numbers, when it fell back, taking up new positions wherever the advantages of ground permitted."[53]

In these last hours of the 30th Pope had weakened his right to shore up the left of the line. The shift in strength freed Jackson enough for him to help Longstreet's attack. Hooker, Kearny, Reno, and Stevens, along with remnants of Sykes and Ricketts, were stingy about yielding ground, but twilight saw them forced back to Buck Hill. Some troops had even crossed Sudley Springs road, which put them as far back as Henry House, though just north of it and the Warrenton pike. The two Confederate wings tried to wedge Pope in, to narrow his escape route eastward across Bull Run. Still the best of the Union troops refused to panic.[54] Piled up on themselves as they were, they managed to keep the right of the line from cracking altogether. To the south Reynolds' men and the others clung to their hill.

The retreat began shortly after 8 o'clock. There was no pursuit. Lee's army was as exhausted as Pope's. As the defeated forces were marching for Centreville, two more corps of the Army of the Potomac had at long last started west to join them. Franklin's and Sumner's men had not fired a shot for two months, and now they came too late. General-in-chief Halleck had prodded and pleaded to get McClellan to send them on. "Send the troops where the fighting is," he wired in final desperation.[55] Gideon Welles, the navy's secretary, thought McClellan's heart was not in the cause, and quoted Lincoln as saying: "There was a design, a purpose in breaking down Pope, without regard of consequences to the country."[56] The original strategy for the campaign had called for McClellan to move up from the Peninsula by land and water to combine with Pope. But whether McClellan really tried to cooperate or whether he stalled, Pope was marching out of the war. So was McDowell. It would be Porter's turn next. A court martial would judge his role at Bull Run and decide against him.

On September 2 Stonewall Jackson fell on Pope's right wing at Chantilly, five miles north of Centreville. It was a short, savage fight, which cost the Union two of its best generals—Philip Kearny and Isaac Stevens. After that the administration handed McClellan the job of reorganizing all the troops around Washington. Lincoln, the cabinet, and the war department had accepted him without enthusiasm, but the soldiers welcomed him back. That was the end of Pope's Army of Virginia. Its casualties totaled more than 8,000 for its month in the field. If losses at Cedar Mountain are included, along with those for the troops Pope did get from McClellan, his total for August exceeded 18,000.[57] In terms of manpower alone the operations proved as costly as they were generally futile.

The Reserves would soon have time to count their own losses. Reynolds had halted them two miles from Centreville on the morning of August 31 and issued hard bread and coffee. This was their first real meal in a week. An officer wrote: "It did not take us long to get our fires burning. These rations were a perfect god-send to us. Every mouthful of coffee we drank, seemed like so much life flowing into the body."[58] About 700 fewer men enjoyed this breakfast than had started north along Warrenton pike on the 27th.[59] The Seven Days' fighting had hurt more, but at that time there were 10,000 troops to absorb the loss. The Reserves went into second Bull Run with only 6,000. Meade felt that the men were so badly used up they ought to be withdrawn from active duty to recruit and reorganize.[60] If the ranks thinned much more, Reynolds would be commanding a division only in name.

At the first opportunity Reynolds wrote his report of the campaign. He also played a prominent role in the reports of others, sometimes more than he wanted. Sigel and his officers complained as much about Reynolds' activity on the 30th as they had about the day before. Sigel said he lost the army its key position when he pulled away from Bald Hill.[61] This was true. Schenck's adjutant said Reynolds left McLean's brigade without support.[62] And this was true. McLean in his turn wrote: "Soon after I had taken my position, much to my surprise, General Reynolds put his troops in motion and marched entirely past and across my right, to what point I am not informed."[63] True again. But all three reports imply that Reynolds acted on his own. It was as if, after being ordered to Bald Hill and after carefully posting his division, he had suddenly decided the place was too hot. Fortunately McDowell came to Reynolds' rescue by taking full responsibility for the order removing him.[64] Reynolds' report showed what he thought of it, especially as a victim of its consequences. But he did not say whether he had informed McLean that he was leaving. It might have helped if he had. The two corps of Sigel and McDowell simply did not cooperate at second Bull Run.

The cost of taking the Reserves from Bald Hill has been agreed on;[65] also the danger in having withdrawn them from Porter to begin with. "Pope had committed his last and his worst blunder," Henderson wrote.[66] The order detaching Reynolds from Porter's front got attention in other reports too, but with a difference. The other troops exposed by this maneuver happened to belong to the Army of the Potomac. Both Sykes's regulars and Hazlett's battery were left in a bad spot, and their commanders said so in positive terms.[67] But Sykes made the careful distinction that Reynolds was withdrawn, not that he withdrew. It was a distinction Reynolds would be grateful for.

That was the debit side of the record on the Reserves' commander. The credit side more than atoned. Pope wrote: "Brigadier General John F. Reynolds, commanding the Pennsylvania Reserves, merits the highest commendation at my hands. Prompt, active, and energetic, he commanded his division with distinguished ability throughout all the operations and performed his duties in all situations with zeal and fidelity."[68] Pope had praise for Meade and Seymour too. He carefully excepted the Reserves, along with Heintzelman's corps and Reno, from his feeling against the rest of McClellan's army. McDowell also showed his gratitude at having Reynolds and the Pennsylvanians under his command.[69] Porter, now under suspicion himself, but always a friend to the division, said: "The Pennsylvania Reserves did beautifully. They show the advantage of being well led by Reynolds, Meade, Seymour, and Jackson."[70]

These were kind words, but except for those last two hours of the 30th there was little to say in favor of Reynolds and his men. An "A" for effort alone would never have satisfied any of them. Their only luck of the whole campaign was finally getting a position that counted. Both armies saw the value of possessing Henry House Hill. For Pope it meant the difference between a successful retreat or virtual destruction. This much was clear to a board of inquiry which re-examined Porter's court martial in 1879: "Sykes with his disciplined brigades and Reynolds, with his gallant Pennsylvania Reserves, seized the commanding ground in rear, and, like a rock, withstood the advance of the victorious army and saved the Union from rout."[71] Writing from the Confederate viewpoint, Henderson said that nothing would have saved Pope's army if the hill had been lost.[72] But at the time it was reward enough for Reynolds that his division at last got a chance to fight and that it fought so well. It helped erase the feeling of wasted effort that had kept up until almost the end.

In his own report Reynolds showed restraint in appraising his division. "The conduct of the officers and men during the several actions and the arduous marches they were subjected to since leaving Fredericksburg, were generally good and commendable. Many straggled from the ranks, unable to keep up, and some few left the ranks on the field."[73] He had good words for his brigadiers, including Colonel Anderson, who had replaced the wounded C. F. Jackson of the 3rd. Meade was more generous to the Reserves than was Reynolds. He wrote his wife that they had saved the left flank and thus Pope's whole army. Then he ended this letter with a strange statement: "General Reynolds has been very kind and civil to me."[74]

Meade felt a little unsure in his relations with his commander. His honest but touchy pride made it hard for him to take orders from an officer five years his junior and six years later than his own class at West Point. Meade had dropped out of the service between 1836 and 1842; otherwise he would outrank Reynolds. It was a sensitive situation for both of them. Each looked forward to higher command and yet their futures were bound up together. They were also friends. Their association would be worth watching.

A significant aftermath of second Bull Run involved General Fitz John Porter. Doubts about his performance led to a court martial before the year ended. Reynolds' position on Pope's left during the two days of the battle made him a key witness, especially in connection with Porter's inactivity on the 29th. Why had this general failed to move the two or three miles west from Dawkins' Branch to join Reynolds? Called as a witness for Porter, Reynolds was pressed hard on two points: the nature of the ground Porter would have had to cover to reach him, and the enemy's position in relation to Porter's front.

On the first point Reynolds was positive: "It was impossible to maneuver troops over that country." He had already described it as broken and wooded. But the defense was trying to show that a Confederate force had overlapped Reynolds' left to keep Porter from closing the gap. If the ground was too rough for Porter, how did the enemy manage to get in there? "Was not the ground equally bad for the enemy as for General Porter?" This was a tough question, and only a careful answer would keep Porter from being hurt. "They could take position there of course," Reynolds admitted, "and they could be attacked in position by troops; but it would have been very difficult to have got artillery up through that broken country, and a very disadvantageous attack would have been made."[75]

The judge advocate was not satisfied. He said: "You do not seem to catch the point of the question. It is simply to inquire whether, in your judgment, the disadvantages were not equally great for the enemy as they would have been for General Porter's troops?" This poser threatened Reynolds with being inconsistent, but he stuck to his point. The Confederates took up a purely defensive position on the 29th, while Porter was expected to attack. Thus, ground suited to one kind of operations did not necessarily serve for another. Although this seemed like simple military logic to Reynolds, the court tested him on the point again. "Did not the enemy, in attacking the left and rear of General Pope, on Saturday, the 30th of August, pass with infantry and artillery over much the same country that General Porter would have to pass on the 29th to attack the right of the Confederates?"[76]

Now the question had a slightly different twist. Granting Reynolds that the enemy were satisfied with a defensive position on the first day, how about the second? The friends of Porter in the courtroom must have felt uneasy for a moment. But Reynolds quickly showed that there was at least no contradiction in his own mind. He said the Confederates did not attack over the same country Porter would have covered. On the 30th the difficult ground already lay behind them. They had passed through it the day before by filing off the Warrenton pike at points which were not available to Porter, who would have had to move up from the south. Reynolds said he knew the country well, having covered most of it on the 29th.[77] His answer finally seemed to satisfy the court. It should have, for no other general officer had gone as far forward on the left as Reynolds did on the two days at second Bull Run. Either he knew the country or nobody in Pope's army knew it.

But in spite of the testimony of Reynolds and others in support of Porter, the trial ended with the findings against him. The court decided that only Jackson was opposite Reynolds and Sigel on the left throughout the 29th. They did not believe Longstreet had come up yet. At the time Reynolds had no way of knowing whose troops they were either, but he knew he was being outflanked and said so. The court's opinion was still that no fresh force had got in between Reynolds and Porter; that Porter refused to move forward "and remained in rear all afternoon contemplating Pope's defeat." So the general was dismissed from the service. His disgrace lasted for sixteen years, until a board of inquiry re-examined the case and exonerated him.[78]

In the new hearing Reynolds' recorded testimony carried more weight than when he gave it in 1862. Now it was known that the troops pressing him back on the left belonged to Longstreet and that on the 29th they got in where Reynolds said they had. The inquiry agreed. Longstreet's position justified Porter in staying where he was. It went even further. By holding his position Porter kept Longstreet from enveloping Pope's left and rear in the first afternoon. Instead of hastening the army's defeat, he had actually postponed it by a day.[79]

So Reynolds had a hand in the reversal of Porter's sentence. At the same time there is no evidence that he deliberately favored his former commander. When the defense asked his opinion of Porter, he had said: "I served under General Porter on the Peninsula and up to the time that we embarked at Harrison's Landing. . . . I have always considered him an energetic, faithful and devoted officer."[80] This was a safe statement based on past record. Porter had come out of the Richmond campaign with a high reputation. For the most part Reynolds' testimony dealt only with what he saw—the terrain under question and the position of opposing troops. The findings on Porter in 1879 showed the accuracy of Reynolds' observations. He may not have been lucky at second Bull Run, but he proved himself to be an alert and thorough soldier.

For two days John Reynolds had been fighting within sixty miles of Pennsylvania, but his sisters had not heard from him since August 25. Too much Lee, Jackson, and Longstreet, and too many grey columns of men. He found his first chance to write on September 6 from Munson's Hill near Alexandria:

> I rec'd your letters, 3 in number, since my arrival at this place but amid all the movements have hardly had time to read them much less

answer them. We are well in health, that is *I* am, but everyone else is sick, *sick,* always when they are wanted. I have only Kingsbury, Lamborn and Riddle with me—and this to command a division is a very small staff. We are on the move to night. . . . I do not know what the movement portends except that the enemy are evidently bent upon an invasion of the north. I saw all this when we evacuated the Peninsula and attempted to hold the line of the Rappahannock. I have not time to write more. God bless you all and believe me . . .

etc.

This was lean coverage for one of the great battles of the war, but Reynolds was already looking ahead—and with good reason. Lee's army began crossing the Potomac above Leesburg on September 5. Its direction was west and north, toward Reynolds' home state. The rich harvest of a 300-mile border lay ripening in the late summer sun. The hungry Confederates and their animals would raise their standard of living. In crossing the river Lee had cut the heavy Union traffic on the Baltimore and Ohio. Now by reaching the Pennsylvania Railroad, he could scramble east-west communications for some time to come. It would bring the war home to the spoiled prosperity of cities like Harrisburg, York, Lancaster, and maybe even Philadelphia.[81] It might weaken the northern stomach for war. Altogether the rewards made invasion a good risk, and Reynolds' concern for Pennsylvania was well taken.

CHAPTER VIII

North of the Fighting

Andrew Gregg Curtin moved even faster than Lee. Before the Confederates reached the Potomac he issued a proclamation from Harrisburg on September 4. It recommended the organization of volunteer companies from every county and urged that all factories and businesses close at three in the afternoons to permit drilling. On the 6th Curtin was in Hagerstown, from where he wired Stanton: ". . . People are greatly alarmed here. . . ."[1] So was Curtin. He had created the Pennsylvania Reserves for exactly this kind of emergency, but he had matched his foresight by his generosity when he gave them up to the national cause. They had done so well since then that Washington would never release them for purely local defense.

Thomas A. Scott, who had returned from the war department to the Pennsylvania Railroad, now tried the next best thing. As an aide to Curtin he wired Stanton on the 8th for at least a brigade of disciplined troops. He said the people needed something to restore their confidence and ensure their continued support of the government.[2] Of course Scott had good reason to be worried about the railroad,[3] but it was also true that adding Pope's defeat to the wasted Peninsula campaign had hurt morale in the state. Pennsylvania already had supplied more then 200,000 men[4] for a war which was going badly. In fact it was going to take some digging into the remaining male population to come up with a force capable of its own defense. Unless the reorganized Army of the Potomac drove the Confederates back south, the border was vulnerable.

There was no cheer either in a dispatch from another of Curtin's

123

aides. On September 7 Colonel A. K. McClure reported 5,000 of the enemy moving up to Hagerstown,[5] which would put them within six miles of the Pennsylvania line. Or any more cheer in McClellan's assurance to Curtin next day: "If they intend advancing toward your State, I shall act with all possible vigor."[6] McClellan had promised vigorous action before. Curtin showed his confidence in the general by informing Stanton an hour later that he would call out the militia on the 9th unless otherwise advised, and he pleaded once more for troops from Washington.

Stanton's answer to appeals for troops became standard for the whole period of Lee's Maryland campaign. He said the best defense for Pennsylvania was the Army of the Potomac, and it needed every available man.[7] While this made military sense it did not encourage a governor who found some 55,000[8] Confederates camped within twenty-five miles of his state. Worse, they lay *between* it and McClellan's army. Scott made Curtin even more nervous by putting Lee's strength at 100,000. Even McClellan granted Lee only 10,000 more.[9]

Scott's estimate had been given out from Philadelphia, which had a bad case of jitters. On the 10th, the same day Curtin issued his call for militia, four frantic dispatches went to Washington from citizens' committees. Their chief cry was for a prominent general: "We implore you to give us one who combines the sagacity of the statesman with the acuteness and skill of the soldier. Give us a man whose heart is in the war."[10] At first they wanted a Philadelphian and named Meade among others. Whoever they got would have to fill a large order. His troops would be militia, recruited from among the older men, mostly heads of families. Many of them were prominent in their communities and represented fine civilian stock, but for overnight military service they would be something else.

McClellan on September 10 was still about two days southeast of Lee. Before the march began Reynolds and the Reserves had been in camp on Munson's Hill near Alexandria. While there they impressed a soldier of the 63rd Pennsylvania. "I think they are the best men in the army," he wrote, "for they care for nothing, nor do they fear anything. There is but little of the human left in them. They carry nothing but their rifles and ammunition." . . . None of them have any tents, overcoats or blankets, nor will they be bothered with them; *but they mean fight,* and they appear to love it."[11] Reynolds' standards for his men were probably higher than those of the admiring volunteer, but he still could be fairly well satisfied as he led them through Washington's streets on the 7th and out to Meridian Hill.

The division got new uniforms and drew fresh rations at Rockville on the 8th and two days later resumed its march north to the Old National Road. This put Reynolds on the right of the army's advance. McClellan was keeping his other flank close to the Potomac. They were all headed for Pennsylvania with a pretty sure chance of picking up where they had left off against Lee.

Riding along at the head of veterans, Reynolds would be hoping for better luck than at second Bull Run. Henry House Hill had been too brief a reminder of what proper fighting was worth. This time the Army of the Potomac would fight again as a single unit. This time Sigel's corps would not be on his right—or on his left or front or in rear. It had been held out with Heintzelman's corps to defend the capital. This time, too, those Reserves who left the field a week ago would think twice before shirking along their own border. As for himself, Reynolds commanded a division but was still only a brigadier. One good fight would make him a major general.

Where he turned onto the National Road, Reynolds was just twenty miles from Baltimore. This put him close to Jennie and George, and it would be easy enough to ride over. Plenty of officers had been ducking off for short leaves, as headquarters was unhappily aware.[12] But there was so much straggling in this reassembled army that no conscientious commander would think of leaving. So Reynolds swung away from the direction of Baltimore. His march also took him west of Philadelphia and the Landis family; even west of Lancaster where Hal and Ellie were visiting; and of Lydia and Nat Evans in Cornwall. At the same time he was riding toward a battle that would take place closer to home than he ever dreamed. This strange war was getting out of hand. Battles were fought far away from home—in Mexico or against Indians in the far west. Yet here he was, within hours of his native city and state, and in rear of the enemy at that.

September 10 turned out to be a long day. While Reynolds moved up through Maryland the rash of dispatches continued between Pennsylvania and Washington. Governor Curtin kept after Lincoln and the war department for help. General Andrew Porter had been in and out of Harrisburg on vague orders to assist in the state's mobilization. But neither Porter nor Curtin liked the arrangement, so Halleck took the general back and promised another to replace him.[13] To make sure of having some say in the next choice, Curtin then sent his adjutant, Colonel John A. Wright, to Washington. Meanwhile Halleck wired the governor that General Wool was going to Philadelphia to organize the forces north of the Susquehanna.[14] At 5 p.m. Curtin reported enemy troops within three miles of Hagerstown.[15] McClellan had an answer for that—concentrate the militia at Chambersburg and harass them. He added: "It is as much my interest as yours to preserve the soil of Pennsylvania from invasion, or, failing in that, to destroy an army that may have the temerity to attempt it."[16] Little Mac was flexing his muscles again.

By now it was obvious to Scott that he could get no troops for Pennsylvania from Washington. But could they at least have a commander? "We want an active, energetic officer to command the forces in the field, and one that could rally Pennsylvanians around him. It is believed that General Reynolds would be the most useful, and I hope you will arrange to send him after your interview with Colonel Wright in the morning, who will explain fully all the reasons."[17] After all, who would make a better choice? A Pennsylvanian commanding the first division in the army to be recruited entirely from a single state. He had certainly proved himself active and energetic, and the governor knew what his men thought of Reynolds. He had their letters from the Peninsula asking that Reynolds command them. So it looked as though Harrisburg had its man.

The next morning Reynolds continued westward on the Old National Road. No one had bothered to ask his opinion about leaving a division on its way to a battle. He had held on to his command in the reorganization after second Bull Run. It was a vote of confidence, and in the fighting that lay ahead he hoped to repay the war department's trust. For the present there was plenty to do. He rode back and forth along the line of march, whipping up laggards to keep the columns closed. He constantly checked headquarters for reports of Lee's movements, and he carefully timed his own advance to keep pace with the rest of the army.

While the unsuspecting Reynolds went his way, the government of his state and the government of his country argued over his role in the coming campaign. This was now September 11. At 10:20 a.m. Halleck wired McClellan: "The Governor of Pennsylvania wishes the services of General John F. Reynolds. Can you order him here for that purpose?"[18] It took McClellan twenty-five minutes to get off an answer: "General Reynolds is now engaged on important service. . . . He has one of the best divisions and is well acquainted with it. I cannot see how his services can be spared at the present time."[19] Halleck wired back at 1:55 p.m.: "General Reynolds' division can be commanded by someone else. He has been designated for other duty, and must report here immediately."[20] Apparently Halleck and Stanton had not yet got together, for the war secretary's 4:30 dispatch read: "General McClellan declines to spare General Reynolds from the field. Who else will you have?"[21] This was Scott, who replied from Harrisburg: "We still hope Reynolds will be ordered here."[22] In the end Halleck's order stuck, so McClellan gave in and promised that Reynolds would report to Curtin at the earliest possible moment.[23]

The governor was pressing Washington hard. He informed Lincoln that the "whole rebel army" was about to invade the state. He called for 80,000 disciplined troops at once. "Do not suppose for one instant that I am alarmed," he said. ". . . The enemy will bring against us not less than 120,000, with a large amount of artillery. The time for decided action by the National Government has arrived. What may we expect?"[24] Curtin sent this message at midafternoon of the 11th. He had already appealed directly to McClellan for troops, to which the latter replied that he could not divide his army but that he was sending Reynolds.[25]

Meanwhile, with the President's sanction, the governor issued his call for 50,000 militia to move to Harrisburg at once. Lincoln had agreed to receive them into the pay and service of the national government to the extent that they could be armed, equipped, and usefully employed. But regarding the 80,000 men Curtin demanded, he said: "Please consider that we have not to exceed 80,000 disciplined troops, properly so called, this side of the mountains."[26]

On the 12th a final try was made to keep Reynolds in the army. General Hooker appealed to headquarters:

> I have been shown an order relieving Brigadier-General Reynolds from the command of a division in my corps. I request that the major-general commanding will not heed this order; a scared Governor ought not to be permitted to destroy the usefulness of an entire division of the army, on the eve of important operations. General Reynolds commands a division of Pennsylvania troops [which are] not of the best character; is well known to them, and I have no officer to fill his place. It is satisfactory to my mind that the rebels have no more intention of going to Harrisburg than they have of going to heaven. It is only in the United States that atrocities like this are entertained.[27]

This was strong talk from a new corps commander, and he seemed to know all about those rowdy veterans that he felt only Reynolds could control. But for all his blistering tone, he failed of results. Curtin was getting his man. "Send Reynolds as soon as possible," he wired Stanton, ". . . an extra train will be provided for him on arrival at Baltimore."[28]

Lincoln could afford to be patient with the personable Andrew Curtin. If the governor asked a great deal, he offered far more in terms of what he could grant. At his bidding the governors of the loyal states would gather at Altoona, Pennsylvania, on the 24th to scout means of further helping the war. But only Lincoln's patience would have held up under some of Curtin's wilder rumors. On the night of the 12th he wired the President that 190,000 rebels were reported to be in Maryland. "The gentleman who gives me this information is vouched for as reliable and truthful by the best citizens of the place where he lives. I give it to you for your consideration."[29] Not that the governor was alarmed of course.

The outcome of all this telegraphic excitement finally caught up with Reynolds at Ridgeville. He was to turn his command over to General Meade at once and report to Harrisburg. There went his chance to fight with the army. There went his division. There went his major general's stars. Instead, he must have thought bitterly, he was about to throw himself away in the political atmosphere of a state capital gone suddenly hysteric with fear. He would be trying to make civilians resemble an army overnight. Then he would have to get this army to the southern border of the state and try to make it fight if it had to. But what else could he do? His obligation was as clear as his orders. Pennsylvania needed the kind of general he happened to be, and Pennsylvania was his own state.

Meade wrote his wife September 13: "Reynolds obeyed the order with alacrity, though very much against his will."[30] But at the moment Meade was more involved with his own pride than with his friend's unlucky order. He had seen Seth Williams of McClellan's staff and found him upset at Reynolds' leaving. "I told Williams very plainly that I saw no occasion for making such an outcry against Reynolds' removal; that I considered it a reflection on my competency to command the division, and that if he came back on any such grounds, I should insist on being relieved. I am now ready to meet the enemy, for I feel I am in the position I am entitled to. I should have been delighted to have gone to Harrisburg in Reynolds' place, as I have no doubt he will get a large command there."[31]

Reynolds' order left no time for a formal leave-taking, "but he was cheered with great enthusiasm as he rode away."[32] This separation was not open to the irony Reynolds used to describe his departure from West Point. He knew how he stood with his Reserves. They forgot his tough discipline because he had made them tough soldiers. They enjoyed their reputation as a fighting outfit, and they gave him full credit. Reynolds took along his two faithful staff officers, Kingsbury and Lamborn. At Baltimore he stopped to see Jennie and George before going north on his special train.

All this was taking too long for Curtin. When could he expect Reynolds? he wired McClellan.[33] Harrisburg was already choked with recruits on the 13th, so he was desperate for help. He had labored the whole day with Colonels Wright and McClure, trying to whip them into some kind of organization pending Reynolds' arrival. The war correspondent Charles Coffin saw this mobilization on the capitol grounds. It was a glorious exhibition of patriotism, he said. He had just come up from Philadelphia by way of Lancaster. "All labor was at a standstill. The fires of the foundries went out; the farmers left their uncut grain in the field. Men worth millions of dollars were in the ranks as privates. Members of Congress, professors of colleges with their classes, iron-masters with their workmen, ministers and the able-bodied men of their congregations, were hastening to the rendezvous."[34] But Coffin had his doubts about how these fine citizens would stand up to Lee. A militiaman who kept a journal at the time agreed. He said the muskets and bayonets were pure novelties to the men,[35] so it was probably just as well that no ammunition was at hand to be distributed.

There was little sleep for the city that night. The militia already on hand welcomed each new company with singing, cheering, speechmaking, and general rowdiness. The railway station was jammed when Reynolds' train came in.[36] One look around was enough to make the new commander think wistfully of his Reserves. That same night he wired Halleck: ". . . I think if the Reserve Corps could be spared from the army . . . and dispatched here, it would be of great assistance in forming and organizing new troops assembling at this point. I have no hope that this request will meet the favor of the commanding general of the troops, yet I cannot but think it would prove a judicious move in the end. . . ."[37] Could he at least have a battery? He knew of one now recruiting in Washington. Of course Halleck's answer to both requests was No.[38] Pennsylvania's best defense was still McClellan's army.

In his first general order on the morning of September 14 Reynolds formally assumed command of the Pennsylvania militia. Men kept piling in from all directions, needing arms, equipment, and most of all, organization. To expect much training was beyond hope. Two regiments were already at the depot of the Cumberland Valley Railroad, bound for Chambersburg fifty miles southwest. Eleven miles farther south and only five miles from the state line was the town of Greencastle. The railroad terminus lay six more miles below at Hagerstown, which a part of Longstreet's corps now held. This single-track line, with no sidings between Chambersburg and Hagerstown, had to serve as the militia's route of advance. Get the men south! was the slogan at Reynolds' headquarters. He hoped to start down himself the next day.

He had no thought of directing operations from Harrisburg. The militia would turn up too many men seeking preferment, and Curtin would have his political obligations. Anyhow commanders belonged in the field.

But the glut of staff work set in too soon to let Reynolds off. Washington constantly demanded information on Lee's movements along the border. Reynolds' progress was of equal interest. A cavalry troop from Carlisle barracks, organized the year before, had been scouting in the vicinity of Hagerstown for several days. It brought in news, but its captain, W. J. Palmer, needed more horses. This was only the beginning. Reynolds saved copies of the telegrams that piled up during these anxious days.[39] Why he did is hard to guess—maybe to warn him against accepting future militia duties.

Then politics began. From Scott: Could a certain private arriving in Harrisburg be given staff or similar work? From Scott again: Should he send up Major Vogdes, U. S. Army, on leave in Philadelphia—good man. From Curtin: Could some special assignment be found for a prominent citizen now a private in the Huntingdon Company? And Palmer's troubles continued: His men would hardly be able to keep their eyes open another night.

This last was not politics and the commanding general knew how to deal with it. Reynolds to Wright: "You will send 500 men to Greencastle at once to report to Captain Palmer for scouting and ranger duty. Select someone if possible familiar with the country." Reynolds to Wright: "Take immediate steps to obtain and transmit to these headquarters all the copies of the map of Franklin and Cumberland Counties to be found in those counties. Let the names and location of each owner be affixed. Report any that may have been seized by the enemy." Reynolds to Wright: "Be particular to give orders to all commanders to arrest and send to the provost marshal of Harrisburg all persons suspected of gathering information for the enemy." Reynolds to Halleck: "Our pickets are across into Maryland 3 miles from Hagerstown. Rebel pickets falling back. Longstreet retired, moving east on Boonsboro Road to-day."[40] Reynolds to Stanton: "Can you direct the Ordnance Bureau to furnish us, at the earliest moment, with equipments and carbines for 3,000 cavalry? Please answer."[41]

A wire from Curtin to Wright seemed obvious: "General Reynolds expects to remain here till to-morrow. He is very busy getting matters in shape. . . ." Reynolds would agree. In fact he would be doing well to get out of Harrisburg at all.

Lee had pulled Longstreet out of Hagerstown to help keep McClellan from breaking through Turner's Gap on South Mountain. The Army of the Potomac was catching up with the invasion at last. Near the end of the day (September 14) Meade took the Reserves up the east slope on the right of the Union line. Supported by a brigade from Ricketts' division, they soon captured the main position on the heights. Their attack impressed Confederate D. H. Hill, who wrote: "Meade was one of our most dreaded foes; he was always in deadly earnest; and he eschewed all trifling. He had under him brigade commanders, officers, and soldiers worthy of his leadership."[42] This was the division Reynolds had brought to its peak, but while somebody else fought it he sat trapped at a desk in Harrisburg.

One way or another Reynolds had found time to write his sisters. Now that he was in the capital he thought the possibility of a Rebel invasion looked more real. "There is nothing in the Valley to stop them and our army is too far behind them to retard or overtake them if they push on boldly." He was glad that the girls were not alarmed in Lancaster—"That's all right, do not allow yourselves to become so. Burn this up and do not let anyone see it."[43] Orders to his sisters apparently meant less than orders to his men. But if Reynolds believed in the danger of invasion, his new assignment made some sense. Besides, it might keep him from fretting about Meade's command.

Messages continued to flow along the Cumberland Valley Railroad on the 15th. Don't detain cars; return them without delay. Colonel Longnecker on way to Chambersburg with eight companies fully supplied with pans and kettles. Engines and cars now at Chambersburg to move 1,000 to Hagerstown. Have you arranged for provisions, etc., at Hagerstown tomorrow? Edward McPherson and Furman Rogers of Philadelphia have been commissioned as volunteer aides. Halleck says do everything you can to harass Longstreet. Palmer wants 800 saddle horses. Governor Curtin will be obliged if Colonels Campbell and Longnecker are assigned brigades. Colonel Benj. Davis of the regular U. S. Army cavalry has captured fifty of Longstreet's ordnance wagons and is cutting his way through from Harpers Ferry. Send cavalry and artillery to protect the captured train. Send horses at once; Harpers Ferry cavalry fagged out.

One order read like good news: "Arrange rooms for General Reynolds and make telegraph connection. Detail operator for the purpose." Chambersburg was not only the first leg south, but it would get Reynolds out of the capital. The combined efforts of himself, of Curtin, Scott, Wright, McClure, and others had managed to move 10,000 militia to the same place by the 15th. Curtin also reported about 2,000 of the state's cavalry operating farther south. With Longstreet's withdrawal from Hagerstown Reynolds had sent in Morton McMichael of Philadelphia to take charge. He was one militia officer who knew how to exercise authority. His orders got prompt results whenever he had the men to carry them out.

The two armies maneuvering in Maryland were closing in on each other. After the defeat at South Mountain Longstreet's corps moved west of Antietam Creek at Sharpsburg. Jackson was also concentrating there following his capture of Harpers Ferry on the 15th. This left only Jeb Stuart's cavalry in the Hagerstown area. His task was to screen the Confederate marches. He must have done well because Reynolds wired McMichael for information three times on the 16th. In his turn Mc-Michael called for infantry to control Hagerstown. He had about sixty prisoners and only twenty men to guard them. He had shut off the sale of liquor and was permitting no one to leave town. But he needed help.

Transportation was the worst bottleneck for Reynolds. It took great ingenuity to get trains south with troops or supplies and then return the empties over the single track for reloading. In the frantic mobilization there had not been time to pick out men with special skills like railroading. Only after a four-day scrambling of trains was Wright able to dig up a private who might help. He was Joseph D. Potts of Williamsport, general manager of the Philadelphia and Erie Railroad. With his experience put to use the traffic soon straightened out. The militia rolling into Chambersburg on the 16th were hurried off the cars into churches and every other available building. Scott wired Reynolds from Harrisburg: "Engines, cars must be here by daylight to move to Chambersburg the large numbers pouring in from all over."

To the south it was more of the same. Curtin to Reynolds: "Eighty-one prisoners on way from Hagerstown to Chambersburg." Captain Lane to Reynolds from Greencastle: "My command is ready and the cars are here. Shall I proceed to Hagerstown?" Captain Kurtz to Reynolds from Greencastle: "Can I get transportation for 80 to-morrow?" Captain Crosby to Reynolds from Greencastle: "Shall I have my pieces unloaded and put into camp near town?" Captain Brown to Reynolds: "My regiment has reached me here and is encamped on road leading to Williamsport." That dispatch got a quick answer, the copy of which was in Reynolds' own hand. Where was HERE he wanted to know!

Transferring headquarters to Chambersburg only meant moving all the nasty detail along with it. Curtin continued to pass on his discreet requests for special assignments to give his political friends. Halleck's needs also followed Reynolds down from the capital. Right now he wanted a regiment to guard the powder mills at Wilmington, Delaware. And Captain Palmer of the state cavalry never let up: "Is it impossible to get saddles and mount my men? I think we are entitled to this small privilege." An artillery officer had no oats, no tents, no cups or camp kettles. "What shall I do?" he asked. Then Curtin again: "Is your cavalry thrown forward to harass the enemy in flank and rear? We now have here and reported on the way about 25,000. I would like your opinion about increasing the number to 50,000, which can readily be done if required."

So it went, and so it had to continue until the Army of the Potomac beat Lee—if it could. If it failed, no telling what would happen in and to Pennsylvania. In the meantime Reynolds could ponder over a message from McClellan to Curtin. It reported the victory of South Mountain and congratulated the governor on the "gallant behavior of the Pennsylvania Reserves."[44]

Early on the 17th McMichael had a message for Reynolds from Hagerstown: "Heavy and constant cannonading in direction of Sharpsburg heard here now." It was the beginning of Antietam. McClellan's army faced west against Jackson and Longstreet, who held a three-mile line extending north and south of Sharpsburg behind the creek. Meade and the Reserves went in on the extreme right almost at the start, and by afternoon Meade had replaced the wounded Hooker. He was now in command of the 1st Corps. Up in Chambersburg Reynolds was busy too. He got another dispatch from the artillery captain wanting to know about his oats. Curtin informed Reynolds about the cooking utensils, small arms ammunition, tents, lint and bandages on the way to Hagerstown. And Scott complained that some regional maps he had hoped to get from General Patterson had been given to General Banks.

Back south, just north of Sharpsburg, General Joseph Mansfield was mortally wounded in an attack on Jackson's left. A little later General Richardson fell in the fight at Bloody Lane. In the afternoon the battle shifted to the south of the little town. General Ambrose Burnside finally got troops across the bridge that took his name, and for a while it looked bad for Lee. But A. P. Hill's Light Division came up panting from Harpers Ferry in time to make a stand. Still another Union general fell, and soon the battle ended.

In Chambersburg the other kind of war went on and on. Reynolds assured McMichael that Captain Dougherty would obtain a sufficient supply of oats for his present use in the neighborhood, keeping account of it and giving the proper receipts for the same. That finished headquarters for Reynolds. He left Kingsbury in charge and took the train for Hagerstown. He would get as close as he could to his own kind of war. It was good that he had moved down because now McClellan wired for help from the militia. Unless the battle was over, this could mean fighting. Reynolds wired back to Chambersburg at 9:15 that night: "Send the troops already in the cars first to this place. Don't let there be any delay at Chambersburg afterwards. Send those men now at camp to this post. Order them to be prepared to move immediately. . . ."

Reynolds stepped up activity in Hagerstown. He wanted two good operators hunted out of the regiments to assist in the telegraph office. He wanted all troops in camp supplied with at least forty rounds of ammunition with extra caps, cartridge boxes, and three days' rations, if possible cooked. Private Potts, the new find from the Philadelphia and Erie, assured Reynolds that all the troops in Chambersburg could be shipped down that night if necessary. Then having done all he could at the moment, Reynolds sent a final message to Kingsbury: "I am going to join McClellan and to get the troops here and to Boonsboro if such a thing is possible. Send Rogers and McPherson on with horses at once. Veil can bring my horse and you can pay my bill at the hotel."

The phrase "if such a thing is possible" showed Reynolds' doubts about his command. His doubts proved well founded even that night. Word came from Chambersburg that large numbers of the militia refused to put foot south of the state line. At seven the next morning Reynolds wired from McClellan's headquarters to Colonel Vogdes at Hagerstown: "Start all the troops out and urge them forward. Tell Governor Curtin to send Wright on to Chambersburg—that I am afraid I cannot get these troops forward. They only move when I am there in person to direct them. Some one ought to be sent to Hagerstown to command. . . ." Vogdes was having his troubles all right. He protested to Halleck in Washington that all but 2,500 of the militia refused to move, though he added that Governor Curtin had just arrived and might be able to persuade the other 4,000 to advance.[45] Colonel McClure, who went down to Antietam with Reynolds, admitted later that no officer could have coaxed the militia into action against Lee's veterans. He described even the few Reynolds managed to bring onto the battlefield as little better than a demoralized mob.[46]

Luckily the battle was not renewed on the 18th. The two armies held to their positions throughout the day, but heavy losses on both sides discouraged further fighting.[47] Now Reynolds could go back to the bulk of his reluctant command at Hagerstown. Before leaving headquarters he wrote Ellie a bitter note, in which he said: "I think if the Pennsylvania Militia did not turn out to fight they had better have remained at home." He said the battle had been terrible but that the Army of the Potomac got a little the better of it, though not much to boast about. Reynolds' on-the-spot judgment turned out to be right.

Although Lee recrossed the Potomac on the night of the 18th, there was still a chance of scattered raids along the Pennsylvania border. Prospects were dim that the militia would do anything to stop them. "I do not think much can be expected of them—not very much," Reynolds said in a dispatch to Halleck. His failure to supply McClellan the reinforcements he wanted[48] was a blow to his pride. These troops from his own state had let him down. Nor did their behavior improve with the fading of the emergency. Rumors of Confederate cavalry in the neighborhood kept the militia alerted for the next two days. Late on Saturday the 21st a skirmish actually took place on the Williamsport pike a mile south of Hagerstown. When it ended, Reynolds penciled a despairing note to the governor: "The enemy cavalry drove in our picket and by great good luck I happened to be on the spot. Under my direction the picket opened fire on them and drove them back. But if I had not just happened to be on the spot the picket would have retired without firing a shot and might have stampeded the whole command. I really do not know what will be the result if they [the enemy] should undertake to charge down the road tonight. I am afraid to leave the command for a moment after what I saw in front this evening."

A militiaman who saw the skirmish agreed with his commander. "I draw a veil over the scene presented at this juncture among a portion of the reserves of General Reynolds. It would take a better soldier than myself to tell what would have been the result of a serious collision at this moment, to the body of this force, whose chief misfortune was that it was entirely undisciplined."[49] Another recruit, from Reynolds' own county, was awed to find his general bunking in the field among the men.[50] If he could have read the note to Curtin he would have known why.

The threat to Pennsylvania was over by Sunday. Now the agonizing process of getting the militia south had to be reversed. Reynolds wired Kingsbury not to send any more troops from Chambersburg. The artillery captain who wanted oats was still there, so Reynolds ordered him put under the infantry. That would take care of the oats. Potts wanted a good dispatcher for Hagerstown. He also wanted to know how many trains had left for Chambersburg and asked for a guard to keep militia without passes from entering the cars. Someone else pleaded with Reynolds to stop unauthorized officers from issuing transportation orders. A Reading regiment was hauled out of camp at two o'clock one morning to board a northbound train. All the next day they watched other trains loaded with troops ride past them. Lieutenant Crosby and his whole battery got lost. The chief surgeon at Hagerstown wanted to close the hospitals but had nowhere to send the convalescent Rebels. Several militiamen had been jailed as deserters, and Curtin hoped Reynolds would counteract the charges. And all the while supplies no longer needed kept piling up at Hagerstown.

But the nightmare was nearly over. The governor's General Order No. 36 discharged the militia on September 25. Reynolds accompanied it by one of his own. In it he thanked exactly one colonel (Henry Mc-Cormick) and his brigade of four regiments. He also had thanks for Morton McMichael, and the two volunteer staff aides, McPherson and Rogers of Philadelphia. He would have his own way of showing grati-tude to his regular staff, and to a volunteer who came to help at Cham-bersburg when Reynolds moved south. That was militia artillery cap-tain Harry Landis.

Real relief went into Reynolds' letter to Ellie on the 26th from Cham-bersburg: "I leave for Hagerstown to-day at 11 o'clock to join Genl. McClellan, having finally dispersed all the militia to their homes—which they were so exceedingly anxious to defend, only they preferred to wait until the enemy actually reached their own doorsteps before they en-countered him. Harry can tell you something about the campaign. He left here yesterday morning for Philadelphia."

The Harrisburg *Patriot* noted that Reynolds had reserved praise for a single brigade of these state soldiers "who have heretofore lived the life of luxurious ease, never having slept on anything harder than a feather bed until now. . . . The Militia will rob hen-roosts, break open spring houses, wander away from camp without permission and hunt squirrels with their muskets," but at least one brigade had been will-ing to fight.[51] Other newspaper accounts of militia began to appear, some written by the late warriors themselves. Reynolds saw them and boiled over in a letter to his sisters:

> . . . The Militia I see are fighting their battles over again at home. I hope they will succeed in it to their own satisfaction at least if not to that of the public. I have no patience in thinking of them and their course while on the field, much less to write about it. My own private opinion is however, that if the militia of Penna. is to be depended upon to defend the State from invasion they had better all stay at home; they can be of no use in any military point of view if they are to act as they did here, every man to decide for himself whether he will obey the order given or not—and take his time at that, to do it or no. . . .[52]

Defiance of orders was the highest sin in Reynolds' military think-ing. No militiaman could have hated any order as much as Reynolds hated the one that put him at their head. But to question the order or to give it anything less than his all was unthinkable. His trouble was the long habit of expecting cooperation from others. The years of regular army service tended to spoil him; they had narrowed his tolerance. He forgot that his militia were soldiers in name only. They still thought of themselves as wheelwrights, harnessmakers, storekeepers, farmers, or whatever. One of them wrote: "In the quality of civilians, which we could not altogether consent to drop, our sense of individual importance was frequently infringed upon in our new capacity. Each in his turn felt disposed to divide with his superiors the responsibility of the command."[53] This kind of soldier Reynolds simply could not understand.

Some of the militia had as much trouble understanding him, as Reynolds began to find out. He enclosed two news clippings in a letter to Ellie:

GEN. REYNOLDS—We hear much complaint of the manner in which this officer treated the militia. He is a "regular," and we believe a good fighter, but West Pointers will not accord with the opinions and education of a newly organized militia. The distinction between them and regulars did not seem to have occurred to him, and his treatment of the former had been very severely commented upon. One of our citizens, a member of Company A, took occasion to rebuke the General, one day, in Chambersburg, in a very wholesome manner, which so startled this magnificent officer that, at the moment of the company's leaving, he had not recovered from it. We can assure the General he made a very narrow escape, and we have no doubt he will be more circumspect in his treatment of the militia hereafter, should he ever have the honor to command them.[54]

At least one thing in this account was accurate—Reynolds' shock at being rebuked by the member of Company A. The second clipping dug even deeper:

FROM ALL ACCOUNTS, given to us by officers and privates who are respected at home for their courtesy and their veracity, Gen. Reynolds did not elevate himself by his conduct towards the militia of Pennsylvania, during their late demonstration on the border. We have the assurance of several gentlemen, that his conduct was outrageous. So much so, that at one time a revolt was actually threatened by some of the men. When will the officers of the regular army learn that the people are their masters, and that when they rouse in their might, as they did in the state a week ago, it is not to be treated as serfs or dogs.[55]

Reynolds cut the clippings from the papers himself, and he had some comment of his own on these men who rose in their might. He said he found the militia impatient beyond all conception and admitted that in more than two instances they exhausted his own patience as well.

They kept coming to headquarters with the most unbelievable requests, one of which he cited. It was from a soldier who had refused to march to Antietam on the morning of the 18th. But once the danger was over he wanted a railway pass to visit the battlefield. Reynolds gave no report of what he said to this would-be tourist, and with the one example he let the matter drop.

He did have a letter to send along with the news stories. "I enclose Gov. Curtin's letter thanking me for the militia business and so ends the chapter for the present. They will not abuse me much for I have rather the advantage of several of them in the shape of written protests to be taken into action. . . . "[56] The governor's letter was in his own hand:

> Executive Chamber
> Harrisburg, Pa.
> 26 Sept. 1862

General

Having relieved you from duty as commander of the Pennsylvania Volunteer Militia recently called for the defense of the State, I deem it proper to express my strong sense of the gratitude which Pennsylvania owes for the zeal, spirit, and ability which you brot[sic] to her service when her homes and safety were threatened. That for this security you left your brave division the Pennsylvania Reserves thus loosing[sic] the opportunity of leading their gallant cause at South Mountain and the Antetam [sic] is a just demonstration of the true affection you bear for your native State which be assured her freemen reciprocate and for which in their behalf I am happy to make this acknowledgment.

> I have the honor to be
> very respectfully
> your obt Svt
> [Signed] A. G. Curtin[57]

Even if all the freemen were not reciprocating, Reynolds knew he had pleased his governor. Curtin had been active enough with the militia himself to know what Reynolds sacrificed in taking the assignment and to appreciate what he put into it. A copy of the letter was released for publication.

In rejoining the army near Sharpsburg Reynolds faced a change in regard to his command. His leaving had given the Reserves to Meade, who then moved up to head the 1st Corps after Hooker was wounded. Meade was still its acting commander. In the meantime he had won honors in two battles. These facts had never escaped Reynolds in spite of his frenzied days with the militia. So in light of Meade's new status Reynolds certainly brought up the question of his own future when he

saw McClellan the day after Antietam. The general probably told him
then not to worry. Anyhow Reynolds wrote his sisters as soon as he
got back to his troops, saying that he would doubtless be assigned a
corps, he thought Hooker's.[58] It was unlike him to be this casual without knowing beforehand how he stood. And he still outranked Meade.
After all, he was the same Reynolds who never let up until he got
Bragg's battery in 1858, and Reno's the year after.

This set Meade down. Nobody in the army could be more stubborn
about what he regarded as his rights—unless Reynolds himself. But
Meade was more likely to explode, as he had to Seth Williams when
Reynolds got his orders for Pennsylvania. Surprisingly though, he took
his demotion in stride:

> Yesterday General Reynolds made his appearance, very much dis-
> gusted with his Pennsylvania campaign and militia, who he says be-
> haved very badly, refused to come forward, and would not have
> stood five minutes if they had been attacked by one-tenth their num-
> ber. He hurried back here as soon as possible, knowing of course he
> would have command of the corps, as I could not expect McClellan
> to put him under my command. We went to see McClellan together.
> He was very civil to me, said he would have to put Reynolds in com-
> mand, but hoped in a few days to announce to both of us that we
> were major generals, which he had strongly urged on the Govern-
> ment. As yet the order has not been issued, but when it comes I shall
> subside gracefully into a division commander, though frankness
> compels me to say, I do wish Reynolds had stayed away, and that I
> could have a chance to command a corps in action. Perhaps it may
> yet occur. At any rate, it would be great ingratitude in me to com-
> plain, after all my recent good fortune. . . .[59]

Meade could be cantankerous, but he was always honest, and in this
affair his treatment of Reynolds showed some improvement. Three days
later he made a further confession. At first he said he had envied Reynolds his Pennsylvania assignment, and secretly thought the governor
might have picked him instead. But after hearing Reynolds' account he
was satisfied, especially as he would have missed the two battles.[60] As
Meade had said himself earlier: "War is a game of chance . . . the accidents and luck of the field."[61] They had been his at South Mountain
and Antietam. It did credit to both Meade and Reynolds that their
friendship held up at all under these conditions. The military virtue that
made them aggressive officers put a strain on their relationship. Equally
confident of their ability they were equally ambitious to prove it. So
far their trouble lay in leading the same troops.

CHAPTER IX

Trouble Near Franklin's Crossing

Special Orders No. 266 from McClellan's headquarters on September 29, 1862, gave Reynolds temporary command of Hooker's 1st Corps.[1] In a year he had risen from brigade command to equal corps officers like Hooker, Couch, and Sedgwick, who had headed divisions in the Army of the Potomac from the start. Among the brigadiers still to come up were some bright names: Hancock, Doubleday, Humphreys, Sickles, Warren, Newton, Butterfield, Howard, and of course Meade, whose tenure in corps command had been too brief to count.[2]

Why had Reynolds moved up so fast? How much of his success was due to merit, how much to luck, how much to political favor? Certainly the last two combined to help him. When McCall went out as commander of the Reserves, Reynolds happened to be the senior brigadier. That was luck. In taking over the command he got Pennsylvania's favorite troops, whose governor was sure to look out for their interests in Washington. Luck again. If Secretary Stanton suspected any lingering Buchananism in Reynolds, Curtin could set him right. And the governor's help might be needed for an officer blessed by McClellan, who was distrusted as a soft-war Democrat. So the luck that gave Reynolds the Reserves also worked for him politically.

But it was on military grounds that McClellan pushed promotion for both Reynolds and Meade. Reynolds had established himself beyond doubt at Mechanicsville and Gaines' Mill. Then after getting the Reserves, he hammered and hardened them into rugged fighting material. Meade, on his part, deserved promotion for his handling of the division in the Maryland battles. And while Meade was making the

140

most of his chance, Reynolds further endeared himself to Curtin in Pennsylvania. He salvaged at least enough from the militia there to make a gesture of opposition along the border. Lee had to reckon with their presence, not knowing how bad they were. For Curtin, who privately regarded his militia as hopeless,[3] Reynolds' performance must have seemed prodigious.

With the promotion of Reynolds, Meade got the Reserves. He complained almost at the start. Reynolds and Seymour had been ignoring an important section of the act setting up the division. It provided for the election of officers by the men. But Reynolds was interested only in merit, and he thought himself and Seymour better qualified than volunteer soldiers to pick their leaders. To the meticulous Meade this was not going by the book, which irritated him. "The trouble is," he wrote, "both Seymour and Reynolds have got into a snarl with the Governor about elections, the Governor maintaining that he will not appoint without elections, and they (in orders) prohibiting elections and getting McClellan to give acting appointments, subject to the approval of the Governor, which appointments are never submitted to the Governor for his approval."[4]

Meade was more uneasy than Reynolds about having officers in his command who were not properly commissioned. Yet all he could do was press Curtin to accept them. This Curtin insisted he could not do as long as the act stood. He said both McClellan and Reynolds had been clamoring for its repeal, that a bill for that purpose had passed the Pennsylvania house but lost out in the senate. So while he deplored the situation he wanted it understood that the fault was not his.[5] There is a fair chance that Curtin was less upset than he could admit publicly. There is no record that the officers Reynolds picked (Seymour left the division on November 16) were ever set down. Reynolds was neither disobedient nor careless of military law, but if by stalling he could make the Reserves stronger it was worth the try.

The 1st Corps looked impressive on paper, numbering 32,087 at the end of September. But the present-for-duty returns gave Reynolds scarcely more than 14,000 men.[6] Meade counted only 9,000 after Antietam. The difference of 5,000, he said, constituted the cowards, skulkers, and stragglers typical of a volunteer army.[7] Other corps reported similar figures for desertion and absenteeism,[8] so bringing the army back to efficiency and strength would take hard work. The first lack was supply. Reynolds wired headquarters on October 15 that his men lacked all manner of clothing, tents, blankets, knapsacks, and that many were without shoes. His requisitions called for 5,251 pairs of shoes.[9] One way to improve morale was to clothe the men.

Army morale was not helped either when the pesky Jeb Stuart led another raid around it. With 1,800 picked men he left Lee on October 10, bypassed Hagerstown, turned into Chambersburg, Pennsylvania, cut east almost to Gettysburg, then south again through Maryland and back across the Potomac above Leesburg.[10] He failed to destroy the important railway bridge at Chambersburg, which would have disrupted McClellan's supply line, and other than taking several hundred horses and a few hostages Stuart cost the North little except a scare. But he hurt McClellan.[11] Just a week before, the President had ordered him to move down after Lee's army,[12] and now Stuart's feat only increased the impatience in Washington.

Reynolds' first reaction was irony: "I think it probably just as well for the south of the State that there were no militia in Chambersburg as I do not think from what I saw of them they would have been any use in preventing the raid of Rebel cavalry—unless a [more] *courteous commander* would have instilled a proportionate amount more of courage in them than I was able to elicit." But the raid itself impressed him. "I must say that their escape has given me quite a shock—I did not expect they could perform such a feat in our own country. On the Chickahominy it was different."[13]

The 1st Corps broke the long encampment near Sharpsburg on October 26, moving down to Berlin [now Brunswick] on the Potomac. The shortage of supply still existed, and both Reynolds and Meade thought there was something strange about it.[14] But the army's able quartermaster, Rufus Ingalls, complained in his turn about the grumbling officers. He said the army would never budge if commanders refused to move until satisfied that all their needs were met.[15] Supplied or not, the army was at last starting out after Lee. Jackson's corps had lingered in the Shenandoah Valley after the retreat from Antietam, while Longstreet lay at Culpeper. If McClellan was quick enough to catch either of them alone he would be in luck. It was the administration's hope that he could, but he had wasted so much time already. Meanwhile the good autumn weather was running out.

As a corps commander Reynolds began to attract wider attention. Newspapermen always attached themselves to corps headquarters to pick up stories and information. But Reynolds had no use for them. "They do more harm than good and are not at all reliable,"[16] he had written his sisters the year before. At camp in Berlin he had warned a reporter, "Your papers give the enemy too much information." The newsman who heard him say this admitted that none of them ever got anything out of him. He cited one try made by a newcomer: "We do not wish you to commit yourself, General . . . but when do you *suppose* the army *might* cross the river?" The end result was a much humbler though in no way a wiser reporter.[17]

Increased attention of course came from others besides correspondents. One officer remembered a lesson in respect for enemy property: "It is resented that some of your men have crossed the river and have been killing sheep. . . . You will take such measures as to prevent this at once."[18] The note came directly from Reynolds and in his own hand instead of through channels. The colonel kept it as a memento and as proof that his general was no stickler for army red tape. When the move south began, this same officer saw another side of the general. One day Reynolds changed the order of march, but in riding back through his columns he found a brigade about to follow the original direction. Colonel M'Coy reported what happened next:

> . . . Before the head of the column reached this point, it was met by a modest looking officer, entirely alone, exhibiting no especial insignia of rank. . . . He addressed the brigade commander in a mild pleasant way. . . . He seemed to have a knowledge that the column had been ordered to leave the road, and said it was a wrong and mistaken order. . . . The strange officer's manner was observed to be somewhat peculiar, as he kept watching the head of the column; and it being near the turning off, and being satisfied that the brigade commander was not going to counter the order . . . decided it would be necessary for him to indicate higher rank and authority. . . . "Direct your orderly to return to the column, and have it continue its advance on the road." The quiet, dignified manner in which these words were uttered made an impression that he might be more than he seemed to be. . . . As the crisis in this little episode had now come, the modest stranger found it necessary to assert more fully his position and authority. In a calm and moderate tone, peculiar to him, he said: "General Reynolds orders that the column shall continue its march in this direction. . . ."[19]

"No sooner said than done," the colonel added, and he sent the orderly off at full speed. Then he took "respectful leave" of the general and was about to retire to his proper place in the column. Instead Reynolds invited him to ride along with him. M'Coy called it one of the pleasantest of his early experiences in the war, "and as his first introduction to an officer who was then eminent, and who afterward became so distinguished." In his ride he found out, as others had, that Reynolds said little. But he liked his gentlemanly manner and put him down as one of the few "old army" officers who held the respect and confidence of the volunteers.[20]

On this same march Colonel Fred Hitchcock practically duplicated

M'Coy's experience. Going into camp one evening, Hitchcock was uncertain about where his regiment should leave the road. He said Reynolds saw him hesitate and came up at once: "Part of your corps has
gone in yonder. If I were you I would go in here and occupy this field
to the right in columns . . . and you may say General Reynolds advised
this if you please." Reynolds' attitude struck Hitchcock. "Had he chosen
to do so, he could have given me orders as the senior officer present,
but with a gentle courtesy he accomplished his purpose without that,
and to reassure me, gave his name and rank in this delicate way. I shall
never forget his pleasant smile as he returned my salute."[21] It was Hitchcock who had called West Point the national snob hatchery,[22] but he
was clearly excepting Reynolds as "one of the few great commanders
developed by the war." He also liked the general's appearance. "He
was a superb-looking man, dark-complexioned, wearing full black
whiskers and sat his horse like a Centaur, tall, straight, and graceful, the
ideal soldier."[23]

Both M'Coy and Hitchcock reacted like the volunteer officers they
were. They frequently got lost in the maze of army routine and pro-
cedure. With little training they were suddenly called on to put thousands of soldiers into camps overnight, provide space for wagon parks
and grazing for the animals. It was their job to look for proper drainage,
fresh water, firewood. They had to ensure their men protection both
in choice of ground and by adequate pickets. On the march they pa-
trolled miles of columns along skimpy roads that choked men with
dust or sucked them with mud—especially Virginia mud. And these
volunteer officers knew even less about battle tactics than they did
about camp or marching. No wonder they looked anxiously for help
from the professionals. When it was offered without contempt or pulling rank, their gratitude was unqualified.

M'Coy had found Reynolds checking the change in orders because
the general knew his volunteers. He spent whole days on the march
riding up and down from front to rear of his strung-out columns. He
worked his staff and the orderlies just as hard.[24] Reynolds had painfully
acquired patience in dealing with inexperience. He tried to anticipate
the resulting confusion. It accounted for the careful post he had taken
up when Hitchcock saw him watching the troops file off the road into
camp. Double-check everything; trust nothing. It also accounted for a
particular Reynolds habit—prowling his picket lines. He never forgot
the two sleeping companies of Kentucky cavalry that had been surrounded one night below Saltillo in 1847.[25] Now his pickets could expect him any hour in any weather—" 'Who ordered that line? How far

out is it? Push it out, push it out farther! . . . Push it out until you feel something.' This was Reynolds."[26]

Sometimes Reynolds despaired over the lack of discipline in his volunteers, but he kept his control in dealing with them (the militia excepted). His friend Meade lacked both Reynolds' tact and dignity in command. When two new regiments finally came into the Reserves in October, a young volunteer was shocked at the veterans' attitude toward Meade. Admitting that the general and his men probably understood each other pretty well, he said the new men could not get used to hearing oldtimers swear and complain about Meade, even within earshot. It was even rumored that Meade had promised to get even with them come the next battle.[27] If the rumor was true, Meade never kept a promise more faithfully. What saved him, in spite of a temper that often reduced him to childishness,[28] was courage—physical courage especially. Volunteers forgave almost anything else in a commander who *took* his men into action instead of *sending* them in while hanging back himself.[92] Soldiers would continue to call Meade "Old Four-Eyes," and ride him for his tantrums and his unmilitary bearing, but he could make them fight.[30]

The army began crossing the Potomac on November 1. The administration was prodding McClellan loose from northern soil, but his time was running out. He had taken too long. Meade had looked for the general to fall ever since Stuart's raid.[31] Coupled with lack of aggressiveness was McClellan's politics. In issuing the Emancipation Proclamation on September 22, Lincoln had committed the North to the kind of war McClellan was suspected of not wanting. There was little hope in Washington that he would give the new line his wholehearted cooperation.

The order relieving McClellan arrived at headquarters November 8. For the Little Napoleon it was the end of the military road. An officer who hated everything about him managed some sympathy in describing the general's last appearance before an army. A nervous and troubled look had replaced his cocky, casual air of the President's review at Sharpsburg. The aplomb and much of the dignity had drained out of him. It was a smaller man who sat his horse on this cold November day.[32] Before he left, Reynolds and the generals of his corps paid a call. Reynolds spoke briefly, expressing regret at his departure and hoping he would return soon. Everybody knew better of course. In reporting the visit Meade said that McClellan was almost in tears, also that the whole army was depressed.[33] As to the army, Reynolds seemed to disagree when he wrote at the end of the month:

... It of course was a surprise to a greater part of the Army here but take it altogether, it created less feeling than I feared such a step would have done. I saw more of him on this march than I have since he has been in command of the army, had been with him most of the time in the advance and think the step taken by the authorities in Washington was as unwise, injudicious, as it was uncalled for, yet the prevailing spirit, with few exceptions, is obedience to the powers that be—and determine [sic] to do all they are capable of under the new chief. . . . [34]

This was the only opinion Reynolds ever recorded on his commanding general, and it remains vague. More than implying praise for McClellan, he was making his usual protest against interference with the army from Washington. Largely unpolitical himself, he refused to take account of the pressures operating to influence the administration. Reynolds was convinced that only generals with complete independence in the field could ever win the war. To that extent he felt McClellan had not been given a fair chance. When he learned that Ambrose Burnside was the army's new head, he called him as noble a spirit as ever existed, but he wondered whether any officer was actually qualified to lead such a large army. "Very few persons are, that I know of, that is under the circumstances."[35] And by circumstances Reynolds meant control from the capital. Burnside, incidentally, had similar doubts about his own qualifications.[36]

The army continued to be bossed from Washington regardless, and Burnside was substituted for McClellan in the hope of getting action. At least they approved of his own plan, which was to advance against Lee by way of Fredericksburg, then move on to Richmond if he retreated. The supply line would be moved from the much harassed Orange and Alexandria Railroad to the Potomac. The army's new base was on Aquia Creek ten miles east of Fredericksburg. On November 14 Burnside organized the army into three grand divisions of two corps each, with Sigel's 11th as a reserve. Reynolds' 1st Corps and the 6th, of W. F. Smith, formed the left grand division under General William B. Franklin. Reynolds' division commanders were Meade, Abner Doubleday, and John Gibbon.

Along with McClellan's removal came another change that gave Reynolds permanent corps command. General Fitz John Porter was ordered to Washington to answer Pope's charges of disobedience and misconduct at second Bull Run. This left the 5th Corps for Hooker on his return to the army, so Reynolds' command was undisturbed. Actually Hooker did even better. He got the center grand division while the 5th went to Butterfield temporarily.

By November 10 Reynolds had gained about 6,000 men over his return of the month before,[37] and he was as tough in the discipline of 20,000 as he had been of his division of Reserves. He was still tough on stealing. On the 20th he held a drumhead court martial for six men who had stolen a cow, killed it, and divided the meat. He had each man stood on a barrel with both the word "thief" and the stolen meat on his back.[38] "No injustice, abuse or wrong went unpunished within his sphere of authority," a soldier correspondent wrote of Reynolds during this period. "He used few words but with a look he could crush an offender. . . . He never neglected his duty and never overlooked neglect in others."

But in spite of Reynolds' near mania for discipline, the soldier gave him credit for a generous heart, strong affections, and constant zeal for the welfare of his men.[39] The general ran a tight command, old army style. Yet nothing except physical courage won troops over like being well cared for. Reynolds' reputation as a good provider was solid throughout the army. Reynolds knew his cow-stealers did not lack for rations.

In the middle of November Burnside started his move from the vicinity of Warrenton, where he had concentrated 120,000 men.[40] The 2nd Corps of Couch and the 9th of Willcox, forming Sumner's right grand division, reached Falmouth on the 17th. Behind them Reynolds had begun his advance in Franklin's left grand division. By the 23rd he was near Aquia Creek, east of Fredericksburg.

This was familiar ground for Reynolds. In the spring he and the Reserves had spent a month here. He had governed the town itself for a spell and in August had assumed division command nearby. Fredericksburg and environs seemed to bring him good luck. And now he got word of his promotion to major general. "So I am informed on pretty good authority," he wrote his sisters on November 30. He was confident enough to nominate his staff for promotion too, and he also added two new officers. One of them was Captain Joseph G. Rosengarten. "I like him very much from what I have seen of him," he said.[41] For Rosengarten this began a lifelong association with the Reynolds family.

Reynolds' new commission was approved by the Senate and dated November 29. Official word of it reached army headquarters on December 2. Meade was with Burnside when it came, and he wrote his wife: "I am very glad Reynolds is promoted, for I have always thought he deserved it for his services at Mechanicsville." This was generous, but being Meade he could not leave it at that: "Reynolds is a man who is very popular and always impresses those around him with a great idea of his superiority."[42] It bothered Meade that Reynolds was better liked, just as he resented his holding higher command. Meade knew himself to be more widely read, more cultivated in his tastes, and more sophisticated than his friend. Still the old quail hunter and horseman from Lancaster possessed an uncomplicated charm that Meade for all his intellect could not approach. Only a week before he had been botherd that Reynolds spent most of his time "pow-wowing with the *big Indians*" at headquarters.[43] A strange man to call himself a friend, and yet he was. Meade's own promotion was confirmed December 6.

In his letter of the 30th Reynolds gave more space to another item than he did to his commission. The photographer Brady had taken several group pictures at headquarters in Warrenton. "I was taken in one with Burnside sitting on the stump of a tree, and it was very good. If you can ever get a copy of it do so—I saw only the plates." He had ridden up too late to be photographed with the other generals, but in the picture of Burnside with his staff he stood above the commanding general's left shoulder.

Since Reynolds liked the picture it apparently showed qualities he saw in himself, take them or leave them. His kepi sat straight and tight over his black hair, no jaunty tilt about it. Partly hidden in the shade of the brim were the eyes, direct as the lens itself. It was easy to believe he could impale a wrongdoer with a glance. But the face showed strength to lean on too, and for all the fighting presence, a hint of sensitivity. The Reynolds of these days was also a proud officer, and proud of his 1st Corps. In fact he had planned to show it off for his brother Will before the army moved south. A day was set for the visit and John kept the mail wagon waiting on each trip to Harpers Ferry. For some reason or other Will had failed to make it. Now it might be a long time before they could get together as Will had just been ordered to duty at Port Royal, South Carolina.[44]

The 1st Corps left Aquia Creek December 9. The weather was cold, with a light snow on the ground and frozen roads, which helped the teams over the ten miles to the Rappahannock. Burnside's long-delayed pontoon trains had arrived at last. They were too late for any chance that a crossing would surprise Lee, but Burnside still intended to put his army over both at Fredericksburg and below. Once on the south bank his great numbers and wider edge in artillery ought to tell. He hoped to break through a Confederate line stretching six miles along a ridge behind and south of the town. Lee had gradually fallen back to this strong position as Burnside made his intentions clear. It would be a defense by 78,500 men against an attack by 120,000.[45] Longstreet held the left on Marye's Heights behind Fredericksburg, with his line ex-

General Ambrose Everett Burnside (seated, center) and officers, 1862. General Reynolds stands at Burnside's left shoulder.

tending somewhat below. Jackson connected with his right and carried his line south along the high ridge to Hamilton's Crossing.

It was opposite Jackson that Reynolds marched his corps down close to the river on the 10th. Sergeant Tom Dick, Company H, 12th Regiment, got orders to be ready at midnight, along with the rest of the 3rd Brigade, Pennsylvania Reserves. Reynolds and Meade were picking men they trusted for a tough job. The brigade was assigned to cover the engineers while the bridges were being thrown. "... We gave up all hopes of sleeping that night and began preparations for the march," the sergeant wrote. But once they were ready he said the talk around the fires turned serious. The men smelled battle. Some of the faces now glowing near the flames would be gone. "Yet," Dick continued, "about 12 o'clock when the Capt. came round with the familiar command fall in boys they fell in ranks as promptly and marched off gaily as ever."[46] These Reserves had come a long way since their first bad days in Virginia. They showed the advantage of being well led, as General Porter had put it.

The first job turned out better than Company H expected. When the men reached the water's edge, they could see enemy lights on the other side in the darkness. But there was no resistance until some time after daylight when the fog lifted. Then several engineers were hit before a battery was brought up to shell the Confederates out. By one o'clock in the afternoon the bridges were down and a brigade of the 6th Corps went over to hold a bridgehead for the night.

Most of the next day was spent in bringing the rest of the left grand division across. Franklin set up headquarters in the Bernard mansion overlooking the river less than a mile south of the bridges. Reynolds had got there first, and the owner was arguing against the use of his premises when the commanding general arrived. "Reynolds on such occasions was a man of a few words," Franklin recalled, "and I presently saw Mr. Bernard hurrying toward the pontoon-bridges between two soldiers, and he was not seen again in that vicinity."[47] There went one citizen of the Fredericksburg area who would not have subscribed to any appeal for Reynolds' release from Libby.

Franklin favored an all-out attack at daylight on the 13th.[48] For this purpose he could throw in 40,000 men. That ought to take care of the left if the other two grand divisions did their work against Longstreet on the right. Reynolds and Smith, the two corps commanders, agreed with Franklin that the best way to beat Lee was to roll up Jackson's front. And when Burnside rode down in the afternoon to inspect the position on the left, the three generals there thought he approved of the plan.[49] So after making their preparations Reynolds and Smith joined Franklin at the mansion to wait for Burnside's go-ahead. They were still waiting at three in the morning. Reynolds gave up then; said he expected a hard day and was turning in.[50]

Not until 7:30 a.m. of the 13th did an order come through. With priceless time already lost, it contained nothing about an all-out attack against Jackson. A division "at least" was to seize the heights near Hamilton's Crossing if possible, taking care to keep it well supported and its line of retreat open.[51] Meanwhile the entire command was to be in position for a rapid move up the old Richmond road. This of course would depend on Jackson's falling back toward Fredericksburg. Altogether it was a vague and cautious order to give Franklin, who was no gambler at best.

Reynolds' 1st Corps was picked for the drive up the heights. His morning returns for the day showed 18,500 men. He would spearhead the attack with one division, supporting it by the other two. Smith's 24,000 were not taking part in the action. Franklin was holding them for the main movement if Reynolds succeeded. If he failed they could secure the line of retreat. Still across the river were the 10,000 men of Sickles' 3rd Corps, and a division of 4,000 from the 9th.[52]

The privilege of opening the assault went to the Reserves. Here was Meade's chance to get even with his men for their disrespect on the march down. But Reynolds had fixed on them for other reasons.[53] He knew and trusted both the men and their commander above any other troops he had. Though only about a third remained of the 15,000 that began the war, their deeds matched their attrition. So, to quote Sergeant Dick, ". . . as usual the Reserves had to kick up the fight."[54] This was no empty boast. The division had absorbed the first shock of the Seven Days on the Peninsula. It went in beside Sigel's corps to open the two days of second Bull Run. And at Antietam, Hooker took the division in with the 1st Corps at daybreak. Starting battles had become routine for the Reserves.

At 8:30 Meade led his three brigades southward along the river for about a half-mile. After passing Bernard's, they swung sharp right and moved up the Richmond road. Reynolds directed Meade to put the columns into a stretch of wood that at one point extended down from the heights and across the tracks of the Richmond, Fredericksburg, and Potomac Railroad.[55] This line ran along the base of the ridge some 500 yards west of where Meade now halted the Reserves. Jackson had troops behind the railway embankment, and they would have to be driven out before Meade's men could climb the ridge. Once they reached the trees, they would have some protection from the artillery which swept the open ground they had to cross first. That was why it was decided to attack here rather than on Jackson's right. The Confederate general's flank was secured by the swampy nature of Massaponax Creek, on which it rested.[56]

By now it was noon. The sun had sucked up most of the fog from the river and the low-lying land around it. The Reserves started forward under a warming December sky. The 1st Brigade faced toward the railroad on the crest of a slight hollow. The other two brigades advanced at intervals of 300 yards in rear. They ran into trouble at once. Major John Pelham of Stuart's cavalry had found himself an ideal spot for two rifled guns near the Richmond road on their left. From this position he began pouring a flank fire into the advancing columns. Meade pulled three of his own batteries out of line to answer Pelham, but his leading brigade had already come to a halt. Reynolds brought up more guns from Doubleday. Pelham gradually was forced back, though he managed to hang on for over half an hour before running out of ammunition.[57] More wasted time for Meade.

Reynolds was doing his best to broaden Franklin's strict interpretation of orders. To send out a division "at least" certainly implied using more than one. He would put in all three.[58] By now he had Gibbon following Meade somewhat to the right. Doubleday was to move up on the left flank. If Meade broke through anywhere on the heights, the rest of the 1st Corps would be close behind. But Reynolds' plans should have taken Jeb Stuart into account. While Reynolds was bringing Doubleday up from the river on the left, two brigades of Stuart's cavalry got in on the flank near Pelham's earlier position. These brigades dismounted and along with fifteen guns began firing from across Massaponax Creek south of Hamilton's Crossing.[59]

From this point on Doubleday's division, including the famed Iron Brigade, was lost to the offensive. Reynolds was forced to swing it toward the south against this threat from the left.[60] Doubleday pushed far enough out to check the Confederate infantry fire, but not the guns. They kept moving from one emplacement to another, tying down Reynolds' left until dark.

Now only Meade and Gibbon could be spared for the attack. With Pelham out of the way, Reynolds turned his attention to Jackson's 47 guns on the heights and woods in front. He had his corps artillery commander, Colonel C. S. Wainwright, bring every available gun to bear on the objective ahead. A little after one o'clock the Confederate artillery there fell silent. Meade moved forward again.[61] This time his leading brigade got a foothold on the tracks and cleared the embankment of resistance for a stretch of more than half a mile. The other two brigades piled in after the first. Although stung by fire on both flanks, regiment after regiment of the division scrambled up the heights.[62]

Back along the Richmond road Reynolds sat his big black mount beside the artillery. His eyes were on Meade's progress. It was obvious that his friend could use help. Burnside had ordered in two divisions from the reserve across the river, and the first of them was arriving on the field under Major General D. B. Birney. These new troops released Gibbon's division for the attack, and Reynolds sent it forward at once. So far, so good, except for having to deflect Doubleday to the left because of Stuart. At 1:25 a staff officer at Franklin's headquarters wired Burnside that Meade was in the wood and holding on. In fifteen minutes the news improved. Meade had carried part of the wood, driving the enemy. Gibbon had gone in on the right. Three hundred prisoners already taken.[63]

But in battles a lot can change in thirty-five minutes. Meade's push was beginning to lose momentum. At first the Reserves had found a gap in Jackson's line. Some of the leading brigade had even got over the crest of the ridge toward the supply road of the Confederates. They cut in between Archer's and Lane's brigades of A. P. Hill. They mortally wounded Brigadier General Maxcy Gregg and threw Jackson's rear into confusion before he was able to shore up his line.[64] That was about it so far as the Reserves were concerned. Few of the 2nd Brigade got as far as the 1st, while the last to go up began passing units of the first troops who were on their way back.

Meade could see what was happening from his position down on the tracks. He sent staff officers back to both Birney and Gibbon, calling for support.[65] Gibbon was having trouble getting his command forward. Two of his brigades had begun to advance at 1:30, and were followed by the third. But by now the Confederates had followed the Reserves down the ridge and regained their position behind the railway embankment. Gibbon's men stood up to their raking fire for a few moments, then fell back in disorder.[66]

At this Reynolds hurried over to Gibbon and urged him to press his men on. He also supplied two aides to help in getting the advance started again.[67] It helped for a time. Root's brigade of Gibbon made a charge with the bayonet. It was joined by the 12th Massachusetts, the 88th Pennsylvania, and the 97th New York, three good regiments from among Gibbon's other two brigades. They got all the way back to the railway, where they took 180 prisoners.[68] But the rally came too late. Meade's Reserves were on the way out.

As early as 2:15 Burnside's staff officer had wired his chief that both Meade and Gibbon were being rolled back. "Things do not look so well on Reynolds' front; still we will have new troops in soon."[69] The new troops included the rest of Birney's division, one brigade of which also went as far as the railroad only to meet the Reserves falling back. The last two messages from the left grand division told their own story—Meade and Gibbon badly used up . . . enemy in force and threatening on left . . . engaged now heavily in front . . . too late to advance either to left or front.[70]

Again the help came too late. A soldier within earshot reported that Meade was boiling when he got back to the Richmond road. His language to Birney "almost made the stones creep."[71] Then Meade saw his corps commander: "My God, General Reynolds, did they think my division could whip Lee's whole army?"[72] Not quite Lee's whole army, but the Reserves had gone in outnumbered six to one and against a strong position.

Both Reynolds and Meade tried to rally them in front of the guns. Sickles' division had now come up from the reserve, and Franklin was finally releasing Newton of Smith's corps to help in another try. But the generals had to give up. The Reserves had seen all the fighting they wanted for so little result. They had lost forty per cent in casualties, including one brigadier killed and one wounded. Their units were completely disorganized. Later Meade defended them. He thought it little wonder they gave way before the punishment they had taken on both flanks and in front.[73]

All the while Reynolds was fighting Jackson down on the left, Sumner's right grand division and troops from Hooker's reserve had stormed Longstreet's defenses. The 2nd Corps divisions of French and Hancock began their march west through the streets of Fredericksburg around eleven in the morning. At one o'clock General Couch sent them up over the exposed ground in front of the stone wall below Marye's Heights. Then Howard's division was added. One of his brigades, along with some of Hancock's troops, got within a hundred yards of the sunken road that ran behind the wall. Few got farther. From this perfect position the Confederates tore the blue lines to pieces. Hancock lost 2,000, French 1,200, and Howard almost 900.[74] More help was called from across the river. Whipple's division went in to support two divisions of the 9th Corps. At 2:30 Andrew A. Humphreys crossed his division to begin a last despairing bayonet charge that ended the fighting on the right. Sykes's regulars steadied its retreat, though only after it had lost over a thousand men in fifteen minutes.[75]

Burnside's offensive was as futile here as on Franklin's wing to the south. His army had lost close to 12,653 as against only 5,309 for Lee.[76] And still Burnside had to be talked out of renewing the attack next

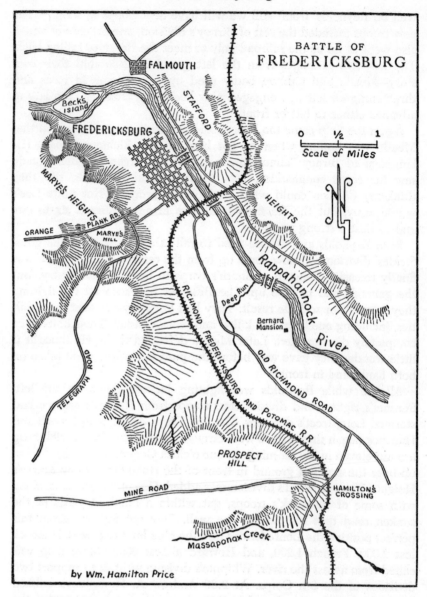

BATTLE OF
FREDERICKSBURG

Scale of Miles

by Wm. Hamilton Price

day. Finally, during a storm on the night of the 15th the army made a skilful recrossing of the river and took up its bridges. Now the battle of Fredericksburg would be fought over in letters home, in official correspondence, and in Congressional investigations. Reynolds wrote his sisters on December 17:

You are no doubt anxious to hear from me since the events of the past few days. The papers give you all the details of the crossing of the Rappahannock as well as the re-crossing, and are not very particular as to the truth of the facts, only so they have a telling effect and read well. My corps, or two divisions of it, made the attack on the left, and after almost gaining the object let it slip. They did not do as well as I expected. Tho' they advanced under artillery fire very well, when it came to the attack of the wooded heights they faltered and failed. We are fortunate it is not worse. The crossing at this point was a failure from the fact that to have been successful it ought to have been a surprise, and we should have advanced at once and carried the heights as was intended. As it was we lost one day by the failure to throw over the bridges at the town without serious opposition—and to have risked more than we did would probably have cost the loss of the whole Army in case of another repulse. You must not show this to anyone.

Reynolds was referring to Burnside's hope of making his crossings a surprise. But the pontoons he needed were far up the Potomac near Harpers Ferry instead of at Washington or Alexandria where Burnside thought they were. When they did arrive it took hours longer to throw bridges across at Fredericksburg than it did below. Lee looked for the main push to come from the city and so offered more resistance there. Reynolds seemed to think this largely accounted for Burnside's defeat, though he sounded philosophical about it. His disappointment over the performance of the Reserves was more surprising. In his official report he merely laid the failure of their attack to Jackson's stout position; also to his advantage in remaining screened while observing every movement on the approaches below.[77]

The letter was closer to his real feelings. He showed this when the Congressional committee on the conduct of the war got around to the battle. They found him more outspoken. Of Gibbon's division, Reynolds said: "They did not advance as vigorously as they should have, I think." And as in his letter he said the Reserves should have done better. But his divisions did lack support. "Should there have been more?" he was asked. "Yes, sir, I think there should." Burnside had already testified that he would have thrown Smith's corps in along with the 1st, and that Franklin had read his orders too narrowly. In his turn Franklin said: "I put in all the troops that I thought it proper and prudent to put in. I fought the whole strength of my command as far as I could, and at the same time keep my connection with the river open."[78]

What did Reynolds think? the committee wanted to know. But Reynolds was an old hand at military inquiries, beginning back in the Mexican War. He refused to pin responsibility on either Burnside or Franklin. Instead, the investigators got a pretty fair summary of how Reynolds saw the situation on the 13th:

> ... The commanding officer of the whole force there must judge for himself as to the manner in which he will carry out the orders he has received. We were fighting with the river to our backs, and in case of a serious reverse there, the army would have been destroyed. I suppose it would be necessary under such circumstances, for a general to hold a pretty large force in reserve. . . . If a larger force had been up there in time, I would have put it into the attack at once. I was going to put General Doubleday's division in behind Meade, and carry the whole thing through as far as my corps was concerned. But the demonstration by the enemy on our left was so strong that I had to turn Doubleday square off to the left to meet it; and he did not succeed in driving the enemy off until it was too late to move up again to support Meade.[79]

Any accusation in these words had to be implied. Reynolds accepted Franklin's holding out of Smith's corps to protect the line of retreat. If more troops had come in time he would have used them. Birney and Sickles should have been crossed over from Hooker's reserve in the morning as Franklin had asked. They would have freed Gibbon sooner to support Meade. Doubleday could have been relieved on the left. The delay in sending Birney and Sickles was Burnside's responsibility. To that extent Reynolds seemed to be involving the commanding general, though only by indirection.

What Reynolds left unsaid covered his feelings about his own role in the battle. He had been the man in the middle. The orders of Burnside and Franklin boxed him in from above, while under him Meade got what credit there was for his brief stand on the heights. About the only satisfaction Reynolds could find was in the handling of his guns. The ex-artilleryman had plenty of them and he knew how to use them. Nominally the corps artillery came under Colonel Wainwright's direction, but the official reports of the battery commanders, as well as Wainwright's own, showed the influence of Reynolds' personal attention.[80]

These same guns also made a Confederate report. Stonewall Jackson admitted being stung by the "warm and well directed fire"[81] from the guns Reynolds had posted to rake the wood in Meade's front before he charged. Then late that afternoon, when the Reserves and Gibbon had been thrown back, Jackson planned a counterattack. But again he paid his respects to the Union guns: "The artillery of the enemy was

Pontoon bridges at Franklin's Crossing, where General Reynolds moved over at the Battle of Fredericksburg.

so judiciously posted as to make an advance of our troops across the plain very hazardous. . . . The first gun had hardly moved forward a hundred yards when the enemy's artillery reopened, and so completely swept our front as to satisfy me that the proposed movement should be abandoned."[82] A Union artilleryman who fought against Jackson on the 13th said that of the eight batteries in position to be of any help on Franklin's left five belonged to the 1st Corps.[83] Another eyewitness, Francis Palfrey, compared the efficiency of the guns here with their failure against Longstreet behind Fredericksburg.[84]

After recrossing the Rappahannock the 1st Corps went into winter quarters near Falmouth. On December 23 it lost a division commander. Meade got the 5th Corps, which had been temporarily under Butterfield. That called for a celebration, so Meade gave a party for Reynolds and some of the other officers. "Whereupon," the new corps commander wrote his wife, "it was unanimously agreed that Congress ought to establish the grade of lieutenant general, and that they would all unite in having me made one, provided I would treat with such good wine."[85]

A day or so later Reynolds went to Philadelphia on leave. While he was there visiting Harry Landis, Kate, Hal and Ellie, he also called on Mrs. Meade. This pleased her husband. "It was very civil in Reynolds to call on you," he said. "I am not surprised he did not indulge in any complimentary remarks about me, because, in the first place, Reynolds is a man who never says or does such things. He is a very good fellow, and I have had much pleasant intercourse with him during the past eighteen months, and considering how closely we have been together and the natural rivalry that might be expected, I think it is saying a good deal for both that we have continued good friends."[86] On January 3 of the new year, after Reynolds had come back to camp, Meade wrote again: ". . . he said he had seen you and the children, but did not have much to say. He is a man of very few words."[87]

CHAPTER X

Hooker's Ablest Officer

After Fredericksburg only a military miracle could have saved Burnside. He knew this of course and tried to get a new offensive of some kind under way. Lincoln disapproved of his first plan, and the second quickly mired down in the lamented "Mud March." It began on January 20, 1863, with the army leaving its camps about Falmouth to strike up the north bank of the Rappahannock. Burnside intended to make a surprise crossing at Banks' Ford, four miles behind and above Fredericksburg. By moving fast and with good weather he hoped to turn Lee's left. But the clear skies under which the march began lowered that night to halt the army and practically sink it in its tracks. Teams had to be cut from the traces of the guns and wagons. Hundreds of mules and horses were shot to save them from strangling in the muck. By evening of the 22nd the troops had splashed and slogged their way back to the camps they had never wanted to leave. Reynolds wrote his sisters the next day:

> We have been on the verge of moving ever since the first of the year and to-day finds us (the whole army) on the banks of the Rapp'k, with the idea of crossing above Fredericksburg. A violent storm interposed, however, and we are now "stuck in the mud," unable to get up our artillery or supplies and Burnside goes to Washington to know what to do!! If we do not get some one soon who can command an Army without consulting "Stanton and Halleck" at Washington I do not know what will become of this Army. No gen'l officer that I can find approved of the move and yet it was made. I have been all along afraid the weather would fall upon us in this way. No one who had not seen the roads in this

158

country we have to move over could conceive of their wretched condition. We are of course anxious to know what is to be done, and it is about as difficult a problem to solve as ever fell to the lot of one man. I do not know how it is that the gen'l in command here is obliged to consult Washington every day, and yet there is no one there responsible for failure of operations here. . . .

To Reynolds' mind the same old problem was plaguing the Army of the Potomac. It had a commanding general only in name. And to make things worse the men who gave directions from the capital shouldered off the blame for what went wrong in the field. Burnside saw this too, and when he was removed on January 25 he apparently recommended to the President that Stanton and Halleck resign.[1] Let Washington share the weight of the army's disasters. The general who succeeded Burnside had no taste for control from Washington either, so Meade said,[2] but Joe Hooker was happy to accept the appointment as chief of command next day.

By now Reynolds himself stood high enough in the army to be a potential candidate for the command. Small wonder he watched relations between its leader and Washington so closely. If Hooker in his turn failed, Reynolds was likely to be considered among others to head the army next—especially if he could get into a battle and do well. But meanwhile Hooker made a change that might have discouraged Reynolds. The center grand division, two corps, went to Meade. This was the first time he had ever topped Reynolds in command. Given Meade's ambition and the rivalry existing between the two, a little preening on his part would not have been surprising. But not at all. He thought of it as purely a temporary arrangement and even doubted its feasibility.[3] Meade was right. The grand divisions went out after only ten days.

The corps were now headed as follows: Reynolds the 1st, D. N. Couch the 2nd, Dan Sickles the 3rd, Meade the 5th, John Sedgwick the 6th, Sigel the 11th, and H. W. Slocum the 12th. General O. O. Howard replaced Sigel a month later when the German decided his corps was being slighted. Hooker put the cavalry under General G. F. Stoneman. This organization of the army left the status of Reynolds and Meade unchanged. But another change that took place did affect Reynolds. He was losing his old division. At long last the Pennsylvania Reserves had been ordered to Washington for rest and recruitment. Both Reynolds and Meade had been pressing for their relief from field duty. After the roughing-up they took at Fredericksburg, Meade appealed to Curtin, who had been trying for several months himself to get them off.[4] The combined pressures finally worked.

Reynolds detached the division from the corps in a special order of February 5: ". . . In separating from the Pennsylvania Reserve Corps, with which the commanding general has been so closely allied for the past eighteen months, he cannot but express his deep regrets. They are, however, lessened by the hope that soon their thin ranks will be filled, and they, once more restored and organized, will be returned to the field prepared to add new lustre to a name already endeared to our patriotic state."[5] To the rank and file this was a stiff and formal statement to describe what they had gone through under their old commander, but in the language of official reports it made its point. And nothing was said about plundering enemy property.

The Reserves were to be stationed in the defenses about Washington. Heintzelman, the general in command there, was directed to send Reynolds an equal number of Pennsylvania troops in exchange. On February 10 Hooker complained that Heintzelman had not obeyed the instructions.[6] Reynolds then assured Heintzelman that the Reserves were worth more than their mere numbers indicated. Besides, they would be further strengthened by the return of absentees.[7] By now Heintzelman's stalling had made Hooker so mad he wired Halleck that he was through with troop exchanges of any kind.[8] In the meantime Doubleday, who had taken the division up to Washington, remained there wrangling with Heintzelman. He wrote back to Reynolds that what the old general really objected to was the shortage of officers. Then Doubleday made the mistake of reminding his commander that this shortage was due to some mixup over Pennsylvania's law for electing them.[9] Instead of winning a longer stay in the capital, Doubleday was abruptly called back to camp in an order that implied a reprimand.[10] Reynolds was still sensitive on the subject of this law, which had finally caught up with the Reserves. He had ignored it to ensure efficiency while he had them, but now he was getting out from under. The problem could be solved in their reorganization, and no officer of his had to bring it up.

With the war grinding on into 1863, Reynolds was still careful about enemy property, whether he forgave his Reserves or not. On February 12 he sent out a foraging expedition with this warning to his colonels: "You will enforce the strictest discipline . . . and summarily punish any unauthorized plundering, it being understood that anything taken is for the Government. Anything more than this is nothing more than robbery."[11] The distinction between stealing and the legitimate confiscation of supplies to support an army was perfectly clear to Reynolds. Only the second had anything to do with waging war.

During the winter Hooker tightened up army discipline over-all. He made himself popular almost at once by improving the food[12] and by setting up a system of furloughs to reduce the disgraceful amount of absenteeism. On taking over the command Hooker listed the absentees as nearly 3,000 officers and about 82,000 men.[13] Correcting this abuse raised morale from its low point under Burnside, but the officers now found it harder to get leaves. Meade finally made it to Philadelphia after the middle of February, and while there called at the Landis home with Mrs. Meade. The sisters wrote Reynolds of the visit, and he answered that he was glad the Meades had been there. Otherwise he hoped the general would hurry back because his own turn came next. He also said he had just heard that brother Sam had applied for a paymaster's post in the army. He would like to see Sam get it.[14] If he did, it would put all four Reynolds brothers in uniform. Will's health had improved enough to give him active duty on the *U.S.S. Vermont* at Port Royal, South Carolina. Jim was an adjutant on Curtin's staff and had recently superintended the draft for the Lancaster area.[15] Sam could round out the family role in the service.

Meade got back to the army at last, and on February 27 Reynolds left for ten days. Two great battles would have to be fought before either of them could expect another leave. Hooker even refused to let them go to Washington for the presentation of swords by the Reserves. Ellie especially had hoped her brother could be there for the event, but he told her the army would be moving by then he was sure. Neither he nor Meade could come up. He thought Jim might be able to accept the sword for him, or maybe some of his old friends in the division.[16]

As for the swords themselves, he and Meade were in agreement. Reynolds had tried to discourage the gift at the start, back in August of 1862.[17] Meade's sword was decided on after he had left the Reserves, but he said he would have preferred their using the money to better purposes.[18] However, they felt it would show poor taste for either general to refuse the swords. The practice of giving them had become so common that one officer called it a mania, though he admitted that they usually went to those who deserved them.[19]

Reynolds was right about the army's moving. Large-scale operations were impossible during early spring. The clinging mud and clay of Virginia's roads made that sure. But Hooker kept his troops sharp by sending them out in small forces whenever the weather allowed. He also held frequent reviews. The first week of April brought the President, his wife, and party down from Washington to see the army. One day Lincoln reviewed the 1st Corps alone. Reynolds wrote that he returned to the capital gratified with everything he saw. ". . . As he ought to have been," he continued, "and if the troops only fight as well as they looked, no expectation however great, need be disappointed."[20] The rise in morale was affecting Reynolds too. Despite his *if*, this was strong praise from him.

He even showed confidence in Hooker. ". . . Our troops here . . . with proper management, which bids fair to be the case, will achieve success undoubtedly."[21] Again a slight qualification, but Reynolds had not looked forward so hopefully to a campaign since the war began. Before April he had felt otherwise. He had made his discouragement known to Hooker in some way or other that brought the following note:

> Headquarters, Army of the Potomac
> April 3, 1863
>
> Dear Gen'l
> Do not fear that I undervalue the services of your corps. At the proper time full justice will be done yourself and them. No words of mine can express the appreciation I feel for your services. It will be right at the proper time. I can say no more now.
>
> Truly yours
> (Signed) Joseph Hooker
> Maj Gen'l
> Comdg [22]

These words in the general's own hand should have been assurance enough, but why did Reynolds need it? He had not been touched when Burnside tried to get Franklin and Smith cashiered for what he called their failure to cooperate on the left at Fredericksburg.[23] Reynolds kept his command in Hooker's reorganization. Excepting the ten-day experiment with grand divisions, nobody had moved past him in promotion. On the record his status looked good, and yet something had bothered him. Whatever it was he said nothing about it in his letters, though he may have talked it out on his leave in Philadelphia. A brief coolness would develop later between Reynolds and Hooker, but for clear enough reasons. At the present there was no suggestion of any strain in their relationship.

Hooker's note contained the only hint of what worried Reynolds. He was afraid of one more wasted battle. This war was getting on. Generals made their reputations by fighting—and winning. Reynolds wanted to come out of the next campaign with honors. He wanted to get his corps into the center of operations. It would be nice too if he was given some freedom. If just once he could put men in according to his own judgment, he was confident of the results. But for the time being the statement from Hooker apparently satisfied him. On April

14 he wrote his sisters: "Our operations may be said to have commenced, and all passes for the Army of the Potomac stopped for the present, tho' I do not know that this has been made public."

In closing his letter he warned the sisters that he would not be writing much for awhile. He was "too full of preparations and business." Reynolds was always stirred by the excitement of a new military move. His old restlessness still hung on; activity was his life. His urge to get going charged him full of energy enough to spare for everybody around him. The officers under him, his aides and orderlies would all feel it— maybe more than they liked. There were sure to be tired men and worn-out horses around headquarters. Reynolds drove his corps hard when there was work to do. Right now he was disappointed over losing another chance to show it off to a member of the family. Harry Landis had wanted to come down all winter, but now that he could get away it was too late. The army was moving.

Hooker had completed plans for his offensive. Stoneman's cavalry were to begin it by crossing the fords twenty-five miles above Fredericksburg. From there they could sweep down behind Lee with the aim of cutting off his supplies from Richmond. The Army of Northern Virginia, except for Longstreet's corps, had spent the winter in their defenses behind Fredericksburg. Hooker wanted to test Lee's strength before starting his main movement, also to thin it out along the Rappahannock if he could. To this end Reynolds got orders to send troops down the north bank to Port Conway, eighteen miles from camp. Doubleday's division made the first march on April 19. When they returned three days later, Reynolds sent the 24th Michigan and 84th New York on the same mission. "The object of this demonstration is to draw the enemy force in that direction," headquarters informed Reynolds.[24] The men should pretend to be concealing their wagon train but to let enough of it show to give the impression of strength.

Like so many clumsy efforts made by both sides to fool each other these two ventures accomplished little. Lee merely noted that eight or ten boats had crossed over to Port Royal and that wagons supposed to contain more boats had come down to the far bank. "It may be an effort to ascertain our position," he concluded.[25] But the second expedition did have importance for Reynolds at least, though he probably never learned of it. He would have been happy if he had. When Lee heard that Reynolds' two regiments completely surprised his cavalry at Port Royal, he wrote Jeb Stuart: ". . . I am afraid the cavalry was negligent. They gave no alarm; did not fire a shot; lost some public horses and two wagons. The citizens gave the alarm. I desire the matter inquired into. . . ."[26]

Reynolds had taken a lot from Stuart's celebrated horsemen. He had begun the war in a vain chase up the railroad tracks behind Stuart. This was on the Peninsula. Then Stuart's men had scared the daylights out of Reynolds' Pennsylvania militia during the Antietam campaign. At Fredericksburg it was Stuart again who pinned down Doubleday's division and kept it from attacking with Meade. Now here at long last was a mite of personal revenge for Reynolds. A small foray on the part of his men had humbled the flamboyant cavalryman. In an army that worshiped its leader as the Confederates did Lee, the general's crisp note must have seared Stuart. It was praise Stuart loved, not censure. Reynolds commended his two regiments for marching thirty-six miles during a single day in bad weather.[27] But if he had only known, he could have added even kinder words.

Hooker's cavalry was having its own troubles. The main force had left camp on April 13 and got bogged down at the upper fords. The streams had suddenly become swollen from recent rains. So the cavalry still had not crossed when Hooker ordered his infantry to begin moving out at sunrise on the 27th. Four corps were to take the nearer crossings above Fredericksburg, leaving one division in camp to divert attention from the march. If everything went well it would put about 50,000 men in position to break down into the Confederate left and rear. This was Hooker's main objective.[28]

But the troops swinging up the river for the big strike did not include the 1st Corps. So far Reynolds' hope to distinguish himself looked dim. Along with the 3rd and 6th, his corps drew only a minor role. As a further attempt to fool Lee they were to make a demonstration below Fredericksburg. If they could keep him occupied he would be unaware of the attack building up in rear of his defenses. The orders for this demonstration contained brave words: "attack and carry the works at all hazards"; "pursue [the enemy] with the utmost vigor, fighting them whenever and wherever he can come up with them." But all this daring-do involved two pretty big *ifs*: "if the enemy detach any considerable part of his force"; "in case the enemy should fall back on Richmond."[29] Suppose the enemy did neither? Suppose Lee refused to be fooled? Then Reynolds, Sickles, and Sedgwick would be reduced to making hostile gestures until Hooker could get behind him.

This plan for a demonstration could only hit Reynolds as a sore reminder of the last battle. Practically the same ground; committed to a mere demonstration (Franklin's interpretation of his orders for September 13); and again under a wing commander. Hooker had put Sedgwick in charge on the left. Sedgwick outranked Reynolds—

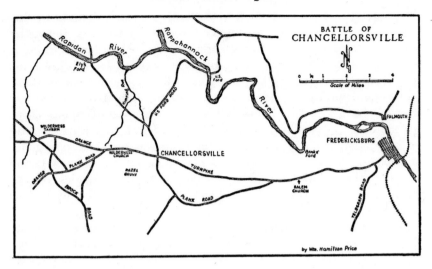

BATTLE OF
CHANCELLORSVILLE

Scale of Miles

by Wm. Hamilton Price

no quarrel there, and he was less cautious than Franklin. But once more another commander was wedged in between him and the top. Hooker's orders would reach him second-hand and subject to Sedgwick's interpretation. Reynolds would have little freedom of action. He could only hope that Lee would be impressed by 55,000 men threatening to cross the river and attack below the city.[30] This was a large number for a demonstration, and it just might look like the real thing. If Lee backtracked at all, then Reynolds could still get into a pretty good fight.

The 1st Corps broke camp at noon of the 28th, near Belle Plain, and marched in the rain toward the Rappahannock. It reached Fitzhugh's Crossing around 5:30 in the afternoon. Reynolds' position on the north bank was a mile below where he had crossed in December. That point had already taken Franklin's name. Sedgwick halted his 6th Corps there, and Sickles moved the 3rd in between Sedgwick and Reynolds, though farther back from the river. Opposite Reynolds on the south bank were the same heights Meade had stormed with the Pennsylvania Reserves. Also the same Confederate troops. Stonewall's men looked down on the now familiar railroad, the old Richmond road, and the approaches from the river.[31] Except for the absence of the Reserves hardly anything was missing to make the new attempt a carbon copy of the last.

General Henry Benham had charge of throwing bridges in front of both Sedgwick and Reynolds. This conscientious but short-tempered engineer came to see Reynolds before 10 o'clock that night. He wanted the pontoon boats carried down to the water by hand. Wagons would make too much noise and give away the point of crossing. Reynolds agreed to this and assigned details from Wadsworth's division to help with the work. Benham's parting instructions called for a brigade to row over in the first forty boats to protect the engineers. The bridges had to be down by 3:30 in the morning of the 29th. Three would be thrown above and two below, where Reynolds was. Responsibility for meeting the deadline lay with Benham.[32] But soon after he left around midnight the job of lugging the boats was switched to wagons and teams. The boats each weighed 1,500 pounds, and to carry them over the poor roadway was asking too much of the men. Besides, Wadsworth doubted whether he could get forty boats in the water by daylight.[33]

Benham found teams being used up at Franklin's Crossing too, so that by the time he returned to Reynolds he was in a bad mood. Already daylight and only half the boats floated. Of course the enemy pickets had discovered the whole movement and were firing from the south bank. Where were the riflemen to protect his engineers? Benham wanted to know. He estimated the Rebel picket at not more than 50 while the 1st Corps had 15,000 men. What was Reynolds waiting for?[34] Well, for one thing Reynolds was waiting for the fog to lift. Unlike the engineer, he refused to guess the number of an enemy force he could not see. Until then he was unwilling to make targets of his men, huddled seventy-five to a boat.[35] Reynolds may not have explained all this to Benham, but he made it clear later in his report.[36]

As soon as Reynolds could spot the rifle pits over the river he ordered Wadsworth to get two regiments across below them and flank them out. They were starting too late to suit Benham—or Hooker,[37] though the work went fast once it began. Wadsworth called on two regiments from the Iron Brigade, 6th Wisconsin and 24th Michigan. They double-quicked down to the boats, fixing bayonets as they ran. While they climbed in under lively fire from the Confederate pickets, Reynolds and Wadsworth sat their horses at the water's edge, calmly chomping cigars as the boats shoved off.[38] Wadsworth then dismounted and jumped into one of the last boats. He held onto the reins of his horse, pulling the animal into the water and forcing him to swim behind. Wadsworth was a political general, not a West Pointer; but this kind of gesture was sure to thrill his volunteers.

The enemy were soon cleared from the rifle pits and about ninety captured. The Iron Brigade regiments lost around sixty in casualties. At 10 a.m. Reynolds wired Sedgwick: "They (engs) say they will have the bridge in order in one hour, which means two."[39] Benham later insisted he laid two bridges for Reynolds in one hour and forty-five minutes.[40] He and Reynolds did not seem to be getting along. But his relations with officers up at Franklin's crossing were even worse—Benham tried to put one of them under arrest for delaying the work there. The engineer was having a tough morning.[41]

Lee anxiously watched this movement on Hooker's left wing. It involved a large number of troops. As the 1st and 6th Corps began crossing he wired Jefferson Davis to this effect. He would like to have Longstreet back from southeastern Virginia. The Union forces seemed to be in earnest below Fredericksburg, he said.[42] If he did expect the main threat at this point, Hooker was off to a good start. But the bridges, instead of being thrown before daylight, were barely finished at noon. It was too late to make a convincing demonstration on the 29th. At the same time any lull in activity would look suspicious. Lee knew by now that Hooker had started crossing other troops far in his rear.[43]

So when Sedgwick should have been piling men over the Rappahannock,[44] he sent only one division of his own corps and one from the 1st to the south bank. By evening Reynolds had brought his other two divisions down near the bridges. They were John C. Robinson's and Doubleday's troops. Wadsworth's was the division across the river. As the grey, foggy day came to a close the only service the left wing had performed was reconnaissance. Poor visibility made even this ineffective. Observation from one of Professor T. S. C. Lowe's balloons reported the enemy line to be thinly held. Reynolds had seen a body of infantry moving along the old Richmond road toward Sedgwick's front.[45] That was about all.

Hooker had to know more than this. Was Sedgwick keeping Lee pinned to his entrenchments below Fredericksburg? On the morning of the 30th he ordered a demonstration by Reynolds to find out. It was to begin at one o'clock—that is, unless Reynolds found the enemy still in full force. In that case the demonstration was off. Two hours before the time set Sedgwick wrote headquarters: "General Reynolds is satisfied that the enemy have not weakened their forces either in infantry or artillery; and that a demonstration will bring on a general engagement on the left."[46] Since Hooker did not want to commit troops to a full-scale battle there, he countermanded the order.

The day dragged on. In the early afternoon Sickles' 3rd Corps was pulled out of reserve to join the right wing near Chancellorsville. Next Hooker wanted a bridge lifted from each of the lower crossings and moved to Banks' Ford above Fredericksburg. Sedgwick protested taking them up before dark. That was all Lee needed—to see the bridges beginning to go. Reynolds had already reported enemy troops moving to the right, and the railroad also seemed to be busy. They might be reinforcements up from Richmond, he thought.[47] Headquarters puffed right back: "General Hooker hopes they are from Richmond, as the greater will be our success."[48]

But by now Reynolds was beginning to suspect the goings on across the river. The enemy might be moving up to the front behind Fredericksburg, leaving only a screen to cover their march. They had never shown their troops in this way before, he said, and it might be mere bravado.[49] For the rest of the day messages kept going up from the left without solving the mystery. Meanwhile the Union front was limited to artillery action. According to Reynolds even that left something to be desired. "The ammunition used in the 3-inch Parrots is not good, or the gunners, I don't know which,"[50] he said in a dispatch to Sedgwick. It would be hard on his gunners if it turned out to be their aim. To an alumnus of Braxton Bragg's old battery perfection was barely acceptable.

For the first time in his life Reynolds wrote the family while a campaign was going on. It was only a note:

> We have got our bridges over the river—and three Corps *have crossed* above and are moving down the *right bank* on the heights and in rear of Fredericksburg. We will cross at our bridges and attack when the heights of Fredericksburg are carried or pursue the enemy if he retreats. The weather has been unfavorable again and has retarded our movements very much or the attack would have been made to-day. The troops are in good spirits and I think will fight well if we meet with any success here. The only thing I do not like about our operations has been that the bridges were thrown too soon by a day and my bridges are not in a good position. I cannot write anymore tonight as I am very busy.[51]

Considering the last two days, Reynolds did not sound discouraged. But he was banking too much on a message just in from Chief-of-Staff Butterfield. Butterfield said Hooker expected to be on the heights behind Fredericksburg by the night of May 1, even against strong opposition.[52] With no way of checking this optimistic forecast Reynolds naturally looked for the left wing to follow up and exploit the main attack. He knew that Meade, Howard, and Slocum were moving down from the upper fords and that Sickles had gone north to join them. If Lee still felt it necessary to keep a large force on the bank opposite Reynolds, there was real reason for hope.

But what about the bridges being thrown too soon? This statement must have puzzled Reynolds' sisters. Generals usually kicked because everything was done too late. Obviously Reynolds saw the situation reversed for once. Half an army had rushed down to a river and thrown five bridges over a span fewer than two hundred yards across.[53] Then they had hustled over some troops in a great show of aggression. After that, nothing. For the rest of the 29th and through the 30th Lee and Jackson waited. When nothing developed they knew they could begin looking somewhere else. Dawdling in front of these two wise commanders merely gave the feint away. That was why Reynolds would have shortened the stalling period by making a later start.[54]

In what he wrote that night of April 30, Reynolds had no help from hindsight. Lee did not feel safe in withdrawing from around Fredericksburg until late in the day. But by midnight the quiet on Sedgwick's front had convinced him. At 3:30 he ordered McLaws to march three of his brigades toward Chancellorsville.[55] So all the next day it was Sedgwick and Reynolds who would be fooled. Reynolds had already got a taste of it the afternoon before. And now Butterfield began asking what Lee was up to. At 9:15 in this morning of May 1 a balloon reported heavy columns of infantry on the way north. Later Reynolds sent a strange message to Sedgwick:

> I think the proper view to take of affairs is this: if they have not detached more than A. P. Hill's division from our front, they have been keeping up appearances with a view of delaying Hooker, in tempting us to make an attack on their fortified position, and hoping to destroy us and strike for our depot over our bridges. We ought, therefore, in my judgment, to know something of what has transpired on the right. Do you not think this the correct view? Let me know, if you please, what you think of it.[56]

This was not a model of military reporting, and it showed Reynolds' state of mind. He had an important fact almost right. One division had left his front. He had another fact exactly right. The enemy were merely keeping up appearances while throwing more strength in the direction of Hooker's advance. He was wrong about the threat to the supply depot, although Hooker had been worried about it himself.[57] Finally there was Reynolds' curiosity about the army's right wing. Hooker now had about 70,000 men and 184 guns up there with him.[58] What were they doing? As long as the real fight was planned for that wing, let it start.

Reynolds was tired of playing a secondary role. Besides, Hooker had just got out a congratulatory order praising the advance made from the upper fords.[59] No word at all about labors on the left. Butterfield knew the feeling down below Fredericksburg and he tried to smooth things over with a note to Sedgwick. He assured him that the

1st and 6th Corps were being counted in, that it would come out all right.[60] This sentence had a familiar sound to Reynolds. It was like the one in Hooker's note of April 3. "It will be all right at the proper time," Hooker had promised him then.

Two o'clock of May 1 gave Reynolds his answer from the right. Hooker wired Butterfield that he was suspending his attack at Chancellorsville, though he hoped the enemy would attack him. "Tell Sedgwick to keep a sharp lookout, and attack if he can succeed."[61] At least for the time being Hooker was switching his hope for offensive action from the right to his left. Reynolds still had Wadsworth across the river, and he ordered the division to feel out the strength opposing it. Wadsworth thought it was about the same as on the 30th, so Reynolds informed Sedgwick at 3 o'clock that an attack would start a battle, though he was keeping his men under arms.[62] But no order came to send them in. Instead, Butterfield wired Hooker an hour later: "They [Sedgwick and Reynolds] consider that to attack before you have accomplished some success, in view of the strong position and numbers in their front . . . might render them unserviceable at the proper time. They are anxious to hear from you."[63] This was the "view" of Reynolds' earlier note and then some. The note only asked what had "transpired on the right."

Hooker had run into more resistance than he expected before reaching the open ground east of Chancellorsville.[64] Except for this clearing, the terrain for several miles to the east, west, and south was a tangle of second-growth pine and thicket. In Hooker's rear between Chancellorsville and the river the ground was also too broken for maneuver. Besides, he had failed to uncover Banks' Ford on his far left so that help could be brought down from the north. Hooker was losing confidence.[65] So with his own attack called off he wanted more pressure on Sedgwick's part. Even before noon he had ordered a demonstration on the left for one o'clock. It was to be severe, though short of an all-out attack. But the telegraph, which had been erratic since the start of the campaign, held the message up till late afternoon. Although Reynolds was called upon to make the demonstration, darkness was so near that Butterfield countermanded the order.

That evening Sedgwick asked Reynolds to come up to see him if he was not tired. So Reynolds rode the mile or more to Tyler's Hill. They had a lot to talk about, not much of it good. If "Uncle John" had a finger or two of brandy about, it would help. Only ten thousand Confederates had bluffed three times their number during this day on the left. Neither Reynolds nor Sedgwick knew this of course, though Reynolds had reported at least a division withdrawn from the other side. Actually, only Early's division of Jackson and Barksdale's brigade of McLaws remained between Hamilton's Crossing and Fredericksburg.[66]

Union reconnaissance had simply failed. The absence of cavalry hurt most,[67] but poor visibility and the frequent breakdown of communications also contributed. The Confederates screened their moves effectively both in the hollow west of the Richmond road and on the heights beyond. Planted information given Sedgwick by "deserters" from Jackson further befuddled the left wing command. Then when Hooker had taken a bridge from each of the lower crossings, he weakened contact between Sedgwick's men on either bank. Taken together, these difficulties accounted for much of the wasted May 1. But Sedgwick himself was partly to blame. Like Franklin six months before, he had taken less leeway than his orders allowed.[68] Once again it was Reynolds' luck to draw a wing commander who underplayed his role.

What Reynolds thought of Sedgwick went unsaid. So far nothing in his dispatches showed impatience or irritation. His note to Sedgwick in the early afternoon had even suggested caution. Up to this point he seemed to be satisfied with whatever was being done, or not done, under existing conditions. After all, the left was not supposed to fight a battle. Its mission was primarily a holding operation. Everybody in Sedgwick's wing knew it, which was bad in itself. Troops fight better when they are convinced that their performance is crucial. Sedgwick and Reynolds both may have been victims of a military axiom.[69]

On May 2 at 1:55 a.m. Hooker sent a message to his chief-of-staff: "Direct all bridges taken up at Franklin's Crossing and below before daylight, and for Reynolds' corps to march at once, with pack train to report to headquarters."[70] Hours passed before this message reached Reynolds, which meant that the bridges would now have to be pulled after daylight and under fire. Sedgwick asked that they be left down until night, but the order stood. Reynolds sent off Robinson's and Doubleday's divisions at 8:30.[71] Wadsworth still had the river to cross. In passing Hooker's instructions on to Reynolds, Butterfield had told him to take the shortest possible route, which was the River road up the north bank. That probably would give the march away, but unless artillery fire drove him to a more roundabout course he could take it. Butterfield was upset about the delay in transmitting the order. He said: "If you were now with the general, I think there would be no doubt as to the result of the operations of to-day."[72]

With a movement beginning hours late, conditions were returning to normal for Reynolds. But at least the order called him up to where the fighting was expected. Maybe Hooker would make good on his promise of April 3. That proper time when full justice would be done to his corps and himself might be here at last. Now the job was to get Wadsworth's men back over the river and started north behind the other two divisions. At first they ran into trouble. Only the first regiments of one brigade got across before Confederate artillery found the range of the single bridge. A shell caught a Pennsylvania regiment in midstream. It sank one pontoon, killing or wounding twenty men and driving the rest back to the south bank.[73] While waiting for the bridge to be repaired, Reynolds sent one brigade up to cross over at Sedgwick's bridge. Then he put a battery in position on the north bank to knock out the enemy's guns. This battery did its work so well that before 10 o'clock Reynolds was able to report all the division over except the skirmishers. At this point he left Wadsworth and rode ahead to catch up with Robinson and Doubleday.[74]

The morning had broken warm and sunny. Before Reynolds ever got his orders a Confederate general had started his own men on a march. Stonewall Jackson was riding to his last battle. During the night he and his commanding general had conferred over a map. Reconnaissance showed Hooker strongly posted in the vicinity of Chancellorsville, ten miles west of Fredericksburg. Meade's 5th Corps anchored Hooker's left on the Rappahannock and extended about two miles south to connect with the 2nd Corps of Couch and Slocum's 12th. These two commands covered the turnpike and the Chancellor mansion itself. Below them Sickles had moved his 3rd Corps to an elevation known as Hazel Grove. To the east Howard's 11th Corps stretched out along the pike to form Hooker's right. This gave the Army of the Potomac a line nearly six miles in all.[75]

Howard's position looked especially weak to the Confederate generals. If they could just find the proper road they could attack his corps in rear. It was during their night conference that Lee and Jackson fixed on the route, and now Jackson was on his way. As Reynolds marched north to fill out Hooker's extended line, Jackson turned south along Sickles' front and disappeared in the wilderness.[76] Reynolds had the longer distance to march, twenty-three miles to Jackson's fourteen. His men also carried eight days' rations while the Confederates went out stripped for fighting. Their supply train moved well to the south. Jackson's departure was no more secret than Reynolds' had been, but there was an important difference. Reynolds was marching toward the point where a battle should be fought. Not Jackson, at least so far as Hooker could see. As late as four in the afternoon Union headquarters thought his march was the beginning of a Confederate retreat.[77] Instead, Lee had split his force of scarcely 45,000 in the face of Hooker's 70,000, and his object was to attack.

Sickles had been ordered to harass Jackson's rear columns shortly after noon, and later Barlow's brigade was detached from Howard to support him. Few moves could have helped Jackson more than weakening Howard. That and Howard's indifference to his exposed position were setting him up for the kill: his corps sprawled out over a mile on the turnpike and the Orange Plank road near their junction at Wilderness Church. Throughout the day Howard had been warned to guard against a possible threat from the west. Although headquarters preferred to believe Lee was dodging a battle, a dispatch alerting Howard went out as early as 9:30 a.m.[78] But almost nothing was done out on the right to protect the flank. At 4 o'clock, the hour of Hooker's greatest optimism, Jackson already had 25,000 men deploying along the pike and in the woods within a mile of Howard. After marching off southward from the front, he had circled back north (via Brock Road) to put his force in this perfect position.

Meanwhile Reynolds had brought the head of his own columns to Banks' Ford, where he looked for a shortcut to Hooker's lines. No bridge had been thrown at that point, so his tired men had to struggle on up to U. S. Ford.[79] The leading brigade crossed there at 5:30 and wearily stacked arms. Many of the men were too tired to eat. The rest of the 2nd and 3rd Divisions had not yet come up, and Wadsworth with the 1st was still several miles behind. Leaving Doubleday in command of the corps, Reynolds rode down to Chancellorsville to report. He reached headquarters about 6 o'clock, at a time when the sunset was taking on an even deeper red from fighting off to the southwest. But as Doubleday wrote later: ". . . knowing Hooker had a large force, we felt no anxiety as to the result, and took it for granted that we would not be wanted until the next day."[80] An aide, dashing back from Reynolds abruptly changed his mind.

Stonewall Jackson had struck. Within a half-hour after arriving at headquarters, Reynolds saw panic-stricken men piling back through the troops being formed to stem Howard's rout. So instead of going into camp after the steaming hike of twenty-three miles, Reynolds was urged to put every available man into position to hold Jackson off. Back to the ford went Reynolds, accompanied by two guides.[81] Once more his men picked up their rifles and filed along through the woods on another march. By now a bright moon dappled their shoulders beneath gaps in the trees,[82] but it was still too dark and too late to establish a fighting line. As brilliant as Jackson's own attack was, it had begun too late. Although he had knocked out Howard's corps, his men soon lost contact and organization.

The Confederate advance halted around nine o'clock. Jackson took a small party out ahead of his position to reconnoiter. In returning to his lines he was shot by some of his own men who mistook the party for Union horsemen. Early next morning Jeb Stuart was given command of Jackson's corps. Stonewall died eight days later. Ironically it became the chief consolation the Army of the Potomac could claim for the campaign.

At the time Jackson was wounded Reynolds had moved Robinson's division two miles south from the ford, with Doubleday close behind. They were forcing their way against the continued backwash of Howard's flight. It took every man on Reynolds' staff to keep the road clear enough for the columns to advance at all.[83] At one point Reynolds had to deploy a regiment across his front to drive the fugitives back. If his morning's order to march had only reached him in time, all this trouble could have been avoided. Butterfield's concern over its delay was proving well founded. It brought Reynolds on the field too late to shore up the collapse of the 11th Corps. It forced his men to push on through the dark in unknown country and against the wake of a disastrous rout. As of Saturday midnight, May 2, the "full justice" Hooker owed Reynolds and the 1st Corps was as remote as ever.

Just to make things worse Reynolds got conflicting orders for taking his new position.[84] He had no sooner got the head of his column near the Chandler house about a half-mile north of Chancellorsville when a change of orders put his footsore men on the road again. The choking dust and the heat of thirteen hours had not been enough. It was one o'clock Sunday morning before Reynolds reached his assigned position. His right began near the mouth of Hunting Run, which empties into the Rapidan a mile or so west of where it joins the Rappahannock. From here the line swept south for about two miles, then it bent back eastward on the Ely's Ford road. This put Reynolds' left in contact with Sykes's division of Meade. It was a strong alignment as it faced toward Jackson's (now Stuart's) left. Meade carried the line down toward the Chandler house, and from there it angled to the Rappahannock on the Mineral Springs road.[85]

The position given to Reynolds and Meade threw their outermost flanks too far from the likely center of action. These ambitious corps commanders might have trouble getting all their men into battle. The choice spots for fighting went to three other corps. Couch with the 2nd Corps fronted generally toward Fredericksburg and Lee's

12,000 troops. Slocum's 12th Corps looked south and west, as did Sickles' 3rd. Sickles held what turned out to be the key point of the whole field. As a placement for guns Hazel Grove had elevation enough to command the approaches both of Lee on the east and Stuart from the west. But if it fell into Confederate hands it could be murder to Hooker's center.[86]

Neither Lee nor Stuart took Hazel Grove by assault. It came to them as a gift when Hooker abandoned it at the start of the main battle. He had gone out to look at the position and decided that Fairview to the north was more promising for his artillery. He ordered Sickles to withdraw.[87] For a short while after that Slocum kept the enemy from taking Hazel Grove, but not for long. Stuart had moved out to the attack at 6 a.m. He struck directly east, with his center on the pike and his flanks a half-mile to right and left. It looked at first as if Reynolds would see action. He had batteries planted where Ely's Ford road faced obliquely toward Stuart's left. Additional guns were brought in from the 11th Corps, but Reynolds found some of their men still full of fright. He made official note of it: "I regret to report that two batteries, or parts of two, left the position assigned to them without orders, and disgracefully retreated in the direction of United States Ford."[88]

At eight in the morning Reynolds still had forty guns on his left, but no call for the use of his infantry. Hard fighting went on to the south, where the big battle he had been waiting for since December was taking place without him. It looked as if the "luck of the field" Meade talked about would evade them both. Aware that Stuart's left was advancing across part of their front, they wondered why they were being held out. Meade finally saw Hooker and begged that he and Reynolds be allowed to go in.[89] Hooker refused. Then Reynolds tried and got the same answer.[90] During the forenoon Hooker gradually pulled one division after another out of the battle in the center, and yet in this crisis he was writing off the help of the 37,000 men under Reynolds and Meade.

Earlier in the morning a shell had hit a pillar on the Chancellor house porch, driving it against Hooker's head and side. For several days from that point on, the general was in too much pain to give full attention to the battle. Thus, to some extent Reynolds and Meade were victims of his present state of mind. Hooker was also waiting for word of Sedgwick's approach from Fredericksburg. If he had followed the timetable of his orders, Sedgwick must already have taken the city. Now pressing westward, he should be about to strike the smaller part of Lee's army from the rear. Once this force was crushed Hooker could turn on Stuart. That would be the time to bring in Reynolds and Meade.

But it worked out differently. Sedgwick was south of the river instead of north where Hooker thought he was when he sent him his orders. As a result the 6th Corps had to move three miles up to the city across Early's front. It was 10 o'clock before he began his assault on Marye's Heights, though Fredericksburg was supposed to be taken at daylight. Five more hours would pass before Sedgwick started west. In the meantime the fighting at Chancellorsville had slacked off by noon. Hooker was constricting his lines to conform with the angle held by Reynolds and Meade, a position they made safe by entrenching. Just before the withdrawal Meade had managed to put one brigade into the battle. He did it without orders, and Hooker protested when he heard about it.[91] This was a liberty Reynolds would never have thought of taking. As Doubleday said of him, he always obeyed his orders literally.[92] But for once Reynolds was disgusted enough to be tempted.

When the battle picked up again in the late afternoon, it shifted east. Lee knew Hooker's position was now too strong to be attacked. He was just as sure Hooker would stay in it. That left him free to detach McLaws to hold off the advancing Sedgwick outside of Fredericksburg. About 4 o'clock fighting commenced around Salem Church, two miles west of the city. The main part of the army, held idle in front of Stuart, could easily hear the firing six miles off. Sedgwick was fighting it out on his own. He held onto his ground, but he practically gave up the idea of ever reaching Hooker. In fact he had Benham throw two bridges across the Rappahannock in his rear to assure his retreat if it became necessary. So Sunday closed with the Army of the Potomac wholly on the defensive. There was little to say in answer to Lincoln's wire of 4:35 p.m.: "Where is General Hooker? Where is Sedgwick? Where is Stoneman?"[93]

For Reynolds, Monday, May 4 merely copied the previous day. Nothing in his own front, and again toward evening a reprise of Lee's attempt to drive Sedgwick back. Reynolds tried once more for permission to attack, then worked out his own way of getting some action. Between four and five in the afternoon he sent a brigade out on reconnaissance. Reynolds knew its commander well. Colonel Roy Stone was an old Bucktail and spoiling for a fight. Of course he had to be given the usual warning about not bringing on a general engagement, but he just might fall into enough trouble to require considerable help. Stone headed his men south along Hunting Run, which brought him in near Stuart's left. Soon afterwards Reynolds heard the sound of firing. It seemed to be coming from the right direction, and as it picked up in intensity so did Reynolds' impatience. Maybe Stone had found his trouble. Major Riddle was hurried off to find out how much the colonel had stirred up. When Riddle came back he brought Major Chamberlin along to describe the action. Stone's brigade had driven Stuart's skirmishers in, then run against a much larger force holding a barricaded road. It looked promising for a few moments until Stone thought of his orders and broke off his advance. It would have been the easiest thing in the world to draw an attack, Chamberlin said. "I wish to God he had!" Reynolds told him.[94] Doubleday was in the tent at the time and said later that if Stone had only got a hint of what was in Reynolds' mind he would have gone in gladly.[95]

It was just not in Reynolds to ask one of his officers to violate an order he would not ignore himself. He did the best he could. He sent in a trigger-happy colonel and hoped. But the events of May 3 had begun his suspicion of Hooker, and by evening of the 4th he was plainly disgusted.[96] He had hardly slept since the campaign started and yet all his efforts and those of his men amounted to nothing. When Hooker called the corps commanders into a midnight conference, it was a moody Reynolds who dragged himself over to headquarters.

Hooker wanted the opinion of his officers on whether the army should now advance or whether it should recross to the north bank of the Rappahannock. Before leaving the tent while a vote was taken, Hooker made it clear that his own inclination was to withdraw. Howard voted to advance. It was a chance to salvage something from the disgrace to his 11th Corps.[97] Meade then voted to advance. Reynolds in his turn said that since his corps had not fought he did not want to urge an opinion, but that he would go along with Meade.[98] Following that he paid his respects to Hooker's irresolution by promptly dozing off.[99] The final vote showed only Sickles and Couch in favor of retreating. Slocum arrived too late to vote, and of course Sedgwick was pinned down six miles to the east. This made it three to two for continuing the fight. Hooker came back in for the result, then announced that he had decided to recross. Someone woke Reynolds and he left the meeting behind Couch. "What was the use of calling us together at this time of night when he intended to retreat anyhow?"[100] Reynolds asked.

Hooker's conference ended the fighting in the Chancellorsville campaign. Sedgwick had already crossed the river after standing off a heavy attack by Lee on the 4th. Now came the labor of preparing roads, collecting artillery and trains, and setting the order of march for the United States Ford and the bridges. On the afternoon of the

5th a downpour held work to a minimum. By midnight the level of the water had risen six feet, and none of the infantry had yet got to the north bank. But Hooker had, and now he suddenly found himself cut off from his army. This left Couch the senior commander south of the river. So at once he took Reynolds and Sickles with him to Meade's headquarters and announced that the crossing was suspended. He said they would stay where they were and fight it out.[101]

These stout words sounded good for a change, but as orders they left Meade in some doubt. He waited until Couch had gone, then sent an aide over the single tottering bridge to find Hooker. Around 2 o'clock in the morning a message came back from Butterfield. The order to retreat still stood! The aide reported that Hooker himself had been asleep. When Reynolds heard the news back at his own tent he said: "Tell General Meade that someone should be waked up to take command of this army."[102] Bitter as Reynolds was, he could not resist the opening.

As the water began to fall on the 6th the withdrawal continued. Reynolds rode out early to find Meade, whose corps was dug in to cover the movement. When they met he said: "General, I will support you. If there is any fighting to be done, we will do it together."[103] These two men had fought the war almost side by side. Whatever anneals soldiers, both under pressure of fighting and in the routine of camp, had worked a near miracle. Their rivalry was giving way to interdependence; they were beginning to think in terms of each other. Whether they knew it or not it would serve them better—and in time, the army too.

Hooker's retreat left the field to Lee, though Confederate losses discouraged any further gambling against a strong position. Lee's casualties were put at 12,821 as compared with Hooker's 17,278. But Reynolds' corps lost only 299 and Meade's 700. Set beside a toll of over 4,000 each for the 3rd and 6th Corps,[104] it became obvious that Reynolds and Meade were scarcely used. Lincoln had cautioned Hooker to get all of his men into the next battle, but two years after Chancellorsville Hooker still could not explain his failure to let the 1st or the 5th Corps fight. Before the war investigating committee of Congress he used up some five hundred words trying to justify his reasons for holding them out.[105] What he said has not convinced military writers[106] any more than it satisfied Reynolds or Meade during the campaign.

Hooker did make one statement Reynolds would have liked except for its implied criticism of another officer. The committee had been questioning Hooker about Sedgwick's delay in taking the heights behind Fredericksburg. At one point he replied: "Had General Reynolds been left with that independent command, I have no doubt the result would have been very different."[107] Some years later Hooker said more: "My army was not beaten. Only a part of it had been engaged. The First corps, commanded by Reynolds, *whom I regarded as the ablest officer under me,* was fresh and ready and eager to be brought into action" [author's italics].[108] So for Reynolds the irony was complete. The corps commander Hooker rated first did the least fighting.

Even at the time, Hooker refused to admit he was beaten. On May 6 he issued congratulatory orders to his army for its "glorious victory."[109] He did tone this down somewhat in a wire to the President,[110] and by the 10th was willing to express disappointment over his cavalry.[111] A force under General Kilpatrick had thrown a brief scare into Richmond during a raid, but over-all, Stoneman's operations accomplished little.

Reynolds had his own opinion of Chancellorsville. "We did not effect much more by our crossing," he wrote, "than to be slaughtered and to slaughter the Rebels. My Corps was very little in action and has of course suffered very little, tho' I do not consider its morale improved by the operations."[112] What the "operations" did to Reynolds' morale could be guessed by remembering the high hopes he took into them.

CHAPTER XI

With a View to an Advance

The soldiers of both armies lapsed back into the routine of their old camps after Chancellorsville. They left the worry to the generals. Lee had to strengthen an army that could no longer afford its losses. Stonewall Jackson of course was irreplaceable. As for Hooker, he had lost the campaign, no matter what he said. To dispel the gloom in the capital Lincoln at first urged Hooker to resume the offensive immediately. But Hooker pleaded the need for partially reorganizing his army. Service expirations were about to lose him 16,000 men, or about the effective strength of a corps. So with characteristic patience Lincoln resigned himself to further waiting. Meanwhile, the only good news kept coming from the west. Grant had Vicksburg invested, and its fall would open the Mississippi for the Union.

In the same letter permitting Hooker to delay operations, the President concluded with some disturbing words. Not all of Hooker's corps and division commanders were giving him their confidence.[1] Hooker tried at once to find out who these officers were. This was on May 14. The next day he called Meade to headquarters. Hooker said he had heard indirectly through Governor Curtin that the army had lost confidence in him—and that Reynolds and Meade especially had.[2] Since Lincoln had not mentioned any names, how had Hooker tracked down the two Pennsylvanians? Meade knew the answer. In visiting the army on the 12th, Curtin admitted to Meade how troubled he was over Chancellorsville.[3] Reynolds would certainly have seen the governor too. Whether or not he left any statement of opinions to the more articulate Meade, Reynolds seemed equally committed in this growing rift with the commanding general.

More difficulty with Hooker followed. Now he was insisting that in the midnight conference of May 4-5 both Meade and Reynolds had voted to retreat. It looked as if Hooker was trying to shore up his own decisions after the fact. Anyhow the charge upset Meade to the point of writing all the officers who had been present, asking for their recollections of what he had said. Reynolds answered first, on May 24. Meade had decidedly favored an advance, he said, an opinion with which he himself had agreed.[4] The assurance pleased Meade, but it would hardly improve the relations of either corps commander with Hooker.

News of the affair went the rounds in the army. On May 25 General Gibbon wrote: "Gen. Hooker is seeking someone upon whose shoulders to place the responsibility of his defeat and to the astonishment of everyone has selected Gens. Meade and Reynolds, more especially the former. This has made an open issue between himself and Gen. Meade, who is known to have urged in the strongest terms an advance. Reynolds would not even join in the discussion, went to sleep during the Council and when waked up said 'We ought not to fall back.' No one whose opinion is worth anything now has any confidence in Gen. Hooker and the President has been told so. . . ."[5]

Later Hooker did admit that Meade had in fact voted for an advance, though, he said, only because he did not think the army could recross the river in the presence of the enemy.[6] But in the wake of Chancellorsville bad blood was showing among the high command. "There has been a misunderstanding between Reynolds and Hooker," a colonel of the 1st Corps wrote. "Reynolds is a thorough soldier and somewhat disgusted with humbug. I am told that either Reynolds or Hooker will be relieved or else our corps will be assigned to duty somewhere else."[7] The colonel was making his own interpretation of the trouble. Reynolds certainly hated humbug, but the word was too hazy to describe what he felt. Like so many others, he had simply lost all confidence in Hooker.

Meade had a more interesting theory to account for Hooker's antagonism. "I suppose he has heard some of the stories flying around camp in regard to my having the command, and these . . . have induced him to believe that I am manoeuvering to get him relieved, that I may step in his shoes."[8] If there was any truth in this suspicion of Meade's it might account, at least in part, for Hooker's feeling against Reynolds. Since Reynolds outranked Meade, no consideration of a change could ignore his own claims to the command. In the meantime Hooker could well be worried by criticism from among his officers. No one had been harder on Burnside than Hooker. And Hooker had superseded Burnside.

While the bickering went on, a good month for fighting was nearing its end without a move by the Army of the Potomac. Activity was limited to small raids, mostly by cavalry. On May 20 Reynolds sent the 24th Michigan and 6th Wisconsin down the Northern Neck beyond King George Court House.[9] In that direction the Potomac was being used to ferry deserters across to the Maryland shore, and also for smuggling. Hooker had called for crack troops, and Reynolds had them in these regiments of the Iron Brigade. The mission was hardly more than a training exercise, but since the best fighting men could be the most restless in camp, they usually drew these assignments.

Anyhow bigger movements would come soon enough. Word already out had the Army of Northern Virginia under marching orders. On May 27 Longstreet was reported about to rejoin Lee for operations against or above Hooker's right.[10] On the same day Reynolds was directed to have his command ready to march and to report himself to headquarters for special instructions. The entire army was alerted on the 28th, even though Hooker wired Stanton that enemy camps appeared to be as numerous and well filled as ever.[11] End of the month returns for the Army of the Potomac showed 104,619 men reporting for duty. Lee's effective total present was 68,352.[12] With such vast numbers astir, June was bound to see fighting somewhere.

On May 31 Doubleday announced himself as commanding the 1st Corps, pending his general's return to camp.[13] Reynolds had suddenly gone up to Washington; nobody but himself knew why. He was just three days away from a critical decision. He had learned that he was being considered for army command.[14] It was a chance to head the largest army in the field. Less than two years ago Reynolds had been only a brigadier. Now, if he moved into Hooker's present spot he would have no military superior except General-in-Chief Halleck, in Washington. Of course he would be responsible also to the civilian heads Stanton and Lincoln. Of course! Among them, these three sat on the Army of the Potomac. At every critical turn they had seemed to dictate policy—for McClellan, for Pope, for McClellan again, then Burnside, and now Hooker. While Hooker had been granted more freedom for a time than the others, at present he would be lucky to hang on to his command.

As John Reynolds sailed up the Potomac to the capital, this matter of who ran the army could only keep turning over and over in his mind. He had hated outside direction from the start. He had complained about it to his sisters in June of 1862.[15] Two months later he had written: "If the army is to be managed from Washington, I am afraid there will be nothing but failures as there has been formerly; no one can conduct a campaign at a distance from the field or without being in the actual presence of the operating armies."[16] He put it more plainly than ever when Burnside had the army: "If we do not get some one soon who can command an army without consulting 'Stanton and Halleck' at Washington, I do not know what will become of this Army."[17]

Eventually the administration might find a general to command in the field without help from Washington. Reynolds might be the man himself, for that matter. But would Lincoln or Stanton or Halleck agree? What would they find in his favor when they looked at his record?

Major General John F. Reynolds was forty-two years old. He had spent twenty-six years in service. He had fought in two wars, as well as against the Indians. His administrative talents had been recognized early by his appointment as Commandant of Cadets at West Point. In the present war he had commanded in succession a brigade, a division, a corps. He had led each of them in battle—the brigade at Mechanicsville, the division at second Bull Run, the corps at both Fredericksburg and Chancellorsville. Whenever his orders had let him fight, he did well. Mechanicsville had been a brilliant beginning. Gaines' Mill showed the tenacity that kept him on the field till it was overrun and his capture lost him to the army for the rest of the Seven Days. At second Bull Run Reynolds' part in the defense of Henry House Hill was brilliant again. Cramped by Franklin's caution at Fredericksburg, he still led the only corps that penetrated Lee's defenses at any considerable point. Only Chancellorsville dimmed the record when Hooker refused to use him.

Reynolds himself had no doubt about his qualifications. Otherwise he would not now be on the way to Washington. No offer of army command had come to him from either the White House or the war department. All he knew was that a friend he trusted had said he was being considered.[18] An offer could be weighed and then accepted or rejected, depending on the conditions. An order to take the command would be something else. For Reynolds such an order would have to be obeyed, if issued. But he could at least forestall the possibility unless he liked the terms. Complete freedom to plan and fight his battles in his own way was one thing; anything less was intolerable.

During Reynolds' stay at the capital his sister Ellie was visiting Jennie and George Gildersleeve in Baltimore. They spent the evening of June 2 at a concert, and as they were nearing home afterwards they saw that someone had turned on the lights in the parlor. Inside they found Brother John reading. He told them he had just come up from Washington. He had been with the President during the day, and Mr. Lincoln had offered him command of the army. No, he could not accept it, John added, because he was not promised a free hand in its direction. That was all he would say about it. The next morning Reynolds left for camp.[19]

Not until ten days later did he see his friend Meade. The army was already beginning its move north to follow Lee, who had pulled out from around Fredericksburg about the time Reynolds got back. As the 1st Corps was passing Meade's 5th up along the Rappahannock Reynolds stopped by to talk about his conference with Lincoln. What he told his friend on that June 12 differed in one respect from what Ellie later remembered of John's brief words in Baltimore.[20] According to Meade, Reynolds had told the President positively that he would not accept the offer. No if's or but's about freedom of control.[21] If this was the correct version, had Reynolds decided that promises from Washington were not to be trusted? At any rate the greatest chance of his career had touched him and he had brushed it off.

Meade had more to report on Reynolds' conference with Lincoln. "He spoke, he says, very freely to the President about Hooker, but the President said he was not disposed to throw away a gun because it missed fire once; that he would pick the lock and try it again."[22] Lincoln seemed to be insisting on Hooker against Reynolds' protests. In refusing the command himself, Reynolds might well have suggested someone else. Meade?[23]

Even the last sentence of Meade's letter carried news of his friend. He had just heard that Reynolds would command the army's right wing, which would include the 1st, Sickles' 3rd, and Meade's 5th.[24] That would put Reynolds over him at the very time Meade was dreaming of full army command. Those early rumors about his own prospects seemed to have died out. It was Reynolds who went up to Washington and now Reynolds who might lead three army corps. So much more gall to Meade's pride.

Word of Reynolds' new command was correct. Butterfield had sent him a confidential message to that effect on June 12. But it stated clearly that his command of the right wing would hold only until such time as Hooker should arrive from the left. This might be a matter of weeks or only of days, depending on the army's need to concentrate. Lee's movements continued north and west. At first Hooker suspected only a raid, and Reynolds had orders not to let enemy troops cross to the upper bank of the Rappahannock. Next day, when Lee's march looked more serious, Reynolds got another wire: "You must keep them from getting in advance of us, through Manassas Gap, between the Army of the Potomac and Washington. . . . You will also realize the important duties intrusted to you."[25] Hooker was putting high faith in an officer he had so recently accused of lacking confidence in his commanding general.

Now the days of hard marching began. Moving out from White Oak Church on June 12, the 1st Corps made twenty miles before dark. They were twenty miles of scorching heat and choking dust. Fourteen miles more on the 13th brought the troops to Bealeton Station on the Orange and Alexandria railroad, but not for long. Reynolds already had orders to press on to Manassas Junction. In a little over three days he pushed his command sixty-four miles.[26] At every break in the march men sagged to the side of the road and slept. Water was scarce or undrinkable. Finally, on the forenoon of the 15th, the command staggered into Centreville for a day and a half of rest.

Reynolds marched his men relentlessly, but he never forgot their needs. A captain in one of his regiments admired the consideration of "that dark, silent, alert man." He wrote: "It was particularly on those trying occasions that we learned to appreciate the superior ability of General Reynolds in caring for his troops and providing for their comfort." No matter how long the march Reynolds' staff carried his order to every regiment in his command: "You will have time to make coffee if you so desire." If no such order came, no fires were started, the captain said. The 1st Corps never built an unused fire, and in this denuded country fuel for fires was in short supply. At night there was no uncertain shifting of weary regiments from one point to another. Reynolds picked the camp in advance, and as each brigade came up it was directed to a site already provided with both wood and water. "It was all very simple," the captain concluded, "but it did require considerable extra care and trouble on the part of the Corps Commander: and we soldiers of the 1st Corps were very fortunate that our general had, not only common sense, but sufficient humanity in his heart to use it."[27]

On June 15 Reynolds set up headquarters in Centreville. Meanwhile Lee had moved north through the Shenandoah Valley, with Stuart carefully screening his advance by holding the passes of Bull Run Mountains. For a second time the enemy were approaching too close to Pennsylvania to suit Governor Curtin. He had issued a proclamation on the 13th. It set up two departments of defense, one at Pittsburgh and the other at Harrisburg. General Couch, who had asked to be relieved of service under Hooker, was in charge of the state capital.

Among other things in his proclamation Curtin had said: "I know too well the gallantry and patriotism of the freemen of this Commonwealth."[28] To this remark Reynolds could say, Amen; but in what irony. He knew all about the gallant and patriotic freemen who refused a year ago to move toward Antietam. And by June 16 Curtin himself was complaining that Philadelphia had not responded.[29] At this point, if nobody else could say where Lee was heading, Curtin could and did.

Hooker now had his army pretty well concentrated along the line of the Orange and Alexandria railroad. In this position he was subscribing to the ritual of keeping the Army of the Potomac between Lee and Washington. A Union force under General Milroy had already been driven out of Winchester, opening the Valley as far north as Harpers Ferry. The threat to Pennsylvania did begin to look real. In a dispatch on June 17 Butterfield said enough enemy cavalry had already been reported there to fill up the whole state without leaving room for the inhabitants.[30] But was Pennsylvania really Lee's objective? "We cannot go boggling around until we know what we are going after," Buttterfield added. Hooker could only keep feeling for the mountain passes to the west, probing for hints as to the direction of the Confederate advance.

Reynolds' temporary command of the right wing ended when Hooker came up with the rest of the army. Meade seemed relieved that Reynolds' "honors" had lasted only two days, as he reckoned it. But he was forgetting an order from Reynolds to have his trains filled with subsistence, an order dated the 16th. So Reynolds had commanded him for a whole four days in June, assuming it mattered. More important was the reaction of Reynolds to the command in the first place. Meade wrote: "Reynolds took it into his head that Hooker expected our withdrawal from the Rappahannock was going to be disputed, and that he had been selected for a scapegoat to bear the brunt of the shock."[31] Apparently Reynolds had not been appeased by Hooker's gesture in assigning him the command. If he continued in this attitude his effectiveness under Hooker in future operations was doubtful.

In a general way the Blue Ridge and the Bull Run Mountains now separated the two armies in mid-June. To the north some of Lee's cavalry and infantry had got as far as Chambersburg in Pennsylvania, while to the south A. P. Hill had yet to pull all of his corps out of Culpeper, Virginia. Longstreet and most of Ewell's corps were in the Shenandoah between these two extremes. Of Hooker's infantry Reynolds' corps was closest to the enemy. Only Kilpatrick's cavalry operated west of him, trying to drive Stuart from Aldie's Gap in order to see where Lee was headed.

On the 19th the 1st Corps pushed farther west along the small railroad between Alexandria and Leesburg. At Guilford Station Reynolds halted for five days, and from there he wrote his sisters:

Ellie's letter of the 15th came yesterday. The Army has moved up so as to cover Washington but we have not yet been able to discern where-abouts the enemy is exactly. Our cavalry has been fighting on our flanks, but no large infantry force of the enemy has been discovered this side of the Blue Ridge. It is possible that Lee is yet in the Shenandoah Valley. Our cavalry drove them back yesterday to Upperville in the direction of Ashby's Gap. We may have to move up after them by the gaps or through Harper's Ferry—tho' it is impossible to say where the enemy is with any certainty. I am well. With much love to all at home and greetings to the newcomer, William R. Landis. Sam I have not seen or heard of since he was in Washington.[32]

The Army of the Potomac still seemed to be boggling around, groping uncertainly after an enemy that threatened the north. The pattern of September 1862 was repeating itself. Once again Reynolds was pushing his command in the direction of his home state. And just as before, Governor Curtin was trying desperately to rally the people of the Commonwealth to their own defense. "I will not insult you by inflammatory appeals," he said in Philadelphia on June 25.[33] No matter what he said this time, the response would be slight. Reynolds could be thankful that General Couch had already taken charge of the troops about Harrisburg.[34] Another stint with the Pennsylvania militia would have been two too many for Reynolds.

By the 25th it was finally clear that Lee was going into Pennsylvania. On the same day Hooker again gave Reynolds additional command, the 3rd and 11th Corps, as well as the cavalry scouting the gaps to the west.[35] The 5th Corps was not included in the order, so Meade escaped his earlier embarrassment over having to report to Reynolds. But just the same, Meade was occupied with matters of command. In a long letter to his wife he rated his chances of leading the army as slim, and teasingly accused her of harboring ambitions for him. He also had the honesty to admit that others were as qualified for the command as himself.[36]

Toward evening of the 25th Reynolds reached Poolesville, where Hooker had his headquarters. The 1st Corps, with Doubleday in command, had crossed the Potomac at Edwards Ferry in the morning and marched ten miles in the rain. Doubleday found Reynolds anxious about Pennsylvania. He said his general was all for attacking Lee at once, before he plundered the whole state.[37] Reynolds' staff felt his

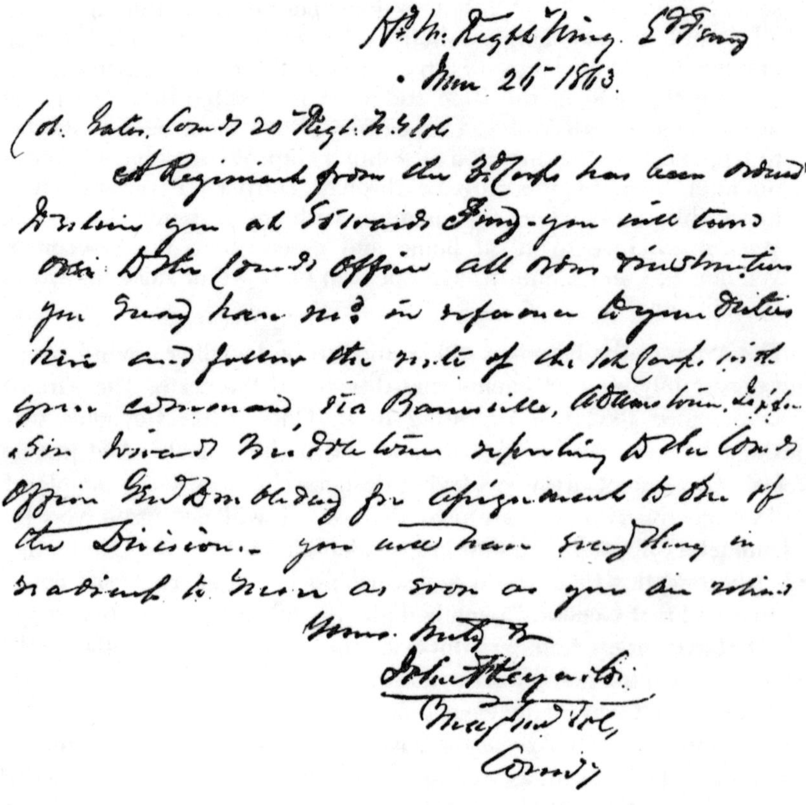
Hd. Qrs. Right Wing Edwards Ferry
June 25 1863.

Col. Gates Comdg 20 Regt. N.Y. Vols

A Regiment from the 3d Corps has been ordered to relieve you at Edwards Ferry - you will turn over to the Comdg Officer all orders and instructions you may have recd in reference to your duties here and follow the route of the 1st Corps with your command via Barnesville, Adamstown, Jefferson and towards Middletown reporting to the Comdg Officer Genl Doubleday for assignment to one of the Divisions - you will have everything in readiness to move as soon as you are relieved

Yours Resply
John F. Reynolds
Maj Genl Vols,
Comdg

Field order from General Reynolds to Colonel Theodore B. Gates, June 25, 1863.

impatience too. "The Old Man," as they called him, was in anything but an amiable mood. They saw him really smile only once during these days of punishing marches. One day exhausted men had begun to drop out of a regiment moving on the left at the head of a column. A private shouted out: "Captain Jones, we're left in front, aren't we?" They were, the captain told him, but why ask? "Because, if we don't soon get a rest, I'm thinking most of us will be left behind."[38] Reynolds overheard his soldier's complaint and at once brought the column to a halt. An old punster himself, Reynolds could forgive it in others. And this one he even rewarded.

But the marching went on. The corps was on the road at four in the morning of the 26th, moving north along the Potomac toward Point of Rocks, in Maryland. The strain worked another of Reynolds' men up to logging his foot-miles for the two years of his service. As of June 26 he put down a total of 1,476 miles.[39] Complaining to his general would have got the soldier little sympathy. In his own time Reynolds had legged it too many miles himself, and under hotter skies. So the chase after Lee pressed forward. On every available road infantry threaded the jam of wagons, batteries, caissons, ambulances. Teamsters swore and lashed at sweating animals; and until it rained on the 25th, dust caked on soldiers' faces to form indistinguishable masks. Sunstroke continued to take its toll, and even officers dropped from their saddles.[40]

Fortunately the 27th called for a march of only eight miles, which brought Reynolds close to Frederick. By now Lee had all his infantry in Pennsylvania. Stuart had been allowed to get off on another raid away from the army. Ewell's corps had moved up the Susquehanna where it threatened Harrisburg from across the river. From his headquarters in Jefferson Reynolds wired Hooker: "General Ewell is with Early's division in person, and this column evidently directed on Gettysburg."[41] This little town in Adams County would draw more attention to itself later. Meanwhile Reynolds got off another wire: "The cavalry sent out by Stahel does nothing."[42] With his home state already invaded, Reynolds was going to be a hard man to please.

In the state capital people were frightened, but they showed far less interest in defending themselves than they had at the beginning of the threat in 1862. The same correspondent who had covered Harrisburg during the Antietam campaign returned to the city. It was bedlam, he reported. "The railroad stations were crowded with an excited people . . . shouting, screaming, as if the Rebels were about to dash into the town and lay it in ashes." Everywhere he found only the desire to escape, never the urge to fight. "In '62 the cry was, 'Drive the enemy from our soil!' in '63, 'Where shall we hide our goods?' "[43] In from the east marched troops of both New York and New Jersey, to protect a state too apathetic to supply enough of its own.[44] Up in Massachusetts young John Codman Ropes was shocked at the "utter imbecility of the People of Pennsylvania. . . . A little ravishing and burning might wake up the lummoxes." But he had only praise for Curtin's efforts to arouse them.[45]

This craven attitude on the part of his state would not surprise Reynolds. His experience with the militia had prepared him. Still, there was another side to this sorry picture, as Reynolds had reason to know. Nearly all the fighting Pennsylvanians seemed to be in service —over 200,000 by the end of 1862.[46] In the Army of the Potomac alone they counted 68 regiments of infantry, ten of cavalry and seven batteries.[47] Included among the infantry were nine regiments Reynolds was proud to claim for the Commonwealth. Those stout Pennsylvania Reserves (except four regiments) had returned to the field. The stay-at-home civilians of their state should have read a sentence or two from the petition of the 2nd Regiment Reserves to their brigade commander, Colonel William McCandless: ". . . Under McCall, Reynolds, Meade, Seymour, Sinclair and yourself we have more than once met and fought the enemy when he was at home. We now wish to meet him again where he threatens our homes, our families and our firesides."[48]

Added to this kind of spirit was the fact that three of Hooker's seven corps and all his cavalry were led by Pennsylvanians. One of them, Reynolds, commanded three corps. Winfield Scott Hancock had the 2nd Corps, and Meade of course the 5th. The cavalry leader was General Pleasonton. So the army moving into Frederick on the night of the 27th did not lack for defenders whose special concern was their invaded state. They would make amends for any shortcomings at home.

That same Saturday evening Reynolds rode eight miles northeast into the city. He had tried ten months before to reach Frederick, though from the opposite direction. On that march Curtin had plucked him from the army before he made it. At the time, his plans had included calling on his cousin Mary Catherine Reynolds, and now he was determined to see her. People with northern sympathies had their troubles in this semisouthern city. Any encouragement he could give her now would be doubly welcome in the wake of an enemy that had just decamped to threaten the Union stronghold. But getting his three corps settled around Middletown had taken too long. It was quite late to expect the maiden ladies of this Reynolds household to remain up. He had better wait until next day.

The early morning hours of Sunday, June 28 affected Reynolds' life far more than merely postponing a visit. The Army of the Potomac had a new commander before daylight. Hooker had wanted Harpers Ferry given up and the 10,000 troops in that garrison added to his own force. This request only capped a conflict that had been going on between Hooker and the general-in-chief in Washington. When Halleck refused to let Harpers Ferry go, Hooker asked to be relieved.[49] Hours later on Sunday Hooker wrote an order which began with these two sentences: "In conformity with orders of the War Department, dated June 27, 1863, I relinquish the command of the Army of the Potomac. It is transferred to Major General George G. Meade, a brave and accomplished soldier, who has nobly earned the confidence and esteem of this army on many a well fought field."[50] The new appointment was by order of the President, and Meade answered in part: "As a soldier, in obeying this order—an order totally unexpected and unsolicited—I have no promises or pledges to make."[51] It was an order, not an offer; and it left Meade virtually no choice.

News of the change riffled swiftly down through the army. The Reserves were reported as generally enthusiastic over the selection of Meade.[52] It took General Alexander Webb's Philadelphia Brigade by surprise, but was received with satisfaction.[53] An officer with Sedgwick described the reaction of the 6th Corps commander when he heard the news. Digging spurs into his horse, he led his staff at a hot gallop for some distance until his feelings simmered down.[54] Like Reynolds, Sedgwick outranked Meade, and it had been rumored earlier that he too had been felt out in Washington regarding army command.[55] He might not want the command for himself, yet the habit of seniority died hard in old soldiers.

Some comment definitely favored others to head the army. A soldier in the 3rd Corps had no use for Meade, at least as a successor to Hooker or others who outranked him.[56] In a 3rd Corps regiment opinion went against Meade until somebody remembered: "It's all right, boys. That's 'Old Pennsylvania Reserves'—they say he's a brick!"[57] General Carl Schurz of Howard's 11th Corps still thought the army would have preferred Reynolds.[58] Others agreed with this opinion.[59]

As might be expected, Reynolds was the commander generally wanted by the men of his own corps, though apparently not by all. His New Jersey regiments left no record of preference. They merely said Meade had yet to be proved and was too little known in the army.[60] The 150th Pennsylvania still liked Hooker, as well as objecting to the swapping of horses in midstream.[61] The 33rd Massachusetts also liked Hooker, though Meade was well regarded.[62] But General James Wadsworth's biographer said the 1st Corps heard the news of Meade's appointment with a pang of regret. "Reynolds, they believed, was the great soldier, clear-sighted, cool, yet full of ardor; a fighter by instinct and master of his art."[63]

In the 24th Michigan of the famed Iron Brigade there could be only one nomination:

> Perhaps few knew him intimately, for he was a strangely reticent man and it may be that the fate of other officers, his equals in rank, taught him more and more the wisdom of guarded speech. But the quiet demeanor could not wholly mask the ardent spirit. His opponents recognized his ability and his soldiers knew that he held in reserve a latent force of clear and coolheadedness that could always be relied upon. They trusted him implicitly. And when the news reached the First Corps that Hooker had been relieved, it was not strange that many of us jumped to the conclusion that our Reynolds would be selected. . . . And yet all the while we felt that we wanted him with us and as our special leader rather than have him gain the higher office, for which he was so pre-eminently qualified.[64]

An artilleryman remembered the feeling in Stewart's battery: "In the First Corps it was reported at the start that General Reynolds had been put in Hooker's place, and, of course there was wild enthusiasm; for no commander in any army ever had the respect and affection of his men to a greater degree than Reynolds had of the old First."[65] But the battery commander did call Meade a rattling good fighter. In time even the enemy got around to appraising the change in leaders for the Army of the Potomac. General E. P. Alexander held Meade an excellent fighter but too lacking in audacity for a commanding general. His quarrelsome disposition also hurt him, the Confederate officer thought. Then he added that the army's real choice would have been Reynolds.[66]

Meade now commanded the army regardless of what anybody thought, including himself for that matter. He was in anything but an enviable position. His army was scattered for some miles about him in Maryland. Stuart on one of his recurrent cavalry raids was annoying it, and Lee had close to 80,000 troops in the rich Cumberland Valley of Pennsylvania. They threatened not only Harrisburg but Philadelphia and Washington as well. The citizens were even digging trenches in Pittsburgh. In this predicament Meade would be grateful for all the help he could get, so Reynolds was sure of a wholehearted welcome when he arrived to congratulate the new commanding general on Sunday morning.[67]

The long rivalry between these two men was ended. Meade could forget his frequent pettiness now that he had the army. And Reynolds had no reason for rancor. It was true that Meade had been offered more freedom of action[68] than Washington apparently had promised

Reynolds, but the administration was in a spot. It had to offer more on June 27 than it had on the 2nd. Besides, in the crisis facing them, these two Pennsylvanians had stature enough to rise above personal vanity. Their own state and with it their own cause could suffer in the days ahead. They had more to worry about than the dead issue of their respective rank. And for once Meade would not begrudge his friend a wing command. As soon as the army moved north again Hooker's old arrangement with Reynolds would be continued.[69] This time Meade was unlikely to raise a jealous eye if the appointment lasted longer than two days.

On Sunday afternoon Reynolds finally managed to squeeze in a call on Cousin Catherine. He would not pass through without seeing her and her sisters. Family counted with Reynolds, and it included these nieces of his father.[70] Like Hal and Ellie, they were unmarried, and now especially they would be grateful for this northern cousin who came riding into the city on the enemy's heels. Surrounded by a friendly army and with his presence, these loyal members of the family would gain confidence and hope. Even in the taut hours when his commanding general was trying to put together a plan of operations, Reynolds had to find time for this visit. Catherine would have a lot to tell the girls in Philadelphia once she got the chance to write.[71]

By Monday morning at four the army was on its way toward Pennsylvania. It rained most of the day, and Doubleday found the march long and toilsome.[72] But the troops seemed to find it otherwise, for all the thirty miles they had to cover. At last they were out of denuded Virginia. Instead of a countryside wasted by two years of war, they saw fertile fields again, ripening orchards, houses bright with paint. Great barns yawned open for the harvest. "Was there any war?" a soldier asked. "The men might have looked at their guns, their dirt, their tents, and at their comrades to convince themselves of it. . . . The dusty roads, the scorching heat, the warm, vapid water from the canteens which had been the experience in Virginia gave way to clear cool wells and to a day of clouds and showers."[73] Others saw these things, and more too. Every village they passed through—Adamsville, Lewistown, Catoctin Furnace, Mechanicstown—brought out the population with flags and cheering. Along the roads women offered water, bread, pastries, and fruit.[74] This was an army moving among its own people at last.

If the happy change struck Reynolds, he gave it little thought. Riding on far in advance of his corps, he reached Emmitsburg by midafternoon. Of all the army, his infantry was closest to Lee, and he was straining to get it closer. His new commanding general would understand the urge. Together they had been held down too long—half an attack under Burnside, then none at all under Hooker. Reynolds knew where he stood with Meade. This time he had only to catch up with the enemy to fight him. At 3:15 he got off a dispatch to headquarters: two of Lee's divisions near Gettysburg, another close to Carlisle, and farther to the west a whole corps said to be moving toward Chambersburg. Reynolds added that he was sending some local citizens to Waynesboro to learn what they could.[75] He had battle on his mind. He had even opened his dispatch with the phrase, "I have the honor to report," a strange formality in a simple message about enemy movements.

The rest of Meade's army moved up more slowly that day and not all as directly as the 1st Corps. In some ways it had not been a good first march for the new commander. Through a clerk's error Hancock's 2nd Corps started three hours late, and Slocum of the 12th complained that Sickles was blocking the roads with his 3rd Corps trains. Former secretary of war Simon Cameron wanted Meade to come up faster. He wired Lincoln from Pennsylvania on the evening of June 29, reminding the President that to let Lee cross the Susquehanna was to accept disaster for the entire North. New Jersey's Governor Parker also had advice for the White House. Bring McClellan back to head the Army of the Potomac. Another self-appointed adviser wanted Little Mac for all the armies, and Don Carlos Buell to replace Meade.[76] This was the same General Buell who had been removed from an army command in Kentucky less than a year before. He had been judged too slow. But no matter how peculiar the suggestions and entreaties, Lincoln could ill afford to have this army fail again—on political as well as military grounds.

Meade felt the weight of the command so abruptly handed him, as he frankly admitted to his wife on June 30.[77] He needed help and he turned to his friend Reynolds. He now assigned him the left wing of the army, which would include Reynolds' own 1st, and the 3rd and 11th Corps.[78] This order placed Sickles, a political general, and Howard, whose 11th had won no friends at Chancellorsville, under leadership that Meade had every reason to trust. The command also embraced John Buford's two cavalry brigades, along with a reserve. Reynolds now was responsible for almost half of Meade's 100,000 men. More important, Reynolds' troops were farthest in advance. Buford was in Gettysburg by noon of the 30th, where he found everybody in a state of excitement. In fact, the force he had just driven out left pickets within five miles of the town.[79]

Before the day ended, Reynolds moved four miles closer to Gettysburg himself. Howard halted his corps near Emmitsburg, from where the 1st Corps had started. Sickles encamped ten or more miles to the east at Taneytown. Around noon Meade had wired Reynolds to fall back again to Emmitsburg if Lee pressed him in any force. "Your present position was given more with a view to an advance on Gettysburg, than on a defensive point."[80] This idea of advancing on Gettysburg sounded good enough to Reynolds that he ordered Sickles to close up toward the other two corps in the left wing. He carried out the new theme in a postscript to the order: "Face towards Gettysburg."[81] But Sickles answered that he had conflicting orders from Meade, who had previously told him to remain where he was.[82] There certainly would be trouble if the commanding general insisted on issuing separate instructions to corps he had placed under Reynolds.[83] With two great armies maneuvering dangerously close to a battle, Meade could not afford the luxury of confusing his orders.

Reynolds had set up headquarters in Moritz Tavern, a small house on the right of Emmitsburg road near Marsh Creek. In the late afternoon a staff officer arrived from Meade. He was to stop by for information before going on to see Buford at Gettysburg. Of Reynolds he said afterwards: "I shall never forget his calm, quiet dignity and true soldierly appearance as he courteously arose to receive me, and offering me a chair, asked whether I was alone, and which way I was going." Reynolds had pushed aside the stack of reports and maps on his table to make room for a cup of tea and several crackers. "A very frugal repast," the officer said to him, "considering the work we may have to do to-morrow." He left Reynolds twenty minutes later, expecting to return with word from Gettysburg on his way back to Meade.[84]

At sunset Howard rode up the six miles from Emmitsburg at his commander's request. He found Reynolds in a back room of the tavern, working at the pile of papers before him. Together the two men discussed Meade's circulars and dispatches, reports from scouts and from citizens of the area. They also studied the maps. As a young instructor at West Point Howard had known Reynolds when he commanded the cadet corps. Reynolds had greatly impressed him then, and still did. He would be a most careful listener to any opinions or advice from his general on fighting the battle that threatened. After several hours, when Howard finally left, he had the feeling that Reynolds definitely expected a battle and that he seemed depressed.[85] That might be. For all his willingness to fight, Reynolds was not rash. He had no stomach for going into battles blind. As of this June 30 evening he knew too little about Lee's positions while knowing only too well the scattered locations of the various corps under Meade.

Around 10 o'clock there was still no late word from Buford. This was ominous because the cavalry leader held the spot of highest tension at the moment. Reluctantly Reynolds wrote army headquarters at Taneytown:

> I have forwarded all the information to you that I have been able to gain to-day. I think if the enemy advances in force from Gettysburg, and we are to fight a defensive battle in this vicinity, that the position to be occupied is just north of the town of Emmitsburg, covering the Plank road to Taneytown. He will undoubtedly endeavor to turn our left by way of Fairfield and the mountain roads leading down into the Frederick and Emmitsburg Pike, near St. Mary's College.
>
> The above is mere surmise on my part. At all events an engineer officer ought to be sent up to reconnoitre this position, as we have reason to believe the main force of the enemy is in the vicinity of Cashtown, or debouching from the Cumberland Valley above it.[86]

Like the obedient soldier he was, Reynolds remembered his instructions earlier in the day—to fall back if attacked in force. It was also the logical move if Lee threatened his left flank. Since Fairfield was directly west of his present position, he would have to withdraw to connect with Howard. Finally, he stressed the approach of the enemy's army as much as he dared, pending further word from Buford. Given what he knew as of this hour on June 30, it was the best Reynolds could do. He gave his aide Major William Riddle the message, along with other reports that might be of interest to Meade, then sent him off to Taneytown.[87]

But John Buford had not forgotten his commander. He sent a staff officer down Emmitsburg road to Moritz Tavern with a dispatch marked 10:30 p.m. The situation was clearer now. A. P. Hill's corps was massed behind Cashtown, with Longstreet on the way to join him. Part of Ewell's corps had moved southwest from Carlisle, and the rest were advancing from York.[88] Unless the pattern shifted abruptly the Army of Northern Virginia ought to converge on Gettysburg sometime next day.

At midnight Reynolds wrapped himself in a blanket and lay down on the floor.[89] He had crammed a day and part of a night with study, consultation, guessing, and advising. No point now in undressing and climbing into bed. Lee was only a few hours distant, and in Reynolds' own Pennsylvania. Lancaster was less than 60 miles off to the east. This war had worked itself back to where John Reynolds used to shoot ducks and quail. It almost encroached on streams where he had fished or swum or skated. The earth-shake of guns might soon roll through valleys and over hills he had covered on horseback in the 1830's.

Beyond this ground lay Philadelphia, with Harry and Kate, the new baby, Hal and Ellie. Beyond them were his sister Jennie and her husband in Baltimore.

But if Buford was right, at least the Reynolds brothers, sisters, and in-laws looked safer now. Lee's present concentration bore away from them toward the little town six miles north of Moritz Tavern, where Reynolds hoped for a few hours' rest. As long as the Confederate leader had brought the war this close to home, it might as well be here. At Gettysburg Reynolds might have some say regarding Lee's intentions. There was still that sentence in Meade's noon order: "Your present position was given more with a view to an advance on Gettysburg, than on a defensive point." Advance was a fine word—a word that could stand more emphasis in the operations of the Army of the Potomac. It was a good word to sleep on. ". . . position was given more with a view to an advance . . ."

CHAPTER VII

"For God's Sake, Forward!"

William Riddle got back from Taneytown at four o'clock on the morning of July 1. He hated to wake Reynolds from his only good sleep in nights, but he had brought an important order. Once roused, the general lay quietly for some time, one hand under his head, his dark eyes staring at the ceiling. He had Riddle read the order three times, and no wonder.[1] The 1st Corps would march to Gettysburg; the 11th to Gettysburg or supporting distance. That much sounded all right. Sickles' 3rd was to move up to Emmitsburg, which was all right too, considering the single available road north from that point. But Meade was holding the 2nd, 5th, 6th, and 12th Corps too far back. Even the small margin of aggressive intent in his first order seemed to have vaporized: ". . . The General believes he has relieved Harrisburg and Philadelphia, and now desires to look to his own army, and assume position for offensive or defensive, as occasion requires, or rest to the troops."[2]

The one positive fact in the order that concerned Reynolds was enough to get him on his feet. He was taking his corps into Gettysburg. If it moved him head-on into Lee and the Confederate general showed fight, there could well be one. Of course fighting was no way to rest troops, nor did Meade's leisurely forward movement look as if he expected to fight. Yet by now he knew of Lee's continuing concentration in the area. He still wanted Reynolds at Gettysburg, and that was where Reynolds would go.

The sooner the 1st Corps started, the sooner room could be made on the road for Howard's 11th. Wadsworth's division, which had led the march on the 30th, expected Robinson's and Rowley's (Doubleday's) to go past them today. But Reynolds rode over to see Wadsworth himself. Never mind the routine marching order; to save time he wanted the division put on the road at once.[3] Shortly after six he heard from Howard, who had received the order from Meade to move up in support of the 1st Corps. Reynolds told Howard to start, and that he hoped both the 1st and 11th Corps might be in Gettysburg by evening. He also sent word for Sickles to come into position north of Emmitsburg.[4] With Buford's two cavalry brigades already in Gettysburg, Reynolds would have fairly tight control of his entire command.

Within the next hour he called in Doubleday, who commanded the 1st Corps now that Reynolds led the left wing. Together they went over the orders and reports. Reynolds said he had already sent Wadsworth on, along with Hall's 2nd Maine Battery. Doubleday was to call in the pickets, and arrange for starting the other two divisions and the rest of the artillery.[5] Then around 8 o'clock Reynolds gathered his staff and with them took to the road. They soon caught up with Wadsworth and moved out ahead on the march. Behind Wadsworth and his staff came Brigadier General Lysander Cutler's 2nd Brigade of the 1st Division. It was led by the 76th New York. Following in order were the 56th Pennsylvania, 147th New York, 95th New York, and the 84th New York (14th Brooklyn).[6] If any excitement lay up ahead, these troops would be the first Union infantry on the field.

The distance from Moritz Tavern to Gettysburg was six miles. Riding along with Reynolds, Captain Edward Baird thought his general was more silent than even his usual self.[7] But to others of the staff he seemed otherwise. In fact, it semed to them that Reynolds had thrown off a great load from the time of Meade's appointment. He had not been in better spirits since the period just before Chancellorsville. Except for Baird, these young men around Reynolds remembered him as having talked and joked far more than commonly during the marches up from Frederick.[8]

Reynolds' improved spirits could be accounted for. He certainly trusted Meade far more than he ever had Hooker, despite the hint of irresolution in this morning's order from Taneytown. Reynolds also knew that Meade trusted him.[9] This trust gave him more elbow room in command than ever before. At the same time, in permitting himself to be passed over for the army command, Reynolds had found both release and relaxation.

These reasons hardly added up to lightheartedness, of course, when there was so much threat in what lay ahead. Pennsylvania was invaded; the North was frightened; the Army of the Potomac would have to close with a foe that usually whipped it; and Reynolds was deeply involved in it all. But the army *was* on the way to meet Lee, and Reynolds led the advance. For once in this war he might have some say about fighting. Reynolds could not help feeling grim satisfaction in that. It may have been the reason why most of his staff found him less dour than they expected.

The silence on Reynolds' part that Captain Baird remembered may well have set in as they approached Gettysburg. The head of the column could hear the boom and roll of guns from the low ridges west of the town. Buford must have made contact. On hearing these sounds, an experienced soldier would begin to eye the kind of ground he was moving toward. By this time Reynolds would have on his right a fair-sized hill and to the north a smaller one. Beyond there he might make out a gentle rise shaping toward a third hill just south of town.[10] With firing in front of him, it was a simple instinctive reflex to look for defensive positions in rear.

Here, about a mile south of Gettysburg, the reliable Buford supplied the answer to what was going on. An aide from the cavalryman brought word that Confederates had been pouring down from the direction of Cashtown since daybreak. Buford had dismounted both Gamble's and Devin's brigades to make a stand about a mile west of Gettysburg. They had Calef's battery with them. The cavalry would need help if Reynolds wanted them to stay there.[11]

Wadsworth had joined Reynolds to learn his decision. It was now about 9 o'clock. The sun already gave off a steaming heat that could raise sweat on the gleaming flanks of Reynolds' big black mount.[12] From this little conclave on the road would come a fateful order. A great battle could take place here if Reynolds decided he did want Buford to stay. And there was Meade's dispatch of the day before: ". . . if they advance against me, I must concentrate at that point where they show the strongest force." Well, the word from Buford certainly sounded like force. Then that other sentence from the same message: "Your present position was given more with a view to an advance on Gettysburg than on a defensive point."[13] Reynolds' newest orders were more positive. Go to Gettysburg, they said.

But what about the town, the people, and their homes? To defend the place from inside would lay it open to destruction. Reynolds was the kind of soldier who would think of that. Besides, his infantry had not begun to come up yet. How long could Buford hold on? Reynolds answered these questions in a matter of moments. He would try to save the town by supporting Buford's position west of it.[14] He sent his aide Captain Joseph G. Rosengarten to warn citizens to stay in their

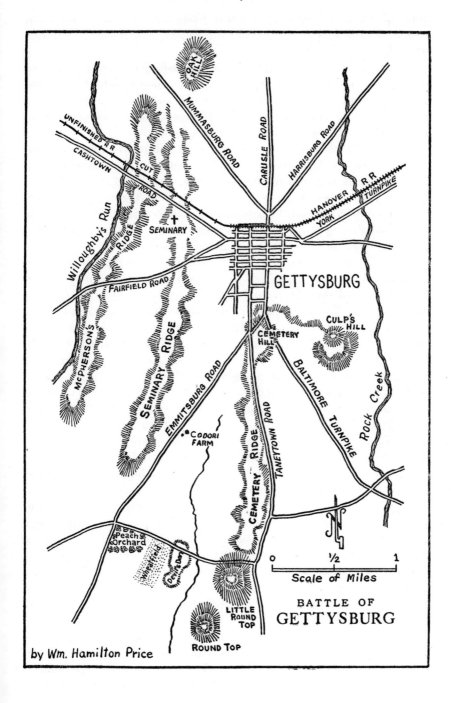

BATTLE OF
GETTYSBURG

by Wm. Hamilton Price

houses.[15] Then leaving Wadsworth to hurry up the column, Reynolds rode into town and turned left for the Lutheran Seminary a half-mile beyond.[16]

Buford saw the general from the cupola, where he had been watching the first of A. P. Hill's divisions deploy along both sides of the Cashtown road. He started down the ladder and was met by Reynolds part way. "What's the matter, John?" Reynolds asked. The cavalryman shook his head, then answered: "The devil's to pay."[17]

Things did look bad—and especially so to Buford. His men had been on horseback for days, scouting or skirmishing, almost without rest.[18] Now here came Hill bearing down on them, and Longstreet was not far behind. Ewell meanwhile was converging from the north and east. Most of Lee's 75,000 men[19] would soon be hammering at this little town. So far, all that opposed the threat were two cavalry brigades and a single battery. Buford's concern was understandable.

Reynolds knew all this too. He asked Buford if he thought he could hang on till the 1st Corps came up. Buford reckoned he could. When Reynolds heard that, he turned to give a verbal message to Captain Stephen Weld. The aide was to ride in all haste to Taneytown and tell the commanding general that the enemy were advancing in force. Reynolds would hold on as long as he could even if driven through Gettysburg from house to house.[20] Next, to an officer just up from Howard, Reynolds sent off an appeal for help.[21] Other aides dashed off with messages to Doubleday and Sickles. Then Reynolds mounted and headed back to where he had left Wadsworth on the Emmitsburg road. Instead of going through town, he cut across the fields to the south, his escort knocking down fences as they rode along. This would make the shortest route for getting troops onto a battlefield.[22]

By now there was furious excitement in Gettysburg. Captain Rosengarten, with two or three burgesses and several clergymen, argued futilely in an effort to get the people off the streets.[23] But they continued to mill about everywhere—some only restless, many frightened, all of them curious. Where facts failed, rumor filled in. The skirmishing already begun on the ridges out to the west was only the start. Nine roads made a wheel leading into the center of town, each pounded by the feet, hooves, and iron tires of two great armies. It was asking too much to expect the citizens of this once quiet town to sit in their houses to-day. At least not yet.

When Reynolds got back to Wadsworth near the Codori farm, his first regiments were coming up. The two generals put their staffs and the "pioneers" with their axes to work completing the destruction of the fences across the fields to the west.[24] As fast as the men reached the point for turning off, they were switched in the direction of Seminary Ridge. Reynolds reined up for a few moments to watch the 1st Corps veterans file by. The same captain who had admired his consideration for troops on the march saw him here. "General Reynolds sat upon his horse on the west side of the highway facing us, and as we marched near the head of the column we had a fair view of his features. . . . The general looked careworn, and we thought, very sad."[25]

Careworn, yes. Riddle had called Reynolds' four-hour sleep of the 30th his best in days. But that was the least of it. Like the captain, other soldiers must have glanced up when they swung to the left in front of him. Few, if any, were likely to look with distrust. Reynolds was known as a commander who took care of his men. They would approach the direction of the firing with confidence. Reynolds knew this, and it was a terrible responsibility. In holding Buford west of Gettysburg, he had offered these men in support. The offer must not become a sacrifice. Reynolds' face could well have shown the extra dimension of anxiety that grew out of his decision. But sadness probably was not the word to describe his feelings. His prompt decision to go in was completely in character. He trusted his own judgment. Lee had to be met, and Reynolds would meet him here.[26] At last this army was getting to the work at hand. The prospect was enough to buoy up a born fighter like Reynolds.[27]

As soon as he was satisfied that all was being done to hurry the column, Reynolds rode ahead to rejoin Buford at the Seminary. At this point Rosengarten appeared to report his troubles with the people in town. Reynolds showed his dissatisfaction at what his aide said, then looked at his spattered glasses. "Oh, they have been throwing dirt in your eyes."[28] If Reynolds still had the urge to pun at a time like this, he must have been feeling all right.

With Buford, Reynolds now rode out to the next ridge, some six hundred yards west of the Seminary. Most of Gamble's brigade was fighting on the left of the Cashtown road, facing perpendicular to it. Against Gamble's men Archer's brigade of Heth's division was trying to cross a small stream called Willoughby's Run. If the Confederates could get over and climb the slope through a grove of trees on the McPherson farm, they would cause trouble. North of the road another brigade of Heth's under Davis was pressing Devin's dismounted brigade. Calef's battery straddled the road itself, with two guns on the right and four on the left, or south side of the road.[29]

For Buford it was a tight spot, as Reynolds could see at once. The morning was getting on toward 10 o'clock by now,[30] and these troopers had stood off the growing assault for around two hours. Behind Archer and Davis two other enemy brigades had formed, while the advance of Pender's division was sending up dust hardly a half-mile in their rear. It would soon bring about 15,000 men to bear on the 2,500 of Buford and 8,200 of the 1st Corps—if they could be brought up in time.[31]

Reynolds wheeled about just as Cutler's brigades began to move out on the Cashtown road north of the Seminary. Next came Captain James Hall with the battery. When Reynolds got to the guns, he picked up their commander and turned west again to show him his position. Later Hall remembered this short ride out to the relief of Calef. He got the very definite impression, he said, that Reynolds was really in earnest, that he had no intention of leaving this battlefield.[32] Every move and gesture Reynolds made in the next feverish moments bore Hall out.

It was a scramble to deploy Cutler's regiments before Davis could strike. From left to right north of the road Reynolds placed the 147th New York, the 56th Pennsylvania, and the 76th New York. To the south of the road he threw in the 14th Brooklyn on the left, and the 95th New York on the right.[33] In this position the 95th would support Hall, who was just across the road to the north. Hall's support on the right would come from the 147th New York. Now the cavalry could retire to protect the flanks, but it would take more than replacing fought-out troopers to hold this line. Reynolds was relieved to see Doubleday ride up and to hear that the Iron Brigade was beginning to come on the field near the Seminary.[34] Yet even with these new arrivals thrown out to the left of Cutler, he would have a front that was far too narrow and thin—nearly a mile from left to right.

Reynolds would do with what he had. He told Doubleday he would hold on to the Cashtown road while Doubleday put the left regiments of the Iron Brigade in position to defend the road from Hagerstown and Fairfield.[35] The enemy driving in from the west might use more than a single road. At this stage nothing could move fast enough to suit Reynolds. Davis had already reached the top of the ridge north of the Cashtown road. If he succeeded in overlapping the right flank, Wadsworth would have his hands full. The immediate need was to get that Iron Brigade on the ridge double-quick. Its right had to connect with the 14th Brooklyn on Cutler's left.

In spite of the firing that stepped up ominously north of the road, Reynolds had to turn his back. The Confederate Archer had broken across the ravine of Willoughby's Run and was getting into McPherson's grove. This small wood had to be held because from it the enemy could be enfiladed on either road.[36] So with his orderly, Reynolds rode over the flat of the ridge to check the new threat. He stopped at a point where the wood ended, about two hundred yards from the McPherson barn. From here he could fairly well control the juncture of his two brigades—that is, if Brigadier General Meredith's Iron Brigade ever got up. Reynolds could see them double-quicking across the depression between the two ridges. But double-quick was too slow.

These were famous troops that Reynolds had never really fought. He had to keep them practically idle on his left flank at Fredericksburg, and had seen them inactive again at Chancellorsville. This morning the brigade had marched up to Gettysburg in high spirits. "Find a good place to camp; be sure and get near a good dry rail fence," was the shout carried along to the column's head. And to troops not yet on the march: "Better stay here till we send for you; climate up there may be unhealthy. . . ."[37] Later, when Doubleday pointed to the grove where Reynolds now sat his horse, and told them they had to secure it, he was told: "If we can't hold it, where will you find men who can?"[38]

Finally—it must have seemed hours to Reynolds—the regiments began their evolutions from column into line. They formed in échelon, the 2nd Wisconsin moving up the gentle slope toward the trees. To their left and at intervals in the rear, came the 7th Wisconsin, 19th Indiana, and 24th Michigan.[39] Now Reynolds had to rein his mount to the west. The first of Archer's men had worked up the opposite slope through the grove. It would be a race between them and the Iron Brigade. Come up, 2nd Wisconsin! Impatient, Reynolds wheeled about and galloped back to where his first line was sweeping over the eastern part of the ridge. He turned in behind them and rode down the line. In they went, then reeled back from Archer's first volley. "Forward, forward men!" Reynolds shouted. "Drive those fellows out of that. Forward! For God's sake, forward!"[40] He followed them in among the first trees. This charge could save the whole position. It had to. But Reynolds wanted more men—more men. He turned in the saddle and looked back anxiously toward the Seminary. It was almost 10:30.[41] Where was Rowley with Doubleday's men? The Iron Brigade needed help out here—now!

Seconds later Reynolds sagged to the ground. Sergeant Charles Veil leaped from his horse and ran over to him. The general had fallen face down, toward the west. The orderly could find no wound; there was no bleeding. Taking hold under Reynolds' arms, he dragged him back out of the immediate range of fire.[42] Meanwhile Reynolds' battle went on. With the 2nd Wisconsin anchoring the brigade and flanked on the left by the 7th, the other two regiments curled slowly forward. The 19th Indiana and the 24th Michigan were swinging west, then around to the north to seal Archer's troops in the grove.[43] The Confed-

erate right soon found itself outflanked. The brigadier himself was captured, along with about a thousand of his men. The impetus of the
attack carried the two left regiments of Meredith down over the run
and up to the far ridge beyond. Later Doubleday pulled them back to
re-establish his line.[44] He had beautifully coordinated his left with Reynold's right. For a while at least the threat south of Cashtown road was
over.

North of the road the battle was not going so well. Davis had got
his brigade onto the ridge there before Cutler was safely deployed.
This gave the Confederates the advantage of first fire. Besides, Cutler's
right was in danger of being outflanked. When Wadsworth saw them
staggered by the volley from Davis and noted their plight, he ordered
a withdrawal. The 76th New York and 56th Pennsylvania began to
pull out. But the 147th New York, nearest the road, missed the order
and now they could be overlapped on their right. Hall's battery was
soon in trouble too.[45]

What saved Cutler at this stage was another regiment of the Iron
Brigade. Doubleday had held the 6th Wisconsin out of action to the
south to act as a reserve. Now he ordered them in from the Seminary
to salvage the 147th. They crossed the Cashtown road at an angle that
brought them in on Davis' flank and forced him to face about. By this
time Hall had been driven out, but the 14th Brooklyn and 95th New
York swept over from south of the road to join the 6th Wisconsin. Some
of the 147th New York, no longer isolated, also went in.[46]

The pressure on Davis forced many of his troops into a railroad cut
about a hundred yards or more north of the road. Then an enfilading
fire directed on the regiments in this trap ended the morning for Davis.
One of his regiments was captured intact.[47] So finally what had looked
bad for both of Wadsworth's brigades turned out all right. For the
present, Reynolds' gamble was paying off. If the rest of his old corps
and all of the 11th and 3rd got up before Lee's full strength was on
the field, the heavy losses among Meredith's and Cutler's men could
be justified.

In the lull that set in around 11 o'clock or a little after, other Reynolds aides were able to join Veil. Mitchell had come up shortly after
his general fell. Together he and Veil had examined him. This time they
found a hole where a rifle ball had struck behind the right ear and
passed through Reynolds' head. When they turned him on his back
they heard him gasp once, then smile. But he never spoke and must
have been dead in the first minute or two after he was hit.[48] Willing
hands carried the general's body back to the Seminary, then away from
the battle to a small stone house on the Emmitsburg road.[49]

Later, in the afternoon, an ambulance bearing the body of John Reynolds moved slowly down through the troops coming up to finish the fighting he had begun. Along with an escort were Rosengarten and Veil. "Their faces showed plainly enough what load their vehicle carried. . . . His death affected us much, for he was one of the *soldier* generals of the army. . . ."[50] This was the 2nd Corps, meeting the ambulance about four miles south of Gettysburg. It was noticed by others of the corps around the same time: "A word tells us that it contains the body of the heroic Reynolds borne from his last battlefield. A deep silence falls upon the galloping staff, and nothing is spoken until . . . the panorama of Gettysburg lies unrolled before them."[51] The ambulance continued south to Westminster, Maryland, where Major William Riddle joined the party for the rail trip to Baltimore.[52]

That same afternoon in Frederick, Catherine Reynolds found time to write her cousin Hal. Hal's brother John had been kind enough to stop by on his way north with the army, and Catherine wanted her to have all the details of the visit:

I have been thinking of writing you for the past 3 days to tell you how much I enjoyed Cousin John's brief visit. Judging of your feelings by my own, the most trivial circumstance of so dearly beloved a brother will be of interest to you. We have been in such a state of excitement and confusion since our capture and recapture that I do not remember what I wrote Ellie but think I gave her particulars of the street skirmishes &c. When we heard the Army of the Potomac was really coming my first and constant thought was, Now I shall see Cousin J.

All day Saturday the Cavalry were passing up Market St. and I inquired of several of the soldiers who stopped to eat the bread and butter the ladies were sending out to them (some rode so fast they snatched a piece and in that process much of it fell to the street) if Gen. Reynolds would be through. All who seemed to know anything about him said that he had gone with the infantry by way of Jefferson, a shorter route than this, so I gave up the hope of seeing him for the time, although I had really been so confident he was coming as to prepare a nice dinner. Saturday night we were kept awake by the noisy wagon trains and such a Sunday I never spent. There was scarcely any possibility of crossing the street for the countless multitudes who came pouring through. Quite unable to read for the noise and wearied with looking, about 3 P. M. I undressed to try to get a nap. A few minutes after Clara came up and said Gen. Reynolds was down stairs. It really seemed in my hurry as if I never should get ready to go down. I told Ann to set a table for lunch. Cousin looked very well, said he had returned from Jefferson the night before and would have come round then but thought it too late (but I had a room ready for him and wish so much he had come). He seemed to enjoy the extemporaneous meal of cold roast beef, yellow pickle and cherry pie, said he had eaten nothing that morning being engaged in finding an encampment for his men (said the biscuits "reminded him of home at Kate's House"), promised to return to late tea, after he had been to see his new Commander in Chief for orders and spoke as though they expected to remain here for some time (Whereupon I thought in that case you and Ellie would come on here to be with him and we should have such nice times) but like many of my other plans this was doomed to a disappointment. We waited for him until ½ past 9 o'clock, meanwhile Ann and I gave supper to 17 soldiers who came in at different times asking to buy bread as the shops had all sold out and they had nothing all day. It was truly a pleasure to supply their wants. One very intelligent old man said he had not eaten a meal at a table for 15 months before and that they would never forget how kind the Frederick ladies were to them, so different from the Virginia ladies who used to throw stones after them. Another heard the church bells ringing and said, that sounded like home, we've had no Sunday for a year. Ann's gallon boiler of coffee seemed quite to rest and revive them. I forgot to mention in the right place that the 3 members of Cousin's staff who accompanied him, remained mounted while he stayed and I sent them a plate of sandwiches which no doubt amused our Secesh neighbors, but no matter.

Cousin did not return to supper, nor have I seen him since. Early the next morning he left with his corps and yet there must have been some confusion in the arrangements for two of his officers came here about 8 o'clock on Monday morning (One I think the original of a picture in Ellie's album) inquiring whether the Gen. was here and if I could inform them where his head quarters were the night before. . . .

Cousin talked more than you led me to expect. He was quite communicative, read me a part of Ellie's last letter announcing the birth of little Chester Landis, laughed heartily when I told him that I had told Ellie it did not seem fair for her to have 4 brothers and me to have none and that I had since thought perhaps you could spare Cous Jim, but that he was not much of a lady's man, to which he replied "Yes, I think they might spare you Jim. I expect he is in Harrisburg now," &c. As usual with me I always remember things I wish to ask after the opportunity is passed. The orders must have been very sudden and no news has reached here from them.[53]

No news had reached Catherine Reynolds, but Hal's late brother and Catherine's late cousin had been making news enough. Although the "architect of the battle had fallen,"[54] his tactical plan still shaped the fighting his death passed on—first to Doubleday, then Howard, then

Hancock, and in the end, to the commanding general who had sent him to Gettysburg in the beginning. And whatever the results, they would have to be matched against a terrible morning. The Iron Brigade had lost well over half its 2,500 men. In Cutler's brigade, the 147th New York lost 207 of 380 men in a half-hour near the railroad cut north of Cashtown road. In the 76th New York, 169 out of 375 went down in the same length of time.[55]

Even with losses like these and more, Reynolds' battle was only fairly begun. The remaining two divisions of the 1st Corps came up at 11 o'clock and were moved into position, Rowley on the left, Robinson out to the right. At one o'clock the 11th Corps began filing out north of town and by two had formed its lines. But by now Lee's army was already on the field in greater numbers. Early afternoon saw A. P. Hill engaged to the west of Gettysburg and Ewell's corps moving down from the north to strike both Howard and the right flank of the 1st. Exploiting a gap of several hundred yards between the two Union corps, Ewell gradually drove Howard back into Gettysburg. When this happened, the 1st Corps also had to give ground to protect itself. Hancock had ridden up at 3 o'clock ahead of his corps to take over the command, but nothing could stem the overwhelming Confederate pressure.[56]

The day that began with Reynolds' decision to support Buford was ending. His old corps followed Howard's through the streets of Gettysburg and took up positions on Cemetery and Culp's Hills. As the rest of their army was moving in, they could count their losses in the gathering dusk. The 1st Corps had shrunk from over 8,000 to around 3,000. The 11th was down to 3,800 from 6,000.[57] They had paid high for whatever objective was in Reynolds' mind at the start.

And Reynolds himself had paid. He was dead now because he had ridden into a grove of trees in the very first line of attack. Three army corps and two brigades of cavalry answered to his orders, but he was killed leading a regiment. Buford was said to have warned the general not to expose himself too much. Reynolds had a fault of doing just that.[58] By contrast, Wadsworth, who commanded only a division, had remained back at the Seminary during Cutler's fight. Yet nobody ever accused Wadsworth of lacking physical courage.[59]

All the action on the morning of July 1 could have been observed from the Seminary cupola. It gave a clear view of both McPherson's Ridge and of those beyond. From it the Cashtown and Fairfield roads could be followed from the point of Confederate approach to their apex in the center of town.[60] But Reynolds not only ignored the cupola; he refused to remain on the ridge itself and to direct his troops as they came on the field. Instead he went out the Cashtown road with Hall. With an old artilleryman's eye he posted those six 3-inch guns himself. Once there he stayed. As Cutler's brigade filed up he assigned its stations, regiment by regiment. Then he crossed the road south to scout Archer's advance, to decide where best to put in the Iron Brigade. This was reconnaissance. He was doing here what he had done on the last day of second Bull Run. And at that time it had shocked a soldier into exclaiming that the general's hour had obviously not yet come.[61]

So Reynolds had begun a battle that in one day ground up two army corps and cost him his own life as well. This all had the look of rashness, and at first the charge was made.[62] But the accusing words died out when the fruits of Gettysburg began to be realized. Reynolds' acting out of his final day could pretty well be accounted for. To begin with, Lee had lost some men on July 1, too. Heth and Pender together took casualties of 4,540 out of some 15,000, most of them to the 1st Corps.[63] Not exactly blow for blow, but Reynolds had not gone out there merely to trade losses.

The position itself was everything. Given the risk, Reynolds had to be sure in his own mind that Meade could fight a battle successfully on this ground. Otherwise why tell Buford to hang on? It was a gamble, of course. If his small force got pushed back into Gettysburg before the rest of the army was up, he had wasted everything—his men, himself, the position. But he took the chance. "Reynolds had planted the advance of the Union army in Lee's route, he had secured a position across all the roads leading east from the mountains at this point, a point where the Confederate army must assemble, if it united east of the mountains."[64]

The first day's holding action included saving the defensive position south of the town. It could not concern Reynolds now that Howard would receive the thanks of Congress for having first recognized its importance.[65] Howard did post the first troops there. Equally it could be of no concern to Reynolds that Howard claimed the credit.[66] If it mattered, Reynolds had his defenders.[67]

Still to be answered is why Reynolds moved so far forward himself. For one thing, he would be extremely sensitive to the danger of sending the few men available against double the numbers of Heth and Pender. These were his own troops and it might help if he took them in. They were volunteers, Iron Brigade or no, and volunteers liked to be led.[68] It could make the difference Reynolds wanted. Add another reason—his urge to break the invasion of his own state. "It was a Pennsylvanian who hurried the left wing into action and lost his life in determining that the battle should be fought at Gettysburg, and not on any line more remote."[69] The pull of home soil made it easier for Reynolds to forget his own safety.

There still might be a third motive for Reynolds' going out to McPherson's Ridge. Meade had commanded the army only four days. It did not make for confidence, and Reynolds had read the doubts in the last order he got from Taneytown: ". . . offensive or defensive, as occasion requires, or rest to the troops."[70] The best way of bringing his old friend around to a choice was to leave him none. Go in, hang on, then inform headquarters that its army was engaged in a battle. Hancock's biographer seemed to think Reynolds did exactly that. DeTrobriand also said that Reynolds' actions, not Hancock's reports of Gettysburg, made the commanding general give up his idea of waiting for Lee along Pipe Creek. Meade himself said so.[71] Reynolds may have felt he could best hold the initial ground by making his personal presence count.[72]

Many thought that if Reynolds had lived, the first day would have gone better. It was natural for the general's own staff to think so, as the Lancaster *Daily Express* reported on July 7. The 1st Corps historian quoted General John C. Robinson of Reynolds' 2nd Division: "If Reynolds had lived there would have been a different story of that battle."[73] The artilleryman Augustus Buell thought so too, as did Colonel Martin Hardin of the 12th Pennsylvania Reserves. And there were others.[74]

No matter what might have happened, Reynolds was dead and his body had arrived in Baltimore. His sister Jennie and her husband met it and the escort early Thursday morning. That evening they accompanied the body to Philadelphia, to the Landis home at 1829 Spruce Street.[75] Rosengarten and Riddle had been joined by other aides, and of course Charles Veil was still in faithful attendance.

The shock would be greatest for Ellie. The baby sister had long been John's favorite, with Hal probably a close second. Hal was next youngest, and both were unmarried. For this reason especially John had made them his particular concern. But during the two years of war most of his letters were directed to Ellie. She was the "you" in them, even when the salutation read "sisters." Not that he lacked affection for the three married girls: Lydia, Jennie, and Kate. The last two he visited whenever he could. He had called "Kate's" his home after Lancaster was given up. Just the same, in these next hard days the others would be watching Ellie with anxiety. Her soldier brother's death took so much away from her—a dedication that stretched over years.

But the family soon learned that John Reynolds' death took a great deal more away from another woman. On the field, after Reynolds fell, Major Riddle had found a Catholic medal hung on a chain around his neck. He remembered then how carefully the general had always guarded it.[76] Also on the chain was a gold ring joined in the shape of clasped hands. On the inner band were inscribed the words "Dear Kate." John's own West Point ring was missing. So there must have been a girl. For how long? This close-mouthed brother had never mentioned a girl. As to the ring and the medal, Jennie said in a letter to Will: ". . . we all thought a lady was the donor and must be prized and wished we could only know who and where she was."[77]

They were not long in finding out. The timing showed the dramatic structure of a novel. Friday morning, July 3, a note that went upstairs announced a Miss Hewitt, who wished to see the remains if agreeable. "Is she Kate?" Ellie asked. When told it was, she and Hal went down for her. They fell in love with her at once. "She seems to be a very superior person," Jennie wrote. "We all regret that he had not told some of us about her, and that we had [not] known her, yet are happy she came and had all the comfort we could offer her. Four years ago they met coming from California (I think in 1860). She had his consent to enter a religious convent should she lose him, and now she intends to do it as the world has no interest for her now. . . . They would have been such a happy couple, were going to Europe after the war. She is a lady of means. I won't send a personal description; you would not be disappointed if you saw her but we ought not to judge the looks under such circumstances. I need not tell you what a thunder clap it was to us all."[78]

It would have been excusable in Ellie to feel some resentment toward this stranger who had suddenly moved in to share her grief. But not at all. "Poor girl she has been a heroic mourner and most worthy of our dear one. I cannot tell you all she said of him but she was in his heart and from her I learned much of him, of his feelings and inner life that I never knew before. . . . She made no parade of her religion, nor in any way that was the least disagreeable. She had been expecting him to visit her in Philadelphia on the 8th of July and she said then he was to bring her to us."[79]

If Katherine Hewitt was worthy of John Reynolds as a wife, Eleanor Reynolds was certainly the strongest and most generous-hearted of sisters.

On Saturday Reynolds' body was taken to Lancaster for burial.

The Pennsylvania Railroad, with their usual liberality, had placed one of their handsomest passenger coaches at the disposal of General Reynolds' relatives, for the purpose of conveying them and the corpse to this place. Upon the arrival of the train, this car was taken in charge by a detachment of the returned Reserves, under command of Captain Barton, who opened a passage way through the dense crowd assembled at the depot, and after the relatives and staff of the deceased were seated in carriages, carried the coffin to the hearse. The various church bells ceased the merry peals they had been ringing in honor of the 4th of July, and as the mournful cortege began to move, they tolled forth a mournful requiem for the lamented brave. The hearse was followed by an immense concourse of citizens, headed by all the clergymen in the city, including the venerable Father Keenan. . . .[80]

The family at the funeral included all the sisters except Kate, whose baby had been too recently born. Her husband, Harry Landis, was being held close to Gettysburg with the militia. Of the brothers only Will was absent, unable to leave his station at Port Royal, South Carolina. It was Will whose presence would have meant most to John. He would have wanted Becky, too. Jennie said that the members of the Pennsylvania Reserves had begged for permission to act as pallbearers, a wish the family was pleased to grant. She listed the general's aides as Riddle, Mitchell, Rosengarten, Willcox, and Stephen Weld. They were glad also to have Veil. They found the eighteen-year-old orderly intelligent and they appreciated his devotion to their brother.[81] They never forgot that he was the one closest to his general when the bullet struck and that he brought the body away from the firing.[82]

Governor Andrew Curtin had telegraphed Jim from Harrisburg on the 3rd:

I have hoped until now to be at the funeral of your brother, Major General John F. Reynolds, and to testify by my presence something of the high esteem in which I held him as a gentleman and a soldier while he lived, and the profound sorrow I feel at his death.

I know however that he would not have wished me in this hour of peril to neglect the safety of the State he loved so well, and in whose defence he so willingly died, even to do honor to his memory.

As a General, the whole nation honored and mourns him, but Pennsylvania has reason to cherish with especial pride, alike the noble qualities of character which led him to his high command, and his chivalric courage on the historic battleground where he closed his life so gloriously.[83]

Also from Harrisburg General Couch wired his regrets "that the present emergency of the service prevent my sending such an escort to the funeral of Major General Reynolds as his high rank and brilliant services so eminently deserve."[84] Reynolds would have understood. After all, he had made sure that the "emergency" took place.

But emergency was hardly the word for what went on at Gettysburg while Reynolds' body lay first at Baltimore and then in Philadelphia. July 2 saw Longstreet's corps move in on Seminary Ridge below A. P. Hill to extend Lee's line to the south. Opposite his position, across Emmitsburg road, he could see the exposed salient of Sickles' 3rd Corps. A fearful four hours later Longstreet had broken its southern flank and forced the Union front back onto the ridge extending down from Cemetery Hill. New place names now belonged to American history: the Peach Orchard, the Wheatfield, Devil's Den, and Little Round Top. Of this line, as it ran east from Emmitsburg road, only the crest of Little Round Top remained in Meade's hands. Lose it and his whole position was gone. Fortunately, General Warren had found it undefended, and managed to bring up troops in time to block the sweep of the Confederate right toward its summit.

From north and east of the town Lee had sent in the left of his line to help Longstreet's attack. The list of place names grew: Cemetery Hill itself, Culp's Hill, Spangler's Spring. Ewell's corps struck these points and made some gains on Culp's. But the defense was well dug in and had the guns to offset the loss of units pulled out by Meade to brace Sickles. Lee had less success here and had to see the day close with the Union line intact though pinched and shaken on both flanks.

On July 3rd Lee hit Meade's center. More historic names: the Angle, the Stone Wall, Ziegler's Grove, the Little Clump of Trees. A reluctant Longstreet let Pickett carry out the commanding general's order that sent 15,000 men from Seminary Ridge down over the Emmitsburg road and up across the open fields to Cemetery Ridge. A few reached it; most died there. It cost nearly 10,000 casualties to make the try. Union cavalry fought off further threats to the east and south. By dusk it was all over. In three days each army had lost more than 20,000 in killed, wounded, and missing. For Lee it meant retreat; for Meade the conviction that his army was too spent to mount a counterattack. But the second two days had proved the strength of the Union position that Reynolds' opening fight had done so much to secure. In Harrisburg, Governor Curtin and General Couch could now relax.

The Lancaster papers were generous in their obituaries. At least one of the three funeral sermons was printed in full,[85] along with accounts of the first day's battle and much praise of the general who was now laid at rest in his native city. "He never fought battles through his orderlies and aides, but always in person."[86] "He was exceedingly severe in his discipline, but passionately devoted to his command. . . . He had no mercy for the delinquent officer, but an ever-present indulgence for the errors of the private soldier. He never asked anybody to go in the way of danger unless he himself was in front. He was not a babbling general."[87]

The *Daily Inquirer* of July 6 quoted an Associated Press correspondent on the occasion when Reynolds first drew a wing assignment from Hooker: "I have often said if you want to know who is a good general, ask the soldier. . . . I must tell you that when it was announced a few evenings ago, to the different divisions, brigades, and regiments composing the First and Third army corps that he [Reynolds] was to take command of them jointly, their cheers were so loud and prolonged that he was compelled to order them to desist."

A hero's death sits well with posterity. It was important to Reynolds' later reputation that he missed the postwar recriminations, jealousies, and the all-too-frequent bitterness that cropped up. It is doubtful, of course, that Reynolds could ever have been drawn into these arguments even if he had survived the war. As it was, he found himself lifted clear of the bickering, though it only helped a record that could stand on its own. Except for the two disgruntled militiamen of 1862, only one other person appears to have attacked Reynolds in print. A Philadelphia newspaperman, John H. Taggart, had helped raise the 12th Pennsylvania Reserves at the beginning of the war. As a result he was elected its colonel and led the regiment until the autumn of 1862. But his brigadier, Truman Seymour, was dissatisfied with his handling of the command, and so apparently was Reynolds.[88] The forced resignation that followed embittered Taggart, who used his Sunday Philadelphia *Times* as an outlet for his feelings.

Ellie Reynolds collected these clippings conscientiously along with the praise. Several of these attacks appeared over a period of years. Typical of their tone was one published on November 4, 1883. In it Taggart suggested that an equestrian statue of the general which was to be placed in front of City Hall be set up instead either before the entrance of the almshouse or the city jail. The reaction was instant. The Reynolds and George H. Thomas posts of the G.A.R. in Philadelphia both answered. One closed with an appeal to boycott the "contemptible sheet"; the other said ". . . we are unable to find language strong enough to express the contempt for the man who has undertaken to . . . assail the character of the noble General Reynolds."[89]

Whether stout defense of Reynolds or his own conscience worked the change in Taggart, he altered his tone completely when he addressed his comrades of the 12th Reserves at the 50th reunion in Gettysburg. Now Reynolds became "the ideal Hotspur, as brave as a lion in battle, and perfectly oblivious of danger. . . . He died defending the soil of his native state, and yonder monument . . ." etc.[90]

Taggart aside, the record is all positive. Men wrote at different times and for different occasions or reasons but with unanimous assent. Hancock thought no officer in the Army of the Potomac had developed a character of usefulness and ability, in the highest grades of command, superior to that of General Reynolds.[91] The Comte de Paris called him undoubtedly the most remarkable man among all the officers that the Army of the Potomac lost in the war.[92] Hooker's biographer named Reynolds as perhaps the best all-round soldier in that same army.[93] Another thought him its most brilliant officer.[94] The contemporary New York *Times* correspondent William Swinton said he was marked for the highest fame.[95] A private soldier called him the most popular officer of his rank in the army.[96] The historian of the New Jersey troops cited Reynolds as one of the ablest and best known of all corps commanders. "He possessed rare personal courage with military ability and skill of a high order."[97] Writing of Gettysburg, America's wartime ambassador to Britain considered him perhaps the most skilful general and the fiercest fighter on the Union side.[98]

When the committee investigating the conduct of the war was trying to get General Gouverneur K. Warren to include Sickles among the great corps commanders of the Army of the Potomac serving in 1863, Warren would name only three: Reynolds, Hancock, and Meade. He said: "They were considered as fighting men by the army. They were men who handled their corps well, and stood well with their commands."[99] Reynolds never would have objected to being placed in this company.

The Confederates added their praise for John Reynolds, too. One of Lee's chief artillerymen at Gettysburg admitted that Reynolds' good handling of his one division won the early part of the fight. "He was an excellent soldier. . . ."[100] And from Archer's men who were taken prisoner by the Iron Brigade in McPherson's wood, Colonel Morrow reported the highest praise expressed for Reynolds' skill and bravery.[101]

A lot more has been said in favor of Reynolds, but he probably would have looked most to his old corps for approval. He had given them a bad July 1. "The First Corps fought that day with no other protection than the flannel blouses that covered their stout hearts."[102] They had gone in without question at his command. What they thought after that day would have been all-important to their general. Reynolds was a corpsman through and through—a 1st Corps man. He would have liked what they said.

One report came in the form of a complaint: "Since General Reynolds was killed, our corps does not seem to be selected for work in the advance. The second corps now does most of the heavy work of making reconnaissances and covering the retreats."[103] But there was worse news to come for the old 1st. In March of 1864 it was discontinued to form a part of the 5th Corps. "This was an act of gross injustice, and a cruel violation of the corps pride," a military writer complained.[104] With Reynolds still at its head this would never have happened.

More positive testimony for Reynolds came in a letter from Captain Mitchell to the family, written from Culpeper Court House on September 17:

> You will I know pardon me for writing to you without permission when I give you my excuse. It is a plea that I urge, in fact it is demanded by those who can never forget the brave old days, when one was living whom we all loved.
>
> Miss Reynolds, the feelings of his old corps remain unchanged. He was our favorite & every day by our camp fires we talk of him & of the days his memory has taught us to love.
>
> It is the wish of the 1st Corps, I mean the whole corps, men and officers, to pay a small tribute to his memory. I was selected as one of a committee & asked to write to you, begging you to allow us the privilege, I mean the honor, to place over our General a monument, which would be done without any public demonstration, & which would please the officers and men of the old Corps.
>
> A tribute of that kind should only be made to our General, by the people he commanded, by those who appreciated his worth.
>
> Please give us this privilege. I think that *I* have a right to demand it in the name of the corps. . . .[105]

Ellie Reynolds already knew how the corps felt about her brother. Riddle had written her a month before:

> I have just received your letter of the 4th inst, Miss Ellie. . . .
>
> I was melancholy indeed to come back to the army and see no more the face of him we so loved and respected; I will never see the man who can fill his place in the hearts of those who knew him; it is pleasant to hear the tributes to his memory from the lips of all in the army here—even our enemies: General Meade in speaking of the General to me said that he would "rather have lost twenty thousand men, for the country's sake, than Reynolds"; and a Rebel Lieut Col taken at Gettysburg, when some one remarked that the greatest loss the Rebels had had was Jackson—said that "they could far better spare Jackson than we could Reynolds," and he spoke truly.[106]

If this was overstatement, at least it was applied to a good soldier.

For all the shared devotion between Reynolds and his corps, he had still older friends. Near the end of June nine regiments, which had been on inactive duty, marched from Fairfax Station to rejoin the army. Four of these regiments brought along a very special sword:

The blade of the sword was of the finest Damascus steel, and the scabbard of pure gold. . . . Upon the grip was a black onyx, in the centre of which was set in diamonds the initials J F R, surrounded by a wreath of precious brilliants. . . . Crowning the grip was a solid globe of gold, chased with the map of the world, around which was the belt of the Union in blue enamel, with thirteen diamond stars. . . . The shield of the hilt was formed of the arms of the state of Pennsylvania, cut from a solid plate of gold.[107]

Inscribed on the scabbard was the following: "Presented to Major-General John Fulton Reynolds, by the enlisted men of the First, Second, Fifth, and Eighth Regiments of the First Brigade of the Pennsylvania Reserves, in testimony of their *love and admiration*, Mechanicsville, June 1862.[108]

These Reserves reached Gettysburg a day too late. But all nine regiments went on to fight their first commander's kind of battle. They spent July 2 in the hot area around the Wheat Field, and after Pickett's charge on the 3rd, closed the fighting by punishing a Longstreet regiment on Lee's right.[109]

A month after Gettysburg the four Reserves regiments which had comprised Reynolds' first command in the Civil War still had the sword. Finally it was decided that one of their men should present it to a member of the family. "A brave and gallant sergeant was chosen to proceed to Philadelphia. . . .":[110]

From Camp near Rappahannock River
Aug 21, 1863

Mrs. Capt H. S. Landis
Dear Madam

In behalf of the Penna Reserves, the Committee through the Chairman, Sergt. W. Hayes Grier, will perform the painful duty of presenting you the sword, sash & belt intended for your deceased Brother. It would have been a pleasant task, could we have been able to present it to the brave and noble General, under whose command we passed through the different engagements of Mechanicsville, Gaines' Mill, 2nd Bull Run and Fredericksburg. Under his command we done all in our power to aid in crushing this unholy rebellion. A strict disciplinarian, attention to the wants of his men, and a brave and fearless commander, combined, united our hearts in willing action to his commands. The cause which he espoused, and for which he yielded his noble life, a willing sacrifice, has in his death lost one of its most earnest supporters. It is unnecessary for me to attempt to eulogize his name, as his history is well known to all who are conversant with the affairs of the present day.

Therefore, to you his cherished Sister, we present this testimonial of esteem from the Penna Reserves, resting assured that it will be preserved, and that in future generations when the donors will be numbered among the things that were, it can be viewed with pride by the Kindred of the brave, beloved & lamented General.

(Signed) Sergt. W. Hayes Grier,
Co. A. 5th Regt. P.R.C.
in behalf of the
Old 1st Brigade, P.R.C.[111]

Reynolds and the Army of the Potomac Command

Specialists in the Civil War would have liked to see the Reynolds Papers turn up final proof that John F. Reynolds either was or was not offered the command of the Army of the Potomac. No letter of Reynolds mentions the subject, which is characteristic of the man. Equally typical was the fact that he did not sign the register of officers arriving in Washington when he went up from camp on June 1, 1863.[1]

The closest the Papers come to giving an answer is a letter written by Eleanor Reynolds. A nephew, Lieutenant Colonel J. F. Landis, persuaded his aunt to put into writing what had been family history for years: The letter, dated August 20, 1913, follows in part:

> Your letter has been received and I hasten to answer it. Your Uncle John spent the evening and night in Baltimore of June 2nd, 1863. I was staying with my sister, Mrs. George Gildersleeve, at that time. We had been at a *"Union Concert"* that evening, and as we approached the house saw lights in the parlor, and found your Uncle John reading there. He told us he had been with the President that day, and that Mr. Lincoln had offered him the command of the Army of the Potomac, which he told the President he would accept, if he was not interfered with from Washington. *This* the President would not promise him, therefore your Uncle declined the offer. I am positive as to the date being June 2nd because it was the *last* time I saw him, and because the next morning, before he left us, a telegram came from your father, announcing the birth of your youngest brother, on the previous day, June 2nd, and your Uncle sent a message by me, to your mother. . . .

Of course as your Uncle had told his family of the interview he had with the President he never alluded to it in any of his letters. His letters were few, between the 2nd of June and July 1st. . . .

I am the only member of my generation, now living, and I am thankful to be able to state the fact of my brother's interview with President Lincoln. If I can give any further information about my brother, to assist General Huidekoper, will be pleased to do so.[2]

Henry S. Huidekoper was preparing the major address to be given in Gettysburg at the unveiling ceremonies for the equestrian statue of General Reynolds.[3] Accompanying Eleanor Reynolds' letter is a statement by Colonel Landis identifying his aunt and Mrs. Gildersleeve, ending: "The baby mentioned is William Reynolds Landis, my youngest brother, whom I know to have been born in Philadelphia, 1829 Spruce St., on June 2, 1863."[4]

Eleanor Reynolds' letter was written 50 years after the event it describes. Conservative judgment hesitates to credit it absolutely, both because of the date and possibly because of the special interest she might have in adding to her brother's fame. As for the date, Eleanor Reynolds lived ten more years after writing the letter, and Mrs. J. F. R. Scott has assured the writer that the general's sister was alert of mind even when she saw her in her last years. Also, dedicated as Eleanor was to her brother, the importance to her of the conversation on that night of June 2 would certainly hold it in her memory. As for integrity, after what is learned about her through her brother's letters, her own, and her relations with the family, it is hard to believe she would either invent or distort the incident.

At the very least, Eleanor Reynolds' letter is good evidence in so far as it correlates with what Meade wrote his wife on June 13, 1863. About Reynolds and the command he had this to say: "He told me that being informed by a friend in Washington, that he was talked of for command of this army, he immediately went to the President and told him he did not want the command and would not take it."[5] The letters differ in two respects. Eleanor implies that the command offer was positively made to her brother, while Meade does not. Eleanor also reports her brother as saying he would accept the command if given a free hand. Meade has Reynolds rejecting it without qualification.

If, as Meade says, Reynolds went up to Washington on the word of a friend, it explains the absence of any written request that he appear. There is nothing in either the Lincoln or Stanton Papers, or in the letters and telegrams sent and received by the then General-in-Chief General Halleck.[6]

So except for the two letters, Eleanor Reynolds' and Meade's, the rest is opinion, though it is not always stated as such. Mention of Reynolds in connection with the Army of the Potomac command started with his death. L. L. Crounse of the New York *Times* wrote on July 3, 1863: "The President, it is well known, hesitated long between the choice of him [Reynolds] and Gen. Meade as successor to Gen. Hooker. Priority of rank finally determined the matter." The second sentence ruins the value of the first, as Reynolds outranked Meade.

Charles F. Benjamin, in *Battles and Leaders*,[7] had the most to say about Reynolds in regard to the command offer. But he places the offer at the time of Burnside's removal. No reliable evidence supports this statement. Further, Benjamin's dramatically detailed account of what went on in connection with the Army of the Potomac command during the first six months of 1863 leads the reader to wonder how he was in a position to know so much. Joseph G. Rosengarten, who had been on Reynolds' staff during much of the period, wondered too. In 1883 he wrote Benjamin, questioning several statements made by him in a letter printed in *The Nation* of the same year.[8] Benjamin's answers are revealing. He admitted having given the wrong date for Meade's acceptance of the command, and said he had inserted the word "Gettysburg" in a conversation of Meade's only because it would make clearer the eventual destination of the march north from Frederick, Maryland. He also confessed that he was writing from memory, having lost what little data he had through petty robberies two or three years before.[9]

Benjamin explained his intimate knowledge of the conversation between Meade and Reynolds on June 28 as follows:

> At the time mentioned I was serving as a clerk at the general headquarters, and was in close attendance upon Seth Williams.
>
> Shortly after taking notice of General Meade in front of his tent, with a group of visiting officers . . . I went back in our little office tent to continue some writing I was doing for General Williams. Whilst engaged the open tent flap was pushed farther back, and General Meade came in, ushering General Reynolds. . . . When I saw who the visitors were I wanted to leave the tent, but being screened by the traveling desk which stood on the table between me and the door, I had not been perceived and Meade began so soon and talked so fast that I concluded the best thing to do was to keep on writing and pay no attention to what was said. . . .[10]

But Benjamin went on to say that Meade made him a listener in spite of himself. The conversation between the two generals follows in quotes. One sentence has Meade saying that he supposed, as everybody in the army did, that the command would fall to Reynolds. Would Meade have made this statement in light of what Reynolds had told him after returning from Washington? And the same with Benjamin's long article in *Battles and Leaders*. There are too many reasons to doubt the accuracy of what he says. But the prominence of *Battles and Leaders* as a source for Civil War material probably has given Benjamin's version more influence than it deserves.[11] Hooker's biographer accepts him, as does one of Meade's; and other writers may have followed the same account.[12]

Another source could have been impressive on this subject of Reynolds and the command offer. One of his aides, Stephen Weld, recorded in his diary on June 28, 1863, that he was with Reynolds when Meade's appointment was announced. Then in a footnote he added: "He [Reynolds] said he was very glad of it and he spoke most highly of Meade. He then told me, confidentially, that the command had been offered to him, but that he had refused it."[13] There are two things wrong with this entry. The footnote could have been added at any time after the war (the book was not published until 1912). It does not sound like Reynolds to confide so important a fact to a young aide who had been with him scarcely more than a month. He would have made such a statement only to quiet a protest on the part of his staff.

Of opinions, the most sensible and most authoritative is probably that given by General Winfield Scott Hancock, in a letter written for inclusion in the *Reynolds Memorial*. Hancock writes:

> It is quite well understood, and I believe it is a matter of history, that he could have had the command of the Army of the Potomac before the battle of Gettysburg, and that it was conferred upon General Meade after General Reynolds' recommendation or suggestion. They were close friends, — a friendship based not upon personal considerations alone, but upon mutual esteem, and appreciation of character and abilities as well. General Reynolds was senior to General Meade in rank, and therefore it can be well understood that, with his well-known merit, he was first considered when command was in question.[14]

Available fact and opinion make it safe to assume that John F. Reynolds was given the opportunity to command the Army of the Potomac.

Notes

1. John F. Reynolds to his father, November 22, 1833. Letter in the unpublished papers of General John Fulton Reynolds, Fackenthal Library, Franklin and Marshall College, Lancaster, Pa. (cited hereafter as Reynolds Papers).
2. I. Daniel Rupp, *History of Lancaster and York Counties,* Lancaster, Pa., 1844, p. 320.
3. *Ibid.,* p. 90n, 96n.
4. *Ibid.,* p. 135n.
5. J. F. R. Scott (Col.), "John Fulton Reynolds," *Papers* of the Lancaster Co. Historical Society (cited hereafter as LCHS *Papers*), Vol. 52, No. 2, 1948, p. 21; Mrs. James D. Landis, "Who Was Who in Lancaster 100 Years Ago," LCHS *Papers,* Vol. 11, No. 10, 1907, p. 390.
6. Alex Harris, *Biographical History of Lancaster County,* Lancaster, Pa., 1872, p. 483; unpublished correspondence of James Buchanan to John Reynolds, Fackenthal Library, Franklin and Marshall College, Lancaster, Pa.
7. D. B. Landis, "The Conestoga River at Lancaster," LCHS *Papers,* Vol. 36, No. 11, 1932, p. 270.
8. Herbert H. Beck, "Historical Sketch of Rural Field Sports in Lancaster County," LCHS *Papers,* Vol. 27, No. 9, 1923, p. 155.
9. Landis, "Conestoga River at Lancaster," *op. cit., p.* 270.
10. F. S. Klein, *Lancaster 1841-1941,* Lancaster, Pa., 1941, p. 3.
11. Dates for the children of John and Lydia Moore Reynolds are as follows:

    1) Samuel, b. April 7, 1814; d. May 29, 1888.
    2) William, b. Dec. 10, 1815; d. Nov. 5, 1879.
    3) Jane Moore, b. April 7, 1817; d. infancy.
    4) Lydia, b. July 27, 1818; d. Dec. 20, 1896.
    5) *John Fulton, b. Sept. 21, 1820; d. July 1, 1863.*
    6) James Lefevre, b. March 8, 1822; d. April 5, 1880.
    7) Mary Jane, b. Feb. 13, 1824; d. Dec. 10, 1901.
    8) Catherine Ferree, b. Dec. 11, 1825; d. Feb. 10, 1905.
    9) Edward C., b. Dec. 26, 1827; d. Sept. 25, 1828.
    10) Anne Elizabeth, b. Dec. 26, 1827; d. June 7, 1832.

11) Edward, b. May 26, 1829; d. July 5, 1829.

12) Harriet, b. July 29, 1832; d. Sept. 4, 1898.

13) Eleanor, b. March 13, 1835; d. Feb. 20, 1923.

This list was supplied from family records by Mrs. J. J. Kline of Fort Wayne, Indiana, in a letter to the author dated April 30, 1955. Mrs. Kline is a granddaughter of Lydia Reynolds and Nathaniel Evans. See also LCHS *Papers*, Vol. 11, No. 10, 1907, p. 401; there Eleanor is incorrectly placed above Harriet, and no dates are given.

12. Scott, "Reynolds," *op. cit.*, p. 27. The house is still clearly recognizable in downtown Lancaster on U.S. Route 30. Stores have occupied the lower floor from at least the early 1860's. A state historical marker has been placed on the sidewalk opposite the entrance.

13. Only that year John Beck had appointed John Rickert and Augustus Christ as assistant teachers, John G. Zook, *Historical and Pictorial Lititz*, Lititz, Pa., 1905, p. 50.

14. JFR to his sister Lydia, December 19, 1833, Reynolds Papers.

15. JFR to his mother, December 7, 1833, Reynolds Papers.

16. Zook, *Historical Lititz*, p. 50.

17. *Ibid.*

18. JFR to his mother, December 7, 1833, Reynolds Papers.

19. JFR to his mother, March 8, 1834, Reynolds Papers.

20. George W. Cullum, *Biographical Register of the Officers and Graduates of the U. S. Military Academy*, 3 Vols., Boston and New York, 1891, Vol. 2, p. 92.

21. JFR to his father, July 5, 1835, Reynolds Papers.

22. JFR to his sister Lydia, December 10, 1835, Reynolds Papers.

23. JFR to his father, October 27, 1835, Reynolds Papers.

24. Beck, "Rural Field Sports in Lancaster County," *op. cit.*, p. 270.

25. JFR to his father, May 14, 1836, Reynolds Papers.

26. James Buchanan to John Reynolds (father), covering letter to Buchanan from Lewis Cass, January 25, 1836, Reynolds Papers. Buchanan's letter seeking the appointment for John is in the National Archives, Records of the Adjutant General's Office, File No. 243, Applications 1805-1897 (hereafter cited as Adjutant General's Office, with file number and description).

27. Allen Johnson and Dumas Malone, eds., *Dictionary of American Biography*, 22 Vols. plus supplements, New York, 1928-1937, Vol. 15, pp. 522-523 (cited hereafter as DAB).

28. JFR letter of attorney, August 17, 1853, appointing his brother Samuel as executor of his share of their father's estate, Reynolds Papers. The counties included are Lancaster, York, Greene, and Clarion.

29. Ulysses S. Grant, *Personal Memoirs of U. S. Grant*, E. B. Long, ed., Cleveland, Ohio, 1952, p. 11.

30. George Gordon Meade, ed., *Life and Letters of George Gordon Meade*, 2 Vols., New York, 1913, Vol. 1, p. 45, Meade to his wife, January 20, 1846 (cited hereafter as Meade, *Letters*).

31. Adjutant General's Office, File No. 243, Applications 1805-1897.

32. *Ibid.*

33. JFR to his brother William, August 20, 1837, Reynolds Papers.

34. *Register of Graduates and Former Cadets United States Military Academy*, published annually by the West Point Alumni Foundation, Inc., New York, 1952, p. 16 (cited hereafter as *Register USMA*, 1952).

35. William H. Baumes, *West Point: Moulder of Men*, New York, 1942, p. 16.

36. Grant, *Memoirs*, p. 15.

37. *Exec. Doc.*, H.R., 29th Cong., 2nd Sess., Vol. 5, No. 4, 1846, p. 135.

38. *Ibid.*, 1st Sess., Vol. 3, No. 660, 1846, p. 2.

39. *Register USMA*, 1952, See class standings.

40. Cullum, *Biographical Register*, Vol. 2, p. 92.

41. Lloyd Lewis, *Sherman: Fighting*

Prophet, New York, 1932, p. 543; William T. Sherman to Samuel Reynolds, February 16, 1883, Reynolds Papers.

42. JFR to his sister Jane, September 26, 1847, Reynolds Papers.

43. Charles Kingsbury wrote a widely printed account of the battle of Buena Vista, in which he praised Reynolds' handling of his guns. It first appeared in Niles' *National Register,* Vol. 72, April 10, 1847, pp. 85-86.

44. Edgar Allan Poe stood near the head of his class for six months in 1830-1831, but soon lost interest and was dismissed, W. A. Croffut, ed., *Fifty Years in Camp and Field: the Diary of Ethan A. Hitchcock,* New York, 1909, p. 63n.

45. JFR to his sister Jane, March 8, 1841, Reynolds Papers.

46. *Register USMA,* 1952, pp. 176-182, see years of graduation.

47. William A. Ganoe, *History of the United States Army,* New York, 1924, p. 191.

48. *Register USMA,* 1952, pp. 166-181, see individual biographies.

49. The girls probably were Sarah and Isabel Coleman, Anne Reigart, and Mary Elizabeth Lane, all of Lancaster.

50. It was due largely to Ringgold's efforts that the new light artillery had taken hold, William E. Birkhimer, *Historical Sketch of the Artillery U. S. Army,* Washington, 1884, p. 50.

51. Braxton Bragg to John Reynolds, Sr., July 23, 1842, Reynolds Papers.

52. *Ibid.,* August 12, 1842.

53. JFR to his sister Eleanor (Ellie), September 20, 1860, Reynolds Papers.

54. Erasmus D. Keyes, *Fifty Years Observation of Men and Events,* New York, 1884, p. 179.

55. *Ibid.,* pp. 178-179.

56. William T. Sherman, "Old Shady with a Moral," *North American Review,* Vol. 147, No. 383, October, 1888, pp. 364-365.

57. Keyes, *Fifty Years,* p. 180.

58. James H. Wilson, *Under the Old Flag,* 2 Vols., New York, 1912, Vol. 1, pp. 68-69. Wilson conceded W. T. Sherman's soldierly qualities but called him a "martinet of violent and ungovernable temper." He was too exacting and too impatient to get along with his men.

59. LCHS *Papers,* Vol. 11, No. 10, 1907, p. 370. As John Reynolds made no mention of his mother's death in his letters, the assumption is that he probably went home at the time or shortly afterwards. Gaps in the correspondence are usually attributable to his leaves.

60. William T. Sherman, *Memoirs of William T. Sherman,* 2 Vols., New York, 1892, pp. 32-33.

61. Grant, *Memoirs,* p. 30.

62. JFR to his sisters, January 4, 1846, Reynolds Papers.

63. Paul E. Beck, "List of Iron Furnaces Formerly Operating in Lancaster County," LCHS *Papers,* Vol. 31, No. 10, 1927, p. 149. The elder John Reynolds and James Buchanan bought Lucinda Furnace in 1843. Its iron had a high reputation with mill and foundrymen but the yield was small. After Reynolds' death in 1853, his son-in-law Nathan Evans continued to operate the furnace until 1858, when it was abandoned because of the scarcity of labor and the low price offered for iron.

64. Augustus Buell, *The Cannoneer,* Washington, 1890, p. 13.

65. Niles' *National Register,* Vol. 70, June 27, 1846, p. 267.

66. George McCall, *Letters from the Frontier,* Philadelphia, 1868, pp. 431-432. The Northers appeared to impress McCall more than they did Reynolds. After one storm, McCall said, the men found themselves icebound in their tents. His servant thawed the flaps of his own tent by pouring boiling water over the opening.

67. JFR to his sisters, January 4, 1846, Reynolds Papers.

68. *Ibid.*

CHAPTER II. RIO GRANDE AND POINTS SOUTH

1. Justin H. Smith, *The War with Mexico*, 2 Vols., New York, 1919, Vol. 1, pp. 143-144.
2. Grant, *Memoirs*, p. 30.
3. John Sedgwick, *Correspondence of General John Sedgwick*, 2 Vols., Boston, 1902, Vol. 1, p. 18. Cf. Arthur Schlesinger, Jr., in his *Age of Jackson*, New York, 1945, p. 450: "General Taylor waited at the head of a rabble army in the disputed land." Schlesinger's description comes closer to fitting the army after the volunteers joined it.
4. Charles J. Peterson, *The Military Heroes of the War with Mexico*, Philadelphia, 1850, pp. 30-31.
5. Smith, *War with Mexico*, Vol. 1, p. 148; McCall, *Letters*, p. 438.
6. McCall, *Letters*, p. 439.
7. Smith, *War with Mexico*, Vol. 1, p. 150.
8. Niles' *National Register*, Vol. 70, June 20, 1846, p. 254.
9. William H. Samson, ed., *Letters of Zachary Taylor from the Battlefields of the Mexican War*, Rochester, New York, 1908, p. 2.
10. McCall, *Letters*, p. 441.
11. Meade, *Letters*, Vol. 1, p. 75, to his wife, May 5, 1846.
12. Grant, *Memoirs*, p. 12.
13. Meade, *Letters*, Vol. 1, pp. 75-76, to his wife, May 5, 1846.
14. *Exec. Doc.*, Senate, 30 Cong., 1 Sess., Vol. 7, No. 60, 1848, p. 293.
15. Niles' *National Register*, Vol. 70, June 20, 1846, p. 254.
16. JFR to sister Jane, June 12, 1846, Reynolds Papers.
17. William S. Henry, *Campaign Sketches of the War with Mexico*, New York, 1847, p. 104.
18. JFR to sister Jane, June 12, 1846, Reynolds Papers.
19. For agreement with Reynolds on Mexican cruelty see Niles' *National Register*, Vol. 72, May 8, 1847, p. 158; James H. Carleton, *The Battle of Buena Vista*, New York, 1848, p. 153.
20. JFR to sister Jane, June 12, 1846, Reynolds Papers.
21. *Ibid.*
22. Meade, *Letters*, Vol. 1, p. 40, to his wife, December 18, 1845.
23. Taylor, *Letters*, p. 18.
24. *Ibid.*
25. Meade, *Letters*, Vol. 1, p. 91, to his wife, May 9, 1846.
26. Luther Giddings, *Campaigns in Northern Mexico*, New York, 1853, p. 81.
27. Niles' *National Register*, Vol. 71, September 26, 1846, p. 58.
28. William P. Johnston, *General Albert Sidney Johnston*, New York, 1878, pp. 242-243.
29. Croffut, *Fifty Years in Camp and Field*, p. 221; Ganoe, *U. S. Army*, pp. 173-174.
30. JFR to sister Jane, September 3, 1846, Reynolds Papers; see also Meade, *Letters*, Vol. 1, p. 94, to his wife, May 28, 1846.
31. Niles' *National Register*, Vol. 70, October 3, 1846, p. 67.
32. Meade, *Letters*, Vol. 1, p. 115, to his wife, July 24, 1846.
33. JFR to sister Jane, September 3, 1846, Reynolds Papers.
34. McCall, *Letters*, pp. 466-470; Niles' *National Register*, Vol. 71, October 31, 1846, pp. 130-131, 167; John R. Kenly, *Memoirs of a Maryland Volunteer*, Phila., 1873, p. 155; Samuel G. French, *Two Wars*, Nashville, Tenn., 1901, pp. 59, 73; Meade, *Letters*, Vol. 1, p. 131, to his wife, September 17, 1846.
35. Giddings, *Campaigns*, p. 171.
36. Niles' *National Register*, Vol. 71, January 30, 1847, p. 343.
37. Grant, *Memoirs*, p. 51.
38. Giddings, *Campaigns*, p. 76.
39. JFR to his sister Jane, September 3, 1846, Reynolds Papers.

40. Smith, *War with Mexico*, Vol. 1, p. 251.
41. Kenly, *Memoirs*, p. 111.
42. French, *Two Wars*, p. 62.
43. Giddings, *Campaigns*, pp. 168-169.
44. *Exec. Doc.*, H.R., 29th Cong., 2nd Sess., Vol. 1, No. 4, 1846, pp. 86-87.
45. Kenly, *Memoirs*, p. 122.
46. French, *Two Wars*, p. 67; Nathaniel W. Stephenson, *Texas and the War with Mexico*, New Haven, Conn., 1921, p. 67. Stephenson notes that the Texans used this same method, breaking holes through the houses in Béxar (San Antonio) on December 12, 1835, against the Mexicans.
47. Joseph G. Rosengarten, (John F.) *Reynolds Memorial*, Addresses, Philadelphia, 1880, p. 14. Captain Rosengarten served for a time as aide to General Reynolds. He later became a close friend of the family and wrote most of the articles and addresses about the general during the late years of the last century. Rosengarten had access to the few letters then collected. The one quoted here is among several that have been lost, but the date is given as December 6, 1846.
48. Meade, *Letters*, Vol. 1, p. 135, to his wife, September 27, 1846.
49. *Exec. Doc.*, H.R., 29th Cong., 2nd Sess., Vol. 1, No. 4, 1846, pp. 78-79.
50. Niles' *National Register*, Vol. 71, January 30, 1847, p. 342.
51. *Exec. Doc.*, H.R., 29th Cong., 2nd Sess., Vol. 1, No. 4, 1846, pp. 78-79.
52. Rosengarten, *Reynolds Memorial*, p. 14, from the same letter dated above, Note 47.
53. Niles' *National Register*, Vol. 71, November 21, 1846, p. 180.
54. Smith, *War with Mexico*, Vol. 1, p. 254.
55. *Ibid.*; Stephenson, *Texas and War with Mexico*, p. 199; Croffut, *Fifty Years in Camp and Field*, p. 215.
56. *Exec. Doc.*, H.R., 29th Cong., 2nd Sess., Vol. 1, No. 4, 1846, p. 89.
57. *Ibid.*, p. 221.
58. French, *Two Wars*, p. 68.
59. JFR to his brother James, January 30, 1847, Reynolds Papers.
60. *Ibid.*
61. *Ibid.*
62. Fred L. Hitchcock, *War from the Inside*, Philadelphia, 1904, p. 102.
63. Cullum, *Biographical Register*, Vol. II, p. 93.
64. Henry Coppée, *General Thomas*, New York, 1893, p. 17.
65. French, *Two Wars*, p. 68; Rosengarten, *Reynolds Memorial*, p. 14.
66. Meade, *Letters*, Vol. 1, p. 157, to his wife, November 24, 1846. Lieutenant Meade was more impressed by the buildings than was Reynolds. His fine description of the cathedral's interior especially shows his appreciation of "an effect you cannot but consider grand."
67. French, *Two Wars*, pp. 69-70. Although French agreed with Reynolds on the poor quality of native liquor, he told of one occasion when they both drank something other than pure water. On the march to Victoria they had stopped for New Year's Day to see in the beginning of 1847. Reynolds somehow found eggs and eggs suggested eggnog. But eggnog required liquor. So they called for the company's doctor and locked him up until he wrote a prescription for a bottle of rum and one of brandy to be sent over from medical supply. The doctor shared the eggnog.
68. JFR to his brother James, February 13, 1847, Reynolds Papers.
69. *Ibid.*

CHAPTER III. SIX-POUNDERS AT BUENA VISTA

1. Edward D. Mansfield, *The Mexican War,* New York, 1848, p. 121.
2. Brantz Mayer, *Mexico,* Hartford 1850, 2 Vols. In Volume 1, page 354, is an old engraving of the Narrows and valley where the battle took place. Though its topography is exaggerated it does represent the rugged nature of the ground. William T. Sherman faced roughly similar ground so far as ravines and ridges are concerned when he tried to dislodge the Confederates north of Vicksburg, Mississippi, in the spring of 1863.
3. Niles' *National Register,* Vol. 72, March 21, 1847, p. 36, reprints from *El Republico* Santa Anna's estimate of his strength as being 21,340 men.
4. JFR to his sister Jane, March 1, 1847, Reynolds Papers.
5. *Ibid.* Praise for the volunteers in this action also appears in Niles' *National Register,* Vol. 72, April 17, 1847, p. 100. Stephenson, *Texas and War with Mexico,* p. 193, more generally commends the courage of the volunteers in these early campaigns.
6. JFR to his sister Jane, September 3, 1846; quoted in Chapter II, p. 28.
7. Smith, *War with Mexico,* Vol. 1, p. 394; Ellen Hardin Walmouth, "The Battle of Buena Vista," *Magazine of American History,* Vol. 3, No. 12, December 1879, p. 736; Carleton, *Buena Vista,* p. 112; *Exec. Doc.,* Senate, 30 Cong., 1 Sess., Vol. 1, No. 1, 1848: Taylor in his report, p. 139, and Wool in his, p. 150, named O'Brien first among the subalterns. Unfortunately, this promising young officer died in 1850.
8. French, *Two Wars,* p. 80.
9. Carleton, *Buena Vista,* p. 93. This part of Reynolds' action in the battle was also commended in Niles' *National Register,* Vol. 72, April 10, 1847, p. 85. The account, which was signed "Buena Vista," was written by Reynolds' friend Charles Kingsbury. See Notes, Chapter I, No. 41.
10. Carleton, *Buena Vista,* p. 96.
11. *Ibid.;* also Niles' *National Register,* Vol. 72, April 10, 1847, p. 85.
12. Walmouth, "Buena Vista," *op. cit.,* p. 726.
13. *Exec. Doc.,* Senate, 30 Cong., 1 Sess., Vol. 1, No. 1, 1848, p. 161. O'Brien took three pages to justify the loss of his three guns. To his commander he summed up by saying: "You are, sir, well aware that it is often the duty of an artillery officer to sacrifice his pieces for the safety of other troops. Such was my position. I could have saved the guns, had I withdrawn them earlier; but in such case, the day might, perhaps, have ben lost. . . ."
14. Smith, *War with Mexico,* Vol. 1, p. 395.
15. JFR to his sister Jane, March 1, 1847, Reynolds Papers.
16. *Exec. Doc.,* Senate, 30 Cong., 1 Sess., Vol. 1, No. 1, 1848, p. 138.
17. JFR to his sister Jane, March 1, 1847, Reynolds Papers. Although Meade was not present at Buena Vista, he had already expressed agreement with Reynolds on the treatment he felt Taylor was receiving from the administration, from Polk in particular, Meade, *Letters,* Vol. 1, pp. 102-103, Meade to his wife, June 12, 1846. A contemporary, Peterson, *Military Heroes,* p. 55, tends to side with Reynolds and Meade, but Stephenson, *Texas and the War with Mexico,* p. 200, defends Polk's distrust of Taylor. Smith, *War with Mexico,* Vol. 1, pp. 368-369, also finds Taylor both unwise and insubordinate.
18. Niles' *National Register,* Vol. 72, April 17, 1847, p. 100. Other opinions, both at the time and later, agree on Taylor's courage but not

on his military skill—e.g., Smith, *War with Mexico*, Vol. 1, p. 395; Stephenson, *Texas and the War with Mexico*, pp. 200, 203; Peterson, *Military Heroes*, p. 137.

19. *Exec. Doc.*, Senate, 30 Cong., 1 Sess., Vol. 1, No. 1, 1848: Taylor's report, pp. 138-139; Wool's, pp. 150-151; May's, pp. 198-200; Sherman's, p. 205. Taylor in a private letter said: "Our artillery did more than wonders," Niles' *National Register*, Vol. 72, May 1, 1847, p. 135.

20. JFR to his brother James, May 23, 1847, Reynolds Papers.

21. See above, Note No. 9.

22. JFR to his brother James, May 23, 1847, Reynolds Papers.

23. John Reynolds (father) to JFR, April 27, 1847, Reynolds Papers.

24. *Ibid.* Buchanan was receptive to a brevet for Lieutenant Reynolds. He wrote John's father on May 10, 1847: "I shall take good care of John when the time arrives. He richly deserves a brevet; but the President without the Senate cannot give it to him." (Unpublished letters of James Buchanan to John Reynolds, Fackenthal Library, Franklin and Marshall College, Lancaster, Pennsylvania.) See beginning Chapter IV.

25. JFR to his brother James, August 6, 1847, Reynolds Papers.

26. Meade, *Letters*, Vol. 1, p. 87, to his wife, May 9, 1846.

27. Oliver L. Spaulding, *The United States Army in War and Peace*, New York, 1937, p. 226; Ganoe, *U. S. Army*, p. 231; Grant, *Memoirs*, p. 96. A book on the Mexican War by A. H. Bill, published in 1947 (New York) is even given the title *Rehearsal for Conflict*.

28. Giddings, *Campaigns*, p. 97n.

29. Kenly, *Memoirs*, p. 263.

30. The core of Scott's defense of the Academy lies in the following sentence: "Hence, I give it as my fixed opinion, that but for our graduated cadets, the war between the United States and Mexico might, and probably would, have lasted some four or five years. . ." *Exec. Doc.*, Senate, Misc., 36th Cong., 2nd Sess., Vol. 1, No. 3, 1860, p. 176. Continued attacks on West Point appear in John Watts DePeyster, *Personal and Military History of Philip Kearny*, New York, 1869, pp. 218, 307; Hitchcock, *War from the Inside*, p. 175. Even as late as the Spanish American War, a Captain James Parker, U.S.A., in the *North American Review*, Vol. 166, No. 499, June 1898, p. 651, felt it necessary to argue that West Point was superior to any other means of producing military talent.

31. JFR to brother James, November 14, 1847, Reynolds Papers.

32. JFR to brother James, May 23, 1847, Reynolds Papers.

33. William Reynolds' wife was formerly Rebecca Krug, daughter of George H. Krug of Lancaster, DAB, Vol. 15, pp. 522-523.

34. William Reynolds to JFR, July 8, 1847, Reynolds Papers.

35. *Ibid.*

36. *Ibid.*

37. JFR to sister Jane, December 26, 1848, Reynolds Papers.

38. *Ibid.*

39. JFR to brother James, November 14, 1847, Reynolds Papers.

40. JFR to sister Jane, January 1, 1848, Reynolds Papers.

41. JFR to brother James, August 6, 1847, Reynolds Papers.

42. William Reynolds to JFR, July 8, 1847, Reynolds Papers.

43. JFR to sister Jane, March 19, 1848, Reynolds Papers.

44. *Ibid.*

CHAPTER IV. MOUNTAINS, MORMONS, AND DUST

1. James Buchanan to John Reynolds (father), May 10, 1847, Buchanan letters to John Reynolds, Fackenthal Library, Franklin and Marshall College, Lancaster, Pa.
2. Francis B. Heitman, *Historical Register and Dictionary of the United States Army*, 2 Vols., Washington, 1903, Vol. 1, p. 825.
3. William F. Wormer, "Dinner Declined by John F. Reynolds," LCHS *Papers*, Vol. 34, No. 9, 1930, p. 213.
4. *Ibid.*
5. *Ibid.*
6. JFR to his brother James, August 6, 1847, Reynolds Papers.
7. JFR to his sister Harriet, January 31, 1849, Reynolds Papers.
8. *Ibid.*
9. Major Anderson was later in command of Fort Sumter when it was fired on to begin the Civil War, April 12, 1861.
10. JFR to his sister Harriet, January 31, 1849, Reynolds Papers.
11. From copy of report, Reynolds Papers. During Anderson's absence Reynolds was temporarily in command.
12. JFR to his sister Harriet, January 31, 1849, Reynolds Papers.
13. JFR to his sister Ellie, October 6, 1849, Reynolds Papers.
14. JFR to his sister Harriet, January 31, 1850, Reynolds Papers.
15. Quartermaster general in Washington to JFR, November 20, 1849, Reynolds Papers.
16. JFR to his sister Ellie, June 23, 1850, Reynolds Papers.
17. *Ibid.*
18. Lewis, *Sherman*, p. 87.
19. *Reynolds Memorial Association*, Unveiling of statue of John F. Reynolds, Philadelphia, September 18, 1884 (pamphlet), p. 17, General Abner Doubleday to Reynolds Memorial Commission, September 14, 1884.
20. *Ibid.*, General W. T. Sherman to ex-Governor Andrew G. Curtin of Pennsylvania, May 8, 1884.
21. The elder John Reynolds was 67 years old. He suffered a stroke at the dock in Baltimore while waiting to take the Philadelphia boat. He died in a few minutes (Lancaster *Intelligencer*, undated clipping, Reynolds Papers).
22. JFR to his sister Ellie, November 1, 1853, Reynolds Papers.
23. JFR to his sister Ellie, March 28, 1854, Reynolds Papers.
24. *Exec. Doc.*, H.R. 34th Cong., 1st Sess., Vol. 1, Pt. 2, 1856, p. 154.
25. *Ibid.*, pp. 152-168.
26. JFR to his sister Ellie or to Hal (Harriet), March 28, 1855, Reynolds Papers.
27. *Exec. Doc.*, H.R., 34th Cong., 1st Sess., Vol. 1, Pt. 2, 1856, p. 167. For Ingalls' views on the Mormons, see also Johnston, *Albert S. Johnston*, p. 239.
28. William A. Linn, *The Story of the Mormons*, New York, 1923, p. 458.
29. JFR to his sister Ellie or to Hal, March 28, 1855, Reynolds Papers. Reynolds' account of this trial is borne out in every way by Ingalls' report to the secretary of war in *Exec. Doc.*, H.R., 34th Cong., 1st Sess., Vol 1, Pt. 2, 1856, p. 167.
30. JFR to sister Ellie or to Hal, March 28, 1855, Reynolds Papers.
31. Heitman, *Historical Register*, Vol. 1, p. 825.
32. JFR to his sisters, May 14, 1855, Reynolds Papers.
33. *Ibid.*
34. James Bassett Moore, *The Works of James Buchanan*, 12 Vols., Philadelphia, 1909, Vol. 9, p. 12. James Reynolds advises Buchanan regarding the latter's chance for an appointment as minister to England.
35. H. M. S. Klein, *Lancaster County: a History*, 4 Vols., Lancaster, Penn-

sylvania, 1924, Vol. II, p. 889.
36. JFR to his sisters, August 27, 1855, Reynolds Papers.
37. *Ibid.*
38. JFR to his sister Ellie, December 18, 1855, Reynolds Papers.
39. Keyes, *Fifty Years*, p. 251.
40. JFR to his sister Ellie, January 11, 1856, Reynolds Papers.
41. DePeyster, *Kearny*, p. 155.
42. General Orders No. 14, Headquarters of the Army, New York, November 13, 1857, copy in Reynolds Papers.
43. JFR to his sisters, June 19, 1856, Reynolds Papers.
44. "Citizens" of Port Orford, Oregon Territory to JFR, July 31, 1856, Reynolds Papers.
45. JFR to his sisters, June 19, 1856, Reynolds Papers.
46. Don C. Seitz, *Braxton Bragg*, Columbia, South Carolina, 1924, p. 14.
47. *Ibid.*, p. 17.
48. JFR to his sisters, April 29, 1857, Reynolds Papers.
49. JFR to his sister Ellie, undated, Reynolds Papers. In her bound volume of her brother's correspondence Eleanor Reynolds placed this letter between those of June 25 and August 23, 1857.
50. JFR to his sister Hal, April 12; and to Ellie, May 6, June 3, June 28, 1858, Reynolds Papers.
51. Johnston, *Albert S. Johnston*, pp. 202ff; J. Cecil Alter, *James Bridger: a Historical Narrative*, Salt Lake City, 1925, pp. 291ff. Alter, without

excusing Mormon intransigence, analyzes the point of view that led to it.
52. JFR to his sister Ellie, May 6, 1858, Reynolds Papers.
53. Birkhimer, *History of Artillery U.S.A.*, pp. 67-68.
54. JFR to his sister Ellie, September 30, 1858, Reynolds Papers; The artilleryman Augustus Buell was equally impressed by the dust, *Cannoneer*, p. 395.
55. Spaulding, *U. S. Army*, p. 234.
56. Albert S. Beveridge, *Abraham Lincoln 1809-1858*, 2 Vols., Boston, 1928, Vol. II, p. 389.
57. Keyes, *Fifty Years*, pp. 429-430; Ganoe, *U. S. Army*, p. 245.
58. JFR to his sister Ellie, February 3, 1859, Reynolds Papers.
59. *Ibid.*
60. JFR to his sister Ellie, March 10, 1859, Reynolds Papers.
61. *Exec. Doc.*, Senate, 36th Cong., 2nd Sess., Vol. 2, No. 1, 1861, pp. 124ff. Both Americans and Canadians had settled on the Island of San Juan in the channel at the southern end of Vancouver Island. By the middle of 1859 troops from both sides landed to contest ownership, but General Scott went out and arranged for a peaceful coexistence until final settlement could be reached.
62. JFR to his sister Ellie, December 23, 1859.
63. *Ibid.*

CHAPTER V. TO SERVE IN ANY CAPACITY

1. Beveridge, *Abraham Lincoln*, Vol. 2, p. 658.
2. Harris, *Lancaster County*, pp. 485nff.
3. John G. Nicolay and John Hay, *Abraham Lincoln: a History*, 10 Vols., New York, 1890, Vol. 2, pp. 340-341.
4. From "Quarterly Return of Clothing, Camp, and Garrison Equipage," September 13, 1856, Reynolds Papers.

5. From recruiting account of Brevet Major John F. Reynolds, February-April, 1849, Reynolds Papers.

6. JFR to his sisters, December 10, 1860, Reynolds Papers.

7. JFR to his brother Sam, November 19, 1860, Reynolds Papers; Joseph P. Farley, *West Point in the Early Sixties*, Troy, N. Y., 1902, p. 25.

8. *Exec. Doc.*, Senate (Misc.), 36th Cong., 2nd Sess., Vol. 1, No. 3, 1861, pp. 200-201.

9. Morris Schaff, *The Spirit of Old West Point*, Boston, 1907, pp. 92-93. Schaff describes Reynolds' smart handling of the cadet corps during a review given for the then Prince of Wales.

10. JFR to his sister Kate, February 13, 1848, Reynolds Papers. See Chapter III, p. 51.

11. JFR to his sisters, November 14, 1845, Reynolds Papers.

12. *Exec. Doc.*, Senate (Misc), 36th Cong., 2nd Sess., Vol. 1, No. 3, 1861, p. 12.

13. *Ibid.*, 37th Cong., 1st Sess., Vol. 1, No. 1, 1861, pp. 45-46.

14. Lewis, *Sherman*, pp. 56, 59.

15. Farley, *West Point*, pp. 74-75; *Register USMA*, 1952, p. 196. Custer was once dismissed but was readmitted and graduated last in his class.

16. *Exec. Doc.*, Senate (Misc.), 37th Cong., 1st Sess., Vol. 1, No. 1, 1861, p. 33.

17. Farley, *West Point*, pp. 68-69.

18. JFR to his sister Ellie, September 20, 1860, Reynolds Papers.

19. Farley, *West Point*, p. 25.

20. JFR to his brother Sam, November 19, 1860, Reynolds Papers.

21. *The College Student*, Franklin and Marshall College, Lancaster, Vol. 14, No. 15, May 1, 1894, pp. 185-186.

22. JFR to his sister Ellie, May 11, 1859, Reynolds Papers.

23. Henry Landis retired in 1875 and lived in Chestnut Hill until his death in 1895. He spent his winters in Florida. Ellie and Hal continued to make their home with the family.

24. JFR to his sisters, December 10, 1860, Reynolds Papers.

25. JFR to his brother James, June 6, 1861, Reynolds Papers.

26. JFR to his sister Ellie, June 11, 1861, Reynolds Papers. The committee Davis headed did a thorough job of investigating West Point, regardless of how Davis himself felt about other matters at the time. Its report, which covers 350 pages in the Senate Documents, included minute inspection of every phase of instruction, discipline, physical plant, etc. Most of the work had been finished when Reynolds arrived, and Colonel Hardee had made some recommendations that should have pleased his successor. Hardee favored a return from the five-year course to one of four years; a system of cadet appointments that would ensure better selection; and the dropping of army organization and administration from the Commandant's teaching load to allow more instruction in strategy.

27. JFR to his sister Ellie, June 11, 1861, Reynolds Papers.

28. JFR to his brother Jim, June 6, 1861, Reynolds Papers.

29. Lieutenant General Winfield Scott to JFR, March 8, 1861, original in Reynolds Papers.

30. Nicolay and Hay, *Lincoln*, Vol. 4, p. 307.

31. Heitman, *Army Register*, Vol. 1, p. 825.

32. JFR to his sister Ellie, July 15, 1862, Reynolds Papers.

33. JFR to his sister Ellie, July 1, 1861, Reynolds Papers. Contemporary evidence did not bear out Reynolds' irony. As Commandant of Cadets he seems to have been both respected and admired. See Morris Schaff, *West Point*, p. 93; Farley, *West Point*, p. 69; *Personal Recollections of the Rebellion*, 4 Vols., Military Order Loyal Legion, New York Commandry, New York, 1891, Vol. 2, p. 196.

34. Heitman, *Army Register*, Vol. 1, p. 825.

35. General George B. McClellan to JFR, September 4, 1861 (telegram),

Reynolds Papers.

36. General John E. Wool to General Scott, September 9, 1861, *The War of the Rebellion: Official Records of the Union and Confederate Armies,* 70 Vols. (in 128), Washington, 1880-1901, Serial 4, p. 581. (Hereafter cited as *O.R.,* with serial and page numbers given. The first 31 serial numbers are not printed on their respective volumes.)

37. George B. McClellan, *McClellan's Own Story,* New York, 1887, p. 107, McClellan to Simon Cameron, September 18, 1861.

38. Copies of these orders are in the Reynolds Papers; also in *O.R.,* Serial 4, pp. 581, 612; Serial 107, pp. 469-480.

39. Scott to Cameron, August 9, August 12, 1861, *O.R.,* Serial 14, pp. 4-6; also Scott to Cameron, October 4, 1861, *O.R.,* Serial 107, pp. 491-492.

40. T. Harry Williams, *Lincoln and His Generals,* New York, 1952, p. 25.

41. See especially *O.R.,* Serial 27, pp. 277ff.

42. J. R. Sypher, *History of the Pennsylvania Reserves Corps,* Lancaster, 1865, p. 17.

43. *Ibid.,* p. 59.

44. *Ibid.,* p. 90.

45. *Ibid.,* p. 94.

46. *Ibid.,* p. 101.

47. Regiments were distributed as follows: 1st Brigade—1st, 2nd, 5th, 8th, Cavalry; 2nd Brigade—3rd, 4th, 7th, 11th, 13th (Bucktails); 3rd Brigade—6th, 9th, 10th, 12th (McCalmont, temporary Commander).

48. None of the three men makes any mention of the other two in covering the Mexican War, but it is improbable that the West Pointers in General Taylor's small command were unacquainted.

49. Reynolds seems to have got as far as Old Point Comfort on the way south. He mentioned seeing old army friends who, he said, regretted that his changed orders would prevent his going to Hatteras.

50. Reynolds Papers.

51. William H. Powell, *The Fifth Army Corps,* New York, 1896, p. 56.

52. William H. Locke, *The Story of the Regiment* (11th Pennsylvania Reserves), Philadelphia, 1868, p. 38.

53. Samuel P. Bates, *History of the Pennsylvania Volunteers,* 5 Vols., Harrisburg, Pennsylvania, 1869, Vol. 1, p. 666.

54. Sypher, *Pennsylvania Reserve Corps,* p. 121.

55. JFR to his sisters, October 14, 1861, Reynolds Papers.

56. Sergeant Thomas W. Dick to a friend, December 24, 1861, in the unpublished letters of Thomas W. Dick, Company "H," 12th Regiment, Pennsylvania Reserves, in the possession of his grandson Dr. J. S. Bowman, State College, Pennsylvania. Thomas Dick survived the war and practiced law in Cambria County, Pennsylvania for many years.

57. Meade, *Letters,* Vol. 1, p. 223, to his wife, October 12, 1861.

58. JFR to his sisters, October 22, 1861, Reynolds Papers.

59. *Ibid.*

60. John D. Billings, *Hard Tack and Coffee,* Boston, 1887, pp. 154-155; Henry N. Blake, *Three Years in the Army of the Potomac,* Boston, 1865, p. 86; T. F. M'Coy, "Recollections of General Reynolds," Alexander K. McClure, ed., *Annals of the War,* Philadelphia, 1879, p. 386.

61. *O.R.,* Serial 5, p. 611, McClellan's General Order No. 19. He complained of ". . . depredations of atrocious character committed on persons and property of citizens in Virginia by troops of his command. . . ."

62. *Ibid.,* p. 308.

63. JFR to his sisters, November 4, 1861, Reynolds Papers.

64. Tyler Dennett, *Lincoln and the Civil War in the Diaries and Letters of John Hay,* New York, 1939 (Hay diary, May 14, 1864, p. 182).

65. *O.R.,* Serial 5, p. 290. McClellan wrote: "My telegram [to Stone] did not contemplate making an attack on the enemy or crossing the river in force by any portion of General Stone's command, and, not anticipating such movement, I had upon

the 20th directed Major General McCall to return with his division on the 21st from Dranesville. . . ."

66. Meade, *Letters*, Vol. 1, p. 225, to his wife, October 24, 1861.

67. JFR to his sisters, November 4, 1861, Reynolds Papers.

68. JFR to his sister Hal, January 3, 1849, Reynolds Papers.

69. Meade, *Letters*, Vol. 1, p. 227, to his son, John S. Meade, November 11, 1861.

70. *O.R.*, Serial 5, pp. 490-495, 476.

71. *Ibid.*, p. 480.

72. *Ibid.*, p. 732.

73. Meade, *Letters*, Vol. 1, pp. 227, 233, 242, to his wife, November 1, 1861, February 2, 1862, February 5, 1862.

74. G. F. R. Henderson, *Stonewall Jackson and the Civil War*, 2 Vols., New York, 1902, Vol. 1, p. 231.

75. JFR to his sister Ellie, March 22, 1862, Reynolds Papers.

76. Meade, *Letters*, Vol. 1, p. 265, to his wife, May 10, 1862.

77. JFR to his sister Ellie, May 4, 1862, Reynolds Papers.

78. Moncure D. Conway, "Fredericksburg First and Last," *Magazine of American History*, Vol. 17, No. 6, March, 1887, p. 453; John T. Goolrick, *Historic Fredericksburg*, Richmond, 1922, p. 37.

79. General Reynolds' Special Order No. 18, issued May 29, 1862, undated clipping, Reynolds Papers. The clipping may be from a newspaper *The Christian Banner* published in the city irregularly by a Union sympathizer, James W. Hunicutt. See Charles A. Cuffel, *Durell's Battery During the Civil War*, Philadelphia, 1903, p. 37; S. J. Quinn, *Historic City of Fredericksburg*, Richmond, 1908, p. 77, identifies this man as a Reverend James V. Hunnicutt.

80. A. P. Smith, *The Seventy-Sixth Regiment New York Volunteers*, Cortland, New York, 1867, p. 75.

81. Sypher, *Pennsylvania Reserve Corps*, pp. 191-192.

82. Reynolds was referring to the behavior of southern women during General Butler's occupation of the city after Admiral Farragut's victory. Butler was so incensed that he issued his celebrated Order No. 28, May 15, which said that women guilty of insulting Union soldiers should be treated as women of the town, Robert U. Johnson and Clarence C. Buel, eds., *Battles and Leaders of the Civil War*, 4 Vols., New York, 1887, Vol. 3, p. 582n (hereafter cited as *B. and L.*).

83. Lieutenant Charles B. Lamborn, one of Reynolds' aides. Reynolds had probably brought Lamborn into Washington to meet Ellie on an earlier occasion.

84. This information was made available through the kindness of Mr. Prentiss Price, Rogersville, Tennessee, in a letter to the writer, July 21, 1957. The home itself is shown by Michler in 1867 as located about a mile and a half north by northeast of Falmouth, Plate 33, Map No. 1, *Atlas to Accompany the Official Records of the Union and Confederate Armies*, Washington, 1891-1895. Mr. George H. S. King of Fredericksburg, who also has been helpful in supplying information on this Washington family, says that the house burned around the turn of the century. However, until recent years the site remained clearly visible from U.S. Route 1, at the top of a long hill known as "Brummetts."

85. Sypher, *Pennsylvania Reserve Corps*, p. 180.

86. JFR to his sisters, April 24, 1862, Reynolds Papers.

87. JFR to his sister Ellie, June 10, 1862, Reynolds Papers.

88. *Ibid.*

89. Meade completely agreed with Reynolds. Jackson had paralyzed McDowell's 40,000 men, he said, when stupidity of the authorities in Washington sent McDowell "on a wild goose chase after a wily foe, who never intended to be caught in a trap. . . ." Meade, *Letters*, Vol. 1, p. 276, to his wife, June 18, 1862. For opposing views see Colin R. Ballard, *The Military Genius of Abraham*

Lincoln, New York, 1952, p. 87; John Codman Ropes, *The Story of the Civil War,* 2 Vols., New York, 1933, Vol. 1, p. 247; Peter S. Michie, *General McClellan,* New York, 1915, pp. 446-447. Michie, who wanted to be fair to McClellan, nevertheless admitted that the administration could not ignore Jackson's threat to the capital and that retaining McDowell to oppose him was justified.

CHAPTER VI. TWO OF SEVEN DAYS

1. Douglas Southall Freeman, *Lee's Lieutenants,* 3 Vols., New York, 1942, Vol. 1, pp. 288, 293.
2. Meade, *Letters,* Vol. 1, p. 273, to his wife, June 11, 1862.
3. *O.R.,* Serial 12, p. 1028.
4. *Ibid.,* p. 1013.
5. *Ibid.,* p. 1028.
6. *Ibid.,* Serial 14, p. 238.
7. *Ibid.,* Serial 12, p. 54.
8. *B. and L.,* Vol. 2, p. 317.
9. *O.R.,* Serial 14, p. 240, McClellan to Stanton, June 17, 1862; p. 259, Lincoln to McClellan, June 26, 1862.
10. *Ibid.,* p. 238.
11. *Ibid.,* Serial 13, p. 400 (Seymour's report); Reports of the Joint Committee on the Conduct of the War, *Senate Doc.,* Senate, 37th Cong., 3rd Sess., Vol. 1 (1863), p. 594 (hereafter cited as *C.C.W.*). In testimony before the Committee Reynolds said: "The position was selected by Porter and the troops disposed in it by Seymour and myself under McCall's direction."
12. *B. and L.,* Vol. 2, p. 238.
13. Details of the battle of Mechanicsville, so far as they involve Reynolds directly, are taken from his official report, which was never completed or published. It was delayed by Reynolds' capture at Gaines' Mill. While in Libby Prison Reynolds wrote two rough drafts and a partially finished copy, all three of them preserved in the Reynolds Papers.
14. *O.R.,* Serial 12, p. 54, McClellan's report.
15. *Ibid.,* Serial 13, p. 490, Lee's report.
16. *Ibid.,* p. 491.
17. JFR to his sisters, April 24, 1862, Reynolds Papers.
18. Reynolds' report of the battle, Reynolds Papers.
19. Sypher, *Pennsylvania Reserve Corps,* p. 198.
20. *O.R.,* Serial 13, pp. 490-491.
21. *Ibid.,* p. 392.
22. *Ibid.,* p. 400.
23. *Ibid.,* Serial 12, p. 54.
24. *Ibid.,* Serial 13, pp. 387, 389.
25. Meade, *Letters,* Vol. 1, p. 265, to his wife, May 10, 1862. However, Meade's disappointment over not rising fast enough was certainly normal in a military officer.
26. Sypher, *Pennsylvania Reserve Corps,* p. 189.
27. Sergeant Thomas W. Dick to his brother, May 29, 1862, unpublished letters.
28. Reynolds' report of the battle, Reynolds Papers.
29. *O.R.,* Serial 14, p. 264. Henderson, *Stonewall Jackson,* Vol. 2, p. 25, also admits that this retreat was ably conducted.
30. *O.R.,* Serial 14, p. 238. McClellan's exaggerated notion of Lee's numbers made him over cautious about weakening his main front opposite Richmond.
31. *B. and L.,* Vol. 2, p. 333.
32. *O.R.,* Serial 13, p. 492, Lee's report.
33. *Ibid.,* Serial 12, p. 56, McClellan's report.
34. *Ibid.,* Serial 13, p. 388, McCall's report.

35. Ropes, *Civil War*, Vol. 2, pp. 179-180; James Ford Rhodes, *History of the Civil War 1861-1865*, New York, 1917, p. 138; Henderson, *Stonewall Jackson*, Vol. 2, p. 39. Contrary to his criticism of McClellan, Henderson has only praise for Porter's tactics.
36. *O.R.*, Serial 14, p. 265.
37. *Ibid.*
38. *Ibid.*
39. *Ibid.*, Serial 13, p. 416.
40. Reynolds' report of the battle, Reynolds Papers.
41. *O.R.*, Serial 13, p. 389.
42. *Ibid.*, p. 225.
43. JFR to his sister Ellie, July 3, 1862, Reynolds Papers.
44. Charles Lamborn to Reynolds' sister Ellie, July 5, 1862, Reynolds Papers.
45. *O.R.*, Serial 13, pp. 565, 571, 587, 626.
46. *B. and L.*, Vol. 2, p. 360.
47. Henderson, *Stonewall Jackson*, Vol. 2, pp. 43-44.
48. Charles Lamborn to Reynolds' sister Ellie, July 18, 1862, Reynolds Papers. Lamborn himself had done well enough in the recent fighting to earn strong praise from the hard-bitten Major Roy Stone, who commanded the Bucktails in the battle of Gaines' Mill, *O.R.*, Serial 13, p. 418.
49. *C.C.W.*, Vol. 1 (1863), pp. 586-588.
50. *O.R.*, Serial 13, pp. 111-115, 391ff.
51. *Ibid.*, p. 397.
52. *Ibid.*, p. 395.
53. Sypher, *Pennsylvania Reserve Corps*, p. 309.
54. *O.R.*, Serial 118, pp. 386-387.
55. *Ibid.*, Serial 117, pp. 795-796.
56. *Ibid.*, p. 457, in General Order No. 118, Washington, Reynolds is listed as having been exchanged for Brigadier General Lloyd Tilghman, although other sources, including Reynolds' family, have said he was exchanged for Brigadier General William Barksdale. But barring some last-minute switch in the arrangements, there is no reason to ignore the wording of this order.
57. Sypher, *Pennsylvania Reserve Corps*, p. 323; Meade, *Letters*, Vol. 1, p. 302, to his wife, August 16, 1862.
58. E. M. Woodward, *History of the Third Pennsylvania Reserves*, Trenton, N.J., 1883, p. 137.
59. *Ibid.*, pp. 137-138.
60. Lancaster *Examiner and Herald*, July 16, 19, 1862.
61. *Ibid.*, July 1, 1862.
62. Meade, *Letters*, Vol. 1, p. 303, to his wife, August 16, 1862.
63. *O.R.*, Serial 107, pp. 752-753.
64. *Ibid.*, Serial 12, p. 61.
65. *Ibid.*, pp. 73-74.
66. *Ibid.*, Serial 18, p. 523.
67. *Ibid.*, Serial 16, pp. 12-13, Pope's report.
68. Warren H. Cudworth, *The First Massachusetts Regiment*, Boston, 1886, p. 263.
69. Massachusetts Historical Society, *Military Papers of the Massachusetts Historical Society*, 14 Vols., Boston, 1881-1918, Vol. 2, p. 132. (Hereafter cited as MHS *Papers*.)
70. Bates, *Pennsylvania Volunteers*, Vol. 1, p. 849.

CHAPTER VII. HEROICS ON HENRY HOUSE HILL

1. *O.R.*, Serial 16, p. 656.
2. *Ibid.*, p. 34. As of August 27 Pope estimated the number of troops under his command at 54,500 infantry and 4,000 cavalry.
3. A. F. Hill, *Our Boys, The Personal Experiences of a Soldier*, Philadelphia, 1865, p. 371. Hill lost a leg at Antietam, then began writing his book almost at once while his mem-

ory of events was clear.

4. *Ibid.*, pp. 371-372.

5. *O.R.*, Serial 15, pp. 148-149.

6. *Ibid.*, Serial 16, p. 665. The Confederate brigade commander was Bradley T. Johnson, who admitted that Reynolds' guns were served with rapidity and accuracy.

7. At McDowell's request a board of inquiry was called on November 21, 1862, to examine charges made against him during the campaign under Pope. At one point in the hearings Meade was asked if he approved of McDowell's leaving the pike after this brush with the enemy, *Ibid.*, Serial 15, p. 198. Meade said he did, that the opposition was thought to be slight. Reynold's report, *Ibid.*, Serial 16, p. 393, describes it as merely a demonstration by the enemy to save a wagon train. McDowell, *Ibid.*, p. 336, called it a rear guard reconnaissance of some cavalry. It should be remembered that at this time neither McDowell or Reynolds had any information to counter their belief that Jackson was still at Manassas Junction.

8. *Ibid.*, p. 393, Reynolds' report. Two orders from Pope were received by McDowell around 4 o'clock, the second of which, *Ibid.*, Serial 15, p. 329, announced the discovery that Jackson was north of Bull Run.

9. Pope, in *B. and L.*, Vol. 2, pp. 469-470, called it unaccountable that Sigel and Reynolds did not reinforce King, though he gives McDowell's absence as the probable reason no orders were given. McDowell had left his command to find Pope in response to the latter's request earlier in the day. But Pope, writing now in the 1880's, was conscious of the need to explain his defeat. In his report and testimony following the battle, he referred to Reynolds twice in connection with the evening of August 28, and without a word of disapproval, *O.R.*, Serial 15, p. 330; *Ibid.*, Serial 16, p. 14. For Pope's unqualified praise of Reynolds' actions at second Bull Run see *Ibid.*, p. 48.

10. John Gibbon, *Personal Recollections of the Civil War*, New York, 1928, p. 57.

11. Ropes, *Civil War*, Vol. 2, pp. 272-273.

12. *B. and L.*, Vol. 2, p. 469n; Henderson, *Stonewall Jackson*, Vol. 2, p. 148, says Jackson lost 725 out of 3,000 engaged. As to when the Iron Brigade got its name, William F. Fox, *Regimental Losses in the American Civil War*, Albany, New York, 1889, p. 117; Gibbon, *Recollections,* p. 93; Kenneth P. Williams, *Lincoln Finds a General*, 4 Vols., New York, 1949-1956, Vol. 1, p. 320, all agree that it came after the battle of Antietam. Henry G. Pearson, *James S. Wadsworth of Geneseo*, New York, 1913, p. 170, says the brigade was named at South Mountain. The subject is of interest in connection with Reynolds because he later commanded this famous unit.

13. Gibbon, *Recollections*, p. 57.

14. *O.R.*, Serial 16, p. 393, Reynolds' report.

15. *Ibid.*, Serial 18, pp. 717-718.

16. *Ibid.*, Serial 16, p. 337.

17. *Ibid.*, p. 38; Serial 15, p. 330.

18. *Ibid.*, Serial 15, pp. 330-331; Henderson, *Stonewall Jackson*, Vol. 2, pp. 149-150; Ropes, *Civil War*, Vol. 2, p. 275.

19. Sypher, *Pennsylvania Reserve Corps*, p. 339.

20. *O.R.*, Serial 16, p. 393, Reynolds' report, for statement that Sigel requested his help; Serial 15, p. 124, for Sigel's insistence that he did not see Reynolds on that day; Serial 16, p. 267, for Sigel's contradictory statement, in which he admits that Reynolds was up on his left by noon of the 29th.

21. *Ibid.*

22. *Ibid.*, Serial 16, p. 76.

23. *Ibid.*, p. 393, Reynolds' report.

24. *Ibid.*, pp. 279-280.

25. *Ibid.*, p. 364.

26. *Ibid.*, pp. 338-339.

27. Ropes, *Civil War*, Vol. 2, pp. 303-304n.

28. *O.R.*, Serial 15, p. 124. In answer to

a question at McDowell's inquiry, Sigel said he did not regard McDowell as treacherous but thought him inattentive to duty.

29. Locke, *Story of the Regiment*, p. 114; Blake, *Three Years*, p. 132; Benjamin F. Cook, *The 12th Massachusetts Volunteers*, Boston, 1882, p. 64.

30. *O.R.*, Serial 16, p. 366.

31. *Ibid.*, p. 39, Pope's report; p. 646, Jackson's report.

32. *Ibid.*, p. 15; see also Theodore B. Gates, *The Ulster Guard and the War of the Rebellion*, New York, 1879, p. 273.

33. Hill, *Our Boys*, p. 377.

34. E. Porter Alexander, *Military Memoirs of a Confederate; A Critical Narrative*, New York, 1907, pp. 211-212; Henderson, *Stonewall Jackson*, Vol. 2, p. 168.

35. Ropes, *Civil War*, Vol. 2, p. 288; Henderson, *Stonewall Jackson*, Vol. 2, p. 170.

36. *O.R.*, Serial 16, p. 393, Reynolds' report.

37. Woodward, *Third Pennsylvania Reserves*, p. 159.

38. George H. Gordon, *History of the Campaign of the Army of Virginia*, Boston, 1880, p. 359.

39. Ropes, *Civil War*, Vol. 2, p. 292; Henderson, *Stonewall Jackson*, Vol. 2, pp. 171-172; Powell, *Fifth Army Corps*, p. 223.

40. O.R. Howard Thomson and William H. Rauch, *History of the "Bucktails,"* Philadelphia, 1906, p. 193.

41. *O.R.*, Serial 16, p. 482; John Codman Ropes, *The Army under Pope*, New York, 1885, p. 136.

42. *Ibid.*, p. 140.

43. *Ibid.*

44. *O.R.*, Serial 16, p. 394, Reynolds' report.

45. Martin D. Hardin, *History of the 12th Regiment* (Pennsylvania Volunteers), New York, 1890, p. 102.

46. *O.R.*, Serial 16, p. 394, Reynolds' report.

47. A. E. Lee, "From Cedar Mountain to Chantilly," *Magazine of American History*, Vol. 16, No. 5, 1886, p. 578.

48. Hill, *Our Boys*, p. 384.

49. A. M. Stewart, *Camp, March and Battlefield*, Philadelphia, 1865, p. 280. Stewart said that veteran soldiers soon learned to laugh at the posturing officers they saw pictured in the popular weeklies.

50. Thomson and Rauch, *Bucktails*, p. 192.

51. Bates, *Pennsylvania Volunteers*, Vol. 1, pp. 583, 697; Woodward, *Third Pennsylvania Reserves*, p. 162; Sypher, *Pennsylvania Reserve Corps*, p. 346; Hill, *Our Boys*, pp. 384-385.

52. *O.R.*, Serial 16, pp. 341-342, 532.

53. *Ibid.*, p. 395, Reynolds report. The final position of this brigade remains vague. Reynolds names only Meade's and Seymour's brigades as fighting on Henry House Hill and states that the division was united after that. McDowell, *Ibid.*, p. 341, mentions only the two brigades as being brought back from the right. Ropes, *Civil War*, Vol. 2, pp. 294n-295n, says the rear brigade under Anderson was not able to cross the pike and that it fought with Warren. He too has only Meade and Seymour on Henry House Hill, as do Thomson and Rauch, *Bucktails*, p. 191. The question of Anderson's position in the late afternoon of the 30th is important because it has been mapped as connecting with the rest of the division in the fighting on Henry House Hill (see the *Illustrative Map of the Battle Grounds of August 28, 29, 30, 1862*, surveyed in June, 1878, by Major General G. K. Warren, copy in the Museum of the Manassas National Battlefield Park). Having fought that day on the left, Warren may have remembered Anderson's position. This brigade could have remained in the angle just south of the pike and west of Sudley Springs road. If so, it may possibly have been close enough to Henry House Hill to justify connecting it with Meade and Seymour. Meade, *O.R.*, Serial 16, p. 398, says: "It was the good fortune of the Reserves to be brought into action at this moment" on the hill.

He makes no mention of a separated brigade. Unfortunately, reports are not available from Seymour or from any of the several officers who took turns leading the 3rd Brigade on August 30.

54. Ropes, *Army under Pope*, p. 142.
55. *O.R.*, Serial 18, p. 746.
56. John T. Morse, Jr., ed., *The Diary of Gideon Welles*, 3 Vols., Boston, 1911, Vol. 1, entry of September 4, 1862, p. 107, and September 7, p. 113. For a defense of McClellan's actions during this period see James G. Randall, *Lincoln the President: Springfield to Gettysburg*, 2 Vols., New York, 1945, Vol. 2, pp. 107, 112; Warren W. Hassler, Jr., *General George B. McClellan: Shield of the Union*, Baton Rouge, Louisiana, 1957, pp. 208ff.
57. Thomas L. Livermore, *Numbers and Losses in the Civil War in America 1861-1865*, Boston, 1901, pp. 87-88. The exact total given is 16,054. Separate losses for troops of McClellan are not shown.
58. Sypher, *Pennsylvania Reserve Corps*, p. 352.
59. *O.R.*, Serial 16, p. 256.
60. Meade, *Letters*, Vol. 1, p. 308, to his wife, September 4, 1862.
61. *O.R.*, Serial 16, p. 269.
62. *Ibid.*, p. 282.
63. *Ibid.*, p. 286.
64. *Ibid.*, p. 341.
65. Ropes, *Civil War*, Vol. 2, pp. 294-295; Alexander, *Memoirs*, p. 213;

Hardin, *12th Regiment*, pp. 100-102.
66. Henderson, *Stonewall Jackson*, Vol. 2, p. 173. Also of this general opinion are Ropes, *Civil War*, Vol. 2, p. 290, and DePeyster, *Philip Kearny*, p. 418.
67. *O.R.*, Serial 16, pp. 469, 482.
68. *Ibid.*, p. 48.
69. *Ibid.*, p. 345.
70. *Ibid.*, p. 768.
71. *Ibid.*, p. 532.
72. Henderson, *Stonewall Jackson*, Vol. 2, p. 181.
73. *O.R.*, Serial 16, p. 395, Reynolds' report.
74. Meade, *Letters*, Vol. 1, pp. 307-308, to his wife, September 3, 1862.
75. *O.R.*, Serial 17, p. 992.
76. *Ibid.*, p. 994.
77. *Ibid.*, pp. 995-996.
78. *Ibid.*, Serial 16, p. 529.
79. Williams, in *Lincoln Finds a General*, Vol. 2, pp. 785-789, comments in detail on the board's vindication of Porter. He objects to its going so far as to make Porter practically the savior of Pope's army.
80. *O.R.*, Serial 17, p. 992.
81. Governor Curtin, *Ibid.*, Serial 28, p. 203, wired General Wool that the Confederates had arrived at Frederick, Maryland. He had heard that Jackson spoke of going through Adams, York, and Lancaster Counties of Pennsylvania and all the way to Philadelphia.

CHAPTER VIII. NORTH OF THE FIGHTING

1. *O.R.*, Serial 107, p. 791.
2. *Ibid.*, Serial 28, p. 214.
3. Samuel R. Kamm, *The Civil War Career of Thomas A. Scott*, Philadelphia, 1940, p. 142. Feeder lines of the Pennsylvania Rail Road extended below the Pennsylvania border at several points.
4. *Pennsylvania Archives*, 138 Vols., Harrisburg, 1852-1935, Series 4, Vol. 8, p. 723, totals for 1861-62.
5. *O.R.*, Serial 28, p. 216.
6. *Ibid.*
7. *Ibid.*, pp. 216-217.
8. Ropes' estimate, *Civil War*, Vol. 2, p. 337n; but Livermore, *Numbers*

and Losses, p. 93, gives Lee close to 60,000 effectives alone by September 15. The number is important chiefly in terms of the exaggerations being circulated in Pennsylvania.

9. *O.R.*, Serial 28, pp. 219, 230.
10. *Ibid.*, p. 251.
11. Letter of a soldier in the 63rd Pennsylvania Volunteers, September 14, 1862, undated clipping from a newspaper, Reynolds Papers.
12. *O.R.*, Serial 28, pp. 225-226. Both a circular and a general order were sent out from McClellan's headquarters on the subject of unauthorized leaves and straggling.
13. *Ibid.*, p. 203, pp. 246-247.
14. *Ibid.*, p. 247.
15. *Ibid.*, p. 248.
16. *Ibid.*, pp. 248-249.
17. *Ibid.*, p. 250.
18. *Ibid.*, p. 252.
19. *Ibid.*
20. *Ibid.*
21. *Ibid.*, p. 270.
22. *Ibid.*
23. *Ibid.*, p. 253.
24. *Ibid.*, p. 268.
25. *Ibid.*, p. 269, both telegrams.
26. *Ibid.*, pp. 267, 276.
27. *Ibid.*, pp. 273-274.
28. *Ibid.*, p. 277.
29. *Ibid.*
30. Meade, *Letters,* Vol. I, p. 310, to his wife, September 13, 1862.
31. *Ibid.*
32. Hill, *Our Boys,* p. 393.
33. *O.R.*, Serial 28, p. 287, telegram of September 13.
34. Charles C. Coffin, *Four Years of Fighting,* Boston, 1866, p. 113.
35. Louis Richards, *Eleven Days in the Militia,* Philadelphia, 1862, p. 19.
36. *Ibid.*, p. 20. Reynolds' expected time of arrival is given in a wire from Governor Curtin to his adjutant, Colonel J. A. Wright, September 13: "General Reynolds is on his way. We expect him at 8'oclock." *O.R.*, Serial 28, p. 287.
37. *O.R.*, Serial 28, p. 288. The message was about 200 words in all, and included Reynolds' statement of conviction that the enemy intended to

invade the state.
38. *Ibid,* p. 292.
39. All the dispatches covering the Pennsylvania militia campaign of 1862, unless otherwise noted, are quoted or extracted from copies contained in the Reynolds Papers.
40. *O.R.*, Serial 28, p. 293.
41. *Ibid.*
42. *B. and L.*, Vol. 2, p. 574.
43. JFR to his sisters, September 14, 1862, Reynolds Papers.
44. *O.R.*, Serial 28, p. 306.
45. *Ibid.*, p. 329.
46. Alexander K. McClure, *Old Time Notes of Pennsylvania,* 2 Vols., Philadelphia, 1905, Vol. 1, pp. 570-571.
47. Livermore, *Numbers and Losses,* pp. 92-93, Union casualties 2,108 killed, 9,549 wounded, 753 missing; Confederate casualties 2,700 killed, 9,024 wounded, an estimated 2,000 missing, mostly stragglers.
48. *O.R.*, Serial 28, p. 332, September 19. Reynolds said that none of the militia regiments would march. In *B. and L.*, Vol. 2, p. 597, General Jacob Cox writes that McClellan had told him he expected 15,000 Pennsylvania troops on the morning of the 18th and that when these reinforcements arrived, he would attack.
49. Richards, *Eleven Days,* p. 44.
50. "David McNeely Stauffer," Elizabeth Clarke Kieffer, LCHS *Papers,* Vol. 56, No. 7, 1952, p. 167.
51. Harrisburg *Patriot,* Harrisburg, Pennsylvania, September 17 and 25, 1862.
52. JFR to his sisters, September 28, 1862, Reynolds Papers.
53. Richards, *Eleven Days,* p. 30.
54. Undated clipping, Reynolds Papers. The exact source and date for this paragraph were not found. The files of the Holidaysburg (Pa.) *Register* and the Blair County (Pa.) *Whig* which were searched contained no issues for the period of the Civil War. It was from a Holidaysburg paper that Reynolds said he had clipped the paragraph.
55. The *Pennsylvania Daily Telegraph,* Harrisburg, Pennsylvania, Septem-

ber 27, 1862. The undated clipping, along with the one mentioned above in Note No. 54, is in the Reynolds Papers.

56. JFR to his sisters, October 5, 1862, Reynolds Papers.

57. Reynolds Papers; also the Harris-burg *Pariot*, October 3, 1862.

58. JFR to his sisters, September 28, 1862, Reynolds Papers.

59. Meade, *Letters,* Vol. 1, pp. 314-315, to his wife, September 29, 1862.

60. *Ibid.,* October 1, 1862.

61. *Ibid.,* May 10, 1862.

CHAPTER IX. TROUBLE NEAR FRANKLIN'S CROSSING

1. *O.R.,* Serial 28, p. 367.

2. *Ibid.,* p. 569. As of September 10, 1862, the other corps commanders were Couch, 2nd; Porter, 5th; Franklin, 6th; Willcox, 9th; Slocum, 12th. The only major generals were Couch, Porter, Franklin, and the absent Hooker.

3. JFR to his sisters, October 14, 1862, Reynolds Papers. He wrote: "I thought the Governor was pretty well convinced that they [the militia] were not to be depended upon in any case."

4. Meade, *Letters,* Vol. 1, p. 316, to his wife, October 1, 1862.

5. *Pennsylvania Archives,* Series 4, Vol. 8, p. 475, Meade to Curtin, September 29, 1862; McClellan to Curtin, September 30, 1862. While Meade said he was not competent to pass judgment on whether the state or the national government had the right to make nominations for officers, his implication was strong. McClellan only pressed for action. Curtin reprinted these letters in his report to the legislature in connection with his defense, given on p. 474.

6. *O.R.,* Serial 28, p. 374.

7. Meade, *Letters,* Vol. 1, p. 318, to his wife, October 5, 1862. In *O.R.,* Serial 28, p. 348, Meade raised the number absent from the field to 8,000.

8. *O.R.,* Serial 28, p. 365.

9. *Ibid.,* p. 430.

10. A detailed and dramatic account is in Freeman, *Lee's Lieutenants,* Vol. 2, pp. 284-309.

11. Peter S. Michie, *General McClellan,* New York, 1915, p. 436; *Diary of Gideon Welles,* Vol. 1, October 11, 1862, p. 169. Welles writes: "We have word that seems reliable that Stuart's cavalry have been to Chambersburg in the rear of McClellan, while he was absent in Philadelphia stopping at the Continental Hotel. I hope neither statement is correct. But am apprehensive that both may be true."

12. *O.R.,* Serial 27, pp. 10-11, the order transmitted through Halleck on Oct. 6.

13. JFR to his sisters, October 14, 1862, Reynolds Papers.

14. *Ibid.;* Meade, *Letters,* Vol. 1, p. 321, to his son John Sergeant Meade, October 23, 1862.

15. *O.R.,* Serial 28, p. 492.

16. JFR to his sisters, November 4, 1862, Reynolds Papers.

17. Philadelphia *Weekly Express,* July 12, 1863.

18. M'Coy, "Recollections of General Reynolds," *Annals of the War,* p. 386.

19. *Ibid.,* pp. 388-389.

20. *Ibid.,* p. 389.

21. Hitchcock, *War from the Inside,* p. 101.

22. *Ibid.,* p. 245.

23. *Ibid.,* p. 101.

24. Hill, *Our Boys,* p. 139. Earlier Hill had tried a spell of serving as one of Reynolds' orderlies, but two days

seem to have been enough. When asked how he liked the duty, he said: ". . . I liked 'over there' very well. But . . . I wasn't there a minute at a time without being sent elsewhere, which was peculiarly unpleasant." Hill was glad to be relieved.

25. See Chapter II, p. 35.

26. Hitchcock,*War from the Inside*, p. 102.

27. *History of the One Hundred and Twenty-First Pennsylvania Volunteers*, "An Account from the Ranks," Philadelphia, 1926, pp. 25-26. In *History of the Corn Exchange Regiment* (118th Pennsylvania Volunteers) by The Survivors Association, Philadelphia, 1892, p. 231, it was said that the berating of Meade took place only out of earshot.

28. Hill, *Our Boys*, pp. 292-293; Billings, *Hard Tack and Coffee*, p. 349. Billings describes how Meade, in a fit of temper, knocked down an exhausted straggler with the flat of his sword. Shortly afterwards, Billings adds, the general was filled with remorse.

29. Buell, *Cannoneer*, p. 80; Cook, *12th Massachusetts*, p. 99; Smith, *Seventy-Sixth New York Volunteers*, p. 107. Frank Wilkeson, *Recollections of a Private Soldier in the Army of the Potomac*, New York, 1887, p. 93, felt differently. He said the only time he ever saw Meade or Grant under fire was at Spottsylvania, and then only in range of rifled cannon fire. But Billings should have been with Meade earlier—say at South Mountain, Antietam, or Fredericksburg.

30. *Corn Exchange Regiment*, p. 231.

31. Meade, *Letters*, Vol. 1, p. 320 to his wife, October 20, 1862.

32. William H. Armstrong ("Citizen Soldier"), *Red-Tape and Pigeon-Hole Generals*, New York, 1864, p. 188.

33. Meade, *Letters*, Vol. 1, pp. 325-326, to his wife, November 9, 1862.

34. JFR to his sisters, November 30, 1862, Reynolds Papers.

35. *Ibid.*

36. *O.R.*, Serial 28, p. 554.

37. *Ibid.*, p. 569.

38. Alfred B. McCalmont, *Extracts from Letters Written by Alfred B. McCalmont, 1862-1865*, printed for private circulation by his son Robert, p. 22.

39. Philadelphia *Weekly Express*, July 12, 1863.

40. *O.R.*, Serial 31, p. 1121.

41. JFR to his sisters, November 30, 1862, Reynolds Papers. It was Captain Rosengarten who became a sort of official biographer of Reynolds during the eighties, nineties, and early nineteen hundreds.

42. Meade, *Letters*, Vol. 1, p. 334, to his wife, December 2, 1862.

43. *Ibid.*, p. 328, November 16, 1862.

44. JFR to his sister Hal, October 25, 1862, Reynolds Papers.

45. Livermore, *Numbers and Losses*, p. 96. These are approximations of total strength. Listed as actually engaged are Union—113,987; Confederate—72,497.

46. Thomas W. Dick to his parents, January 8, 1862, unpublished letters.

47. *B. and L.*, Vol. 3, p. 136n. B. O. Curtis, *History of the 24th Michigan of the Iron Brigade*, Detroit, 1891, p. 90, added regarding Reynolds: "This officer was noted for his reticence and made no reply."

48. *C.C.W.*, Vol. 1 (1863), pp. 709-710, Franklin's testimony before the committee investigating the conduct of the war.

49. *B. and L.*, Vol. 3, p. 133.

50. *Ibid.*, pp. 133-134.

51. *O.R.*, Serial 31, p. 71.

52. *Ibid.*, p. 90. These numbers do not include Sickles' 10,000 in reserve or Brig. Gen. George Bayard's 3,500 cavalry. Franklin's left grand division totaled 56,000.

53. Reynolds, in his testimony before the committee, said he chose the Reserves because they showed the largest return for that morning, but the difference in strength hardly justifies their selection on that basis, *C.C.W.*, Vol. 1 (1863), p. 698.

54. Thomas W. Dick to his parents, January 8, 1863, unpublished letters.

55. O.R., Serial 31, p. 454, Reynolds' report.
56. Henderson, *Stonewall Jackson*, Vol. 2, p. 311.
57. *Ibid.*, p. 314.
58. *C.C.W.*, Vol. 1 (1863), p. 699, Reynolds' testimony.
59. *O.R.*, Serial 31, p. 638, Jackson's report.
60. *C.C.W.*, Vol. 1 (1863), p. 699, Reynolds' testimony.
61. *O.R.*, Serial 31, p. 92.
62. Henderson, *Stonewall Jackson*, Vol. 2, p. 317.
63. *O.R.*, Serial 31, p. 92.
64. *Ibid.*, p. 632, Jackson's report.
65. *Ibid.*, p. 512, Meade's report.
66. *Ibid.*, p. 485.
67. *C.C.W.*, Vol. 1 (1863), p. 700, Reynolds' testimony.
68. *O.R.*, Serial 31, pp. 480, 485.
69. *Ibid.*, p. 92.
70. *Ibid.*
71. Hitchcock, *War from the Inside*, p. 134.
72. Thomson and Rauch, *The Bucktails*, p. 236.
73. *O.R.*, Serial 31, pp. 512-513, Meade's report.
74. *Ibid.*, pp. 129-131.
75. *Ibid.*, p. 137.
76. Livermore, *Numbers and Losses*, p. 98.
77. *O.R.*, Serial 31, p. 455, Reynolds' report.
78. *C.C.W.*, Vol. 1 (1863), pp. 700-701, Reynolds' testimony; pp. 723-724, Burnside's testimony; p. 661, Franklin's testimony.
79. *Ibid.*, p. 699, Reynolds' testimony.
80. *O.R.*, Serial 31, pp. 458-459, Wainwright's report; p. 483, Captain James Hall's report; p. 515, Cooper's report; p. 517, Amsden's report; p. 518, Ramson's report.
81. *Ibid.*, p. 632, Jackson's report.
82. *Ibid.*
83. Buell, *Cannoneer*, p. 45.
84. Francis W. Palfrey, *The Antietam and Fredericksburg*, New York, 1882, p. 147.
85. Meade, *Letters*, Vol. 1, p. 341 to his wife, December 23, 1862.
86. *Ibid.*, pp. 342-343, December 30, 1862.
87. *Ibid.*, p. 346, January 4, 1863.

CHAPTER X. HOOKER'S ABLEST OFFICER

1. *O.R.*, Serial 31, p. 1009. Halleck, writing to Franklin on May 29 said that Burnside did not deny it. See also pp. 1006-1012.
2. Meade, *Letters*, Vol. 1, pp. 346, 351, to his wife, January 4, 28, 1863.
3. *Ibid.*, pp. 350-351, January 26, 1863.
4. Meade's letter, dated December 25, 1862, is reprinted in the Lancaster *Examiner and Herald*, January 21, 1863. Curtin's appeal is in *Pennsylvania Archives*, Series 4, Vol. 8, p. 487.
5. *O.R.*, Serial 107, pp. 981-982.
6. *Ibid.*, Serial 40, p. 63.
7. *Ibid.*
8. *Ibid.*, p. 83, the message dated February 17, 1863.
9. *Ibid.*, pp. 90-91, the message dated February 20, 1863.
10. *Ibid.*
11. *Ibid.*, Serial 107, pp. 986-987.
12. Cook, *12th Massachusetts*, p. 99; Locke, *Story of the Regiment*, p. 187.
13. *C.C.W.*, Vol. 1 (1865), p. 112.
14. JFR to his sisters, February 24, 1863, Reynolds Papers.
15. Lancaster *Examiner and Herald*, December 3, 1862.
16. JFR to his sisters, April 11, 1863, Reynolds Papers.
17. See Chapter VI, p. 101.
18. Meade, *Letters*, Vol. 1, p. 363, to

his wife, April 5, 1863.

19. Armstrong, *Red-Tape and Pigeon-Hole Generals*, p. 283. Armstrong's general bitterness against high-ranking officers makes this admission on his part impressive.
20. JFR to his sisters, April 11, 1863, Reynolds Papers.
21. *Ibid.*
22. Original in Hooker's hand, Reynolds Papers.
23. *O.R.*, Serial 31, pp. 998-999.
24. *Ibid.*, Serial 40, p. 234.
25. *Ibid.*, p. 774.
26. *Ibid.*, p. 750.
27. *Ibid.*, Serial 107, pp. 1009-1010, April 4, 1863.
28. John Bigelow, Jr., *The Campaign of Chancellorsville: A Strategic and Tactical Study*, New Haven, 1910, p. 224, gives these acceptable numbers for Hooker's right wing; Abner Doubleday, *Chancellorsville and Gettysburg*, New York, 1885, pp. 4-5, describes Hooker's plans.
29. *O.R.*, Serial 40, p. 228.
30. *Ibid.*, p. 320. The April 30 present-for-duty-equipped returns for the 1st, 3rd, and 6th Corps totaled 55,677.
31. Bigelow, *Chancellorsville*, p. 273, gives Jackson's total strength as 31,740.
32. *O.R.*, Serial 39, pp. 204-205. Headquarters came down hard on Benham for what they considered his failure to meet the deadline. Benham in turn took up ten pages (205-214) in trying to defend himself.
33. Pearson, *Wadsworth*, p. 179. Wadsworth proved right; only twenty boats had been floated by daybreak. Men staggered and fell from the weight of the pontoons, and before they resorted to wagons even the officers were lending a hand.
34. *O.R.*, Serial 39, p. 208.
35. Pearson, *Wadsworth*, p. 180.
36. *O.R.*, Serial 39, p. 253.
37. *Ibid.*, pp. 204 - 205 (see above, Note 32).
38. Pearson, *Wadsworth*, p. 181.

39. *O.R.*, Serial 40, p. 288.
40. *Ibid.*, Serial 39, p. 213.
41. Bigelow, *Chancellorsville*, p. 192, says Benham's trouble lay in his believing he was over Wadsworth at the lower crossing and over Brigadier General W. T. H. Brooks at the one above.
42. *O.R.*, Serial 40, pp. 757-758.
43. *Ibid.*, p. 759.
44. Bigelow, *Chancellorsville*, p. 234, feels that Sedgwick should at least have thrown additional troops across the river by the 30th, though he thought Hooker was at fault for restricting Sedgwick's action.
45. *O.R.*, Serial 40, p. 290.
46. *Ibid.*, p. 310.
47. *Ibid.*, p. 309.
48. *Ibid.*, p. 310.
49. *Ibid.*, p. 313.
50. *Ibid.*, pp. 310-311.
51. JFR to his sisters, April 30, 1863, Reynolds Papers.
52. *O.R.*, Serial 40, p. 312.
53. Pearson, *Wadsworth*, p. 178.
54. Bigelow, *Chancellorsville*, p. 234. (See above, Note 44.)
55. *O.R.*, Serial 40, p. 824.
56. *Ibid.*, p. 337.
57. *C.C.W.*, Vol. 1 (1865), p. 145.
58. Henderson, *Stonewall Jackson*, Vol. 2, p. 417.
59. *O.R.*, Serial 39, p. 171.
60. *Ibid.*, Serial 40, p. 312.
61. *Ibid.*, p. 326.
62. *Ibid.*, p. 340.
63. *Ibid.*, p. 326.
64. *B. and L.*, Vol. 3, p. 176; Doubleday, *Chancellorsville and Gettysburg*, pp. 13-14; Henderson, *Stonewall Jackson*, Vol. 2, p. 419.
65. Bigelow, *Chancellorsville*, p. 478n; *B. and L.*, Vol. 3, p. 161.
66. *O.R.*, Serial 40, p. 337, for Reynolds to Sedgwick on A. P. Hill's withdrawal; Henderson, *Stonewall Jackson*, Vol. 2, p. 416, for Confederate troops left opposite Sedgwick and Reynolds. Henderson gives the number as 10,000.
67. Doubleday, *Chancellorsville and Gettysburg*, p. 68; Freeman, *Lee's Lieutenants*, Vol. 2, p. 646.
68. Henderson, *Stonewall Jackson*, Vol.

2, p. 428; Freeman, *Lee's Lieu-tenants*, Vol. 2, p. 645.

69. G. W. Redway, *The War of Secession 1861-1862*, London, 1910, p. 348.

70. *O.R.*, Serial 40, p. 351.

71. *Ibid.*, p. 353.

72. *Ibid.*, pp. 368-369.

73. Pearson, *Wadsworth*, p. 187.

74. *O.R.*, Serial 39, p. 254, Reynolds' report; *Ibid.*, Serial 40, p. 362.

75. Henderson, *Stonewall Jackson*, Vol. 2, p. 427.

76. *Ibid.*, pp. 429, 432-433.

77. *O.R.*, Serial 40, p. 363.

78. *Ibid.*, p. 360. This is the disputed dispatch that Howard denied ever having received. See *B and L.*, Vol 3, p. 219.

79. *O.R.*, Serial 39, pp. 254-255, Reynolds' report.

80. Doubleday, *Chancellorsville and Gettysburg*, p. 42.

81. *O.R.*, Serial 39, p. 254, Reynolds' report.

82. Bigelow, *Chancellorsville*, p. 307.

83. *O.R.*, Serial 39, p. 255, Reynolds' report.

84. *Ibid.*, Serial 40, pp. 364, 369.

85. Bigelow, *Chancellorsville*, p. 346.

86. Doubleday, *Chancellorsville and Gettysburg*, p. 44.

87. *O.R.*, Serial 39, p. 390, Sickles' report.

88. *Ibid.*, p. 255, Reynolds' report.

89. Meade, *Letters*, Vol. 1, p. 372, to his wife, May 8, 1863; Doubleday, *Chancellorsville and Gettysburg*, p. 54.

90. A. R. Small, *The Sixteenth Maine Regiment in the War of the Rebellion*, Portland, Maine, 1886, p. 106; Bigelow, *Chancellorsville*, p. 364.

91. Meade, *Letters*, Vol. 1, p. 372, to his wife, May 8, 1863.

92. *C.C.W.*, Vol. 1 (1865), p. 311.

93. *O.R.*, Serial 40, p. 378.

94. Thomas Chamberlin, *History of the 150th Regiment Pennsylvania Volunteers*, Philadelphia, 1905, pp. 94-95. Reynolds' report, *O.R.*, Serial 39, p. 255, merely describes the reconnaissance, concluding: ". . . as it was nearly dark the brigade returned."

95. Doubleday, *Chancellorsville and Gettysburg*, pp. 55-56. Doubleday confuses the date of Stone's reconnaissance, placing it vaguely on May 3 instead of 4.

96. Samuel P. Bates, *Martial Deeds of Pennsylvania*, Philadelphia, 1875, p. 473; Gibbon, *Recollections*, p. 119. Gibbon said that in seeking information from a reliable source, he had gone to Reynolds' tent on the morning of May 6: "He was the picture of woe and disgust and said plainly that we had been badly outgeneraled and whipped by half our number."

97. Doubleday, *Chancellorsville and Gettysburg*, p. 68.

98. *O.R.*, Serial 39, p. 510. Reynolds made this statement in a letter on May 24 to Meade, supporting him in a controversy with Hooker over what Meade and others had decided in the conference of the 4th.

99. *C.C.W.*, Vol. 1 (1865), p. 135, for Hooker's own testimony as to Reynolds' falling asleep; Doubleday, *Chancellorsville and Gettysburg*, p. 68. In *B. and L.*, Vol. 3, p. 171, Couch says only that Reynolds lay down on the ground very fatigued.

100. *B. and L.*, Vol. 3, p. 171.

101. *Ibid.*

102. Richard M. Bache, *General George Gordon Meade*, Philadelphia, 1897, p. 277.

103. *Ibid.*, p. 278.

104. Bigelow, *Chancellorsville*, pp. 473, 475.

105. *C.C.W.*, Vol. 1 (1865), p. 144. Hooker discusses the point again in *B. and L.*, Vol. 3, p. 222.

106. Theodore A. Dodge, *The Campaign of Chancellorsville*, Boston, 1881, p. 14; Doubleday, *Chancellorsville and Gettysburg*, pp. 53-55; Bigelow, *Chancellorsville*, p. 477; Gibbon, *Recollections*, p. 107; Henderson, *Stonewall Jackson*, Vol. 2, p. 468 (though qualified).

107. *C.C.W.*, Vol. 1 (1865), p. 146.

108. *B. and L.*, Vol. 3, p. 222.

109. *O.R.*, Serial 39, p. 171.

110. *Ibid.*, Serial 40, p. 438.

111. *C.C.W.*, Vol. 1 (1865), p. 237.

112. JFR to his sisters, May 9, 1863, Reynolds Papers.

CHAPTER XI. WITH A VIEW TO AN ADVANCE

1. *O.R.*, Serial 40, p. 479.
2. Meade, *Letters*, Vol. 1, p. 376, to his wife, May 15, 1863.
3. *Ibid.*, p. 374, May 12, 1863.
4. *O.R.*, Serial 39, p. 510. In testimony before the committee on the conduct of the war, *C.C.W.*, Vol. 1 (1865), pp. 135-136, Hooker produced only two of the letters Meade had requested from officers present at the conference. He cited those of Sickles and Howard, who supported him, though with reservations. Why he did not mention the one Reynolds wrote two days before the others is not clear.
5. Gibbon, *Recollections*, p. 120.
6. *C.C.W.*, Vol. 1 (1865), pp. 135-136.
7. McCalmont, *Letters*, pp. 41-42.
8. Meade, *Letters*, Vol. 1, p. 378, to his wife, May 19, 1863.
9. *O.R.*, Serial 40, p. 511.
10. *Ibid*, p. 528.
11. *Ibid.*, p. 542.
12. *Ibid.*, pp. 574, 846.
13. *Ibid.*, Serial 107, p. 1043.
14. Meade, *Letters*, Vol. 1, p. 385, to his wife, June 13, 1863.
15. JFR to Ellie, June 10, 1862, Reynolds Papers.
16. JFR to his sisters, August 25, 1862, Reynolds Papers.
17. JFR to his sisters, January 23, 1863, Reynolds Papers.
18. Reynolds' friend may have been Colonel William G. Freeman, of Cornwall, Pennsylvania. After closing out his career in 1856 in the adjutant general's office in Washington, he had remained in the city. He was a family friend, to whom Reynolds appealed indirectly through a letter to his sisters, May 14, 1855 (Reynolds Papers), when he felt that Jefferson Davis was overlooking him. During the war Freeman may have kept in touch with affairs at the war department.

He lived until 1866, Cullum, *Biographical Register*, Vol. 1, p. 574.
19. Eleanor Reynolds to Colonel J.F.R. Landis, August 20, 1913, Reynolds Papers. See Appendix.
20. *Ibid.*
21. Meade, *Letters*, Vol. 1, p. 385, to his wife, June 13, 1863.
22. *Ibid.*
23. The only contemporary statement found regarding Reynolds' suggestion of Meade for the command is in the New York *Times*, July 3, 1863. But it crept into later accounts: Rosengarten, *Reynolds Memorial*, p. 20; a letter to the *Memorial* by Winfield S. Hancock, March 4, 1880, p. 92; George Meade, ed., in Meade, *Letters*, Vol. 2, p. 6; Bache, *Meade*, p. 64. Eleanor Reynolds also wrote that her brother had recommended Meade, letter to Colonel Landis, August 20, 1913, Reynolds Papers.
24. Meade *Letters*, Vol. 1, p. 385, to his wife, June 13, 1863.
25. *O.R.*, Serial 45, pp. 86-87.
26. Pearson, *Wadsworth*, p. 196.
27. R. K. Beecham, *Gettysburg: Pivotal Battle of the Civil War*. Chicago, 1911, pp. 119-120.
28. *O.R.*, Serial 45, p. 79.
29. *Ibid.*, pp. 137, 169.
30. *Ibid.*, p. 175.
31. Meade, *Letters*, Vol. 1, p. 387, to his wife, June 25, 1863.
32. JFR to his sisters, June 22, 1863, Reynolds Papers. This letter, his last to the family, is undated but is addressed from Guilford Station, where the 1st Corps camped from June 19 to the 24th. The cavalry action mentioned by Reynolds was reported to headquarters at 4:30 p.m. June 21 (*O.R.*, Serial 45, p. 248). As he reported it as taking place "yesterday," the date of his letter would be the 22nd. This is also the date fixed by his grandnephew Colonel Scott.
33. *O.R.*, Serial 45, p. 347.

34. *Ibid.*, p. 343. Reynolds might have been horrified to know that both Curtin and Couch were trying to get a general released from the army to assist in Pennsylvania's defense.

35. *Ibid.*, pp. 305, 307.

36. Meade, *Letters*, Vol. 1, p. 388, to his wife, June 25, 1863.

37. Doubleday, *Chancellorsville* and *Gettysburg*, p. 122.

38. Chamberlin, *150th Pennsylvania Volunteers*, pp. 111-112. For Reynolds' general habit of silence during marches, see Bates, *Martial Deeds*, p. 476. But of this particular march there is some contradiction in a letter from Eleanor Reynolds to William Reynolds written on July 5, 1863, Reynolds Papers. All of John's staff, she says, had told her how lighthearted he became once Meade was given command of the army. They remembered him as having talked and joked freely on the road north toward Gettysburg.

39. Cook, *Twelfth Massachusetts Volunteers*, p. 97.

40. Smith, *Seventy-Sixth Regiment N.Y. Volunteers*, p. 227.

41. *O.R.*, Serial 45, p. 347.

42. *Ibid.*, p. 324.

43. Coffin, *Four Years of Fighting*, p. 259. M. Jacobs in *Notes on the Rebel Invasion of Maryland, Pennsylvania, and the Battle of Gettysburg*, Philadelphia, 1863, pp. 9-10, agrees that military ardor was slight in Harrisburg at this time. But although an attempt to form an infantry company in the state capital failed, the people were at least reluctant to leave their homes.

44. Toombs, *New Jersey Troops at Gettysburg*, Newark, N.J., 1887, p. 86.

45. John C. Gray, John C. Ropes, *War Letters 1862-1865*, Boston, 1927, pp. 133-134.

46. Howard M. Jenkins, *Pennsylvania Colonial and Federal*, 3 Vols., Philadelphia, 1903, Vol. 2, p. 400.

47. John P. Nicholson, ed., *Pennsylvania at Gettysburg*, 3 Vols., Harrisburg, 1914, Vol. 1, pp. 1-2; Fox, *Regimental Losses*, p. 536, gives the total number of troops furnished by Pennsylvania during the war as 366,107. This was the second highest percentage enrolled from a major state. Ohio was first.

48. *Pennsylvania at Gettysburg*, Vol. 1, p. 226, letter dated June 17, 1863.

49. *O.R.*, Serial 43, p. 60.

50. *Ibid.*, Serial 45, pp. 373-374.

51. *Ibid.*, p. 374.

52. Sypher, *Pennsylvania Reserves*, p. 499.

53. Charles H. Banes, *History of the Philadelphia Brigade*, Philadelphia, 1876, p. 175.

54. T. W. Hyde, *Following the Greek Cross*, Boston, 1894, p. 140.

55. Alexander McClure, *Recollections of Half a Century*, Salem, Massachusetts, 1902, p. 346. McClure reports Burnside as having told him that after his resignation, Reynolds, Meade, and Sedgwick all were felt out in regard to the army command. In *B. and L.*, Vol. 3, pp. 239-240, Charles F. Benjamin also notes Washington's interest in Reynolds and Meade, though doubting that any offer was made to Sedgwick. Bigelow, *Chancellorsville*, p. 487, adds General Darius Couch to the list. See Appendix.

56. Blake, *Three Years in the Army of the Potomac*, p. 201.

57. Charles H. Weygant, *History of the One Hundred and Twenty-Fourth New York Volunteers*, Newburgh, New York, 1877, p. 170.

58. Carl Schurz, *Reminiscences of Carl Schurz*, 3 Vols., New York, 1908, Vol. 3, p. 6.

59. Jesse B. Young, *Battle of Gettysburg*, New York, 1913, p. 340; Walter E. Day ("Miles"), *Campaign of Gettysburg*, Boston, 1912, p. 58n; Spaulding, *U. S. Army*, p. 299; Alexander, *Memoirs*, p. 383 (see Note 64).

60. Toombs, *New Jersey Troops at Gettysburg*, pp. 120, 129.

61. Chamberlin, *150th Pennsylvania Volunteers*, p. 119.

62. Andrew J. Boies, *Record of the 33rd Massachusetts Volunteer Infantry*, Fitchburg, Massachusetts, 1880, p. 35.

63. Pearson, *Wadsworth*, p. 201.

64. Curtis, *Twenty-Fourth Michigan*, p. 422.
65. Buell, *Cannoneer*, p. 61.
66. Alexander, *Memoirs*, pp. 377-378, 383. (See Note 57.) For an understanding and sympathetic characterization of Meade, see Bruce Catton, *Mr. Lincoln's Army*, New York, 1951, pp. 116-117.
67. Meade, *Letters*, Vol. 2, p. 33, Captain George Meade's biographical account of his father.
68. *O.R.*, Serial 43, p. 61.
69. *Ibid.*, Serial 45, pp. 414-415. Meade's order establishing a left wing under Reynolds was dated June 30.
70. The four daughters of John's uncle, Samuel Reynolds, were Mary Catherine, Margareta, Lydia Eleanor, and Sarah. None married. This information was supplied from the Reynolds' family records by Mrs. J. J. Kline in a letter to the author, May 14, 1955. In his letter of April 5, 1957, Mr. Charles F. Bowers of Frederick, Maryland, has generously furnished the following information —that at the time of Reynolds' visit his cousins lived in a two-story brick L-shaped structure, listed as 9 West Second Street. The house was torn down in 1925 and the site is now occupied by an Elks Lodge building.
71. See Mary Catherine Reynolds to her cousin Hal (Harriet), July 1, 1863, Chapter XII.
72. *O.R.*, Serial 43, p. 243.
73. *One Hundred and Twenty-First Pennsylvania*, pp. 50-51.
74. Pearson, *Wadsworth*, p. 202; Hyde, *Following the Greek Cross*, p. 141; Smith, *The Seventy-Sixth New York*, p. 232.
75. *O.R.*, Serial 45, p. 397.
76. *Ibid.*, pp. 409-410.

77. Meade, *Letters*, Vol. 2, p. 18, to his wife, June 30, 1863.
78. *O.R.*, Serial 45, pp. 414-415.
79. *Ibid.*, Serial 43, pp. 923, 926. Jacobs, *Notes on the Rebel Invasion*, said the Confederates were not driven out, but Buford's evidence is more trustworthy on this point.
80. *O.R.*, Serial 45, pp. 419-420.
81. *Ibid.*, p. 424.
82. *Ibid.*, p. 425.
83. Williams, *Lincoln Finds a General*, Vol. 2, pp. 676-677, cites these orders as one sign of Meade's confusion and irresolution.
84. *Proceedings of the Buford Memorial Association*, New York, 1895, pp. 23-24, oration by Major General James H. Wilson.
85. Oliver Otis Howard, *Autobiography of Oliver Otis Howard*, 2 Vols., New York, 1907, Vol. 1, pp. 107, 403. In *O.R.*, Serial 43, p. 701, Howard confirms this meeting. Colonel Chapman Biddle, in *Reynolds Memorial*, p. 58, thinks too little was made of the conference between Reynolds and Howard, for it could have helped the latter in making his dispositions the next day.
86. *O.R.*, Serial 45, pp. 417-418.
87. Copy of letter from William Riddle, one of Reynolds' aides at Gettysburg, to a Le Bouvier [Sp?] from Headquarters, Army of the Potomac, near Warrenton Junction, August 4, 1863, Reynolds Papers. The name of the addressee in this copy has been scratched out and the correction written above in such a way as to blur the spelling. Since Riddle's letter contains important contemporary information it would be interesting to know whom he wrote to.
88. *O.R.*, Serial 43, p. 923.
89. William Riddle to Le Bouvier, August 4, 1863, Reynolds Papers.

CHAPTER XII. "FOR GOD'S SAKE, FORWARD!"

1. Riddle to Le Bouvier, August 4, 1863, Reynolds Papers.
2. *O.R.*, Serial 45, p. 416. This was almost certainly the last order Reynolds received. In *C.C.W.*, Vol. 1 (1865), p. 316, Doubleday testified that he did not know of Reynolds' ever having received the controversial Pipe Creek circular (*O.R.*, Serial 45, pp. 458-459), in which Meade designated a defense line just below the Pennsylvania-Maryland line. Captain George Meade in Meade, *Letters*, Vol. 2, p. 30, said Reynolds did not receive it. Others who thought he never got it were General Henry J. Hunt, *B. and L.*, Vol. 3, p. 291; General James Wadsworth in *C.C.W.*, Vol. 1 (1865), p. 413.
3. Pearson, *Wadsworth*, p. 204.
4. *O.R.*, Serial 45, p. 457; Serial 107, p. 1066.
5. *Ibid.*, Serial 43, p. 244, Doubleday's report.
6. *Pennsylvania at Gettysburg*, Vol. 1, p. 343.
7. Bates, *Martial Deeds*, p. 204.
8. Ellie Reynolds to her brother Will, July 5, 1863, Reynolds Papers. In many particulars regarding her brother's last words and actions Eleanor Reynolds relied on the account given her orally by orderly Charles Veil. He was in closest contact with his general, especially during the early forenoon of July 1. Veil's published account did not appear in full until March 19, 1911, in the Philadelphia *Public Ledger*. His version was also considered accurate by the late J.F.R. Scott, grandnephew of John Reynolds.
9. *O.R.*, Serial 45, pp. 460-461. In this long message Meade reminded Reynolds that he (Meade) had had little time to appraise the situation concerning the Gettysburg

area and asked for his views and suggestions. "He feels that you know more of the condition of the troops in your vicinity and the country than he does." Reynolds did not receive the message.
10. See Note 67. These hills, from south to north as Reynolds would have viewed them, are Big Round Top, Little Round Top, Cemetery Hill, and east of it, Culp's Hill.
11. Meade, *Letters*, Vol. 2, p. 32; Pearson, *Wadsworth*, p. 205.
12. J. D. de Roulhac Hamilton, *The Papers of Randolph Abbott Shotwell*, 3 Vols., Raleigh, North Carolina, 1929, Vol. 1, p. 500. Shotwell saw the horse being led by one of Reynolds' men later in the forenoon: ". . . a fine black charger. He was much admired by those who noticed him."
13. *O.R.*, Serial 45, p. 320.
14. *C.C.W.*, Vol. 1 (1865), p. 413, Wadsworth's testimony; Lancaster *Daily Inquirer*, July 8, 1863.
15. Joseph G. Rosengarten to M. Jacobs, October 5, 1863, Reynolds Papers.
16. Ellie Reynolds to her brother Will, July 5, 1863, Reynolds Papers.
17. John Watts de Peyster, *Decisive Conflicts of the Late Civil War*, New York, 1867, "The Battle of Oak (or Seminary) Ridge and Gettysburg," p. 153. De Peyster quotes the account of this meeting between Reynolds and Buford from that of a signal corps lieutenant assigned to Buford. The account is signed by General Winfield S. Hancock, below which are the initials A. B. J., which fit the name of Aaron Brainard Jerome, acting assistant signal officer. Buford praised him in his report of the battle, *O.R.*, Serial 43, p. 930. There seems to be good reason for accepting Jerome's version.

18. *O.R.*, Serial 43, p. 923. Buford reported both his men and horses as fagged out.
19. Livermore, *Numbers and Losses,* p. 102.
20. Stephen Minot Weld, *War Diary and Letters of Stephen Minot Weld 1861-1865*, privately printed (Riverside Press), 1912, pp. 230, 232. Captain George Meade, who was on his father's staff at Taneytown, differs with Weld on what the general said on receiving Reynolds' message. Captain Meade's version reads: "Good! That is just like Reynolds; he will hold on to the bitter end," Meade, *Letters,* Vol. 2, p. 36. Weld's entry for July 1 shows these words: "Good God! If the enemy get Gettysburg, I am lost." But in his summary written later, Weld is closer to the son's account—thus: "Good! That is just like Reynolds."
21. Doubleday, *Chancellorsville and Gettysburg,* pp. 126-127; Howard, *Autobiography,* Vol. 1, p. 407. But Howard does not mention receiving the kind of order Doubleday says Howard got: to bring his corps forward at once and *form them on Cemetery Hill* as a reserve [italics Doubleday's].
22. Pearson, *Wadsworth,* p. 207; de Peyster, *Decisive Conflicts,* p. 34. Bates, *Martial Deeds,* p. 209, says John Burns led Reynolds across the fields. But although the activities of this civilian hero were carefully accounted for on July 1, no other writer mentions his having aided Reynolds. See *B. and L.,* Vol. 3, p. 284.
23. Rosengarten to Jacobs, October 15, 1863, Reynolds Papers. Rosengarten is objecting to Jacob's statement in *Notes on the Rebel Invasion,* p. 29, that Reynolds advised the residents of the town to leave their homes.
24. Gates, *Ulster Guard,* p. 425; Smith, *76th New York,* p. 23.
25. Beecham, *Gettysburg,* p. 134.
26. *C.C.W.,* Vol. 1 (1865), p. 404. Hancock said: "General Reynolds at once advanced to the relief of Buford, and engaged the enemy, knowing that it was no time to inquire about future operations, and that the only thing was to attack the enemy and delay him until the commander of the army should come to some decision."
27. J. F. C. Fuller, *Decisive Battles of the U.S.A.,* New York, 1942, p. 229.
28. Ellie Reynolds to her brother Will, July 5, 1863, Reynolds Papers.
29. *Buford Memorial,* p. 27.
30. *O.R.,* Serial 43, pp. 273, 278. Officers of both the 2nd and 7th Wisconsin report approaching Gettysburg about 10 a.m. Reynolds would have preceded them on Seminary Ridge by some moments. Pearson, *Wadsworth,* p. 265, puts the time a little later. The reporting of time varies widely for events on July 1.
31. *Pennsylvania at Gettysburg,* Vol. 1, p. 483. For the 1st Corps, Doubleday's estimate is usually accepted, *O.R.,* Serial 43, p. 251. He put the full strength of Heth and Pender combined at 25,000. Lee's returns for Gettysburg itself are not in the official records.
32. Rosengarten, *Reynolds Memorial,* p. 29. Hall, *O.R.,* Serial 43, p. 359, says that Reynolds placed him in position.
33. *Pennsylvania at Gettysburg,* Vol. 1, pp. 343-344.
34. *O.R.* Serial 43, p. 244, Doubleday's report.
35. *C.C.W.,* Vol. 1 (1865), p. 306, Doubleday's testimony.
36. *O.R.,* Serial 43, p. 244, Doubleday's report.
37. Buell, *Cannoneer,* p. 64.
38. *O.R.,* Serial 43, p. 244, Doubleday's report.
39. *Ibid.,* pp. 273, 279, reports of Major John Mansfield, 2nd Wisconsin, and Colonel William W. Robinson, 7th Wisconsin. Robinson makes it clear that the right of his regiment was close to McPherson's grove and that the 2nd Wisconsin fronted it. Mansfield says

the 2nd Wisconsin went into the woods. Doubleday, *Ibid.*, p. 245, confirms this. William Wade Dudley, the *Iron Brigade at Gettysburg*, Cincinnati, 1879, p. 6, also puts the 2nd Wisconsin "into the northern edge of McPherson's woods." As Reynolds also fronted this woods, he took in the 2nd Wisconsin, as his aide Major William Riddle said he did (letter to Le Bouvier, August 4, 1863, Reynolds Papers). There is no basis for saying that Reynolds led the 19th Indiana in this charge, as do both William F. Fox, ed., *New York at Gettysburg*, 3 Vols., Albany, New York, 1902, Vol. 1, p. 11; and de Peyster, *Decisive Conflicts*, p. 37. The 19th Indiana was, in fact, far to Reynolds' left.

40. Ellie Reynolds to her brother Will, July 5, 1863, Reynolds Papers, reporting Veil's account to her.

41. *O.R.*, Serial 43, p. 266, Wadsworth's report. This is the most acceptable contemporary source for the time at which Reynolds fell. Wadsworth was the highest ranking officer near the scene, Doubleday having gone to the far left.

42. Ellie Reynolds to her brother Will, July 5, 1863, Reynolds Papers. Veil's word that he was alone with Reynolds when he was hit was not disputed at the time by the aides who attended the general's funeral. Later confusion as to who else was present is probably over a matter of moments. R. W. Mitchell and Edward Baird certainly joined Veil very shortly, as noted by de Peyster, *Decisive Conflicts*, p. 38; Bates, *Martial Deeds*, p. 474; and others.

43. *O.R.*, Serial 43, p. 279, Robinson's report. That Reynolds fell as the assault began and not later is strongly supported: Riddle to Le Bouvier, August 4, 1863; Ellie to her brother Will, July 5, 1863; Rosengarten to Jacobs, October 15, 1863 (these three letters in the Reynolds Papers); Willcox, *Philadelphia Inquirer*, July 5, 1863; Jacobs, *Notes on the Rebel Inva-*

sion, p. 26; Pearson, *Wadsworth*, p. 209; Doubleday, *Chancellorsville and Gettysburg*, pp. 131-132; Meade, *Letters*, Vol. 2, p. 46.

44. *O.R.*, Serial 43, p. 245.

45. *B. and L.*, Vol. 3, p. 277.

46. *New York at Gettysburg*, Vol. 3, p. 1002.

47. *O.R.*, Serial 43, p. 246, Doubleday's report.

48. The bullet that killed Reynolds was described by Veil at the time as a stray shot, Ellie to her brother Will, July 5, 1863, Reynolds Papers. Neither Rosengarten's letter to Jacobs of October 15, 1863, nor Riddle's to Le Bouvier of August 4, 1863 (both in Reynolds Papers) mentions the possibility of Reynolds' having been killed by a sharpshooter. This story grew out of an article published in the Lancaster *Intelligencer* of November 7, 1902, and reprinted elsewhere. It was reprinted in the Lancaster *Sunday News*, November 23, 1952. In it a Leander T. Hensel of Quarryville, Pennsylvania, claimed to have talked to a soldier named Benjamin Thorpe in North Carolina. Thorpe was supposed to have described in detail how, as a sharpshooter in the 55th North Carolina, he fired from a cherry tree next to a stone house on a hill and killed Reynolds from a distance of 800 yards. He said the general was posting artillery at the time. But in a letter to a nephew of the General's, from Satterwhite, North Carolina, on May 20, 1903 (the original in the Reynolds Papers), Benjamin Thorpe himself said he regretted publication by friends of the claim that he shot Reynolds, though admitting that he did knock some officer from a horse at 900 yards. Charles Veil to "Friend Conevery," November 11, 1902, Reynolds Papers, refuted on three counts the claim that Thorpe could have shot Reynolds: (1) there was no cherry tree in McPherson's woods; (2) Reynolds was not posting artillery when

shot; (3) sharpshooters usually operate only in open country. Dr. Frederick Tilberg, the Gettysburg historian, also believes it is most unlikely that Thorpe killed Reynolds. The Confederate General Henry Heth wrote in his official report that Reynolds was hit by an artillery shell, *O.R.*, Serial 44, p. 637. He may have accepted an artilleryman's similar statement, *Ibid.*, p. 677. The sum of available evidence seems to throw doubt on the story of Reynolds as a sharpshooter's victim, although it has been widely accepted, notably in *B. and L.*, Vol. 3, p. 277; Schurz, *Reminiscences*, Vol. 3, p. 6; *Pennsylvania at Gettysburg*, Vol. 1, p. 291; *Ibid.*, Vol. 2, p. 994; John D. Vautier, *History of the 88th Pennsylvania Volunteers*, Philadelphia, 1894, p. 119; John R. Boyle, *Soldiers True: Story of the 11th Pennsylvania Veteran Volunteer Infantry*, New York, 1903, p. 115.

49. Veil, Philadelphia *Public Ledger*, March 19, 1911. J. H. Stine, *History of the Army of the Potomac*, Philadelphia, 1892, p. 455, names four soldiers of the 76th New York as carrying Reynolds' body to the stone house. But in *New York at Gettysburg*, Vol. 2, p. 688, the 84th New York (14th Brooklyn) claims the honor of having borne the "heroic Reynolds" from the field.

50. Frank A. Haskell, *The Battle of Gettysburg*, Boston, 1908, p. 8.

51. Francis A. Walker, *General Hancock*, New York, 1894, p. 109; *Pennsylvania at Gettysburg*, Vol. 1, p. 333. The claim made by several companies of the 2nd Pennsylvania Cavalry that they escorted Reynolds' body is suspect because two different accounts, *Ibid.*, Vol. 2, pp. 806, 812, give the date as July 3 and the time of starting as near midnight.

52. Riddle to Le Bouvier, August 4, 1863, Reynolds Papers.

53. This letter from the Reynolds Papers has been quoted at length because of its vivid contemporary description of a city in war times.

54. Curtis, *24th Michigan*, p. 157; *Pennsylvania at Gettysburg*, Vol. 2, p. 702; Pearson, *Wadsworth*, p. 208.

55. *O.R.*, Serial 43, pp. 281-282, 291.

56. *B. and L.*, Vol. 3, pp. 278-280.

57. These estimates from Rosengarten, in *Pennsylvania at Gettysburg*, Vol. 1, p. 37, seem more useful than those of Fox, *Regimental Losses*, p. 25. Fox admits that probably no more than four-fifths of the present-for-duty equipped ever saw action. *OR.*, Serial 43, p. 172, gives 1st Corp losses as 6,059.

58. Bates, *Martial Deeds*, pp. 209, 475. Schurz, *Reminiscences*, Vol. 3, p. 6, also thinks Reynolds was too far forward.

59. Pearson, *Wadsworth*, p. 209. See Chapter X, Note 38.

60. Dr. Tilberg pointed out to the writer the advantages of this observation post as of 1863. They are also noted in J. Willard Brown, *The Signal Corps U.S.A. in the War of the Rebellion*, Boston, 1896, p. 359.

61. Woodward, *3rd Pennsylvania Reserves*, p. 159. See Chapter VII, Note 31.

62. War correspondents G. W. Hosmer in the New York *Herald*, July 3, 1863; and L. L. Crounse in the New York *Times*, July 4, 1863, the latter in milder terms.

63. Reliable breakdowns of the Confederate losses on the first day at Gettysburg are hard to find, but detailed figures given by Lieutenant Colonel George E. Wagner in *Pennsylvania at Gettysburg*, Vol. 1, p. 483, have been accepted here as at least helpful.

64. *Ibid.*, p. 292. This address was given by Brigadier General Martin D. Hardin, a West Pointer, who at Gettysburg commanded the 12th Pennsylvania Reserves.

65. Objection to this honor for Howard was made by Cook, *12th Massachusetts*, p. 106; Small, *The Sixteenth, Maine*, p. 133; Gibbon,

Recollections, p. 202; Williams, *Lincoln Finds a General*, Vol. 2, p. 685.

66. Howard, *Autobiography*, Vol. 1, p. 410.

67. Rosengarten was the first to insist on Reynolds' awareness of the value of Cemetery Hill. In his letter to Jacobs, October 15, 1863, Reynolds Papers, he writes: "Reynolds ordered up all his troops with the express purpose of holding the town and Cemetery Hill. . . ." Rosengarten told Doubleday that he heard Reynolds give an order to Howard, directing him to post troops on the hill, Doubleday, *Chancellorsville and Gettysburg*, pp. 126-127. Doubleday adds: "It is quite possible that Reynolds chose the hill simply as a position upon which his force could rally if driven back, and Howard selected it as a suitable battle-field for an Army." A number of writers believe that Reynolds saw the value of the hills south of Gettysburg: Comte de Paris, *History of the Civil War in America*, 4 Vols., Philadelphia, 1875-1888, Vol. 3, p. 550; William Swinton, *Campaigns of the Army of the Potomac*, New York, 1866, p. 331; Young, *Gettysburg*, p. 191; Beecham, *Gettysburg*, p. 125; Francis Marshal, *The Battle of Gettysburg: the Crest-Wave of the American Civil War*, New York, 1914, p. 111; Gates, *Ulster Guard*, p. 425; Nicolay and Hay, *Lincoln*, Vol. 7, p. 239.

68. Cook, *12th Massachusetts*, p. 99; Buell, *Cannoneer*, p. 80.

69. *B. and L.*, Vol. 3, p. 407; Young, *Gettysburg*, p. 177; Day, *Gettysburg*, p. 65n, also believe Reynolds felt a special urgency over Pennsylvania's invasion.

70. *O.R.*, Serial 45, p. 216.

71. Walker's statement, *B. and L.*, Vol. 3, p. 408; Regis de Trobriand, *Four Years with the Army of the Potomac*, Boston, 1889, pp. 489-490; *C.C.W.*, Vol. 1 (1865), p. 348, in which Meade says he did not wait for Hancock's report after hearing of Reynolds' fight.

72. *B. and L.*, Vol. 3, p. 277. Meade's artillery chief, General Henry Hunt, thought Reynolds' presence sparked the assault.

73. Stine, *Army of the Potomac*, p. 457.

74. Hardin, *12th Pennsylvania Volunteers*, p. 148; Buell, *Cannoneer*, p. 61; Chamberlin, *One Hundred and Fiftieth Pennsylvania*, p. 118.

75. Jennie Gildersleeve to her brother Will, July 5, 1863, Reynolds Papers.

76. Riddle to Le Bouvier, August 4, 1863, Reynolds Papers.

77. Jennie Gildersleeve to her brother Will, July 5, 1863, Reynolds Papers.

78. *Ibid.* John V. Miller, M.D., of Dillsburg, Pennsylvania, grandnephew of Charles Veil, was helpful in furnishing the following information which in turn was supplied him from records of the Sisters of Charity, Saint Joseph's Central House, Emmitsburg, Maryland. Katherine Hewitt was born in Oswego, New York, April 1, 1836, and as a resident of Huntingdon, New York, applied to enter St. Joseph's on July 12, 1863. It is not clear whether she was accepted there, but she later spent several years at St. Joseph's School, Albany. She left September 3, 1868, without taking Vows.

79. Ellie Reynolds to her brother Will, July 5, 1863, Reynolds Papers.

80. Lancaster *Daily Inquirer*, July 6, 1863.

81. Jennie Gildersleeve to her brother Will, July 5, 1863, Reynolds Papers.

82. The Reynolds Papers include three letters from Veil, one dated November 10, 1863, and two January 5, 1864. The first thanks the family for the gift of a watch; the second for help toward a commission. The third letter begins: "At the request of the Secretary of War, I have taken the liberty of addressing you. He wished me to state to you . . . the facts concerning the

delay in my nomination for lieutenancy in the 1st U. S. Cavalry. . . ." Again Veil thanks the family for their great kindness to him. Ellie Reynolds, in particular, deserved Veil's gratitude. She had taken him to see President Lincoln to ask that the boy be rewarded for his services to her late brother. Lincoln referred Veil to Stanton with the request that he be given a commission. Eleanor Reynolds' thanks for this favor are found in a letter to the President, June 11, 1864, Lincoln Papers, letter pages 29372-29373, Library of Congress Annex. Veil later fought in the wilderness campaign, where he was promoted for gallantry. At Five Forks he was breveted captain for conspicuous bravery, and later as major for meritorious services during the war, Philadelphia *Public Ledger,* March 19, 1911.

83. Copy in the Reynolds Papers.
84. Copy in the Reynolds Papers.
85. Lancaster *Daily Express,* July 6, 1863.
86. *Ibid.,* July 7, 1863.
87. Lancaster *Weekly Examiner and Herald,* July 8, 1863. Both the New York *Times* and the *Herald* carried long obituaries on July 3.
88. General Seymour in a letter to Rosengarten, March 9, 1883, took credit for having forced Taggart's resignation. But he switched the responsibility to Reynolds on August 8, 1886, in writing to Sam Reynolds, who had sent him one of Taggart's articles. Both Seymour letters are in the Reynolds Papers.
89. Philadelphia *Press,* November 14 and December 2, 1883.
90. *Pennsylvania at Gettysburg,* Vol. 1, p. 83.
91. Rosengarten, *Reynolds Memorial,* p. 92. Hancock's letter is dated March 4, 1880.
92. Paris, *Civil War in America,* Vol. 3, p. 553.
93. Walter H. Hebert, *Fighting Joe Hooker,* Indianapolis, 1944, p. 175.
94. Day ("Miles"), *Campaign of Gettysburg,* p. 69.
95. Swinton, *Army of the Potomac,* p. 331.
96. John W. Urban, *In Defense of the Union,* Washington, 1887, p. 299.
97. Toombs, *New Jersey Troops at Gettysburg,* p. 152.
98. Charles Francis Adams, *Studies Military and Diplomatic,* New York, 1911, p. 309.
99. *C.C.W.,* Vol. 1 (1865), p. 384.
100. Alexander, *Memoirs,* pp. 282-283.
101. *O.R.,* Serial 43, p. 273.
102. Fox, *Regimental Losses,* p. 66.
103. Rufus R. Dawes, *Service with the Sixth Wisconsin Volunteers,* Marietta, Ohio, 1890, p. 219.
104. Fox, *Regimental Losses,* p. 66.
105. Original in Reynolds Papers.
106. Riddle to Ellie Reynolds, August 6, 1863, Reynolds Papers.
107. E. M. Woodward, *Our Campaigns,* Philadelphia, 1865, p. 277.
108. *Ibid.*
109. *B. and L.,* Vol. 3, p. 330.
110. Woodward, *Our Campaigns,* p. 278.
111. The original in Reynolds Papers.

APPENDIX

1. Records of the Adjutant General's Office, Register of Officers Arriving in Washington 1814-1917, File No. 324.
2. Eleanor Reynolds to J. F. Landis, Colonel U. S. Army (Retired), August 20, 1913, Reynolds Papers.
3. *Pennsylvania at Gettysburg,* Vol. 2, pp. 986-996.
4. Statement by Colonel Landis ap-

pended to letter of Eleanor Reynolds of August 20, 1913. The statement is dated August 21, 1913. John Reynolds sent his "greetings to the newcomer, William R. Landis," in a letter to his sisters on June 22, 1863, Reynolds Papers.

5. Meade, *Letters*, Vol. 1, p. 385.

6. Lincoln Papers, Vols. 111, 112, 113; and Stanton Papers, Letter Books No. 6, 12, 13, Division of Manuscripts, Library of Congress, Annex; Records of the Adjutant General's Office, Generals' Papers and Books, File No. 159.

7. "Hooker's Appointment and Removal," Vol. 3, pp. 239-243.

8. "Meade Before Gettysburg," Vol. 37, No. 994, August 2, 1883, p. 96. The letter was unsigned, but Benjamin gave his address and invited correspondence from readers.

9. Charles F. Benjamin to Joseph G. Rosengarten, August 13, 1883, Reynolds Papers.

10. *Ibid.*, August 7, 1883.

11. K. P. Williams, *Lincoln Finds a General*, Vol. 2, p. 829n, also questions Benjamin's authority.

12. Hebert, *Fighting Joe Hooker*, p. 166; Isaac R. Pennypacker, *General Meade*, New York, 1901, pp. 130-131. Others, in order of publication, are Stine, *Army of the Potomac* (1892), p. 455; Bache, *Meade* (1897), p. 281; James F. Rusling, *Men and Things I Saw in Civil War Days*, Cincinnati, 1899, p. 68; Bruce Catton, *Glory Road*, New York, 1952, p. 295. On the other hand, Pearson, *Wadsworth* (1913), p. 201, cites Huidekoper (see Note 3); Rhodes, *Civil War* (1917), p. 224, cites Meade's letter (see Note 5). Marshal, *Gettysburg* (1914), p. 91, has a full discussion of the command problem that seems to be independent of Benjamin. The statement in Cullum *Biographical Register* (1891), Vol. 1, p. 92, was undoubtedly prepared for an edition that appeared before *Battles and Leaders*. McClure, *Recollections* (1902), p. 346, places the offer of command to Reynolds at the same time Benjamin does, but gives a conversation with Burnside as his source.

13. *War Diary and Letters*, p. 227n.

14. March 4, 1880, p. 94.

Bibliography[*]

Adams, Charles Francis, *Studies Military and Diplomatic,* New York, 1911.

Alexander, E. Porter, *Military Memoirs of a Confederate: A Critical Narrative,* New York, 1907.

Alter, J. Cecil, *James Bridger: A Historical Narrative,* Salt Lake City, 1925.

Armstrong, William H. ("Citizen Soldier"), *Red-Tape and Pigeon-Hole Generals,* New York, 1864.

Bache, Richard M., *General George Gordon Meade,* Philadelphia, 1897.

Ballard, Colin R., *The Military Genius of Abraham Lincoln,* New York, 1952.

Banes, Charles H., *History of the Philadelphia Brigade,* Philadelphia, 1876.

Bates, Samuel P., *History of the Pennsylvania Volunteers,* 5 Vols., Harrisburg, 1869.

—————, *Martial Deeds of Pennsylvania,* Philadelphia, 1875.

Baumes, William H., *West Point: Moulder of Men,* New York, 1942.

Beecham, R. K., *Gettysburg: Pivotal Battle of the Civil War,* Chicago, 1911.

Beveridge, Albert S., *Abraham Lincoln 1809-1858,* 2 Vols., Boston, 1928.

Bigelow, John, Jr., *The Campaign of Chancellorsville: A Strategic and Tactical Study,* New Haven, Conn., 1910.

Billings, John D., *Hard Tack and Coffee,* Boston, 1887.

Birkhimer, William E., *Historical Sketch of the Artillery U. S. Army,* Washington, D.C., 1884.

Blake, Henry N., *Three Years in the Army of the Potomac,* Boston, 1865.

Boies, Andrew J., *Record of the 33rd Massachusetts Volunteer Infantry,* Fitchburg, Mass., 1880.

Boyle, John R., *Soldiers True: The Story of the 11th Pennsylvania Veteran Volunteer Infantry,* New York, 1903.

Brown, J. Willard, *The Signal Corps U.S.A. in the War of the Rebellion,* Boston, 1896.

Buchanan, James, Unpublished correspondence of James Buchanan to John Reynolds, Fackenthal Library, Franklin and Marshall College, Lancaster, Pa.

---

[*]Only sources cited.

Buell, Augustus, *The Cannoneer*, Washington, D.C., 1890.

Carleton, James H., *The Battle of Buena Vista*, New York, 1848.

Catton, Bruce, *Mr. Lincoln's Army*, New York, 1951.

Chamberlin, Thomas, *The History of the 150th Regiment Pennsylvania Volunteers*, Philadelphia, 1905.

Coffin, Charles C., *Four Years of Fighting: A Volume of Personal Observation with the Army and Navy, from the First Battle of Bull Run to the Fall of Richmond*, Boston, 1866.

Cook, Benjamin F., *The 12th Massachusetts Volunteers*, Boston, 1882.

Coppée, Henry, *General Thomas*, New York, 1893.

Croffut, W. A., ed., *Fifty Years in Camp and Field, Diary of Major-General Ethan Allen Hitchcock, U.S.A.*, New York, 1909.

Cudworth, Warren H., *The First Massachusetts Regiment*, Boston, 1886.

Cuffel, Charles A., *Durell's Battery During the Civil War*, Philadelphia, 1903.

Cullum, George W., *Biographical Register of the Officers and Graduates of the U. S. Military Academy*, 3 Vols., Boston and New York, 1891.

Curtis, B. O., *History of the 24th Michigan of the Iron Brigade*, Detroit, 1891.

Dawes, Rufus, R., *Service with the Sixth Wisconsin Volunteers*, Marietta, Ohio, 1890.

Day, Walter E. ("Miles"), *The Campaign of Gettysburg*, Boston, 1912.

Dennett, Tyler, *Lincoln and the Civil War in the Diaries and Letters of John Hay*, New York, 1939.

De Peyster, John Watts, *Decisive Conflicts of the Late Civil War*, New York, 1867.

————, *Personal and Military History of Philip Kearny*, New York, 1869.

Dick, Thomas W., Unpublished letters of Thomas W. Dick, Company H, 12th Regiment, Pennsylvania Reserves, in the possession of his grandson Dr. J. S. Bowman, State College, Pa.

Dodge, Theodore A., *The Campaign of Chancellorsville*, Boston, 1881.

Doubleday, Abner, *Chancellorsville and Gettysburg*, New York, 1885.

Dudley, William Wade, *The Iron Brigade at Gettysburg*, Cincinnati, Ohio, 1879.

Executive Documents, Publications of the Senate and House of Representatives, Washington, D.C.

Farley, Joseph P., *West Point in the Early Sixties*, Troy, N.Y., 1902.

Fox, William F., ed., *New York at Gettysburg*, 3 Vols., Albany, N.Y., 1902.

————, *Regimental Losses in the American Civil War*, Albany, N.Y., 1889.

Freeman, Douglas Southall, *Lee's Lieutenants*, 3 Vols., New York, 1942.

French, Samuel G., *Two Wars*, Nashville, Tenn., 1901.

Fuller, J. F. C., *Decisive Battles of the U.S.A.*, New York, 1942.

Ganoe, William A., *History of the United States Army*, New York, 1924.

Gates, Theodore B., *The Ulster Guard and the War of the Rebellion*, New York, 1879.

Gibbon, John, *Personal Recollections of the Civil War*, New York, 1928.

Giddings, Luther, *Campaigns in Northern Mexico*, New York, 1853.

Goolrick, John T. *Historic Fredericksburg*, Richmond, 1922.

Gordon, George H., *History of the Campaign of the Army of Virginia*, Boston, 1880.

Grant, Ulysses S., *Personal Memoirs of U. S. Grant*, ed. by E. B. Long, Cleveland, Ohio, 1952.

Gray, John C., and John C. Ropes, *War Letters 1862-1865*, Boston, 1927.

Halleck Letter Books, National Archives, Washington, D.C.

Hamilton, J. D., de Roulhac, *The Papers of Randolph Abbott Shotwell*, 3 Vols., Raleigh, N.C., 1929.

Hardin, Martin D., *History of the 12th Regiment (Pennsylvania Reserves)*, New York, 1890.

Harris, Alex, *Biographical History of Lancaster County*, Lancaster, Pa., 1872.

Harrisburg *Patriot*.

Haskell, Frank A., *The Battle of Gettysburg*, Boston, 1908.

Hardin, Martin D., *History of the 12th Regiment (Pennsylvania Reserves)*, Baton Rouge, La., 1957.

Hebert, Walter H., *Fighting Joe Hooker*, Indianapolis, Ind., 1944.

Heitman, Francis B., *Historical Register and Dictionary of the United States Army*, 2 Vols., Washington, D.C., 1903.

Henderson, G. F. R., *Stonewall Jackson and the Civil War*, 2 Vols., New York, 1902.

Henry, William S., *Campaign Sketches of the War with Mexico*, New York, 1847.

Hill, A. F., *Our Boys, The Personal Experiences of a Soldier*, Philadelphia, 1865.

History of the Corn Exchange Regiment (118th Pennsylvania Volunteers), by the Survivors Association, Philadelphia, 1892.

History of the One Hundred and Twenty-First Pennsylvania Volunteers, "An Account from the Ranks," Philadelphia, 1926.

Hitchcock, Frederick L., *War from the Inside*, Philadelphia, 1904.

Howard, Oliver Otis, *Autobiography of Oliver Otis Howard*, 2 Vols., New York, 1907.

Hyde, T. W., *Following the Greek Cross*, Boston, 1894.

Jacobs, M., *Notes on the Rebel Invasion of Maryland, Pennsylvania, and the Battle of Gettysburg*, Philadelphia, 1863.

Jenkins, Howard M., *Pennsylvania Colonial and Federal*, 3 Vols., Philadelphia, 1903.

Johnson, Allen, and Dumas Malone, eds., *Dictionary of American Biography*, 22 Vols. plus supplements, New York, 1928-1937.

Johnson, Robert U., and Clarence C. Buel, eds., *Battles and Leaders of the Civil War*, 4 Vols., New York, 1887.

Johnston, William P., *General Albert Sidney Johnston*, New York, 1878.

Kamm, Samuel R., *The Civil War Career of Thomas A. Scott*, Philadelphia, 1940.

Kenly, John R., *Memoirs of a Maryland Volunteer*, Philadelphia, 1873.

Keyes, Erasmus D., *Fifty Years Observation of Men and Events*, New York, 1884.

Klein, F. S., *Lancaster 1841-1941*, Lancaster, Pa., 1941.

Klein, H. M. S., *Lancaster County: A History*, 4 Vols., Lancaster, Pa., 1924.

Lancaster *Daily Express*.

Lancaster *Daily Inquirer*.

Lancaster *Examiner and Herald*.

Lancaster *Intelligencer.*

Lancaster, *Papers of the Lancaster Historical Society,* Lancaster, Pa.

Lancaster *Sunday News.*

Lancaster *Weekly Examiner and Herald.*

Lewis, Lloyd, *Sherman: Fighting Prophet,* New York, 1932.

Lincoln Papers, *Library of Congress Annex,* Washington, D.C.

Linn, William A., *The Story of the Mormons,* New York, 1923.

Livermore, Thomas L., *Numbers and Losses in the Civil War in America 1861-1865,* Boston, 1901.

Locke, William H., *The Story of the Regiment* (11th Pennsylvania Reserves), Philadelphia, 1868.

McCall, George, *Letters from the Frontier,* Philadelphia, 1868.

McCalmont, Alfred B., *Extracts from Letters Written by Alfred B. McCalmont 1862-1865,* Printed for private circulation by his son Robert. (No copyright date, but introduction is dated 1908.)

McClellan, George B., *McClellan's Own Story,* New York, 1887.

McClure, Alexander K., ed., *Annals of the War, Written by Leading Participants North and South,* Philadelphia, 1879.

————, *Old Time Notes of Pennsylvania,* 2 Vols., Philadelphia, 1905.

————, *Recollections of Half a Century,* Salem, Mass., 1902.

Magazine of American History.

Mansfield, Edward D., *The Mexican War,* New York, 1848.

Marshal, Francis, *The Battle of Gettysburg: The Crest-Wave of the American Civil War,* New York, 1914.

Massachusetts Historical Society, *Military Papers of the Massachusetts Historical Society,* 14 Vols., Boston, 1881-1918.

Mayer, Brantz, *Mexico,* 2 Vols., Hartford, Conn., 1850.

Meade, George Gordon, ed., *Life and Letters of George Gordon Meade,* 2 Vols., New York, 1913.

Michie, Peter S., *General McClellan,* New York, 1915.

Moore, James Bassett, *The Works of James Buchanan,* 12 Vols., Philadelphia, 1909.

Morse, John T., Jr., ed., *The Diary of Gideon Welles,* 3 Vols., Boston, 1911.

New York *Herald.*

New York *Times.*

Nicholson, John P., ed., *Pennsylvania at Gettysburg,* 3 Vols., Harrisburg, 1914.

Nicolay, John G. and John Hay, *Abraham Lincoln: A History,* 10 Vols., New York, 1890.

Niles' *National Register,* Baltimore, 1846-1847.

North American Review.

Palfrey, Francis W., *The Antietam and Fredericksburg,* New York, 1882.

Paris, Comte de, *History of the Civil War in America,* 4 Vols., Philadelphia, 1875-1888.

Pearson, Henry G., *James S. Wadsworth of Geneseo,* New York, 1913.

Pennsylvania Archives, 138 Vols., Harrisburg, 1852-1935.

Pennypacker, Isaac R., *General Meade,* New York, 1901.

Personal Recollections of the Rebellion, 4 Vols., Military Order Loyal Legion, New York Commandry, New York, 1891.

Peterson, Charles J., *The Military Heroes of the War with Mexico*. Philadelphia, 1850.

Philadelphia *Inquirer*.

Philadelphia *Press*.

Philadelphia *Public Ledger*.

Philadelphia *Weekly Express*.

Powell, William H., *The Fifth Army Corps*, New York, 1896.

Proceedings of the Buford Memorial Association, New York 1895.

Quinn, S. J., *Historic City of Fredericksburg*, Richmond, 1908.

Randall, James G., *Lincoln the President: Springfield to Gettysburg*, 2 Vols., New York, 1945.

Redway, G. W., *The War of Secession 1861-1862*, London, 1910.

Register of Graduates and Former Cadets United States Military Academy (published annually), New York, 1952.

Reports of the Committee on the Conduct of the War, Senate Documents, 37th Congress, 3rd Session, Washington, 1863; 38th Congress, 2nd Session, 1865.

Reynolds, John Fulton, Unpublished papers of General John Fulton Reynolds, Fackenthal Library, Franklin and Marshall College, Lancaster, Pa.

Reynolds Memorial Association, Unveiling of Statue of General John F. Reynolds (pamphlet), Philadelphia, September 18, 1884.

Rhodes, James Ford, *History of the Civil War 1861-1865*, New York, 1917.

Richards, Louis, *Eleven Days in the Militia*, Philadelphia, 1862.

Ropes, John Codman, *The Army under Pope*, New York, 1885.

——, *The Story of the Civil War*, 2 Vols., New York, 1933.

Rosengarten, Joseph G., *Reynolds Memorial* (Addresses), Philadelphia, 1880.

Rupp, I. Daniel, *History of Lancaster and York Counties*, Lancaster, Pa., 1844.

Rusling, James F., *Men and Things I Saw in Civil War Times*, Cincinnati, Ohio, 1899.

Samson, William H., ed., *Letters of Zachary Taylor from the Battlefields of the Mexican War*, Rochester, New York, 1908.

Schaff, Morris, *Spirit of Old West Point*, Boston 1907.

Schlesinger, Arthur, Jr., *Age of Jackson*, New York, 1945.

Schurz, Carl, *Reminiscences of Carl Schurz*, 3 Vols., New York, 1908.

Sedgwick, John, *Correspondence of General John Sedgwick*, 2 Vols., Boston, 1902.

Seitz, Don C., *Braxton Bragg*, Columbia, S.C., 1924.

Sherman, William T., *Memoirs of William T. Sherman*, 2 Vols., New York, 1892.

Small, A. R., *The Sixteenth Maine Regiment in the War of the Rebellion*, Portland, Me., 1886.

Smith, A. P., *The Seventy-Sixth Regiment New York Volunteers*, Cortland, N.Y., 1867.

Smith, Justin H., *War with Mexico*, 2 Vols., New York, 1919.

Spaulding, Oliver L., *The United States Army in War and Peace*, New York, 1937.

Stanton Papers, Library of Congress Annex, Washington, D.C.

Stephenson, Nathaniel W., *Texas and the War with Mexico*, New Haven, Conn., 1921.

Stewart, A. M., *Camp, March and Battlefield*, Philadelphia, 1865.

Stine, J. H., *History of the Army of the Potomac*, Philadelphia, 1892.

Swinton, William, *Campaigns of the Army of the Potomac*, New York, 1866.

Sypher, J. R., *History of the Pennsylvania Reserves Corps*, Lancaster, Pa., 1865.

Thomson, O. R. Howard, and William H. Rauch, *History of the "Bucktails,"* Philadelphia, 1906.

Toombs, Samuel, *New Jersey Troops at Gettysburg*, Newark, N.J., 1887.

Trobriand, Regis de, *Four Years with the Army of the Potomac*, Boston, 1889.

Urban, John W., *In Defense of the Union*, Washington, D.C., 1887.

Vautier, John D., *History of the 88th Pennsylvania Volunteers*, Philadelphia, 1894.

Walker, Francis A., *General Hancock*, New York, 1894.

War of the Rebellion: Official Records of the Union and Confederate Armies, 70 Vols. (in 128), Washington, D.C., 1880-1901.

Weld, Stephen M., *War Diary and Letters of Stephen Minot Weld*, privately printed, Riverside Press, 1912.

Weygant, Charles H., *History of the One Hundred and Twenty-Fourth New York Volunteers*, Newburgh, N.Y., 1877.

Wilkeson, Frank, *Recollections of a Private Soldier in the Army of the Potomac*, New York, 1887.

Williams, Kenneth P., *Lincoln Finds a General*, 4 Vols., New York, 1949-1956.

Williams, T. Harry, *Lincoln and His Generals*, New York, 1952.

Wilson, James Harrison, *Under the Old Flag*, 2 Vols., New York, 1912.

Woodward, E. M., *History of the Third Pennsylvania Reserves*, Trenton, N.J., 1883.

——, *Our Campaigns*, Philadelphia, 1865.

Young, Jesse Bowman, *The Battle of Gettysburg*, New York, 1913.

Zook, John G., *Historical and Pictorial Lititz*, Lititz, Pa., 1905.

Index